Glory in the Cross

The Letter of Paul to the Galatians

Hamilton Moore

T0349777

FAITHBUILDERS LTD

Glory in the Cross: The Letter of Paul to the Galatians by Hamilton Moore

First Published in Great Britain in 2019

Faithbuilders Ltd,
7 Park View, Freeholdland Road
Pontnewynydd
Pontypool, Torfaen NP4 8LP
www.faithbuilders.org.uk

British Library Cataloguing-in-Publication Data

A catalogue record for this book is available from the British Library

ISBN: 9781912120345

Cover Design by Faithbuilders. Image 112210488 © Oleg Dudko | Dreamstime.com

Printed and bound in Great Britain by Marston Book Services Limited, Oxfordshire.

This book is dedicated to my faithful and loving wife Shirley who has been such an encouragement in my writing and in the ministry of Tell Romania during the past years.

PREFACE

My first serious introduction to the Galatian letter was as a mature student, where my focus, as often when studying an academic course, was centered more on matters of destination, date and the original intended recipients. During the early years of ministry, I had passed over the letter in my own personal reading without recognition of its precious teaching on the sufficiency of the cross, the regenerating and empowering work of the Holy Spirit, and its practical guidance for living out the Christian life. Later, when teaching on Galatians at the Slavic Gospel Association School of the Prophets in Austria, Hungary, and Romania I was encouraged to write this book. Having been involved in mission in Romania for 19 years, aware of critical issues in Pauline theology both at home and abroad and how God has been working in my own personal life, I believe it is time to publish this commentary.

Paul writes in Galatians 6:14 "But far be it from me to boast except in the cross of our Lord Jesus Christ, by which the world has been crucified to me, and I to the world." This is a crucial verse in understanding the whole purpose and message of Galatians. Paul urges his readers, to *Glory in the Cross*. In fact, it can be affirmed, as the Introduction claims, this title actually reflects its underlying or central theme. Regeneration through the Holy Spirit, deliverance from this present evil age, justification, being "in Christ," sonship, heirship, new creation, and a Christian lifestyle in the enabling power of the Holy Spirit are blessings that come to us because "the Son of God loved me and gave himself for me" (2:20). In the context of the situation among the Galatian churches, it was trusting in the Christ of the cross, what he had accomplished, not circumcision, with its commitment to law keeping, which is plainly set out in the letter, first, as the only way of salvation, and also, as the source of all the spiritual blessings which have become ours in Christ alone.

This commentary on Galatians will be useful, particularly where its teaching focuses on some of the real problems facing the church today. Firstly, many in the Christian community are lacking the assurance of salvation, which can possibly be attributed to several factors such as a superficial "conversion" experience, persecution, or serious illness, which can lead to nagging doubts concerning one's acceptance before God. On many occasions, this lack of assurance has been caused by a failure to grasp the wonder of what was accomplished for sinners at the cross. Attempting to follow the Lord with no real understanding of the all-sufficiency of his sacrifice can lead to a deficient spiritual experience. In my opinion, the teaching of Galatians is particularly helpful here. The basic message of the book is that our salvation is not about our work – any obedience, sacrament, kindness etc., but about *his* work. We were helpless; but when we could do nothing to get right with God, he did everything; taking the initiative in love, he sent his Son to pay the full price for us – to redeem (3:13; 4:4–5). As Rom 4:5 states – if we desire to be accepted by God, we must not *start* working in some way; but rather *stop*. The blessing of justification comes to "the one who does not work" but "believes" in a work done, an all-sufficient work completed on the cross. Our faith is placed in Christ and his death for us, not in ourselves. Therefore, Galatians brings us back to basics, encouraging us to believe (and proclaim) the true gospel, in contrast to some modern "perspectives" which are also highlighted. The whole basis of our acceptance is here in this letter – we glory in the cross. It is all-sufficient. We know peace and joy in Christ, seeing he has done all for us and we are delivered, free, accepted.

A second problem in the church today, is the need for power, the power of the Holy Spirit. We find in any study of Galatians a clear emphasis – often missed – on the presence and enabling power of the Holy Spirit (3:3, 6; 5:5–6, 16–26; 6:8). Paul begins by affirming that Christ, "gave himself for our sins, to deliver us from the present evil age" (1:4). The Lord Jesus came from heaven, invaded the present age and through the cross brought to us the blessings of the age to come, *including* not only as we saw above, justification, being "in Christ," sonship, etc., but *the gift of the Holy Spirit.* We are now living in the age of the Spirit! Paul sets out in Galatians not just that we are regenerated by the Spirit (3:29), a new creation (6:15), but we have the promise of his power! Having "begun by the Spirit" (3:3), the Galatians continued to know his enduement, "he who supplies the Spirit and works miracles among you" (3:5). Note that "supplies" is present continuous, emphasising that they must continue to know that same power in all their future walk and witness! Do not be content until you know this enabling and experience this power!

Finally, two further problems for twenty first century believers are disunity in the church and hypocrisy in the workplace. Here again, Galatians provides direction, exhorting believers to exhibit a true Christian lifestyle. Rather than "gratifying the desires of the flesh ... provoking one another, envying one another" (5:16–26), they can begin to manifest "the fruit of the Spirit," a Christlikeness which means that their lives will be different from that of the world. There is a sweetness, a godliness, a submissiveness when the Holy Spirit is in control, as one seeks to follow the teaching and "law of Christ" (6:2).

I pray that God may use your study of this commentary on Galatians to bring you first to a renewed assurance or to heart-felt praise to God for the sufficiency of the cross in your salvation; to challenge you to know and experience the power of the Holy Spirit in your daily witness; and finally, as you submit to the practical teaching of these chapters to make an impact for the Lord by your Christian lifestyle in your local church and in a dark and needy world.

CONTENTS

ABBREVIATIONS

A Against Apion (Josephus)

Abr. De Abrahamo (Philo)

AD Anno Domini

Aet. Mund. De Aeternitate Mundi (Philo)

ANE Ancient Near East

Ant. Antiquities (Josephus)

AT Author's Translation (Moo)

2 Bar 2 Baruch

BCE Before Common Era

Bib Biblica

BJRL British Journal of Religious Literature

BJRL Bulletin of the John Rylands Library

BST The Bible Speaks Today

BZNW Beihefte zur Zeitschrift für Neutestamentliche Wissenschaft

CE Common Era

CA California

CalvTheoJourn Calvin Theological Journal

CD Damascus Document from the Cairo Genizah

Clem. Clement

CNTC Calvin's New Testament Commentaries

Decal. De Decalogo (Philo)

1 En. 1 Enoch

ESV English Standard Version

Ex T. Expository Times

4 Ezr. 4th Ezra

FS Festschrift

Fug. De Fuga et Inventione (Philo)

Hom. E Pet. Homilies, Epistle to Peter Pseudo-Clement

HTKNT Herders theologischer Kommentar zum Neuen Testament

ICC International Critical Commentary

IVP Inter Varsity Press

JB Jerusalem Bible

JBP J. B. Phillips

JSNT Journal of the Study of the New Testament

Jub. Jubilees

Macc. Maccabees

Magn. Letter to the Magnesians (Ignatius)

MI Michigan

MSS Manuscripts

MT Masoretic Text

Mut. Nom. De Mutatione Nominum (Philo)

NEB New English Bible

NIC New International Commentary

NICNT New International Commentary on the New Testament

NIDNTT New International Dictionary of New Testament Theology

NIGTC New International Greek Testament Commentary

NIV New International Version

NLT New Living Translation

NTS New Testament Studies

PG Patrologia Graeca

Ps.-Philo, LAB Pseudo-Philo's Liber Antiquitatum Biblicarum

Ps. Sol. Psalms of Solomon

4QMMT Miqṣat Maʿaśe ha-Torah

QpHab Pesher on Habakkuk

Quaest. Rom Quaestionews Romanae (Plutarch)

Recog. Recognitions Pseudo-Clement

SBLDS SBL Dissertation Series

Sir. Sirach

SJT Scottish Journal of Theology

SNTSM Society for New Testament Studies Monograph

Som. De Somniis (Philo)

SPCK Society for the Preservation of Christian Knowledge

TDNT Theological Dictionary of the New Testament

TNIV Today's New International Version

TNTC Tyndale New Testament Commentaries

Vit. Cont. De Vita Contemplativa (Philo)

War Jewish War (Josephus)

WBC Word Biblical Commentary

Wis. Book of Wisdom

WUNT Wissenschaftliche Untersuchungen zum Neuen Testament

ZNW Zeitschrift für die neutestamentliche Wissenschaft

INTRODUCTION

On a first reading of the Epistle to the Galatians, one might assume that it should be quite straightforward to write a commentary on this letter. There appear to be no serious difficulties regarding matters of authorship, significant textual problems, or the unity of the book. However, with further reading, research, and reflection things can be very different. As Witherington[1] notes, almost everything about the letter, genre, audience, date, structure, relationship with the Acts of the Apostles, theme of the book, and crucially the interpretation of leading concepts, are widely discussed and disputed. The approach adopted in this book is to recognise that these issues cannot be ignored: one must not just write a "devotional" work. The major matters of introduction and the crucial theological arguments must be clearly treated.

There are three main aims in this book. Firstly, to provide a resource for students, preachers and pastors, bringing together material which will be helpful for those seeking to understand the message of the book. Therefore, a selected number of influential commentaries are referred to, often quoted, with various passages discussed, and footnoted, aimed at providing either a negative or positive assessment of their understanding of Paul's teaching. I trust that the information gathered and the suggested interpretation will prove a helpful resource for those with limited access to library facilities. Secondly, to highlight the importance of Paul's teaching. I submit that the letter to the Galatians, with its affirmation about justification by faith alone and the assurance of acceptance with God which the work of the cross brings believers, is crucial. The third aim is to highlight as part of that acceptance, as we noted in the Preface, not only the blessing of being "born of the Spirit," as a "new creation" (Gal 4: 28–29; 6:15), possessing sonship or heirship, but also the empowering of the Holy Spirit to energise the Christian's new life in Christ (Gal 5:16–25). This is a vital emphasis for the Church today. Galatians is not just about justification; it is about power to live! Both are blessings available through the cross.

The Title of the Book

Various titles have been given to commentaries on Galatians. I now propose a new one – *Glory in the Cross.* The reason for choosing this title is because the cross, or the work of Christ on the cross, is fundamental to all the blessings in Galatians, and the theme of the cross runs like an unbroken thread throughout the letter. The saviour's finished work is all the original recipients needed, not the cross plus circumcision,[2] with its commitment to law keeping, days or feasts, but Christ's work alone. And Christ's work on the cross is sufficient for us, too.

---

[1] B. Witherington, 111, *Grace in Galatia: A Commentary on Paul's Letter to the Galatians* (Edinburgh: T & T Clark, 1998), 1.
[2] The reference to circumcision in Galatians is of course always literal (contrast Phil 3:3; Rom 2:25–29; Col 2:11). Circumcision was practiced among many different races in the ancient world as an initiation rite at puberty or marriage. For the Jewish people the importance of circumcision was that it was first

In employing this title one can see that it is not without significance that the cross is the focus in the opening salutation (1:4), delivering us from "the present evil age" and can be seen to form the climax to the whole letter when highlighted again in 6:14: "Far be it from me to boast except in the cross of our Lord Jesus Christ, by which the world has been crucified to me and I to the world."[3] As we will see later, some scholars identify this letter as a rhetorical composition, *either* as a whole or in part, involving significant elements throughout. These suggestions will need further evaluation. While there are differences of opinion regarding the type of rhetoric employed, the extent of its use in Galatians, or alternatively, if we should find here more teaching within an epistolary framework, there seems to be agreement on the significance for the whole letter of 6:12–17, which of course includes Paul's affirmation about the cross in v. 14. Note how Witherington[4] is clear that 6:12–17 gives us the "essential clarification and summing up of the real issue prompting this letter," and Betz[5] that this passage "contains the interpretative clues to the understanding of Paul's major concerns in the letter as a whole and should be employed as the hermeneutical key to the intentions of the apostle." Again, Longenecker[6] can affirm that "The self-giving of Christ through death on a cross is *the central soteriological theme of Galatians* (cf. 1:4; 3:1, 13; 6:12, 14) just as it was the focus of early Christian preaching" (italics mine).

Two more references need to be given here. Firstly, Weima[7] identified these final verses in Galatians 6 (vv. 13–17) as being vitally important for the whole theme of the letter. In fact, he also sees the cross as a major focus. The views of the Judaizers regarding the works of the law were totally incompatible with what was accomplished by the cross of Christ.

Another work to be highlighted is the commentary by Moo[8] on Galatians. In his Introduction he highlights a number of theological themes in the letter, including "The Gospel" and "Christ." The noun "gospel" is in 1:6, 7, 11; 2:2, 5, 7, 14 and the verb "preach the good news" is in 1:8, 9, 11, 16, 23. For Moo, it is clear that the

---

commanded by God to Abraham as a sign of the covenant between God and Israel (Gen 17:9–14). Any uncircumcised male whether freeborn Israelite or household slave would be cut off from his chosen people. The rite was reaffirmed in the law, to be faithfully observed on the eighth day (Lev 12:3). In the Hellenistic period circumcision became the distinguishing mark of Jewish identity. The practice was enforced on all Jews during the Maccabean revolt (1 Macc. ii.46) and was integral with the emergence of Judaism. Only the circumcised were regarded as Jews, members of the covenant with a commitment to keep the law and were seen as belonging to the people of God. In NT times for a Gentile Christian to submit to circumcision implied the acceptance of a whole way of life under the law. For a fuller treatment see T. George, *Galatians*, The New American Commentary, Vol. 30 (Nashville, Tennessee: Broadman & Holdman Publishers, 1994), 142–45; R. Meyer, "Περιτέμνω" *TDNT*, 6. 72–84.

[3] Quotations of Scripture in this book will be taken from the English Standard Version (Wheaton, Ill: Crossway, 2001).

[4] Witherington, 111, *Grace in Galatia*, 445.

[5] H. D. Betz, *Galatians: A Commentary on Paul's Letter to the Churches in Galatia* (Philadelphia: Hermeneia, 1979), 313.

[6] R. N. Longenecker, *Galatians,* WBC 41 (Dallas: Word, 1990), 264.

[7] J.A.D. Weima, "Gal 6:11–18: A Hermeneutical Key to the Galatian Letter," *CalvTheoJourn* 28 (1993), 90–107.

[8] D. J. Moo, *Galatians* (Grand Rapids, Michigan: Baker Academic, 2013), 32.

language is prominent in the crucial opening section (1:6–10). The incidents set out in 2:1–14 involve Paul's battle for "the truth of the gospel" (2:2, 14). The important of this phrase leads Moo to identify 2:15–21 – a section introducing key vocabulary and the central argument *to follow in the letter* – as a "summary" of the "truth of the gospel." (italics mine) He claims:

> The good news about the 'apocalypse' of Jesus Christ (1:12; cl. 4:4–6), his death on behalf of sinners (1:4; 3:13), the inauguration of a new creation (6:15: see 3:28), and above all, justification by grace and faith alone (2:15–21) – this gospel is the bedrock on which Paul builds his argument in Galatians and the critical truth that he uses to counteract the teaching of the agitators.

This "gospel" which Paul preached and defended in Galatians, as we see even from the above references, was clearly focused upon the cross as its foundational and central theme. I will return to this below and offer my own summary.

Moo[9] further points out that while Galatians gives us no formal Christological teaching (as Phil 2:5–11), yet we find "Christology understood in the sense of the epochal significance of the Christ event, is at the heart of Paul's argument in the letter.... Within that 'Christ event,' it is *the death of Christ* that draws Paul's particular attention in Galatians." (Italics mine). I concur with Moo, in that Paul's focus is on the cosmic significance of that death. He maintains, "The agitators' teaching stands in fundamental contrast to the 'cross of Christ' (5:11; 6:12). It was by 'hanging on a pole' in crucifixion that Christ 'redeemed us from the curse of the law' (3:13)."

Matters of introduction, purpose, audience, date, structure and genre will be treated only briefly,[10] as there are a plethora of other notable publications that deal with the detail. Furthermore most readers wish to focus more immediately on the chosen theme and the text itself.

In light of the statement in 6:14, we need to ask what it means to boast or glory in the cross? Paul is writing about the object of your confidence – what is it you depend upon, trust in, or what brings to you the sense that you can be accepted with God? The emphasis of this book is that the cross, the work of Christ is the perfect answer to all your sin and need. All that needs to be done has been done. We are urged only to believe the good news, repent, and receive salvation without legal works like circumcision and law keeping through the mercy of God. It was this which was really the crucial issue for the Christian communities in Galatia. They did not require grace plus circumcision, or faith plus law keeping; the way of salvation was faith alone in Christ crucified.

---

[9] Moo, *Galatians*, 33.
[10] For a fuller treatment, see D. Guthrie, *New Testament Introduction*, 4th ed. (Downers Grove, IL.: InterVarsity, 1990), 465–83; Longenecker, *Galatians*, lxi-lxxxviii.

People put confidence in many things. For example, in the parable of the Pharisee and the tax collector in Luke 18:9–14, the Pharisee had his confidence placed in himself and his own law keeping: "God, I thank you that I am not like other men … extortioners, unjust, adulterers … I fast twice a week, I give tithes of all that I get." Yet, Jesus said, it was the despised tax collector who beat his breast, saying, "God be merciful to me a sinner!" who "went down to his house justified, rather than the other." Paul could write in Phil 3:4–6 about where he had formerly placed his confidence: "If anyone else thinks he has reason for confidence in the flesh, I have more." He had been circumcised eight days after birth; he was from the tribe of Benjamin, with Hebrew parents; a Pharisee, who had kept all the tradition of the elders – "as to righteousness under the law, blameless." Yet he came to the place where he had "no confidence in the flesh"; he had learned that he must trust rather in the cross of Christ, than in his own good works or religious involvement.

Paul, of course, was aware of the fears and suspicions which his preaching had aroused among some Jewish Christians. On one of his later visits to Jerusalem, while he was sincerely welcomed by James and the elders, it is clear that there were others who had misconceptions concerning his "law-free" mission. In Acts 21:20–22 he is informed that there are "many thousands among the Jews who have believed … and they have been told that you teach all the Jews who are among the Gentiles to forsake Moses, telling them not to circumcise their children or walk according to our customs." Luke explains that in order to demonstrate his solidarity with the Jewish believers Paul willingly submitted himself to the Jewish ritual of purification with four others who had taken a Nazarite vow. One can also note that in 1 Cor 7:17–19 Paul affirms that he never encouraged Jewish Christians to forgo the circumcision of their children. "Was anyone at the time of his call already circumcised? Let him not seek to remove the marks of circumcision. Was anyone at the time of his call uncircumcised? Let him not seek circumcision. For neither circumcision counts for anything nor uncircumcision, but keeping the commandments of God." He takes a similar position in Gal 6:15, "For neither circumcision counts for anything, nor uncircumcision, but a new creation." Jewish men could in some situations e.g., because of attending the public baths or competing in an athletic competition, submit to a surgical procedure which would cover up cosmetically one's circumcision. George[11] makes the point that "Paul had no sympathy for this kind of radical Hellenizing of Jewish culture and spoke against it. He honoured circumcision as a sign of Jewish identity and encouraged Jewish Christians to continue to circumcise their male offspring." However, it is important to note that while he had no problems with personal compatibility as a Jew with Jewish traditions, there was no movement or shift of his position as far as the gospel of Christ and the preaching of the cross was concerned. Christian believers were not just some kind of new Jewish sect.

It will become clear in Galatians that even at the very moment Paul sends his warnings to the Christian communities, there were some among them (normally described as "agitators" or "Judaizers") who wished the Galatian churches to be

---

[11] George, *Galatians*, The New American Commentary, 145.

reconstructed in the Jewish mould. They would then be seen as just a part of early Judaism, those who would respect and observe the law. Paul in 4:10 is concerned that they had already gone to the extent of observing "days and months and seasons and years." If circumcision was to follow, for the Judaizers the believers would then be "true" children of Abraham or part of the "Israel of God."

The letter itself will show how Paul[12] responds to this vision of the Judaizers, with his emphasis that their message is in fact "another gospel" (1:6–9); salvation is by grace,[13] not law keeping. The emphasis throughout is that the cross work of Christ is all-sufficient for their acceptance with God. Through regeneration of the Spirit, by the hearing of faith, the Galatians have already received the promise of Abraham; they are justified and are "in Christ." Having been born again (Gal 4:28–29; 6:15), the Holy Spirit empowers and enables the true children of Abraham to live a life of holiness, service, and care of others, especially the household of faith (6:2, 10). Paul insists that all this is possible without circumcision and its commitment to law keeping, or observing special days, as the false teachers were advocating. As far as these false teachers were concerned, in 4:30, where Paul refers to Hagar the slave girl and her son, who will not inherit, but were "sent away" (Gen 21:10–14), Witherington[14] comments that, "already there Paul begins to tell them what they must do to correct matters – cast the agitators out of the Galatian churches!" It appears that they were still active and influential.

It must be emphasised again that "the cross" stands for Christ's work. When it comes to the matter of salvation, it is not our work but his. In fact, the glorious news is that all that needs to be done (apart from our repentance and trust in Christ the saviour), has been done. The Christian communities in Galatia needed to be persuaded again of this. They must not be led astray by the false teachers. Acceptance is not through circumcision with its commitment to keep the law but his crucifixion and the faith in Christ they already had exercised when they first heard the gospel.

In reality, no-one is able to keep the law. Yet, as we will see in Gal 3:10, failure to keep any part of it means to be condemned by the law as a transgressor. In Deut 21:22 it is explained that if a man committed a sin "punishable by death," when he was put to death, the direction was to, "hang him on a tree." Hanging the person upon a tree was a sign that they had been condemned, cursed by God. Although the Galatians had broken the law and come under its condemnation, the glorious message of the gospel is that Christ took their condemnation upon himself to deliver them and the sign of this was his death on the cross. "Christ redeemed us from the curse of the law by becoming a curse for us – for it is written, 'Cursed is everyone who is hanged on a tree'" (3:13). This and nothing more was the answer to their (and our) sin.

---

[12] One important point to make at the very beginning here. The issue is between Jewish "Christian" missionaries (Judaizers) and *another* Jewish Christian, Paul. It is *not* between Jews and Christians. There is no anti-Semitism in Galatians.

[13] Grace should be understood not simply as God giving us blessing when we do not deserve it (unmerited favour), but blessing us when we only deserve the opposite i.e., his wrath (favour *against* merit).

[14] Witherington, 111, *Grace in Galatia*, 198.

Therefore, it can be maintained that this focus upon the cross (i.e., the effectiveness of Christ's work for us, not any of our works or law keeping) is the underlying theme of Galatians. It is crucial in understanding the letter for this to be emphasised more than it has been – hence the title of this commentary: *Glory in the Cross.*

Turning to the letter itself, it will be beneficial to note and comment briefly upon the following verses which refer directly to the cross. It can be maintained that these references to his death on behalf of sinners can be found in every chapter, where they are central and fundamental to Paul's whole argument.

1:4 who gave himself for our sins, to deliver us from the present evil age, according to the will of our God and Father.

It is the cross, Christ's voluntary self-giving of himself for us that brings us deliverance from our sins and from this present evil age! Christ actually invaded this present age at his first advent and on the cross became accountable for our sins and brought to his people already the blessings of the new age! They are part of the "new creation" (6:15) – its fullness is in the future, but for those in Christ, its blessings are already being realized in part through the regenerating and enabling Holy Spirit. Paul is also making the point that the Jewish law which the Galatian Christian community was being required to submit to, as we will stress later, belonged to *this* age. It was part of that to which they had been enslaved (and condemned by). Paul is affirming right at the beginning of the letter that Christ by his cross, dying for their sins, has delivered them from the law. He actually affirms that this was in God's will and plan!

2:20 I have been crucified with Christ. It is no longer I who live, but Christ who lives in me. And the life I now live in the flesh I live by faith in the Son of God, who loved me and gave himself for me.

The Galatians died with him, or rather "in" him and were delivered from condemnation; now as believers, Christ lives in them. His cross, his death as us, in our place, means that they (and we) have a new life which they live to God!

2:21 I do not nullify the grace of God; for if righteousness were through the law, then Christ died for no purpose.

Paul will emphasise that Christ's death would have been for no purpose if in fact righteousness is possible through the law. If justification is by works/obedience of the law, which amounts to earning salvation by one's own efforts, the result is to really make the death of Christ and faith in that death superfluous. Trust in one's self is really an insult both to the grace of God and to the cross of Christ, for it, in effect, affirms that both were unnecessary.

3:1 O foolish Galatians! Who has bewitched you? It was before your eyes that Jesus Christ was publically portrayed as crucified?

Christ crucified was Paul's message when he first preached to them. They had believed Paul's preaching of the cross, that Christ's work was altogether sufficient in giving them acceptance. They were regenerated through faith, not through law, as a new creation of the Holy Spirit. Having been blessed in this way it was surely foolish to think that they must now take a different road and go back to law keeping. Had they not been accepted already through faith?

3:13–14 Christ redeemed us from the curse of the law, by becoming a curse for us – for it is written, 'Cursed is everyone who is hanged on a tree.'

The Galatian Christians, who had transgressed God's law, needed to remember that Christ was condemned on the cross in their place. Thus he is the one who has delivered those who have faith in him from the wrath of God, bringing them the blessing of Abraham, justification or acceptance "in Christ" and the enabling Holy Spirit.[15] We need to note that these blessings did not come through circumcision and a commitment to law keeping.

4:4–7 But when the fullness of time had come, God sent forth his Son, born of woman, born under the law, to redeem … so that we might receive adoption as sons. And because you are sons, God has sent the Spirit of his Son into our hearts.

He was the unique Son sent to pay the price on the cross to deliver us from the bondage of the law and to impart to us by his death the blessing of sonship and the promised Holy Spirit – without works, through grace alone.

5:11 But if I, brothers, still preach circumcision, why am I still being persecuted? In that case the offense of the cross has been removed.

If Paul, as some apparently were claiming, was still preaching circumcision, why was he being persecuted? He would surely have avoided this; as his message would have been acceptable to the Jews. But if circumcision was enough there would have been no need for the cross. Alternatively, it is the message of the cross, without circumcision, that is a stumbling block and led to the rejection of his gospel and persecution.

5:22–25 But the fruit of the Spirit is love, joy, peace…. And those who belong to Christ Jesus have crucified the flesh with its passions and desires.

Being "crucified with Christ" (see 2:20) i.e., having died in him, they must crucify the desires of the flesh and walk in the Spirit. The cross has by grace brought them not only justification but liberty from the law. This liberty does not lead to licence but loving service, as it has opened up the experience of a new life of fruitfulness through

---

[15] Bruce proposes that justification before God by faith, apart from legal works and the gift of the Holy Spirit, the one who is the source of the new life in Christ are "two dominant themes in Galatians," F. F. Bruce, *The Epistle to the Galatians: A Commentary on the Greek Text*, NIGTC (Exeter: Paternoster Press, 1982), 2. The cross is foundational for both.

regeneration and the enabling of the Holy Spirit. Having died in Christ at the cross, they now refuse to live in a fleshly manner, but instead walk in the Spirit's power. This is the new Christian lifestyle.

6:12 It is those who want to make a good showing in the flesh, who would force you to be circumcised, and only in order that they may not suffer persecution for the cross of Christ.

Preaching circumcision and a commitment to keep the law would of course, as we noted, have delivered those who preached it and those who accepted it from persecution by Jewish Zealots.[16] On the other hand, Paul makes clear (as he knows from experience) that preaching the work of the cross alone as the way of salvation and acceptance with God will attract suffering.

6:14 But far be it for me to boast except in the cross of our Lord Jesus Christ, by which the world has been crucified to me and I to the world.

Paul had been crucified to the world (as had the Galatian Christians) by Christ's substitutionary death. "The world" here includes all its philosophies of how to be accepted with God. Neither they, nor we, need anything more that the cross. Christ's work is all sufficient for us. In this alone we can "boast" or place our confidence. In fact, being crucified to the world reminds us, as we will see, that the cross introduces us to the new creation and delivers us effectively from the old world. We are transplanted from the one into the other in our experience of conversion. We must live as people of the new age, in holiness, service and loving care of others.

These brief comments will all of course be expanded as we make our way through the book. However, the point here is that the cross is a fundamental theme throughout the letter – it is the basis of all Paul's argument and our hope for eternity.

It is true that people generally do not enjoy hearing the preaching of the cross because it is a message that really is affirming issues concerning them that are not positive but condemnatory. It makes clear to them that their situation is hopeless without Christ. Therefore, some will prefer a Christianity without a cross, which really is proposing salvation through their works/obedience rather than through the death of Jesus Christ. So, it will be no more by grace (which is not just unmerited favour or acceptance, but favour *against* merit, when they deserve the opposite i.e., judgment). For Paul it is clear that if some would "boast in the flesh" at Galatia (6:13), they were in effect denying Christ's all-sufficient and completed sacrifice, and rejecting the gospel of the grace of God. Galatians emphasises the seriousness of this denial and rejection.

---

[16] Jewett suggests there was a resurgence of zealot activity in this period (AD 46–52). Jewish Christians who "fraternized" with their Gentile brethren would be exposed to reprisals. Not only was this a good reason to persuade the Gentile Christians to accept circumcision, but if they could also see and be persuaded that it was required by God for their acceptance. See R. Jewett, "The Agitators and the Galatian Congregation," NTS 17 (1970–71), 198–212, in Bruce, *The Epistle to the Galatians*, 31; Moo, *Galatians*, Baker Exegetical Commentary on the New Testament, 20.

Salvation is by faith alone in Christ, not faith plus circumcision and a commitment to observe the law. Paul is affirming that for those who take this road, their damnation would be certain, for they cannot keep the law perfectly and so would be condemned as lawbreakers. The only way of salvation is through the cross, i.e., Christ taking our condemnation upon himself, dying for us and we placing our trust in him and what he has done. We can only be saved by the grace of God. This is the message of Galatians. It is a message about the cross and only the cross. How that emphasis needs to be clearly made from pulpits today!

Commenting on preaching the cross, Mark Dever[17] states:

> We desire you to preach the cross. Build your church by preaching the cross. Be encouraged and a source of encouragement by preaching the cross. Build friendships with ministers who preach the cross.... That is what a minister of the Word of God is called to do, from the New Testament and the Old, and in a way that is understandable and penetrating, faithful to the truth of justification by faith alone, visibly and verbally exulting in God's grace, reflected in our lives, and shown over the years and decades of ministry that God may give you. Preach the cross.

I concur with Dever that within the preaching of the local church the cross must be central for it is the source of all that the disciple requires to live a Christian life.

I will now turn to the traditional matters of introduction. The conclusions will confirm that although there are a number of arguments to the contrary, that Galatians was addressed to churches in the south Galatian area and was actually Paul's earliest letter.

Why was Galatians Written?

Paul had heard of the arrival of visiting preachers, Jews, who while professing to be Christians, had not been fully delivered from Jewish legalism. They were misleading his Galatian converts. A look back to the beginning of the church in Galatia will help us understand what was happening in these embryonic years. Acts 13–14 recounts how Paul and Barnabas came to Antioch on their first missionary journey. The basic teaching the synagogue worshippers heard is recorded in 13:16–41. God had a purpose for the family of Abraham and "those among you who fear God" and to them he had sent the "message of this salvation" that people could know forgiveness of sins and be justified. God's purpose extends through Abraham and the Exodus, with God's choice of Israel, brought out of Egypt, cared for, given a king after God's own heart and then Jesus, as son of David, and John the Baptist's witness to him. God has raised him from the dead and the words of Ps 2:7; 16:10, and Isa 55:3, apply to him. Therefore, Jesus is the one through whom God's salvation/forgiveness/justification is

---

[17] M. Dever, J. L. Duncan III, R. A. Mohler Jr., C. J. Mahaney, *Preaching the Cross* (Illinois: Crossway, 2007), 16.

to be found. Those who believe in him could be freed from everything they could not be freed from by the law of Moses. The outcome of this preaching, by the effective moving of God's Spirit, led to Jews, proselytes, but also many Gentiles believing and the "word of the Lord was spreading throughout the whole region" (13:42–50).

Not all believed. The people throughout the whole province were idolaters, and while the Roman authorities had brought peace they were still in the grip of fear and superstition and ignorant of God. The Jews raised up such persecution against Paul and Barnabas that they were expelled from the area. Such was the strength of their opposition that the Jews caused the same persecution in Iconium, Lystra, and Derbe, with Paul first considered as a god but then actually stoned and left for dead. In visiting the believers again in the various towns, Paul exhorts them to continue in the faith saying that "through many tribulations we must enter the kingdom of God" (14:22).

It is a fact that when fierce persecution does not stop the advance of the kingdom, the devil employs other methods to "bewitch" (Gal 3:1) the churches with a perverted gospel, which was really no gospel. This is what had happened in Galatia. No doubt the new Galatian converts in the whole area had a real desire to live a holy life and were open to be taught how this was possible. In order to really advance in the faith, they were now being told that they must be circumcised and keep the law of Moses (Gal 4:10–11; 5:2, 3). As already noted, Jewett has suggested that there was a resurgence of zealot activity in this period (AD 46–52). Jewish Christians who "fraternized" with their Gentile brethren would be exposed to attack. Here was another good reason for Gentile Christians to accept circumcision. Again, as Witherington[18] has explained:

It is possible that the agitators had come to Galatia and preyed upon the Galatian's fears that they were not doing enough to be real Christians. For Greco-Roman persons ritual, ceremonies, festivals, and sacrifices were of the essence of true religion and were seen as the proper manner to express one's piety. The agitators may have come to Galatia and discovered their audience was primed for the very sort of arguments they wanted to present.

So, in various subtle ways they were being led back to the law and its prescribed celebrations as a means of being accepted by God. These teachers Paul calls "some who trouble you" (1:7); "make much of you" (4:17); "the one who is troubling you" (5:10); "those who unsettle you" (5:12); "force you to be circumcised" (6:12), and they are usually described as "Judaizers" or "agitators." They were insisting that it was essential for salvation and membership in the community of the people of God for the Galatian Christians to submit to the Jewish rite of circumcision, observe the special days and seasons of the Jewish calendar (4:10), the Jewish regulations regarding meals (2:11–14), and keep the law of Moses (3:19; 5:2f, 6:13). So as

---

[18] Witherington, 111, *Grace in Galatia*, 204, n. 19.

McKnight[19] explains, the term "Judaizers" does not refer to Jews in general but "to a specific movement in earliest Christianity that believed conversion to Christ also involved *a further conversion* (italics mine) to their (Pharisaic) form of Judaism."

To maximise their own influence with the believers, these preachers were also casting doubts upon Paul's standing as an apostle and the apostolic authority of his message. This is clearly why Paul begins the letter as he does with a personal section, stressing the divine authority of his message, his call to preach it, his clear acceptance by the leaders of the Jerusalem church and the affirmation of his deeply held convictions in his confrontation with Peter (1:11–2:18). The Galatians who had been influenced by the "agitators" had become estranged from Paul, if not actually hostile to him. In 4:16 Paul challenges them to consider why they had changed their attitude to him, "Have I then become your enemy by telling you the truth?"

This really was a critical moment for the Galatian churches. If others did not see it, Paul had the insight to realise that the message of the gospel and the future of the church of Christ were at stake! This is why he writes with such seriousness. In the opening salutation there is no praise or commendation of the readers, or, in the concluding comments, no request they pray for others or for him. Bruce[20] makes clear the reality of the situation. This "full" gospel of the Judaizers (adding circumcision with the commitment to law-keeping) for Paul was not the true gospel. The apostle knew that it really denied the all-sufficiency of Christ's sacrifice and the grace of God. A commitment to keep the law, which in reality they could not do, was a return to legal bondage and a denial of the message of justification by grace through faith. The law as Moo[21] explains, was only for a limited period, revealing the true nature of sin (3:19) and intended to be in effect only until the "seed" of Abraham should come (3:19, 24). Human beings were unable to obey it but found themselves condemned by it. Calling upon the Galatians to be circumcised and submit to the law, rather than the true gospel was a perversion (1:7) and did not come from God (5:8). Such a message was in reality apostasy from Christ; to submit to it was to turn away from God and fall from grace (5:4), its propagators were incurring a curse (1:8f) and exposing themselves to divine judgment (5:10). For us, as with them, the stark differences need to be clear.

From the comments he makes about circumcision, for Paul, the rite was now only a physical act without religious significance (5:6; 6:15). Yet it was being enforced as a legal obligation, essential to salvation and for membership in the community of the people of God! As the letter affirms, for the Galatian believers, what was all-important was not the cutting of the flesh but getting a clear grasp of their justification by faith, their freedom from condemnation through the cross of Christ and by the grace of God. God had brought them into liberty; they were regenerated and enabled by the Holy Spirit. But liberty was not licence to live in sin. This danger

---

[19] S. McKnight, *Galatians*, The NIV Application Commentary (Grand Rapids, Michigan: Zondervan Publishing House, 1995), 21.
[20] Bruce, *The Epistle to the Galatians*, 79.
[21] Moo, *Galatians*, 35.

seems to have been a problem, not simply caused by the Judaizers after he left, but even from the very beginning (see 5:21 "I warn you, as I warned you before"). As stated above, having been "born of the Spirit" (Gal 4:29), justified, like the first disciples, they had been endued with power from on high (Luke 24:48–49; Gal 3:3–4; 5:5). They must now go on to live their new life in the power of the Holy Spirit (5:16–18), producing the fruit of the Spirit, serving and caring for others. Christ now lives "in" them (2:20), is being "formed" in them (4:19) and so by that same Holy Spirit can be seen in them. OT prophesies like Ezek 36:22–32 focus in this time of fulfilment on the way the Spirit can enable the born again believer to live an empowered life that pleases God: "I will put my Spirit in you, and cause you to walk in my statutes and be careful to obey my rules." As we will discuss later, this is for many scholars what it means to "fulfil the law of Christ" (6:2). Dunn,[22] using the language one finds in New Perspective ideas (see later notes on Gal 2) suggested that as to purpose, Galatians was not about "getting in" or "staying in" but "going on," i.e., how the believers were to live out their faith. This is true, as we have just discussed, but it is vital not to forget how one "got in" to begin with. They must get back to the cross; they need to grasp again the completeness of what Christ has done for them there. Nothing can be added to the work and words of Jesus; "It is finished" (John 19:30). This completed work has so many implications as to how one "goes on." No circumcision, no works, are required; instead regeneration, justification and the power of the Holy Spirit (sanctification) are necessary. As Moo points out, "The 'promise of the Spirit' in 3:14, then, both circles back to the theme of the initial reception of the Spirit in 3:1–5 as well as hinting at Paul's argument about the Spirit's work in sanctification in 5:13–6:10."

So, Paul outlines in the letter that the Galatians have become a new creation of the Holy Spirit, were blessed in Abraham, recipients of the promise of justification, are "in Christ," sons and heirs, and it is in the power of the Holy Spirit that they "go on" to live a life of holiness, service and sacrifice for others. The challenge for them is to grasp the completeness of their acceptance and live out their lives in the power of that same Spirit. The question for us is – have we found that same acceptance and are we also manifesting a true Christian lifestyle, living in the enabling power of the Spirit of God?

Where Was it Sent?

The epistle is addressed to "the churches of Galatia" (1:2). But the question is, where was Galatia? Is this a reference to the earlier kingdom of Galatia or to the more extensive Roman province of Galatia? Here the territory is larger but still included the former kingdom. In other words, were those to whom Paul was writing Galatians in the ethnic sense, or in the political sense, living in the Roman province of that name? King Amyntas had ruled Galatia from 36–25 BCE, but upon his death Galatia became a Roman province. The Romans included in the province parts of Lycaonia

---

[22] J. D. G. Dunn, *The Theology of Paul's Letter to the Galatians* (Cambridge, Cambridge University Press, 1993), 104, n. 6.

and Phrygia, i.e. territory to the south that had never belonged to ethnic Galatia. So, when Paul writes to the "churches in Galatia" does he mean this northern area, strictly speaking ancient Galatia, sometimes call "tribal" or "regional" Galatia, or the whole province, called "provincial," including the southern cities of Antioch, Iconium, Lystra and Derbe?

The traditional view until the 19th century was that the letter concerned the churches in the north. More recently, it is commonly understood that Paul refers to the whole province and includes the cities in the south visited on Paul's first missionary journey. A decision concerning who the recipients were can have a bearing on when to date the letter. If the older view is accepted then it was written probably during the apostle's third missionary journey. However, if one holds the second view it could have been written much earlier and, in fact, could have been Paul's first epistle. This is the view which is followed in this commentary. The arguments are now summarised in the following excursus.

Excursus: The North Galatian Hypothesis and The South Galatian/Province Theory

The North Galatian Hypothesis

Some scholars, notably Lightfoot[23] and Betz[24], following the majority of patristic, medieval and Reformation commentators, argue that the letter was written to churches in or near Ancyra, Pessinus, and Tavium, three cities in northern Asia Minor (modern Turkey). This territory was originally conquered and settled by a distinct ethnic group of Celtic (Gaulish) descent in the third century BCE. Reasons for the North Galatian hypothesis are summarised below:

(1) Luke uses popular, ethnic and not the official, provincial language as he describes where Paul went. So, the reference was to old Galatia. Lightfoot understands both Acts 16:6 and 18:23 as references to the north Galatian area, the land of the Gauls. "The region of Phrygia and Galatia" therefore refers not to one area but two.

(2) Note the reference in Gal 4:13 to Paul's bodily ailment which he had when he visited these churches. In the Acts of the Apostles Luke does not mention that Paul had been sick during his first and second missionary journeys.

(3) Paul's use of τὸ πρότερον *to proteron* "at the first" in Gal 4:13, alluding to two visits to them, fits the situation suggested by the references of Acts 16:6 and 18:23.

(4) Paul doesn't mention the stoning at Lystra referred to in Acts 14:19–20. He would surely have made reference to it if he was writing to south Galatia.

---

[23] J. B. Lightfoot, *Saint Paul's Epistle to the Galatians* (London: Macmillan and Co. Ltd., 1921), 18–35.

[24] Betz, *Galatians*, 3–5.

(5) The letter to the Galatians states that the recipients were fickle, a people who were liable to change their minds and could be easily influenced. Certain character traits may appear in one group of people more than in another. Fickleness was a characteristic of the Gauls. Caesar's[25] *De Bello Gallico* makes this point in 2.1; 4.5; 6.16.

(6) Paul would not have written to cities of the south using the words "O foolish Galatians."

Earlier commentators, including Lightfoot, dismissed the South Galatian theory because at that time it had not yet been given a secure footing. This was to change through Sir William Ramsay[26] (1851–1939).

South Galatian Theory or the Province Hypothesis

Ramsay was a classics expert and had personally surveyed Asia Minor. His writings produced a change of direction in thinking about the first readers. In summary, the South Galatian theory is generally supported by the following points:

(1) Acts 16:6 actually refers to Phrygia Galatica. Witherington[27] explains that "there is now very clear evidence for the adjectival use of Phrygia in Greek. So, Paul is revisiting churches which he has already established in the south Galatian region. In Acts 18:23 the Greek is slightly different and Witherington[28] again suggests that Luke wishes to point out that Phrygia did extend beyond the Galatian province. Yet we must not think that this means that, "Luke assumed that Paul took a major detour after Lystra, going far to the north after Ancyra before coming to Ephesus." It is maintained that neither reference suggests that Paul evangelised north Galatia.

(2) It is clear from elsewhere that the Galatian churches shared in the collection for the poor in Jerusalem. In 1 Cor 16:6 they are singled out as those to whom Paul had already given instructions. Acts 20:4 includes in the list of the men who accompanied the gift, men from the south Galatian area, not the northern region.

(3) South Galatia would have been more easily reached by Judaizers from Palestine who would have found journeying through the difficult terrain to reach the northern area forbidding. The south had the Via Sebaste, the great Roman road, which linked the major colonies established in Pisidian Antioch, Iconium and Lystra. Hendriksen[29]

---

[25] Caesar's Gallic War – *De Bello Gallico* ET by W. A. McDevitte and W. S. Bohn (New York: Harper & Brothers, 1869), 6.16 e.g., states that the Gauls were, "a superstitious people given over to ritual observances."
[26] W. Ramsay, The Church in the Roman Empire before A.D. 170 (London: 1897), pxii; 8ff., 97ff. *Cities and Bishoprics of Phrygia*, 1–11 (Oxford: 1895–97).
[27] Witherington, 111, *Grace in Galatia*, 6.
[28] Witherington, 111, *Grace in Galatia*, 6.
[29] W. Hendriksen, *Galatians* (Edinburgh: Banner of Truth Trust, 1974), 13.

questions if the Judaizers "with their sinister propaganda, would have bypassed *South* Galatia on their way to *North* Galatia." And then there is Barnabas.

(4) Barnabas is mentioned in Gal 2:13. We know from Acts 13–14 and 15:36 that he was Paul's fellow-labourer in south Galatia. Afterwards Paul and Barnabas did not travel together as he was no longer Paul's companion.

(5) Considering Paul's illness, it is unlikely that he would have gone off the beaten track and over difficult country to north Galatia. In fact, this was not his usual strategy. Paul moved along the main trade routes and preached in the centres of communication. He would not have gone into a remote rural part like northern Galatia. His only contact would be with cities in the south.

(6) 1 Pet 1:1 suggests that it is likely that north Galatia was evangelised from Pontus i.e., from the west, and not by Paul coming up from the south.

(7) When Paul describes the churches he founded he describes them by reference to the Roman provinces. Therefore, when he speaks of "the churches of Galatia" (1:2) he means the Roman province.

(8) In Gal 4:14 the reference to "an angel of God" is taken by some as an allusion to the incident in Acts 14:11f. "The gods have come down to us in the likeness of men." Certainly, the statement of Gal 6:17 "the marks of Jesus" may be a reference which would include Paul's stoning at Lystra in Acts 14:21.

(9) While one can accept the characteristic of "fickleness" may be applied to the north Galatians, there are many Christian communities in the various Pauline churches that were easily influenced by false teachers, see e.g., Phil 1:15–18; 3:18–19; Col 2:8–23; 2 Thess 2:1; 1 Tim 1:3–7; 4:1–5; Titus 1:10–16; Rom 16:17–18. The massive change in attitude of those in south Galatian Lystra, first worshipping, then stoning Paul is surely clear evidence of inconsistency or fickleness among them (Acts 14:8–20).

One should add that J. M. Scott[30] refers to Josephus, who in a discussion of Gomer in his exposition of the biblical table of the nations, identifies the Gomerites with the contemporary Galatians. This reference to all the inhabitants of the Roman province of Galatia provides additional support for the South Galatian hypothesis. Again, we should note that the southern side of the Anatolian Plateau was more important than the northern under the earlier Roman Empire. The full development of the northern side did not take place until the time of Diocletian, who transferred the centre of imperial administration to Nicomedeia in AD 292.

---

[30] J. M. Scott, "Galatia, Galatians," in A. C. Evans & S. E. Porter (eds.) *Dictionary of New Testament Background* (Downers Grove, Illinois: InterVarsity Press, 2000), 390.

It appears that Ramsay's view holds sway with most modern scholars but there are also points to be said in favour of the North Galatian theory (see Kümmel[31]).

Longenecker[32] discusses both views and some of their weaknesses in his Introduction, and agrees with E. de W. Burton's conclusions, which can be summarised as follows:

(1) The evidence of the Pauline epistles is that Paul means the whole Roman province.

(2) Paul could not have addressed the churches of Derbe, Lystra, Iconium, and Antioch by a single term except "Galatians."

(3) The Greek of Acts 16:6 and 18:23 must be read as referring to one locality since only one article is used. It points to the Phrygic-Galactic region.

Therefore, there is a large amount of evidence seemingly in favour of a south Galatian location. The position of Hemer,[33] should also be considered. During Paul's time, Galatia was the name for the entire Roman province stretching from Pontus in the north to Pamphylia in the south. All the residents of this province were properly called Galatians, whatever their ethnic origin. By the third century, the province of Galatia was reduced to approximately its ancient ethnological dimensions, the original northern territory of the Celtic invaders. It is not surprising that patristic commentators, followed by medieval and Reformation commentators, assumed that Paul had addressed his letter to churches in north Galatia, since that was the only Galatia that existed at that time.

Paul normally classified the churches he founded according to Roman provinces: "churches of Asia" (1 Cor 16:19), "churches of Macedonia" (2 Cor 8:1), "Achaia has been ready" (2 Cor 9:2). So, it would be natural for Paul to refer to churches in Iconium, Antioch of Pisidia, Lystra, and Derbe (all cities within the Roman province of Galatia during his lifetime) as "the churches in Galatia"[34] and to refer to the members of those churches as Galatians. Indeed, as suggested above, no other single name would have been appropriate for them. Since there is no clear evidence that Paul founded churches in north Galatia,[35] it seems best to take the account of Acts

---

[31] W. G. Kümmel, *Introduction to the New Testament* (London: SCM Press, 1982), 296–98.

[32] E. de W. Burton, *A Critical and Exegetical Commentary on the Epistle to the Galatians*, ICC (Edinburgh: T & T Clark, 1921), p xxv-xliv, in R. N. Longenecker, *Galatians*, lxx.

[33] C. Hemer, *The Book of Acts in the Setting of Hellenistic History* (Winona Lake: Eisenbrauns, 1990), 227–307. Witherington also makes reference to this work in support of a south-Galatian destination. He makes the point that now there is clear evidence of the use of the word Phrygian as an adjective in Greek and archaeologists with knowledge of that region all identify south Galatia as the region in view in Paul's correspondence. Witherington, 111, *Grace in Galatia*, 6, n. 12.

[34] This is the point made by Hendriksen who explains that in 1 Cor 16 Paul can refer to churches in the Roman provinces of Macedonia (v. 5); Achaia (v. 15) and Asia (v. 19). In 16:1 when he refers to "the churches in Galatia" it is logical to assume that here as well he has the province in mind. He concludes, "Why should the identical phrase in Gal 1:2 have a different meaning?" Hendriksen, *Galatians*, 10.

[35] Fung also mentions, as we noted earlier, Paul's "evangelical strategy" which took him along the main roads to centres of communication in the Roman Empire and the silence in Acts regarding the establishing

13–14 as a record of the founding of the churches in south Galatia that are addressed in Paul's letter to the Galatians.

* * *

When Was it Written?

The dating of the letter depends to some extent on whether the addressees are considered to be southern Galatians or Galatians of the northern region. If it was sent to the believers in south Galatia the letter could have been written any time after the end of the missionary journey recorded in Acts 13:4–14:26. If one accepts this view then the reference in 4:13 needs to be explained. Some have suggested that τò πρότερον *to proteron* in this text is equivalent in Koine Greek to πρῶτος *prōtos*, "first." We noted already that advocates of the North Galatian theory understand this as implying composition of the letter after a second visit, interpreting this to mean that it must follow Acts 16:6 or 18:23.

One should note that as for 4:13, it is not necessary to translate "first." There are other possibilities. Bruce[36] quotes Askwith, who suggests that τò πρότερον *to proteron* must be interpreted in relation to the implied "now" of v. 16. "Formally (τò πρότερον *to proteron*) you congratulated yourselves on my coming to you; *now* you seem to regard me as your enemy."[37] Note also the suggested translation, "It was bodily illness that *originally* led to my bringing you the gospel."[38] However, Bruce,[39] while quoting Askwith, also points out that the second visit could be understood as taking place when Paul and Barnabas retraced their steps on their way back to Antioch, appointing elders for the young churches and commending them to the Lord's care (Acts 14:21–23). In that case it would be possible to date Galatians before the council at Jerusalem in Acts 15:6ff (soon after the last event mentioned in Gal 1:13–2:14). It would also explain Paul's comment in Gal 1:6 of the Galatians "so quickly" turning away from the true gospel. This could be a year or two from the time they were initially evangelised during the first missionary journey by Paul and Barnabas. This view would certainly explain why Paul could not in Galatians use the decision of the council to counteract the Judaizers. Therefore, if we follow the South Galatian theory, the date of the letter could be AD 50 or AD 49 on this evidence. If one favours the North Galatian theory and accept two visits by Paul then the date must be after Acts 16:6 or 18:23 and therefore must be AD 53–56.

---

of the churches in north Galatia. R. Y. Fung, *The Epistle to the Galatians*, NICNT (Michigan, Grand Rapids: Wm. B. Eerdmans Publishing Company, 1988), 2.

[36] E. H. Askwith, *The Epistle to the Galatians* (London: MacMillan, 1902), 73ff. in Bruce, *The Epistle to the Galatians*, 209.

[37] See also Longenecker, *Galatians*, 190; again, note Witherington, 111, *Grace in Galatia*, 13.

[38] The translation in the NEB, although the footnote has two other alternatives, "formally" or "on the first of my two visits."

[39] Bruce, *The Epistle to the Galatians*, 209.

Some make reference to Marcion who assigned Galatians in his canon in the following sequence: Galatians, 1 and 2 Corinthians and Romans. However, Marcion may not have been simply moved by chronological considerations, but rather theological factors.[40] Comparisons with these other epistles (1 and 2 Cor and Rom) as to vocabulary and theological thought are also "not decisive"; other factors must support such a suggestion.[41] These will be explored in due course.

Another important pointer in determining the date is our understanding of Paul's visits to Jerusalem. Galatians 1:18 and 2:1 has two visits; Acts 9:26, 11:27, 15:2 has three visits. Almost certainly Gal 1:18 can be compared to Acts 9:26, which is Paul's initial visit after his conversion. The issue here is whether the Gal 2:1 visit which was 14 years later, is the Acts 11:27–30 visit or the Acts 15:2 visit? This question requires further consideration.

Traditional View: Jerusalem Council Acts 15:2–29

Objections to this View

The most widely accepted view until the early 20th century was that Gal 2:1f. refers to the Acts 15:2–29 visit. This would mean that there is no mention of the famine visit (Acts 11:27–30). Regarding Acts 15, certainly the people and subject of the dispute were the same: both speak of a meeting held at Jerusalem to deal with the question of Gentile Christians having to observe the Jewish law. Again, in both the main participants are Paul and Barnabas on the one hand and Peter and James on the other hand and the decision reached was a "law-free mission"[42] to Gentiles. But there are a number of difficulties in seeing the two passages as referring to the same event.

Objection 1

Galatians 2 is really a private conference; Acts 15 is a public conference. Some have noted that in Acts 11:30 and 12:25 the famine visit account is very brief while in Gal 2 the visit is explained more fully. How could they have happened at the same time? We note how Paul states in Galatians that he "set before them (though privately)" (2:2). This was a private meeting with the leading apostles. It is understandable then that Luke does not highlight this meeting. It is also likely that the Galatians had no knowledge of it until they heard of it in this letter. As Witherington[43] has explained, Luke is recording significant events that were "of a broader and more public character." Also, the agreement in Gal 2:9 "did not settle the crucial issues of food and circumcision for the church as a whole.... A further public conclave was required." This was to happen later as recorded in Acts 15.

---

[40] Bruce, *The Epistle to the Galatians*, 45.
[41] See Bruce, *The Epistle to the Galatians*, 45–55.
[42] Longenecker, *Galatians*, lxxvii.
[43] Witherington, 111, *Grace in Galatia*, 18.

It should be noted that Galatians does not mention the restrictions of Acts 15:19–20. Some however suggest Galatians may have been a record of the preliminary conference which then developed into a public conference. However, the problem remains as to why Paul does not mention the major decision of the Council, which would have supported his arguments that circumcision should not be required of Gentile Christians. How could he have avoided mentioning this landmark decision? Longenecker[44] considers this "inconceivable."

Objection 2

The Gal 2:11 passage gives us the confrontation with Peter. Would Peter have withdrawn from the Gentiles after the Council's decision? Would Barnabas also have withdrawn? Or is Gal 2:11 out of chronological order i.e., did it really happen before Gal 2:1? Again, Peter was very changeable by nature. If Paul's clash with Peter took place after the Jerusalem Council, Paul's account of that clash undercuts his whole argument and is to the advantage of his Judaizing opponents. It would show that a chasm still existed between himself and the Jerusalem apostles and that it had only been superficially bridged over at the Jerusalem Council. The mention of the clash with Peter at a time before the Council is understandable.

Objection 3

The role of Paul. He was a major participant and at the centre of the discussion in Galatians 2 but is overshadowed by Barnabas, Peter and James in Acts 15. Luke can only mention him in one verse.

Objection 4

The relationship (or lack of it) between Barnabas and Paul in Galatians. Barnabas had been Paul's companion and fellow-worker in evangelising the Galatians in Acts 13:1–14:28. However, they had a relationship for many years before this (Acts 9:26–30; 11:19–30; 12:25). Yet Barnabas does not co-author Galatians; in fact, 2:13 reveals Paul's shock not just at Peter's withdrawal from fellowship with the Gentile believers in Antioch, but that "even Barnabas was led astray by their hypocrisy." Paul had to confront them. Now it would have strengthened his argument if he could have made mention of Barnabas' agreement with Paul in this letter; but that did not happen. Yet in Acts 15:1–2, 12, 22–35 Paul and Barnabas share ministry and a common theological viewpoint. Again, soon after the Jerusalem Council they go their separate ways over John Mark (Acts 15:36–41). This data points to Galatians being composed *before* the Jerusalem Council – perhaps not long before, as we are suggesting – in AD 49 or early AD 50.

---

[44] Longenecker, *Galatians*, lxxix.

Objection 5

Galatians 2:2 mentions that the Jerusalem trip was made in response to a revelation. In Acts 15:1–3 the visit was because of a sending by the Antioch church.

Objection 6

Paul's affirmation in 1:20 "I do not lie!" It is difficult to imagine how Paul, who affirms his truthfulness so vehemently here, could have failed to mention the Famine Visit in the account of the contacts he had with the Jerusalem leaders in Gal 1 and 2. This of course is the case if Gal 2 refers to the Jerusalem Council.

Famine Visit View: Acts 11:27–30

Objections to this View

Gal 2:1–10 is to be paralleled with Acts 11:27–30, whereas the Jerusalem Council of Acts 15 takes place after Galatians was written. This explains why Galatians does not mention the decrees of Acts 15. If Paul mentions every visit then Gal 2 must be the Acts 11 visit.

But perhaps Galatians mentions only the times when he meets apostles. In Acts 11 only elders are mentioned. However, as we noted, this was probably a private meeting, despite certain similarities between the conflict reported in Gal 2:11–14 and the occasion for the convening of the Jerusalem Council as explained in Acts 15. In both the agitators come from Jerusalem and stir up controversy at Antioch. However, when Paul took Titus, who was never circumcised (2:3–6) to Jerusalem and the problems brought by the visitors from Jerusalem in Acts 15:1, these were pointers to the fact that the matters over which they disagreed would need a later, larger meeting to settle them. So, the later council of Acts 15 would be required, but this is not in Gal 2.

Objection 1

In Gal 2:7–10 the Jerusalem apostles endorse the apostle's call to preach to Gentiles. If this happened at the time of the famine visit in Acts 11, Paul did not begin ministry to them until Acts 13. In other words, would he be recognised as being a missionary to the Gentiles at the time of the famine visit? His missionary travels had not yet begun. But Paul's call to preach the gospel came to him at his conversion (see Gal 1:15–16). Also, he was preaching to Gentiles before the Acts 11 famine visit – Gal 1:21–24 records preaching in the regions of Syria and Cilicia, again, before the first missionary trip of Acts 13, Barnabas brought him from Tarsus to Antioch, where he shared for a full year in ministry (Acts 11:25–26).

Objection 2 The Chronological Problem

This problem is not straightforward as we are not fully certain about the actual dates when events took place. We should note first of all in Acts 11:27 Luke writes, "Now in those days," which is not a precise reference. Herod's persecution in Acts 12:1 and his unexpected death is usually dated AD 44. Was Paul's visit to Jerusalem *before* AD 44 since it is recorded in Acts 11? We should note the visit is also referred to at the end of 12:24–25. Paul says his first visit to Jerusalem was three years after his conversion (Gal 1:18–19); then "fourteen years" can be understood as the famine visit (Gal 2:1). If these numbers are to be taken *consecutively* seventeen years before AD 44 would bring us back to AD 27, and Jesus had barely begun his ministry then.

It is difficult to firmly establish when the famine mentioned in Acts 11:28 should be dated. Josephus[45] does refer to it but how the text is to be translated is not clear. In the Anglo-Saxon Chronicle, the fifth century historian Orosius[46] mentions this famine in Syria as having occurred in AD 47.

Here are a couple of alternatives. There is first the precise date when the visit occurred. It may be that the three years and fourteen years should be taken as concurrent not consecutively. Witherington,[47] who looks at both numbers in 1:18 and 2:1 from the point of view of "inclusive" reckoning suggests:

> Fourteen years could mean as little as twelve years and a few months (twelve full years plus parts of two others), and when added to the previous number mentioned, we could in fact arrive at a total of fourteen years for the entire period since Paul's conversion (one and a half years plus twelve and a half years). On the other hand, it could be as much as seventeen years. I suspect it is closer to the former than to the latter.

Peterson[48] also discusses the Acts 11:27–30 passage. He notes the vague time reference "in those days." He refers to AD 47 as the time of the great famine in Judea, when Alexander was Procurator (AD 46–48). The poor harvest of AD 45 in Egypt – the breadbasket for the whole area – resulted in Judea feeling the impact.

> It is likely that their trip to Jerusalem on this occasion took place in AD 48 and was the one described somewhat differently in Galatians 2:1–10, when the opportunity for a serious theological engagement with the apostles in Jerusalem was taken. Chronologically, it appears that 11:30 foreshadows the visit, which actually took place after the death of Herod Agrippa 1 in AD 44.

---

[45] Antiquities 20.5.2 101 states: "The successor of Fadus was Tiberius Alexander ... it was in that (or their) administration that the great famine occurred in Judea, during which Queen Helen bought grain from Egypt for large sums and distributed it to the needy." The text is therefore uncertain. If it was under Alexander the date may be AD 46–48; but it may have begun in Fadus' reign, from AD 44. Claudius was Emperor from AD 41–54.

[46] This introductory part of "The Anglo-Saxon Chronicle." See M. J. Swanton *The Anglo-Saxon Chronicle* (New York: Routledge, 1998).

[47] Witherington, 111, *Grace in Galatia*, 127.

[48] D. Peterson, *The Acts of the Apostles* (Grand Rapids, Michigan: W. B. Eerdmans Publishing Co., Nottingham: Apollos, 2009), 358.

He quotes Witherington[49] who suggests that the prophecy of Agabus may have been given in AD 44. He also refers to the vague reference mentioned earlier which shows that Luke's sources are not precise at this point and the famine visit he sees as happening by the sabbatical year in AD 47–48, when the effects of the famine were at their worst. However we consider the records, it seems that we can fit the time of the Famine Visit around AD 48 and in the opinion of a number of scholars this is the time when the Gal 2 visit occurred.

Objection 3

Acts 11 and 15 are duplicates of the one visit referred to in Gal 2. This appears to be still the view of a majority of scholars. It is claimed that the two Acts accounts in 11 and 15 are derived from different sources. Taking this approach will challenge Luke's accuracy as an historian, but such scepticism is not required to work out the accounts. The Acts of the Apostles is a theological work, but this does not mean that it has no historical basis – see the claim that the two-volume work Luke/Acts has involved careful research (Luke 1:1–4) that includes consulting eyewitnesses. This is a hotly debated subject, but there are many scholars who have affirmed Luke's historical accuracy in Acts.

Objection 4

Would there be a need for a Council in Acts 15 if the matter was settled on the Acts 11 visit? It is important to see that the private discussions and the agreement on the first occasion still needed greater ratification later in Acts 15:2–29. In Gal 2:1–10 the leading or 'pillar' apostles *privately* affirmed Paul's law-free gospel. But until as Witherington[50] explains there was a public pronouncement the Judaizing controversy could and would remain.

Paul was gone from Antioch for some time, but returned to the city after the first missionary journey of Acts 13–14. It appears, as will be suggested later, that the incident with Peter in 2:11ff. occurred at that time. Everything before that as far as the relationship with Peter and also Barnabas is concerned was positive (as it appears to be later at the Jerusalem Council in Acts 15:7–12, 22, 35). However, at this point Peter now has not been true to the former understanding with the pillar apostles and more so, acted contrary to his former relationships with Gentile believers, Acts 10:24–35; Gal 2:1–11. Gal 2:12 reveals that when certain men came "from James" Peter *refused fellowship* with the Gentile believers "fearing the circumcision party." Note that this issue over fellowship fits best with the problems *before* the time of the Council highlighted by Luke in Acts 10–11 i.e., the issue is *table-fellowship not circumcision.* Paul had to speak out because Peter's conduct "was not in step with the truth of the gospel" (2:14). We are not told in Galatians how Peter and Barnabas

---

[49] B. Witherington, 111. *The Acts of the Apostles. A Socio-Rhetorical Commentary* (Grand Rapids: Eerdmans, Carlisle: Paternoster, 1998), 80–83.
[50] Witherington, 111, *Grace in Galatia*, 9.

responded to Paul's challenge in the fellowship incident. However, in Acts 15:1–4 which happened soon after when "some men came down from Judaea" insisting that Gentile Christians be circumcised, shows Barnabas now supporting Paul – and also Peter, as mentioned above, at the forth-coming Council, which took things further to settle the whole issue in the matter of circumcision and in regulations regarding food restrictions and purity.

The main issue still needs to be made clear – when was Galatians written? I suggest that it is after this incident with Peter and around the time the trouble came to the Antioch church as mentioned in Acts 15:1–2, which finally led to the Council being called. Paul, while at Antioch, apparently learned of the presence of agitators in Galatia. Witherington[51] suggests that it seems that Paul had not a great deal of information about those who were bewitching them (3:1), unsettling them (5:12), and troubling them, "whoever he is" (5:10). In writing it is clear that Paul has his Galatian converts in view and only indirectly the Judaizers (see Gal 2:1–14). In the letter he makes a comparison between how *on an earlier occasion* he stood against Peter, Barnabas and the others who withdrew their fellowship from the Gentile believers; they themselves must now oppose the agitators who were seeking to persuade them to turn away from the gospel to one that demanded circumcision, which was not the true gospel. Therefore, I am suggesting that the letter should be dated around AD 49 or very early 50, as just prior to or as part of the events of Acts 15:1–3 and before Paul and Barnabas journey from Antioch to the forthcoming Jerusalem Council. This would make Galatians Paul's first letter and the first of the New Testament documents to be written (AD 49), i.e., after the first missionary journey and before the Council of Jerusalem. This date is supported by Longenecker,[52] who maintains that Paul's theological thought in this letter indicates an early date. He finds support in Drane who suggests that in certain ways Galatians can be seen as earlier than 1 Corinthians and Romans. Moo[53] also discusses the clear parallels between Galatians and Romans. He considers that while some major themes may overlap, Paul is developing them in different ways and that the reason for the similarities is that Paul was dealing with the same issues. In support of this position of an early composition we note Paul in 1:6 can write how his converts in Galatia are "so quickly" deserting the one who called them – implying that the letter was sent soon after his planting of the churches. This raises the question of whether or not suitable leadership had emerged in the Galatian churches; if they had Paul does not engage with the leaders but with the church in general.

So Bruce[54] in summarizing, makes the point that when Luke records in Acts 15:1 that Judean visitors – "some men" – came to Syrian Antioch and began to preach a different gospel which centred on the need for Gentile Christians to be circumcised in accordance with the law of Moses. It is probable that others, promoting the same

---

[51] Witherington, 111, *Grace in Galatia*, 23.
[52] See Longenecker, *Galatians*, lxxxiv. He refers in support to J. Drane, *Paul, Libertine or Legalist?* (London: SPCK, 1975), 140–43.
[53] Moo, *Galatians*, 18.
[54] Bruce, *The Epistle to the Galatians*, 55–65.

false gospel, visited the recently formed daughter-churches of Antioch, not only in Syria and Cilicia, as the apostolic letter indicates (Acts 15:23), but also among Paul's Gentile converts in south Galatia. Bruce continues:

> If so, then the letter to the Galatians was written as soon as Paul got news of what was afoot on the eve of the Jerusalem meeting described in Acts 15:6ff. This, it is suggested would yield the most satisfactory correlation of the data of Galatians and Acts and the most satisfactory dating of Galatians. It must be conceded that, if this is so, Galatians is the earliest among the extant letters of Paul. I know of no evidence to make this conclusion impossible, or even improbable ... if it is the earliest extant Christian document, its importance is enhanced.

How is Galatians Structured?

In recent times there has been much interest in analysing Galatians as a rhetorical document. It has often been explained how ancient writers used various forms of rhetoric to seek to persuade their hearers. First, "forensic" or judicial rhetoric, involving a past action, which often will have a courtroom setting, generally with the intention of establishing guilt or innocence; "deliberative," which endeavours to persuade or convince an individual to take a particular course of action in the near future; or again, "epideictic," a form of rhetoric which could be described as praise or blame rhetoric. This could happen at speeches on ceremonial occasions or funerals. Often the focus would be on social issues and on persuading people to affirm a particular view in the here and now.[55] Aristotle[56] writes:

> Further, to each of these a special time is appropriate: to the deliberative the future, for the speaker, whether he exhorts or dissuades, always advises about things to come; to the forensic the past, for it is always in reference to things done that one party accuses and the other defends; to the epideictic most appropriately the present, for it is the existing condition of things that all those who praise or blame have in view. It is not uncommon, however, for epideictic speakers to avail themselves of other times, of the past by way of recalling it, or of the future by way of anticipating it.

All three have been identified at various times in the past by scholars as the interpretative lens for reading Galatians. Betz[57] argued that Paul used forensic

---

[55] G. A. Kennedy, *New Testament Interpretation through Rhetorical Criticism* (Chapel Hill: University of North Carolina, 1984), 19; A *New History of Classical Rhetoric* (Princetown, NJ: Princetown University Press, 1994), 4, both point out that these three classifications were first set out by Aristotle, *On Rhetoric*, 3.1.1358a.

[56] For Aristotle, "The Art of Rhetoric," see trans. J. H. Freese, Loeb Classical Library, *Aristotle*, vol. 22, no. 193 (Cambridge, MA: Harvard University Press, 1926), 1.3.3–4, 34–35.

[57] H. D. Betz, "The Literary Composition and Function of Paul's Letter to the Galatians," NTS, 21 (1975), 353–79; *Galatians: A Commentary on Paul's letter to the Churches in Galatia,* 14–25. He proposes an Epistolary Prescript (1:1–5); *Exordium* (Introduction, 1:6–11); *Narratio* (Statement of Facts (1:12–2:14);

rhetoric. The apostle seeks to defend himself, with the false teachers his accusers and the Galatians the jury, whom Paul aims to win back to the truth. Kennedy, and more recently Witherington,[58] have rather classified Galatians as deliberative rhetoric. Witherington refers to how in Galatians the arguments are not of a forensic nature, on proving something true or false, but presenting reasons for following a certain course of action. There are the examples of Abraham or Paul himself (3:1–4:12); Paul is seeking to persuade his readers that certain actions or a particular course suggested will be honourable or beneficial and that his argumentation has all the elements of deliberative rhetoric. On the other hand, Longenecker[59] proposed that Paul used forensic rhetoric in the first half with "the courtroom scene a feasible backdrop," largely following Betz and then switched to deliberative in the second half, seeing 4:12 as a significant turning point in the letter with Paul moving from accusation and defence to seek "to persuade his Galatian converts to adopt a certain course of action."

Should these differences of opinion not lead us to go forward with caution? No doubt Paul, in seeking to communicate his message in a first-century setting, will use certain familiar forms of argumentation. But this does not mean that we must identify one particular rhetorical genre as the letter's all-pervasive hermeneutical key. Silva[60] observes that:

> If capable scholars cannot come to a firm agreement on so basic a question as identifying the genre of Galatians, those of us without expertise in the field may be forgiven for withholding judgment.... It would seem unproductive to draw exegetical inferences before a solid consensus is reached.

Dunn did not discuss the issue in his commentary and in a later article[61] comments on the fact of Paul's creativity:

> In particular it seems to me fairly pointless to argue about whether Paul's letters are "epideictic" or "deliberative," or whatever, when most are agreed that Paul's creative genius has adapted to his own ends whatever model he may have started with, and has done so to such an extent that the parallels are as likely to be misleading as helpful. And as for some of the elaborate structures which have been proposed for Paul's letters one might simply observe that there seems to be an inverse ratio between the length of the proposed chiasms in an individual letter and the light they shed upon on either the argument or its point. The vigour of Paul's theology evidently did

---

Propositio (Transitional Summary of Material (2:15–21); *Probatio* (Proof 3:1–4:31); *Exhortatio* (Epistolary Parenesis (5:1–6:10); *Conclusio* (Epistolary Postscript (6:11–18).
[58] Witherington 111, *Grace in Galatia*, 33, 198.
[59] Longenecker, *Galatians*, 11–12; 184, see also 197.
[60] M. Silva, *Explorations in Exegetical Method*: Galatians as a Test Case (Grand Rapids, MI: Baker Books, 1996), 94.
[61] J.D.G. Dunn, "Prolegomena to a Theology of Paul," NTS 40 (1994), 414–15.

not allow it to be easily contained within regular grammatical and compositional structures.

Witherington[62] does admit that Paul felt free to "modify" epistolary and rhetorical conventions of the time; he demonstrates a "certain flexibility" while still working within their "general framework." He is still persuaded that Galatians is "more like an ancient speech than any other in the NT."[63] He maintains that the work lacks the general features of the letter-genre i.e., thanksgiving, greetings from and to different individuals, travelogues and has only the briefest letter form at the beginning and end, 1:1–5; 6:11–18. However, in reply, one can say that for a small epistle the opening letter form seems entirely what you might expect – except for a telling omission (i.e., no commendation) which is fully intentional (I will return to this later). Was it not expected that letters were to be read aloud and heard by the community, with the intention to persuade?

We should not forget the lack of interest among earlier interpreters of Galatians in claiming that ancient rhetoric is determinative for any reading of Galatians.[64] It should be noted, although Longenecker can acknowledge that while the rhetorical features of Galatians are "of great value," scholars like Betz "have not given sufficient attention to an epistolary analysis of Galatians."[65] He also affirms that Paul seems much more influenced at times (e.g., in 3:6–4:11) by Jewish forms of argumentation, Jewish exegetical practices using Scripture, rather than Greco-Roman rhetorical conventions.[66] He therefore sets out the letter as having a basic epistolary structure: 1:1–5 Salutation 1:6–4:11; Rebuke Section 4:12–6:10; Request Section; 6:11–18 Subscription, using it as a basis for his exegesis throughout his commentary.[67] Fung[68] also considers that the arguments for some form of rhetorical structure is not "the most appropriate category to apply to the letter as a whole." So,

---

[62] Witherington 111, *Grace in Galatia*, 69.

[63] Witherington 111, *Grace in Galatia*, xi.

[64] See H. Kern, *Rhetoric and Galatians: Assessing an Approach to Paul's Epistle*, Society for New Testament Studies Monograph Series 101 (Cambridge: Cambridge University Press, 1998), 167–203; J. Riches, *Galatians Through the Centuries* (Oxford: Blackwell, 2008), 67; F. Tolmie, *Persuading the Galatians: A Text-Centered Rhetorical Analysis of a Pauline Letter*, Wissenschaftliche Untersuchungen zum Neuen Testament 190 (Tübingen: Mohr Siebeck, 2005), 1–30; M. C. de Boer, *Galatians: a Commentary*, New Testament Library (Louisville: Westminster, John Knox, 2011), 66–71.

[65] Longenecker, *Galatians*, cv.

[66] Longenecker, *Galatians*, 97. He of course, acknowledges, as Hengel in the past has demonstrated, that even Palestinian Judaism was not sheltered from the influence of its Hellenistic environment (M. Hengel, *Judaism and Hellenism: Studies in Their Encounter in Palestine during the Early Hellenistic Period*, vol. 1 Tr. J. Bowden (Philadelphia: Fortress, 1974), 312. For Longenecker Paul seems to have been influenced "unconsciously" by these forms of classical rhetoric which were "in the air," *Galatians*, cxiii.

[67] Longenecker, *Galatians*, cix. Longenecker examines first Deissmann's "private" letter theory, A. Deissmann, *Light from the Ancient East: The New Testament Illustrated by Recently Discovered Texts of the Graeco-Roman World*, Tr. A. R. M. Strachan (London: Hodder & Stoughton, 1909), 244–46; Betz's "apologetic letter" genre, "The Literary Composition and Function of Paul's Letter to the Galatians," *NTS*, 21 and *Galatians: A Commentary on Paul's Letter to the Churches in Galatia*; and B.H. Brinsmead's *Galatians as Dialogical Response to Opponents*, SBLDS 65 (Chico, CA: Scholars, 1982), plus Hellenistic epistolary structures and formulae in ci-cix before suggesting his own.

[68] Fung, *The Epistle to the Galatians*, 32.

his commentary will "adopt a more traditional way of analysis while taking note of the new approach." A telling point in all of this is made by Bruce,[69] who understanding the situation which called for Paul's intervention can question whether "in the excitement and urgency of the crisis with which he was suddenly confronted Paul would have been consciously careful to construct his letter according to the canons of the rhetorical schools."

It is clear as Fung suggests that we ought not to ignore the various suggestions of modern commentators that the work has certain rhetorical features. These will need to be acknowledged in the exegesis below. For the purpose of this commentary it is important to recognising that every written work will have some basic structural form. The important issue is that one seeks to highlight the flow of the argument so that the work holds together with all the parts relating to each other. At this point one can notice that commentators have generally found three major sections and given the work a common tripartite division. Silva[70] observes, "Indeed, no alternative structure has established itself broadly among Pauline scholars." This may be a sufficient division to note concerning the letter at this point. Our own divisions (see Contents pages) will be given as we work our way through the text. The following are simply examples of using the main headings:

Chapter 1–2: PERSONAL. Paul affirms his apostolic authority, writes about the gospel, how it came to him directly from God, his confrontation with Peter, and his personal convictions concerning the message.

Chapter 3–4: DOCTRINAL. Paul goes on the offensive and positively presents his arguments. He insists that salvation is not Christ plus the law. It is not Christ plus anything; it is by faith in Christ and his cross alone that we are saved. This is the true gospel. We are part of the true family of faith – born of the Spirit, sharing Abraham's faith, we receive the promise of justification; also chapter 4 will reveal that being "in Christ" we are adopted as sons and heirs of God.

Chapter 5–6: PRACTICAL. Paul writes about living the Christian life. We are a new creation, brought to the hearing of faith by the regenerating power of the Holy Spirit, who empowers and enables us (Gal 3:2–5, 29; 5:16–24; 6:15). He sets out what it means to be free "in Christ" – the result can be a life of loving service, holiness, and power (Gal 5:13–14, 25–26), fulfilling the "law of Christ" (Gal 6:1–10), a genuine Christian lifestyle.

Some commentators have used these basic divisions, just giving them different titles: The Truth of the Gospel; The Children of Promise; Living by the Spirit. Or as George,[71] History; Theology; Ethics. Sometimes it is suggested that the third section

---

[69] Bruce, *The Epistle to the Galatians*, 58.
[70] Silva, *Explorations in Exegetical Method*, 97.
[71] George, *Galatians*, 350.

really should begin at 5:13, rather than 5:1. Silva[72] also sets out an outline which is very similar to the above. Its main points are:

I. Introduction (1:1–10); II. Paul's Apostleship (1:11–2:21); III. Paul's Gospel (3:1–4:31); IV. Paul's Commands (5:1–6:10); V. Epilogue (6:11–18).

He also includes a number of useful subheadings, some of which he admits may be slightly forced. Although I have not included these in my exegesis, I will highlight some of Silva's insights when appropriate.

The last outline to note is that by Hendriksen,[73] who understands that letter's theme is the gospel of justification apart from law-works defended against its detractors.

Ch. 1 and 2 give us: The Gospel's Origination: It is not of human but of divine origin. Ch. 3 and 4: Its Vindication: both Scripture – the OT – and life (experience, past history) bear testimony to its truth. Ch. 5 and 6: Its Application: it produces true liberty. Let the Galatians stand firm, therefore, as does Paul, who glories in the cross of Christ.

It appears that in recent approaches there is not as strong an emphasis as there could be on the importance of 6:12–18, the final summary, or v. 14 glorying in the cross (see however Hendriksen's outline which makes mention of this). Witherington[74] in discussing what he refers to as the argument from chapter 5:2f. helpfully maintains that "the real bone of contention" in the letter is "the issue of circumcision and the Galatians' contemplation of submitting to it." He affirms:

> Clear proof that this is indeed *the* issue generating all the rhetoric is that Paul revisits this very matter of circumcision in a prominent way in his *peroratio* (or conclusion) in 6:12–17. In other words, Paul has followed the indirect strategy known as *insinuatio* (a subtle approach), reserving his direct comments about the problem in Galatia until near the end of his arguments.

If circumcision is *the* theme of Galatians – or at least identified as the major problem – and the final conclusion is in 6:12–17, then one can surely see the importance of Paul's affirmation in v. 14. The proposal of this book is basically that *boasting in the cross* is set over against depending upon circumcision and the commitment to law-keeping.

Actually, it can be maintained that the most important matter is not whether one is enthusiastic about a rhetorical structure (deliberative or forensic) but, as we are discussing, what the letter itself presents as its main theme. One can refer to

---

[72] Silva, *Explorations in Exegetical Method*, 98.
[73] Hendriksen, *Galatians*, 22.
[74] Witherington 111, *Grace in Galatia*, 364.

Witherington[75] again who in finding the *peroratio* here in chapter 6, in the summary for his whole presentation of the rhetorical features of Galatians, can actually state that:

> It must be stressed that what the *peroratio* tells us is that the *most* fundamental thing that Paul wants his audience to understand and embrace is not the experience of the Spirit or even justification but rather the cross. Justification is only possible, and the Spirit can only be experienced, because of the prior reality of the cross.

Therefore, the main point to accept here is that however much Paul has adopted popular methods of persuasion in the culture of the time, or has combined these with epistolary features in certain ways, we ought to note that undergirding all of the argumentation *contra* circumcision is the fact that we should put our trust in what Christ has accomplished on the cross alone; everything has been achieved through the cross and experienced by God's grace not works. As we have seen, Betz also accepts that as far as 6:12–17 is concerned, these verses can be seen as indicators of Paul's major concerns in the letter and must be employed as a hermeneutical key to all that Paul is seeking to set before his Galatian converts. In seeking therefore to interpret the letter we will endeavour to emphasise the importance of the cross in all of Paul's argument. We will keep in mind 6:14 and the three divisions generally accepted, will draw upon and quote a range of commentators where thought helpful, but will present our own headings as Paul seeks to convince the Galatians to resist the persuasive Judaizers.

In summary, it appears that in Galatians we have the earliest of Paul's letters, written in "large letters" (see 6:6). It was produced likely in Antioch, certainly before the Council of Jerusalem in AD 49 (Acts 15), or Paul would no doubt have referred to this in his argument. The problem involves the OT law. The men who had come to Antioch – as we have seen, they are usually called Judaizers – insisted that in order to be saved the new converts had to be circumcised and keep the law. It appears that they had also questioned Paul's authority as a teacher, his apostolic authority. Paul had been also made aware that the same message had been taken to the churches throughout Galatia. Now we have Paul's response – the way of salvation for condemned sinners is by grace through faith in Christ crucified, not through circumcision and submission to the works of the law. The law in fact, was given for a limited time and its purpose was not to give life (3:21) but to reveal the true nature of sin. Since no one can keep it cannot save but brings people under the curse. Therefore, to repeat, acceptance with God is not through following the path affirmed by the Judaizers (circumcision and law-keeping} but through the cross! The message of Galatians is that we can be – and have been – born of the Spirit and, through the hearing of faith, brought to the justification and adoption proclaimed in the gospel and to the new life empowered by the Holy Spirit. Paul emphasises that all has been accomplished through the completeness of the work of Christ on the cross – we glory

---

[75] Witherington 111, *Grace in Galatia*, 445.

in the cross. In him we are justified, free, no longer under God's wrath, with power to live a new Christian lifestyle through the Spirit's enabling.

The letter to the Galatians, therefore brings to us *assurance of acceptance*; Christ by his work on the cross, "the Son of God who gave himself for me," has done all that God required to be done. You can rest in him.

Also, that same cross work has brought to us, as we will see, the *power of the Holy Spirit.* Christ delivers us from this evil age; he invaded this age and now spiritually the blessings of the new age have come to us in advance. Therefore, at present, this is the age of the Spirit, who can empower us and create a Christ-like character in us, the fruit of the Spirit.

Finally, our lives can be different; by that same Spirit, who enables us to submit to the teaching of the Scriptures and follow the example of the Lord Jesus, we can fulfil the law of Christ i.e., we can manifest *a Christian lifestyle* and make an impact for God in society and the world at large.

GALATIANS ONE

Gal 1:1–5 Paul's Introductory Greeting

In this first chapter Paul greets the churches in Galatia, reminding them that he was "an apostle" and emphasising the divine source of his commission. He had also been independent of the other apostles, and stresses the point that he only had made one visit to Jerusalem in fourteen years and that for fifteen days. Further, he will write about the gospel, how it came to him directly from God and not from man.

Bruce[1] entitles 1:1–5, "salutation," and 6–10, "No Other Gospel"; Moo[2] calls 1:1–10, "The Cross and the New Age" – which is a very important insight, as we shall see for the whole of the letter. Both these commentators divide the opening into two parts: vv. 1–5, Epistolary Salutation; and vv. 6–10, the Letter's Occasion. Regarding this introduction to the letter, Witherington[3] maintains that Paul can consider himself free to modify epistolary and rhetorical conventions of his time to suit his own purpose.

Letters in ANE were regularly introduced by the formula "X to Y, greetings." Most epistles follow this pattern, with one or more elements expanded as appropriate. All three can be identified here: "Paul … the brothers … to the churches of Galatia … grace to you and peace." However, these are followed by a notable omission – there is no commendation of the readers. First:

He Reminds Them of His Divine Calling

This reminder was to reassure those in the Galatian churches and to challenge any who were questioning his authority. Only in this salutation the negative and the positive are used to make all things clear. In what Hendriksen[4] calls "an unequivocal and double denial," v. 1 reads "Paul an apostle, not from men nor through man but…." Paul clearly emphasises that his calling was from God. In 2:12, Paul reveals that, "certain men came from James," which indicates that they claimed to have been commissioned by a human being; but it was not so for Paul. Of course, there was human involvement as well (Ananias, Acts 9:10–19; the leaders of the church in Antioch, 13:1–3), but the point here is his sense of having an ultimate authority from God. Witherington[5] explains, "The ἀλλὰ (*alla* "but") is strongly adversative here and indicates that in contrast to human commission, Paul's was divine in origin and character."

---

[1] Bruce, *The Epistle to the Galatians*, 71.

[2] Moo, *Galatians*, 65–66. Later we will see that the letter's closing section is also "The Cross and the New Creation," 6v6–11.

[3] Witherington 111, *Grace in Galatia*, 17, 69.

[4] Hendriksen, *Galatians*, 30.

[5] Witherington 111, *Grace in Galatia*, 73. Hendriksen makes the point that Paul received office from the one who was "the historical Jesus, who is at the same time the Anointed One," 30.

Paul intentionally uses ἀποστολος *apostolos* to remind his audience that he is one who is sent, who has received a divine commission. It was not his habit to magnify his office and he says elsewhere that he was the very least of the apostles (1 Cor 15:8) but he was an apostle just the same, for he had seen the risen Lord. This is one reason at least for the reference to the resurrection here in v. 1 which reminds us of his Damascus Road experience – also alluded to in v. 15f.

Paul further emphasises that he was commissioned "through Jesus Christ and God the Father."[6] He is not arguing here, he is making a statement of fact. Usually in Paul the order is the Father and then Christ (Rom 1:7; 1 Cor 1:3; 2 Cor 1:2; Phil 1:2). Witherington[7] again suggests that this odd order is perhaps to be explained by the fact that Paul "is already thinking that he received both his call and conversion through a Christophany" (see v. 16 below). Note that for Bruce,[8] "the unselfconscious way in which Paul repeatedly couples God and Christ together bears eloquent witness to his understanding of the person and status of Christ."[9] We should note that to reject Paul's message was to reject Christ and the Father who had sent him. God the Father also "raised him from the dead." The resurrection is the Father's seal of affirmation of the acceptance of the work of the cross as all-sufficient for our sin. As has been said, it is God's "Amen" to Christ's "It is finished!" All that needed to be done for us he has done; no other work is required; we can rest in this assurance. Here also Paul is announcing not just the fact that God has raised Christ from the dead but the soteriological significance of that event. "In Christ," risen from the dead, God has inaugurated the blessings of the new age – those blessings have invaded this present age (see 1:4). Again, in the letter, Paul will make clear that the Mosaic law belongs to the old age not the new.

He can add "all the brothers who are with me," v. 2. Hendriksen,[10] because of his convictions about the place and time of writing, advocates that Galatians was likely written from Corinth before 1 & 2 Thessalonians. This reference would then be for him the church members of Corinth, who came to inform him what was going on (as 1 Cor 1:11), plus the Galatian delegates with Paul at the time. However, if we accept the earlier date which I have advocated in the introduction, then this reference is to *his fellow workers in the church at Antioch* who concur with his claim to apostleship and no doubt share the views he expresses in this letter. It is emphasised that Paul was just as much an apostle as Peter, James and John, who were apostles before him (1:17).

The authority of the person commissioned is delegated from the one who commissions, and so Paul's authority came from Christ and God. Paul knew of other

---

[6] Here και Θεοῦ παρτὸς *kai theou patros* "and God the Father" is omitted by Marcion.
[7] Witherington 111, *Grace in Galatia*, 73.
[8] Bruce, *The Epistle to the Galatians*, 73.
[9] The Fatherhood of God is an important theme in Galatians (1:3, 4; 4:2, 6), as is sonship and adoption (3v7, 26–29; 4v 5–6; 22–31). Paul will affirm that rather than the notion that one needs to be circumcised or be a Jew to be a son or daughter of Abraham or be sons of God, all men, whether Jew our Gentile, can have this status through the work of Christ on the cross and by faith.
[10] Hendriksen, *Galatians*, 16.

apostles who were commissioned by men, such as the apostles of the churches in 1 Cor 8:23. This may have been a valid commission, but it took its character from those who undertook the commissioning. As we noted, Paul's commission was not from men, not even through a human intermediary – οὐδὲ δι'ἀνθρώπου ἀλλὰ *houde di'anthrōpou alla*, "not through man," but directly from Christ. It is likely that his Galatian converts had been given a different account of his apostleship. So, Paul had experienced a "Christophany"; he met the risen Christ who commissioned him. The first stage in the resurrection (expected by all Jews) had already happened.

He Reminds Them of Divine Grace

Paul will emphasise throughout this letter that salvation is not of works but is all of God's grace. But note first that Paul had a concern for the people of God. "To the churches of Galatia." It seems clear that we have a circular letter to be read in all the churches. These will be the churches Paul had first founded. Regarding the location of the churches to which the letter is addressed, note the two positions discussed above in the Introduction:

South Galatia – supported by Bruce, Guthrie, Longenecker, McDonald, Ridderbos, Ramsay, Stott and Witherington. This view is also known as the "Province" Theory, and included the towns that Paul had visited on his first missionary journey set out in Acts 13–14.

North Galatia – with Lightfoot, Kümmel, Betz. This is the "Territory" Theory, which includes ethnic Galatia in the north.

I have taken the reference to the "churches" to be addressed as the church communities in the south. Witherington[11] maintains that the greater number of Paul's Galatian converts in that region will be Gentiles, and not Jews. It is clear from the pressure they were under to adopt a nomistic lifestyle and be circumcised, that they:

> Already had some exposure to Judaism before becoming Christians…. Paul feels he can use an elaborate Jewish allegory in Gal 4 and arguments about covenants … suggests an audience conversant with Judaism and perhaps the basic lineaments of the Hebrew Scriptures as well.

It appears that at the time of writing, as we will see below, they were at the point of defection. But, if we accept an early date to the letter, it is possible to see, in Paul's second missionary journey, the positive outcome of Paul's warnings and his appeal to them. On this journey he could come again to Lystra and Derbe and Timothy could be commissioned to join his missionary team. At that time Luke tells us that the churches in that area were "strengthened in the faith and they increased in number daily" (Acts 16:5).

---

[11] Witherington 111, *Grace in Galatia*, 7.

For the readers, he prays for "grace and peace." Are these just included because they were common greetings in the Greek and Jewish cultures – χαίρειν *chairein* and שׁלוֹם *shalom*? Perhaps. But there is certainly more here, since these words do not stand alone and are followed by "from God our Father and the Lord Jesus Christ" i.e., they have theological significance as well. Grace is Paul's special word. The fountainhead is the Father, the channel is Christ.[12] Grace is the undeserved favour of God. The Galatians had been saved by grace and knew peace with God. Not once in the epistles is the order reversed. Peace is the state of life[13] enjoyed by those who have effectively experienced divine grace. For Hendriksen,[14] "peace" is both a state, of reconciliation with God, and a condition, "the inner conviction that consequently all is well." This is so important here, for it is a blessing that is emphasised throughout the epistle – through Christ's death for us on the cross we have that assurance that we are accepted, free, in fact, in Christ, we are actually sons of God. Note here the stress at the very beginning of the letter that God is "God *our* Father." You must accept it, believe it and live in the good of it!

Bruce[15] points out that God and Christ are completely at one in the bestowal of salvation. First, "grace" is called "the grace of Christ" (1:6) and "the grace of God" (2:21); the "peace" to which salvation leads is "the peace of God" (Phil 4:7) and "the peace of Christ" (Col 3:15). Fung[16] suggests that the triple designation "Lord Jesus Christ" here points to, respectively, his exalted rank, his saving significance (cf. Matt 1:21), and his divine commission (cf. Luke 4:17–21; Acts 10:38). The Lord Jesus brings as Messiah the blessings of that final kingdom, mentioned in 5:21, as these blessings have invaded "in Christ" this evil age (Acts 14:22; Gal 1:4).

But this is where things were being challenged at Galatia – salvation by grace through the cross – and it can be claimed that this is the burden of the letter. George[17] has reminded us that "[grace] runs like a scarlet thread throughout the epistle from start to finish (1:15; 2:9, 21; 3:18; 5:4; 6:18)." In fact, we should note that the grace and peace greeting may form an *incluso* with 6:16 "peace and mercy" on the Israel of God. Remaining faithful to the apostolic gospel will demonstrate the confidence Paul had in them (5:10) that they are truly part of this Christian community and will continue to experience the grace and peace God imparts to his people. We will find the burden of the letter is that the Galatians must reject the Judaizers and, being called (saved) by grace alone (1:6), continue to know sustaining grace, live in the

---

[12] Fung highlights M. J. Harris, "Prepositions and Theology in the Greek New Testament" *NIDNTT* 111 ed. C Brown (Grand Rapids: Zondervan, 1975–78), 1178, who suggests that the juxtaposition of both Father and Son using one preposition as in v. 1, rather than pointing to source and channel, envisages both as a joint source of grace and peace. See Fung, *The Epistle to the Galatians*, 39.

[13] Bruce, *The Epistle to the Galatians*, 74. Witherington reminds us of the "divisive character of submitting to Judaizing suggestions," and of the "strife … quarrels and divisions that exist in the assemblies," Witherington 111, *Grace in Galatia*, 76. Note 2:12 13; 5:22–26, cf. also Acts 15:1. Experiencing peace with God should be followed by peace in the churches, truly manifesting the fruit of the Spirit.

[14] Hendriksen, *Galatians*, 33.

[15] Bruce, *The Epistle to the Galatians*, 75.

[16] Fung, *The Epistle to the Galatians*, 39.

[17] George, *Galatians,*, 92. Moo also affirms that "'the grace of Christ' summarizes the argument of the letter," Moo, *Galatians*, 30.

power of the Spirit and know daily peace. Paul now reminds them that these blessings were purchased at great cost.

He Reminds Them of the Divine Plan

In v. 4 Paul highlights Christ's voluntary surrender of himself for us; Jesus gave himself for our sins. This is the earliest statement in the letter about the significance of the death of Christ. Witherington[18] states, "it is clear that what Christ accomplished on the cross is very important to Paul's overall argument in this document." Therefore, it is not surprising to see it already emphasised in v. 4.

The phrase is τοῦ δόντος ἑαυτὸν ὑπὲρ *tou dontos heauton huper*, "who gave himself for." See 2:20 also. Note that in v. 4 ὑπὲρ *huper* is replaced by περι *peri* in some texts. However, the first may be best here since it is used in 1 Cor 15:3, part of the apostolic message, and occurs again in Gal 3:13, "with the vicarious idea of 'in place of' being connoted in all these passages."[19] So he gave himself "for our sins" i.e., to pay the penalty for them, in our place. The phrase will reflect Jesus' statement, given to us in Mark 10:45, "to give his life a ransom for many," which in turn reveals Jesus' own consciousness of his role as God's Righteous Servant of Isa 53:5–6, 12. Regarding the phrase "for our sins" some scholars suggest that Paul is quoting a form of words they would be already familiar with in a Christian hymn or confession. Generally this can be linked with the view that apostle only seldom uses the plural form "sins" in the "undisputed" Pauline epistles. But if we include all the writings attributed to him the plural can be then found nine times, apart from quotations from the OT (Rom 7:5; 1 Cor 15:3, 17; Eph 2:1; Col 1:14; 1 Thess 2:16; 1 Tim 5:22; 2 Tim 3:6). For Moo,[20] the language is rooted in the Isaiah "servant" prophesies of Christ, especially Isa 53. Is this chapter, see vv. 6, 10, 13 where we find Christ "giving himself" for sins following the will of the Lord. Here at the very beginning of this letter Paul can affirm that Christ has fully dealt will the sins of all his people. You have nothing to fear. Luther[21] made the same observation:

> How may we obtain remission of our sins? Paul answereth, that the man … called Jesus Christ, the Son of God, hath given himself for them…. For if our sins may be taken away by our own works, merits and satisfactions, what needed the Son of God to be given for them? But seeing he was given for them, it followeth that we cannot put them away by our own works.

Paul proclaims early in the letter the ground of God's acceptance of sinful men which had been virtually forgotten. The cross, Calvary alone is all that is required; his work not ours. Note again that this was God's plan. Christ's death for us, his atoning

---

[18] Witherington 111, *Grace in Galatia*, 76.

[19] Longenecker, *Galatians*, 8.

[20] Moo, *Galatians*, 72.

[21] M. Luther, *A Commentary on St. Paul's Epistle to the Galatians*, ETr. A revised and completed translation based on the "Middleton" edition of the English version of 1575 (ed.), S. Watson (London: James Clarke and Co. Ltd. 1953), 47.

sacrifice, was "according to the will of our God and Father." The redemptive acts of Christ; his coming and cross were all through the initiative of God; it was the divine purpose. God's decree in eternity concerning his people has now been fulfilled in time. Father and son acted in perfect harmony.[22] This is essential as Luther[23] explained:

> When thou shalt acknowledge this to be the will of God through Christ, then wrath ceaseth, fear and trembling vanisheth away, neither doth God appear any other than merciful, who by his determinate counsel would that his Son should die for us, that we might live through Him.

Consequently, we need not fear acceptance when we turn to God, since he himself gave his own son for us to make us his children. We can glory in the cross, in the initiative of God! What can the Judaizers add to that source of salvation?

He Reminds Them of Their Divine Deliverance

He gave himself "to deliver us from this present evil age." Salvation is of the nature of a deliverance, a rescue. This is the only occurrence of ἐξαιρέομαι *exaireomai* in Paul, but it is often in the LXX. Note that αἰών *aiōn* "age" refers not so much to a period of time as to what fills that time period. The history of the world is divided into great periods or "ages" and this present evil age refers to the time until Christ returns – which was understood as inaugurating the age to come. This distinction was a common one in Second Temple Judaism. Longenecker[24] quotes from 4 Ezra 7:50, which explained the thinking. "The Most High made not one age but two" and the present age was "already grown old,… already past the strength of youth," 4 Ezra 5:55; because of Adam's sin, the world "became narrow and sorrowful and painful, and full of perils coupled with great toils … but the ways of the future world are broad and safe, and yield the fruit of immortality" 4 Ezra 7:12–13. He also refers to the Qumran literature which has many such similar references, identifying the present age as the "epoch of wickedness" during which Belial has free rein, 1QpHab 5.7–8.

It is clear that this idea of an evil age was part of Paul's Jewish background, his apocalyptic perspective. The Galatians would also be familiar with this perspective. However, what is Paul affirming when he states that Christ has delivered us from this evil age? His understanding is similar to that of other writers in the NT, namely that at his first advent, Christ invaded this age and through the cross brought to his people already the blessings of the new age. In Gal 6:16 Paul affirms that they are part of the "new creation" – its fullness is in the future, but for those "in Christ" its blessings are already realized through the regenerating Holy Spirit. So, it is not just a future deliverance here when Christ comes, but a present deliverance of which Paul writes. In using the phrase "evil age" the apostle is writing of an evil way of life, the evil

---

[22] Fung, *The Epistle to the Galatians*, 40.
[23] Luther, *A Commentary on St. Paul's Epistle to the Galatians*, 56.
[24] Longenecker, *Galatians*, 8.

way people live alienated from God (actually, the god of this age is the devil). We are rescued from this way of living; not delivered out of the world, but from the evil which dominates it. This complements the action of atonement which deals with our sins. His giving himself for us delivers us from condemnation; but also through the cross and by the Holy Spirit we are regenerated – as above, a "new creation" (see Ezek 36:26–27; John 3:6), enabling us to live a different life – a godly life through the Spirit's power. Bruce[25] explains:

> Here then is Paul's "realized eschatology" ... The indwelling Spirit not only helps them to look forward in confidence to the life of the age to come (5:5); he enables them to enjoy it even while in mortal body they live in the present age. Thanks to the work of the Spirit, applying to believers the redemption and victory won by Christ, the "not yet" has become for them the "already."

This is part of what it means to "glory in the cross," the deliverance through the "walk by the Spirit" of which (5:16) speaks. The letter, as was emphasised in the Introduction is about power; the Christian should seek this power.

Also, what has this deliverance from the "old" evil age got to do with this present problem of submission to the law? What is important to note is that the law to which the Galatian Christians were being asked to submit by the Judaizers belonged to this present age. As we will see later, it is also associated with "the elemental powers of the world" under which they were enslaved before they actually came to faith in Christ (4:3, 9). Paul is saying that Christ has delivered them from all of this. Why should they go back to being enslaved again? Moo[26] can insightfully affirm:

> The cross, and especially the epochal significance of the cross, is the fulcrum of Paul's strategy for persuading the Galatians to reject the overtures of the false teachers (see esp. 2:19–30; 3:1, 13; 6:14).

One should not miss the mention of the resurrection in v. 1. Its significance should not be overlooked as it also:

Serves to underline the fundamental break in salvation history that the coming of Christ has created, for resurrection, against the background of the OT and Jewish theology, also signals the arrival of the new age.[27]

This is an important theological argument in Galatians. The new age has broken into history. "In Christ" therefore, the inauguration of a new age effects in a fundamental way, as we noted, any interpretation and application of the law. Again, the different

---

[25] Bruce, *The Epistle to the Galatians*, 76. So also Fung, *The Epistle to the Galatians*, 41–42. Again, Silva explains that Paul is speaking of liberation out of, not the change of the aeons themselves, but "an overlapping of the ages," Silva, *Explorations in Exegetical Method* , 172, n. 10.

[26] Moo, *Galatians*, 66.

[27] Moo, *Galatians*, 66.

opening of the letter here lays down an emphasis for the argument of the letter i.e., that Christ's work is an "apocalyptic rescue operation,"[28] with the cross playing the central role. As George affirms, "The Christian now lives in profound tension between the *no longer* and the *not yet* ... we must not be drawn back into 'a yoke of slavery' (Gal 5:1)." Yet while Christ has rescued us from this evil age he has not taken us out of it. We must remember that "liberty must not degenerate into licence nor the gift of the Spirit be abused by selfish carnal behaviour (Gal 5:16–26)."[29]

As we have stressed, v. 4 is a crucial statement for all that is to come regarding the people of God and what the cross had done for them. Moo[30] maintains that:

> Central to Paul's attempt to woo the Galatians back to the true gospel is his insistence throughout the letter that the cross of Christ is the decisive and uniquely sufficient means to rescue sinners from death. Embracing Christ's cross through faith is all that is needed to effect this rescue and to bring believers into the "new creation" (6:15). The law program advocated by the agitators *effectively underplays the decisive turning point in all of human history.* [italics mine]

The cross is that turning point. Yet the real significance of this early teaching in Galatians is often left out, or certainly not given due prominence in many of the modern commentaries with their "rhetorical structures."

He Reminds Them of the Divine Doxology

Verse 5: "to whom be the glory forever and ever. Amen." A doxology at the end of a salutation is rare in Paul except in Ephesians 1:3. The relative pronoun ᾧ *hō* "to whom," has of course the antecedent in v. 4, "our God and Father." The phrase literally, "unto the age of the ages" emphasises the unlimited extent of the doxology.

Note all that Paul has affirmed about God in this salutation. He is the source of Paul's apostleship; the one who raised Jesus from the dead; the fountainhead of grace and peace; at whose initiative and by whose decree Christ came to die in our place; and the one who is our Father and we his children by adoption (3:7, 26; 4:4–7, 22–31). This is arguably the highest blessing of all, won for us through the cross and made effective in us by his Holy Spirit, who has made us a "new creation." These blessings, plus all that Paul reveals about Jesus Christ as the channel of grace and peace, are grounded in all that he suffered for us as the true Servant of the Lord, who came to do the Father's will concerning his people. He has brought us deliverance from the present age and imparted to us the blessings of the new age. It is not to be wondered at that here we find this ascription of praise! Hendriksen[31] affirms that,

---

[28] R. B. Hays, "The Letter to the Galatians: Introduction, Commentary, and Reflection," vol. XI 181–348 in *The New Interpreter's Bible* (ed.) L.E. Keck (Nashville: Abingdon, 2000), 202.

[29] George, *Galatians*, The New American Commentary, 88.

[30] Moo, *Galatians,*, 72.

[31] Hendriksen, *Galatians*, 35.

"When the wicked infiltrators *minimise* God's work of redemption, Paul will *magnify* it, calling all men to do this with him." Do the blessings God has given to us and what Christ suffered for us not move us in a similar way? Can we not add our "Amen," to that which would be the response of the first hearers, affirming this ascription, giving "glory" to God?

In leaving this section it must be noted that the significance of the introduction for the whole of the letter should not be played down, for it sets the tone for all Paul wants to magnify the gospel as the only means of enjoying salvation.

Gal 1:6–9 Only One Gospel

These verses introduce the reason for writing – the Galatians' departure from the true gospel. We should note that this is the usual place in other epistles where, after the initial greetings have been brought, Paul commends the readers and gives thanks for the spiritual progress they have made. The pattern was common in Greek letter writing; Paul had "baptised" it into Christ and developed it in his own distinctive way. Here we find the opposite. Instead of delight at their consistency, there is dismay at their compromise. Instead of thanksgiving there is the pronouncement of a curse. This severity of tone and urgency of purpose is carried on throughout the letter. As Hendriksen[32] explains, while it was usually his custom to commend, even the Corinthians with all their failings, here the very essence of the gospel was at stake; "the issue is momentous – God's glory and man's salvation – tolerance has its limits." But as we will see, with Paul there was *amazement* rather than *resentment*; *reproach* not *rejection.*

Those who emphasise rhetoric as a hermeneutical key for Galatians, find in 1:6–11 the *exordium*, the statement of the cause or the reason why Paul wrote. Here the Galatians are being faced with a clear choice. As Witherington[33] explains, "They must either choose the gospel which Paul had already proclaimed to them or the message which the agitators had offered them. They could not have it both ways."

Astonishment is Expressed

v. 6 "I am astonished." The word is best understood as an actual "astonishment rebuke,"[34] not just some kind of literary indicator. The present continuous tense of the verb, stresses the on-going concern of the one who first preached the good news in Galatia. Paul writes of them, "you are so quickly deserting." It seems almost that at the very first opportunity, with no real stand against the false teachers, they were considering turning from the way of faith.[35] There are possible echoes here from the

---

[32] Hendriksen, *Galatians*, 37.

[33] Witherington 111, *Grace in Galatia*, 80.

[34] Longenecker, *Galatians,* 14.

[35] Here "so quickly" is best understood as "a temporal marker," Moo, *Galatians*, 76. "Quickly deserting" as we noted earlier in the Introduction, supports an early date for the letter.

OT when the people of Israel, just out of Egypt, turned from the living God (Exod 32:8; Deut 9:16). As Witherington[36] points out, "The Galatians have not yet completely defected from the true Gospel, but they are in the process of doing so."

When someone is young in the faith and anxious to please God, there is the danger of being open to the influence of others who will claim to set before them further steps they can take to please God. Here the word "quickly" suggests that there had been a failure to give time and thought to these doctrines with no one to guide them. Paul now writes to warn them that they were on a false path. We have to go deeper in our comprehension once we have turned to the Lord and not be "carried about by every wind of doctrine, by human cunning, by craftiness in deceitful schemes" (Eph 4:14). The use of the continuous (present) tense suggests that the process has begun but it might still be arrested. They were in the act of turning (see also 4:9–10; 5:2–4) and Paul wants to stop them on their course away from the truth. We are being warned here against rashly accepting the teaching of any man. Just because religious teachers are in positions of importance does not mean that they come from God (2 Cor 11:13–15). We live in an age of hurry and haste. We need to be warned about quickly accepting the latest fad. You need time to study God's word, form your convictions, becoming settled in your understanding.

They are turning from him who called them into the grace of Christ. The ἐν *en* is probably instrumental, meaning "by" the grace of Christ. Paul notes that it is "him" i.e., God the Father – he had called them, that internal and effectual call as God through the Holy Spirit applies the good news of the gospel invitation bringing us to faith and to a miracle of spiritual transformation. This is how we are saved. To abandon the gospel is to therefore forsake God (see 5:4). God's salvation is all of grace and it is brought to us through Jesus Christ alone. The emphasis here on grace is significant. This was what was at stake in the new teaching – they were being turned away from grace to law. Bruce[37] explains about grace, "it is demonstrated in the death of Christ, by which the undeserving, the 'ungodly' (Rom 5:6), are redeemed, justified and reconciled." Note that χριστου *christou* is omitted by some texts, but it is best retained. The spiritual direction in which they were moving was that they are turning[38] to another gospel – a gospel of which God is not the source and Christ is not the author. Paul writes of it as a new sort of gospel, stuff of another brand.

In any focus upon the background to εὐαγγέλιον *euangelion* "gospel" one should begin at Isa 40:9, the good news of Zion's liberation and restoration; Isa 52:7, the good news of peace applied by Paul in Rom 10:15 to preachers of the Christian gospel;[39] Isa 61:1, the good news to the poor read by Jesus in Luke 4:17–19 and

---

[36] Witherington 111, *Grace in Galatia*, 82.
[37] Bruce, *The Epistle to the Galatians*, 80.
[38] Of course, those who have known God's effectual calling will not be finally turned aside – see 5:10, Paul has the "confidence" they will not in the end follow this road and forsake the truth.
[39] Some recent scholars have pointed out a possible contrast by Paul with Roman imperialism – the reign of the emporer, good news for the world, contrasted with the truth that "God reigns" i.e., the reign/lordship of

applied to himself. There are seven occurrences of the word "gospel" in Galatians, six in the first chapter. Witherington[40] sees this as "A telltale sign that the major issue is the message Paul preaches." Again, that message is the message of the cross.

The expression παρ' ὃ (*par'ho*) will mean "beyond that which" or "contrary to" what they had received.

Assurance is Given

Paul continues in v. 7 "not that there is another one (another gospel)." The apostle asserts that there is no other gospel apart from the one he preached. Paul will not allow the conclusion to be drawn that there are various gospels and that the Galatians can pass harmlessly from one to another. There are two Greek words for "another" and, if they are used strictly, the one in v. 6 means "another of a different kind" and the one here, "another of the same kind." It is likely that the false teachers were claiming that their message and activity should be seen as complementary to Paul's preaching and ministry. Paul stresses that in no sense is this true. What they were teaching was really just a perversion of the gospel of Christ. In no sense is it Paul's gospel and in no sense therefore is it the gospel of Christ. "Gospel it is not: it is a message of bondage, not of freedom. It is a form of the doctrine of salvation by law keeping from which Paul had been liberated by the true gospel he had received on the Damascus road by 'revelation of Jesus Christ (v. 12).'"[41] There is only the one gospel of justification by faith in Christ, and this alone leads to a life lived in the power of the Holy Spirit.

It seems to have taken time to fully appreciate the wonder of what God had done in Christ through the cross and all that this meant for Jew and Gentile in Christ – see the great reservations expressed by "the circumcision party" in Acts 11:1–18 about Peter's entrance into and fellowship with the Roman centurion Cornelius. Galatians is also evidence of this. It took the Jerusalem Council of Acts 15:6–29 and the plain responses of both Peter and James to persuade the whole community. As James said in Acts 15:19 "Therefore my judgment is that we should not trouble those of the Gentiles who turn to God." Also 15:24, 28, "since we have heard that some persons have gone out from us and troubled you with words, unsettling your minds, although we gave them no instructions…. For it has seemed good to the Holy Spirit and to us to lay on you no greater burden." In my judgment, this consensus *follows* the trouble in Antioch, also in the Galatian churches and the writing of the letter.

Paul now focuses upon the false teachers (the "some men" or "some persons" of Acts 15:1, 24) who were influencing his converts. He has two things to say about them. Firstly, they were troublers of the church. The verb here is ταράσσοντες *tarassontes*

Christ. Here in Galatians there is not much evidence that Paul had this contrast in mind. The reference to the gospel from Isaiah is stressing the blessing of peace.

[40] Witherington 111, *Grace in Galatia*, 72.
[41] Bruce, *The Epistle to the Galatians*, 82.

which means to trouble, confuse or agitate, to upset the mind.[42] Paul could see that these teachers were out to disturb the loyalty of the Galatians to the apostle and their teachings were perplexing them with regard to their relationship to the Lord. Secondly, they were really perverting, μεταστρέψαι *metastrepsai*, meaning to reverse, twist, change to the opposite, the gospel of Christ. Both verbs were used in a political sense of agitators who caused turmoil and revolutionary action; here now in the NT they are used more figuratively (Acts 2:20; James 4:9).

The present tense of the verbs and participles point to the fact that the false teachers were still in Galatia when Paul was writing. They needed to be stopped. By their legalistic demands they were binding men to the yoke of external conditions for salvation. This was the exact opposite to the full and free salvation in Christ through the work of the cross, which was Paul's gospel, as presented in this letter.

Anathema is Pronounced

Concerning v. 8, the Greek implies a case which has never occurred; indeed this "if" construction is common in the letter. For Longenecker,[43] "The subjunctive mood is used because Paul is making a statement which is somewhat doubtful, though theoretically possible." If it were possible that he or an angel (the most authoritative preacher imaginable)[44] were to preach another message different from what they had received, they are accursed. It is the message, not the messenger, that ultimately matters. As Bruce makes clear,[45] "The gospel preached by Paul is not the true gospel because it is Paul who preaches it; it is the true gospel because the risen Christ gave it to Paul to preach." The gospel of Christ cannot be changed. The gospel is Christ's and no-one, neither an apostle on earth nor a ministering spirit from heaven, can alter it. Any *other* message and its messengers were to be seen as under God's condemnation.

These references are probably because the false teachers would claim to have impeccable credentials as members in good standing in the Jerusalem church, or that they had the authority of the Jerusalem elders behind them, which was not the case. Longenecker[46] explains that, "Paul saw the preacher's authority as derived from the gospel, and not vice versa." The word "accursed" *anathema* is related to the Hebrew *herem* meaning devoted to God for destruction; it is the strongest expression of separation from God, his divine disapproval.

In v. 9 Paul moves from the impossibility of the "should preach" (v. 8) to the "is preaching." It was actually being done. This is therefore not just a repetition of the

---

[42] We find the verb used of Herod (Matt 2:3); the disciples in the storm when Jesus walks upon the sea (Matt 14.26); Zechariah on seeing the angel in the temple (Luke 1:12).
[43] Longenecker, *Galatians*, 16.
[44] Did the agitators stress the connection between the law and angels? Gal 3:19 states it was "put in place through angels through an intermediary." See Fung, *The Epistle to the Galatians*, 47.
[45] Bruce, *The Epistle to the Galatians*, 83.
[46] Longenecker, *Galatians*, 17.

previous statement. Paul had said this before (see also 2 Cor 7:3), the occasion perhaps being the second visit of Acts 14:21f. Paul makes clear that any other gospel is false and will only lead to condemnation. Those who preach and those who accept such a gospel have no hope of escape. The word "*anathema*," as Fung[47] points out cannot simply mean "excommunicated" from a church since an "angel" is also mentioned. The idea is of being "delivered up and devoted to the judicial wrath of God." Hendriksen[48] mentions its similar use in Acts 23:14 Rom 9:3 and 1 Cor 12:3. Witherington[49] explains, "Paul is not himself banning or cursing the agitators but asking God ("let him be") to act against them." The Judaizers, by re-imposing the requirements of the law as necessary for salvation, were actually denying the gospel of justification and presenting a way which brought no hope. As Witherington[50] affirms, noting Paul's reference to angels, "The Gospel of Moses even though mediated through angels should not be received. In Paul's view it is no Gospel at all." Bruce[51] makes clear here the stark reality:

If Christ displaced the law as the activating centre of Paul's own life, he equally displaced the law in the economy of God, in the ordering of salvation-history. Therefore, if the law was still in force as the way of salvation and life, the messianic age had not yet dawned and Jesus accordingly was not the Messiah. It that case Jesus had been rightly convicted and sentenced because his messianic claims were false. Any teaching which logically led to such a conclusion was, for Paul, self-evidently perverse: anyone who implied by such teaching that Jesus was anathema (cf. 1 Cor 12:3) was himself anathema.

Paul affirms this fact again in Gal 3:10. "For all who rely on works of the law are under a curse." This is really another attempt to get to heaven by one's own efforts rather than the all-sufficient work of Christ on the cross. You must realise the stark alternatives. Either one is relying on his own works or the work Christ has already done. God's initiative in Christ or their own?

Gal 1:10–24: Paul's Gospel – A Gospel from God

Suggestions that at this point (particularly from vv. 11 or 12) we should see the beginning of a chiastic structure covering most of Galatians (as Jeremias or Mussner[52] have affirmed) are difficult to accept, as any clear repetitions or parts of a balanced structure are not evident for most scholars. Even so, the meaning of the verses is clear. Paul is still insisting that the gospel he brought to the Galatians, the gospel of grace is the only true gospel. Moo[53] states that Paul's overall purpose in 1:13–2:14 is

---

[47] Fung, *The Epistle to the Galatians*, 48.
[48] Hendriksen, *Galatians*, 41 n. 22.
[49] Witherington 111, *Grace in Galatia*, 83.
[50] Witherington 111, *Grace in Galatia*, 83.
[51] Bruce, *The Epistle to the Galatians*, 84.
[52] J. Jeremias, "Chiasmus in den Paulusbriefen," *ZNW*, 49 (1958) 152–53; F. Mussner, *Der Galaterbrief*, HTKNT, 9 (Freiburg, Basel and Vienna: Herder, 1974), vii-viii, 77.
[53] Moo, *Galatians*, Baker Exegetical Commentary on the New Testament, 90.

to assure the Galatians that they had received the true gospel. "'Gospel' language is, of course, central in the rebuke passage of verses 6–9; but it is also central in verses 11–12 … and it crops up repeatedly in the subsequent argument (1:16, 23; 2:2, 5, 7, 14). 'The truth of the gospel' (2:5, 14) is Paul's focus in this section."

The Gospel was Brought by Him

Paul had proclaimed this message to the Galatians when he first came. In vv. 10–11 he still refers to them as ἀδελφοί *adelphoi* "brothers" (1:11; 4:12, 28, 31; 5:11, 13; 6:1, 18), expressing his love and concern for them, even although they may have been moving away from him. Literally, he says, "I make known to you" and the direct object is the gospel. This message is of course, as we have already affirmed, centred upon the cross (3:1). Paul's preaching was focussed on "Christ crucified" emphasising the need to "glory in the Cross," a message completely distinct from that of the Judaizers i.e., the work of Christ needed nothing added to it, whereas they wanted at the least to supplement it with circumcision and special days. In this gospel he was not just telling the people what they wanted to hear. He was not just seeking to "please man" so that they would look after him well. In his preaching he needed to be Christ's servant even in this; to be bringing the true message to please God and he insists that he was. One should note the context and his use of the strong anathema language in vv. 8–9 – they certainly could not accuse him of seeking to compromise his message. In v. 10 πείθω *peithō* means "persuade" men, rather than "conciliate," which would imply relaxing the relationship with those who insisted upon the circumcision requirement. But Paul would not change or soften his message.

The Gospel was Revealed to Him

The connecting particle in v. 11 suggests a new beginning. Here also we find a "disclosure formula," "I want you to know…." Longenecker, Silva[54] and other scholars take vv. 11–12 as setting forth the thesis of the letter in formal and solemn terms. Note how at this point Paul uses the first person singular "I." Witherington[55] makes two points here. This is "a personal letter from Paul alone, not a joint communication." In calling his readers "brothers," he claims that, "The family language which he uses is not just conciliatory but it makes clear a fundamental conviction of Paul's … that the family of God is composed on the basis of faith, not heredity or other factors."

Paul affirms that the message was not his gospel, nor did he receive it from any man or human source who taught it to him – it came by direct revelation. Paul has already stressed this in v. 1, with both verses focussing upon source and denying that his

---

[54] Longenecker, *Galatians*, 20–21; Silva, accepts 1:6–10 as setting out the occasion of the letter, *Explorations in Exegetical Method*, 153. Moo suggests first the thesis statement (1:11–12); elaboration and justification of that statement (1:13–2:14) – the Antioch incident is an add-on to the narrative. Moo, *Galatians*, 89.

[55] Witherington 111, *Grace in Galatia*, 91. He mentions Jesus' own teaching about the family of God, Mark 3:31–35 par. Matt 23v8.

message originated in mere human ideas or any human tradition. Paul is insisting that he did not invent it nor was he taught it, at the feet of an earthly teacher, but it was revealed directly from God.

The phrase "a revelation of Jesus Christ" – is it objective or subjective? Silva,[56] after a careful discussion of the options, suggests that it should be interpreted as an objective genitive, i.e., it is Jesus Christ who is revealed. Elsewhere Paul views God as the source of revelation, when he expresses the subject of ἀποκαλύπτω *apokaluptō* it is always God (1 Cor 2:10; Gal 1:16; Phil 3:15). Note where Paul speaks of the revelation of the Lord (Jesus) twice in 1 Cor 1:7; 2 Thess 1:7 there it is clearly not the message from Jesus but rather *the second coming* i.e., it is Jesus Christ himself who is revealed or appears.

So, for v. 12, many modern commentators[57] may be persuaded to accept Silva's objective sense; this also will affect how they interpret v. 16 (see below). However, the main point here is the source of the revelation – it has a divine origin.

One should note the argument of those who advocate for a subjective genitive. Elsewhere in certain letters Paul can write of having received certain traditions from those who were before him (e.g., 1 Cor 11:23–26; 15:3–11). Also, Longenecker[58] makes the point that when it comes to Gentiles living as Christians apart from the regulations of the Jewish law and especially with no requirement of circumcision, "Paul saw this as a 'mystery' enigmatically rooted in the prophetic Scriptures but now made known to him by revelation (cf. Rom 16:25–26; Eph 3:2–10; Col 1:26–27), and so uniquely his."

However, do we have to choose between the one and the other? Bruce[59] makes the point that when we take this statement along with v. 16, with reference to Paul on the Damascus Road, "God the Father was the revealer; it was Jesus Christ who was revealed, and in that revelation Paul received his gospel.... The gospel and the risen Christ were inseparable; both were revealed to Paul at the same moment." Moo[60] also discusses this point. He considers that we ought to take note of the eschatological connotations, the use of the word "came." He states:

> It seems relatively clear that the "revelation" Paul had in view is particularly the "revealing" (ἀποκαλύψαι) [*apokalypsai*] of Jesus Christ to Paul at the time of his conversion (see v. 16). This being the case, it would seem likely that we should construe the genitive Ιησοῦ Χριστοῦ as an objective genitive:

[56] Silva, *Explorations in Exegetical Method*, 64–68.

[57] So Fung, *The Epistle to the Galatians*, v. 54. Longenecker, *Galatians*, 24, differs from others in that he sees this statement of the revelation as setting out the *means* rather than the *content* i.e., Jesus Christ is the agent and God the Father is the source. So the emphasis is on the authority of the message – who gave it rather than the content. See also the following footnote.

[58] Longenecker, *Galatians*, 24.

[59] Bruce, *The Epistle to the Galatians*, 89.

[60] Moo, *Galatians*, 95.

the truth of the gospel came to Paul when God revealed Jesus Christ to him.... But the immediate context of the phrase, with its emphasis the source of knowledge, could indeed suggest a source or subjective genitive: the truth of the gospel came to Paul when Jesus Christ revealed it to him ... hence the "from" in many English versions.

Moo finally suggests, as Bruce above, that it is better for us not to lock the meaning into either option. Paul is perhaps meaning that the revelation he received is bound up with, and has to do with, Jesus Christ. We will return to this in v. 16.

The Gospel was Experienced by Him

Paul writes, in vv. 13–14, "You have heard," which makes clear that others (the Judaizers) will have given them information about him. He of course wishes to outline the crucial events in his life to make sure that they know the real facts, especially as they relate to his affirmation in vv. 11–12 concerning the revelation he received from God and not from any human agency. Witherington[61] makes the important point that "Paul is not writing an autobiography here; he is arguing a particular case and trying to persuade his audience to adhere to the one true gospel of grace, adhering to his own personal example." There are three chapters in his life – although the narration of Paul's "story" continues through 2:1–21.

(a) In the Jewish Religion

In vv. 13 and 14 Paul uses the word "Judaism" which is found only here in the NT. We note that it is used in the Jewish literature of the times (cf. 2 Macc. 2.21; 8.1; 14.38; 4 Macc. 4.26), as Witherington[62] points out. He also sees the word as describing "a Torah-true Jewish lifestyle and belief system as contrasted to Seleucid Hellenism." This was where Paul once was, but he had now come to see that, birth as a Jew, Torah observance or living under the Mosaic law was not what fitted him to be a member of the people of God. The true "Israel of God" (6:16), as we will see, is comprised of those who are a new creation (6:15), having been born again (4:29–31), delivered from the condemnation of the law by the cross, sharing Abraham's faith and living a Spirit enabled lifestyle. The term used to describe his "former life" is ἀναστροφήν *anastrophēn* which, while it will be grounded in certain belief systems, emphasises more praxis. For a Jew, it was essential to submit in God's statutes, endeavour to keep all God's commandments or "walk in them" (1 Kings 6:12). The problem is that our fallenness means we have no power to do this (Rom 8:3). But now for the true children of faith we have the enabling Holy Spirit (Jer 31:33; Rom 8:4; Gal 5:16–26).

---

[61] Witherington 111, *Grace in Galatia*, 96. See also Hendriksen, *Galatians*, 47, who finds here a recounting of certain events and only those which focus on points he wishes to emphasise, rather than a complete autobiography.
[62] Witherington 111, *Grace in Galatia*, 98.

Paul writes about the dark history of his former life before he met the Lord. The memory of it must have grieved and humbled him many times. He was fanatical about persecuting the church. Note that ἐδίωκον *ediōkon* and ἐπόρθουν *eporthoun* are both imperfects, "persecuting" and "seeking to destroy," suggest a period of persistent persecution, whereas the phrase καθ' ὑπερβολήν *kath' huperbolēn*, "violently" (lit., "according to excess"), which is only in Paul in the NT (Rom 7:13; 1 Cor 12:31; 2 Cor 1:8, 4:17) signals that the "intensity" of his persecution never diminished. Witherington[63] explains that the above adverbial phrase, "indicates the level to which the persecution reached. Paul went to extremes, the persecutions being not merely extensive (in and beyond Jerusalem) but also intensive." We also know that when he had ravaged Jerusalem, he set out for Damascus (Acts 9:1–2). So, he "tried to destroy" ESV, but did not succeed[64] the church he now knew to be "the church of God" (Acts 8:1–3; 9:1, 13; 22:4).[65] It was God's church and he had come to see that he had dared to set himself against God!

Paul also was "extremely zealous" (1:14), a "zealot," not part of the actual Zealot party for political ends but clearly passionately zealous[66] for the traditions of his fathers, advancing in Judaism, outstripping his young friends as he progressed as a Pharisee in the "strictest party" of the Jewish religion. Fung makes the point that to a Jew, a crucified Messiah was in itself a decisive refutation of any claim to messiahship – as in effect, Paul himself points out in 1 Cor 1:17–24. In fact, it was an insult to every Jew and "impelled him (Paul) to give himself wholeheartedly to what he considered the unmistakable duty and sacred duty of uprooting the pernicious sect of Jesus' followers."[67]

The ferocity of Saul the Pharisee against the church provides us with an example of the strength of feeling and conviction among Jews at the time concerning the appearance of early Christian communities. It explains why the Judaizers came to Antioch urging the Galatian converts to adopt a Torah lifestyle and (according to Jewett[68]) the dangers of fraternisation with Gentiles. Witherington[69] comments on how seriously Jewish conversions to Christianity would be taken:

Especially in view of texts like 2 Cor 11:4 which refers to multiple disciplinary whippings Paul received at the hand of Jews. In short, the social context out of which Christianity arose, especially during the period when there was close association or at least regular contact with the synagogue was a volatile one, which may explain a

---

[63] Witherington 111, *Grace in Galatia*, 100. In Acts 26:11 Paul speaks of his "raging fury" against the believers, "even to foreign cities."

[64] See also Silva, *Explorations in Exegetical Method*, 71.

[65] Note Paul's use of the phrase "the church of God" of a number of local communities which help to make it up i.e., beginning to think more "universally" of a single entity existing over against Judaism rather than as in 1:2, 22.

[66] Rom 10:2 reveals that ultimately he came to see that this zeal which many of his friends continued to have was "not according to knowledge."

[67] Fung, *The Epistle to the Galatians*, 59.

[68] See Introduction note 13.

[69] Witherington 111, *Grace in Galatia*, 101.

good deal about the behaviour and suggestions of the Jerusalem church to other churches.

The verb προκόπτω *prokoptō* in its imperfect form (προέκοπτον *proekopton*) "advancing" will express the continuing religious and moral progress of Paul's development in Judaism in his early life which was unparalleled among his contemporaries. The same word is used of Jesus' advancement as he grew "in wisdom and stature, and in favour with God and man" (Luke 2:52). Regarding the reference to the "traditions of my fathers" Longenecker[70] suggests that Paul will be referring to: (1) the teachings and practices developed in the Pharisaic schools of Second Temple Judaism, later codified in the Mishnah, Palestinian and Babylonian Gemaras, Midrashim, and various individual halakhic and haggadic collections of rabbinic lore; (2) the more popular interpretations in the synagogues of the time, represented in the extant Targumim. For Hendriksen,[71] it is clear that the law was "buried under a load of human traditions." This was the Jewish oral law and Jesus himself affirms that some actually of these traditions were so interpreted that they ended up "directly contrary to the very intention of the law as originally given." Regarding Paul, Stott[72] affirms, "No conditioned reflex or other psychological device could convert a man in that state. Only God could reach him – and God did!"

One should also note that if Paul the Jew had made such a radical break with Judaism then the Galatians, as McDonald[73] points out, "should realise that to allow themselves to be induced into supposing that the gospel needed any Judaistic additions was sheer folly." The fact was they were moving in exactly the opposite direction from Paul in his conversion from Judaism to Christ. How could they turn from the Christian freedom to the slavery of the law (2:4; 4:9, 22–31; 5:1, 13)?

(b) On the Damascus Road

Before this it was "I," "I" (vv. 13–14); now the subject of the two participles is no doubt "God" (vv. 15–16) – recognised by this addition in ℵ A, D and *et al.*[74] In every stage of Paul's experience the initiative and grace of God are mentioned.

In v. 15 Paul was the object of God's special electing purpose. Moo[75] explains that the verb "was pleased" often has the additional nuance "take pleasure in and so

---

[70] Longenecker, *Galatians*, 30. Fung sees the "tradition of the fathers" as "Pharisaic traditions and more particularly those enshrined in the oral law transmitted and expounded in Pharisaic schools, which comprised the 613 prescriptions (248 positive commands and 365 prohibitions) of rabbinic exegesis," *The Epistle to the Galatians*, 57.

[71] Hendriksen, *Galatians*, 51. He points out, for example, that God's command of loving your neighbour (Lev 19:18; Exod 23:4, 5; Prov 25:21) was understood as loving your neighbour and "hate your enemy" (Matt 5:43). Cf. also Exod 20:12; Deut 5:16, "similarly emasculated" in Matt 15:1–6 with regard to honouring father and mother. In every case the demands of the commandment were altered and reduced.

[72] J.R.W. Stott, *The One Way: The Message of Galatians* BST (London: Inter-Varsity Press, 1974), 32.

[73] H. D. McDonald, *Freedom in Faith*: A Commentary on Paul's Epistle to the Galatians (London: Pickering and Inglis, 1973), 29.

[74] See the Additional Note re. MSS evidence in Moo, *Galatians*, 107.

decide to do." He was once a Pharisee, a separatist, now he discovers that he himself was destined, "separated" before he was born, like Jeremiah (Jer 1:4f.) the prophet to the nations and the Servant of the Lord (Isa 49:1–6)[76], to be God's chosen instrument, a light to the Gentiles.[77] It may be that two stages are suggested here. Paul was separated before he was born to salvation, in the purpose of God, but called when God revealed his Son to him on the Damascus Road. Here the point to stress is that we have a calling by grace to preach the gospel of grace.

Verse 16 needs careful comment in light of v. 12 above. There was a revelation made ἐν ἐμοί *en emoi* literally, "in him." We do know that there was also a great revelation made *to him* on the Damascus road – he saw the risen Christ (Acts 9:5, 27; 1 Cor 9:1; 15:8). But in addition, this moment involved an inner illumination – something like 2 Cor 4:6, or the removal of the veil from his heart, 2 Cor 3:14. Paul on the way to Damascus also received a new understanding of Jesus Christ, his person, the reason for his death and of course was made aware of his gracious calling to be the apostle to the Gentiles. As noted above, for Bruce,[78] Jesus Christ is revealed, but the gospel and Jesus Christ are inseparable. The ESV uses the simple dative in the text i.e., "to me," but "in me" as the footnote. Are there not two aspects to the one revelation? Fung[79] insists that:

> The phrase should not however, be taken to suggest a merely inward revelation without a corresponding external object, for there is little doubt that the preceding phrase ("to reveal his Son") refers to Paul's vision of the risen Christ (also attested in 1 Cor 9:1; 15:8) on the road to Damascus ... the inward illumination and the physical vision were alike part of God's revelation to him.

In continuing our discussion of the statement that the revelation by God was of "his Son," note the other references to Jesus as "Son of God" (2:20; 4:4, 6). This should not be understood as merely a reference to the incarnation, for it is used in a resurrection context – here on the Damascus road and in chapter 4, where God sends "the Spirit of his Son" into our hearts – a sending subsequent to the redemption of v. 4. It is Sonship in the ontological sense (see also Rom 1:3f; 1 Cor 1:9; 15:20–28; 1 Thess 1:10). Fung[80] explains, "Paul is claiming that he received insight into the unique nature of Jesus' sonship." One recalls the record of Acts 9:20, when Paul had

---

[75] Moo, *Galatians*, 102.

[76] Moo discusses the idea in the text of Paul set apart from or before birth. The dependance on the Jeremiah reference and the parallelism with Isaiah 49 "makes it very likely that he (Paul) is claiming to have been 'set apart' 'before he was born'." Moo, *Galatians*, Baker Exegetical Commentary on the New Testament, 104.

[77] Witherington, 111, *Grace in Galatia*, 105; Fung, *The Epistle to the Galatians*, 64, points to other similar references, cf. Rom 15:21 with Isa 52:15; Acts 13:47 with Isa 49:6; Acts 18:9f. with Isa 43:5.

[78] Bruce, *The Epistle to the Galatians*, 89.

[79] Fung, *The Epistle to the Galatians*, 64. Hendriksen, *Galatians*, 52, explains that Paul's conversion is told "from the inside." There was an outward or physical side (he saw him, heard him, cf. Acts 22;15 "a witness of what you have seen and heard") but it also pleased God to remove the scales from his heart.

[80] Fung, *The Epistle to the Galatians*, 65.

entered Damascus "immediately he proclaimed Jesus in the synagogues, saying, 'He is the Son of God.'" Note also that Moo[81] claims:

> Sonship plays a critical and indeed central role in Galatians.... Paul's choice to identify the one who was revealed to him as the Son of God therefore implies that his experience has been, in a certain basic sense, similar to the Galatians: in both cases, God worked in grace through his Son to make them his sons.

Stendhal[82] is an example of those scholars who consider that what happened on the Damascus road was only a call, like other prophetic calls in the OT (e.g., Jer 1:5–6; Isa 6; Ezek 1). It is true that the experience involved a call, but it was first of all primarily a conversion. The reason why he writes of his calling is because his focus in his autobiography at this point is upon mission (v. 17).

Excursus: The All-Importance of Damascus for Paul's Life and Theology

In this discussion of what Damascus is about and how it influenced Paul, particularly his world-view and theology, one is reminded of Jeremias[83] who affirmed, "There is only one key to Pauline Theology. It is called Damascus."

Jeremias understands Paul as one of those men who had experienced a sharp break with their past. He affirmed that Paul's theology is a theology rooted in a sudden conversion. I summarise his main insights are here – with additional comments.

(a) His fellowship with Christ had its roots in the Damascus experience. Paul could insist that on the way to Damascus he saw the risen Christ. "Last of all ... he appeared also to me" (1 Cor 15:8). See also Gal 1:12, 16 – a revelation of truth and Christ himself. From the time he saw Jesus in his glory, the exalted Lord became the great reality of his life.

(b) His understanding of the cross and its saving power is anchored in the Damascus experience. His previous convictions were that the Christians were adherents of a false Messiah. He understood that God has cursed Jesus by death on a cross. But now he saw Jesus risen, alive as the exalted Christ. At that moment, by the enlightenment of the Holy Spirit, it became clear to Paul that the persecuted Christians were right in claiming that Jesus as the Servant of God, died on the cross as a substitute for the sins of many. Paul expressed this truth in Gal 2:20 "Christ loved me and gave himself for me" and 3:13 "Christ has redeemed us from the curse of the law, *by becoming a curse for us.*" Paul's whole confidence for acceptance with God was in the cross work of

---

[81] Moo, *Galatians*, 104.

[82] K. Stendal, *Paul among Jews and Gentiles* (Philadelphia: Fortress, 1976), 7–23.

[83] J. Jeremias, "The Key to Pauline Theology," *Ex T.* Oct. 1964, 27–30.

Christ. Again, he came to understand that the resurrection of Christ marked, as we already noted the beginning of a new epoch.

(c) His knowledge of the omnipotence of grace, or the greatness of God's mercy and God's gracious selection and predestination, was born on the Damascus Road. Formally, his hands were stained with Christian blood (Acts 22:4). He tells us, "I not only locked up many of the saints in prison … but when they were put to death I cast my vote against them…. In raging fury against them I persecuted them even to foreign cities" (Acts 26:10–11). Yet through grace he had received mercy. God had actually chosen him!

(d) His understanding of the fearfulness of sin stems from Damascus. He had believed he was "blameless" by the law's standards (Phil 3:6). Now suddenly he sees he has blasphemed the Messiah and endeavoured to wipe out his community. When it came to sin, he was "the foremost" (1 Tim 1:15).

(e) From Damascus we understand his radical opposition to legalism. We can comment that there are two aspects to Paul's convictions. Firstly, there is a negative aspect – it was not through his law keeping he found acceptance. Compared to his contemporaries he had reached the highest achievement, but in seeking to "establish" his own righteousness he had missed "God's righteousness" (Rom 10:3). then there is a positive aspect – he came to realise that he was actually justified by faith, on the basis of Christ's sacrifice for him. The "we know" of Gal 2:16 that he was not justified through law but through faith in Jesus Christ and his cross goes back to this time.

(f) His future hope was rooted here. He had met the risen Lord as the firstfruits of them that sleep. He had seen the glory of God in the face of Jesus Christ (1 Cor 15:20, 2 Cor 4:6 and Gal 5:4).

(g) His sense of missionary obligation and his role as an apostle stem from Damascus. He was converted on the road to Damascus but also called to be the apostle to the Gentiles. See Acts 9:15 where Ananias is informed about Paul that in spite of the "evil" he did to the Lord's people, "Go, for he is a chosen instrument of mine to carry my name before the Gentiles and kings and the children of Israel." But the Lord had already told Paul this on the Damascus Road (Acts 26:17–18; Gal 1:16).

(h) His doctrine of the church has at least one root here (Acts 9:4; 22:7; 26:14). The Lord identifies himself with his church, "Saul, Saul, why are you persecuting me?" How wonderfully Paul develops this unity of the 'head" and the "body" concept e.g., 1 Cor 12:12–31; Eph 1:22–23; 4:12–16. In Gal 3:28 Paul can affirm that "we are all one in Christ Jesus."

There is no sense in which Paul's Damascus road experience as merely a call "a call"; it is much more, as O'Brien[84] affirms:

> To describe the Damascus road experience as *simply* Paul's "call" to the Gentiles does not account for the revelation of Christ and his gospel in which there was a radical change in Paul's thinking about Jesus as the Messiah and the Son, about the Torah, the messianic salvation, and not least Israel's and the Gentiles' place within the divine plan. In the Damascus encounter Paul underwent a significant "paradigm shift" in his life and thought; his own self-consciousness was that of having undergone a conversion.

Thus I concur with Witherington[85] that:

> Paul's Gospel of grace is bound up with Paul's experience of grace and is grounded in the content of God's revelation of his son in Paul, which Paul then worked out the implications of for his beliefs about God, messiah, law, salvation, who God's people are and a host of other subjects.

As we have already noticed above, many of these are actually worked out in this letter. His symbolic universe was radically effected; we could say "turned upside down."[86] So his conversion and call coincided in time, and the sightless days at Damascus gave him opportunity to reflect on his experience and confirmed to him all that Jeremias mentions above. In fact, as we noted, Luke tells us that when he was with the disciples at Damascus, he is preaching about Jesus in the synagogues as "the Son of God" (Acts 9:19b–20)!

The purpose of his call was "to preach him among the Gentiles" (v. 16). Note the present tense (compared to the aorists, "set apart" and "called") affirms Paul's continual preaching of Christ – or more precisely "Christ crucified" (1 Cor 1:23; 2:2; Gal 3:1). The area of his ministry is identified as a Gentile area (2:2, 8). Luther[87] makes the point concerning Paul:

> As if he would say: I will not burden the Gentiles with the law, because I am the Apostle and evangelist of the Gentiles, and not their lawgiver.... Therefore ought you to hear no teacher that teacheth the law. For among the Gentiles, the law ought not to be preached, but the gospel; not Moses but the Son of God; not the righteousness of works, but the righteousness of faith.

---

[81] I. O'Brien, "Was Paul Converted?" in D. A. Carson, T O'Brien, and M. A. Seifrid, *The Paradoxes of Paul*, Vol. 2 (Waco: Baylor University Press, 2004), 390. See also 1v6 where Paul describes the "conversion" of the Gentiles as their "calling" by God.
[85] Witherington, 111, *Grace in Galatia*, 115.
[86] Witherington, 111, *Grace in Galatia*, 115.
[87] Luther, *A Commentary on St. Paul's Epistle to the Galatians*, 85.

He is claiming that his conversion and calling has been all of God. But what about the events which followed it? Again Paul denies following merely human guidance in relation to his subsequent actions.

* * *

(c) On the Missionary Trail

In vv. 17–24 Paul reveals that first there were some things he did NOT do. Since his conversion he had remained independent of all human authority. What he did not do was to confer with flesh and blood. Nor did he go up to Jerusalem. The mention of apostles "before me" implies that he is also as much an apostle as they are (the words πρὸ ἐμοῦ *pro emou* are temporal – time – not status). But then there were things which he DID do. Instead of "going up," he "went away." He travels to Arabia – see Acts 9:19, 23, and note the "some days" he was with the disciples in Damascus, followed by the "many days," implying a leaving from and a returning again to Damascus after his time away from the city.[88]

Arabia is generally understood as the Nabataean kingdom east of the Jordan valley established in the 2nd century BCE. Bruce[89] points out that there were many Gentiles settled there, as well as Bedouin, and no doubt Paul preached to them. If his presence there was only for "a contemplative retreat," this would not explain why in 2 Cor 11:32 he attracted the hostile attention of the governor. There was a time around AD 37, when Caligula was emperor, that Aretas was in control of the city of Damascus and because of Paul's preaching in Arabia the Ethnarch of king Aretas was intent on killing Paul so he had to escape in a basket. At that time he had returned from Arabia with his commission and message confirmed to the very city he had formally set out for intent upon the destruction of the church (Acts 9:1–2). Now again he must secretly leave (Acts 9:23–25).

In v. 18 Paul uses ἔπειτα *epeita* "then" (the first of 3 successive occurrences of the word as he emphasises the chronological or temporal sequence of events, with no gaps between, 1:18, 21; 2:1), to inform his readers that after three years[90] (from the time of his first Damascus road experience) he "went up" (a reference to the city's geographical location) to Jerusalem "to visit Cephas."[91] While some scholars suggest

---

[88] Witherington, 111, *Grace in Galatia*, 116 suggests that the word "immediately" v. 16 has an emphatic position and seems to go with what follows it. "Paul is denying any immediate consulting with humans including any immediate going up to Jerusalem. And by contrast an immediate departure to Arabia."

[89] Bruce, *The Epistle to the Galatians*, 96. See also Fung, *The Epistle to the Galatians*, 69.

[90] Witherington suggests that we should understand this time reference to be an example of "inclusive reckoning" i.e., "in the third year," not "after three full years," which was an important point and a significant figure when collecting data to help determine the date of Galatians (see the discussion in the Introduction).

[91] Paul often called him Cephas, "rock" or "stone" (Gal 2:9, 11, 14; 1 Cor 1:12; 15:5). Only in Gal 2:7–8 is he "Peter." Note also that there are some scholars who propose that the word "visit" would be better read as "to get acquainted with." "Visit" is the strict meaning of the verb, rather than the idea that he went to receive instruction, which would surely contradict the whole argument of the passage. Fung, who is

(see Fung below) that among other things this must have been for a history lesson about Jesus, McDonald[92] proposes that not much could be learned in such a short time. "Indeed, he came knowing for himself the gospel as God's ordained apostle. It was not to be instructed that he came, but to inform." Both Paul and Peter would surely benefit in such a moment. The visit was short – fifteen days – then he went off (with nothing intervening) to Cilicia (see Acts 9:30) – to Tarsus – through Syria and so no doubt via Damascus. Therefore, he is far north and nowhere near Jerusalem. Paul is making clear that for ministry there he had not received nor did he require any authorization or commission from the leaders of the Jerusalem church (see v. 16 "I did not immediately consult with anyone," literally "flesh and blood" – perhaps denoting human frailty over against God). So, no directions or commands as to ministry opportunities were given.

His total isolation from the Jerusalem church leaders demonstrates that his message was not from man but from God. The "three years" can intentionally be contrasted with the "fifteen days." There is no dependence here or major influence from Peter – nor James "the Lord's brother" in such a short time – in fact the text says Paul only "saw" James, but did not consult with him, contra Fung (n. 82). "James" is not to be confused with two other disciples similarly called, one who by the time of writing was already dead (Mark 6:3; Matt 13:55; Mark 3:17–18; Acts 1:13; 12:2). James was resistant to or at least in doubt about Jesus during his earthly ministry (Mark 3:21, 31–35; John 7:3–5), but was transformed by a resurrection appearance of Jesus to him (1 Cor 15:7) and was among the members of Jesus' family[93] in the Jerusalem church (Acts 1:14). A brother of Jesus now also in the full spiritual sense, he had risen to leadership among the early believers (Acts 12:17; 15:13; 21:18–19; Gal 2:1–10). The point here is that Paul did not get his gospel from either of them. As Witherington[94] notes, it is clear that by identifying James as "the Lord's brother," Paul is giving him a "highly honorific" title. Commenting upon what he will reveal in chapter 2 of the pressures brought to bear from "false brothers" (2:4) he maintains that:

> If Paul really had believed that deliberate attacks against his Gospel were coming from James himself, it is very doubtful that he would have spoken in this way about James, whom he clearly distinguishes from the false brothers, who receive a pejorative title unlike the label "the Lord's brother."

---

attracted to this alternative idea, also points out that however we translate, no doubt Paul would learn from Peter the early traditions about Jesus. Also from James who is mentioned here – see the references in 1 Cor 15:1–7 where both are highlighted in a passage about what Paul had "received." "The theory of Paul's lack of interest in the historical Jesus lacks a substantial basis," Fung, *The Epistle to the Galatians*, 74. The fact is that any examination of Paul's epistles will clearly demonstrate that the apostle gives us *both* – the historical Jesus and the exalted Christ.

[92] McDonald, *Freedom in Faith*, 34.

[93] There is no reason to regard Jesus' "brothers" as really first cousins, children of Alphaeus and Mary of Cleopas (Jerome AD 347–420) or sons of Joseph by a previous marriage (Protoevangelium of James AD 145, see 9.2). But, with Tertullian (AD 160–220) in *Adv. Marc.* and Helvidius (before AD 383), there is also an insistence that one does not need to uphold the perpetual virginity of the virgin Mary subsequent to Jesus' birth.

[94] Witherington, 111, *Grace in Galatia*, 122.

Paul was "still unknown" (v. 22) – the grammatical sense is continuance in that state,[95] to the churches in Judea. The apostle is still insisting that the readers needed to accept the divine origin of his message. His commission and gospel are based upon a revelation from God rooted in a direct encounter with Jesus Christ who called him on the Damascus road and there was at that time no contact with the leaders in Jerusalem. His message of grace, of salvation without works apart from law, was from God and was the only gospel! In v. 20, Paul had reaffirmed these facts by an oath "before God"[96] that his statements are totally trustworthy, "I do not lie." In this way he responds to the claims of the Judaizers that he had received his authority and learned his gospel from the Jerusalem leaders during his first visit there. This was not the case.

Clearly Paul is not in any area where he would be under the supervision of the leaders in Jerusalem, nor were they aware of his movements. Paul uses the second "then" although this time, he does not mention the time period involved. Witherington[97] makes the point that "Antioch was the capital of the Roman province of Syria-Cilicia at the time and the next most prominent city therein was Tarsus, and so we should certainly compare this text to what is said in Acts 9:30, 11:25–26."

The adverb μόνον *monon* "only" makes clear that there was only one exception to their lack of knowledge (v. 22) concerning Paul. They "kept hearing" (the grammatical sense of the Greek phrase, which can imply a considerable period of time) that the former persecutor (νῦν *nun* "now" emphasises the transformation) was preaching "the faith" he had formally "tried" to destroy. The term "faith" here with the article is a reference to the gospel or the content of the apostolic message, rather than the act of trusting. Moo[98] informs us that while Paul "normally" can use this word for the act of believing, it also came to be used as a way of referring "objectively, to the movement itself" i.e., the gospel (see also Rom 12:6; 1 Cor 16:13; 2 Cor 13:5; Gal 1:23; 3:23–25; 6:10, 21; Eph 4:13; Phil 1:27; Col 1:23; 2:7; 1 Tim 1:2, 19; 3:9; 4:1, 6; 5:8; 6:10, 21; 2 Tim 3:8; 4:7; Titus 1:4, 13; 3:15; Phlm 6). We should also note, with Hendriksen[99] that the churches of Judaea actually approved of the message Paul was preaching, recognising it as the same gospel they themselves had heard from the start. "What a crushing argument against the Judaizers, who were slandering the apostle for proclaiming the wrong kind of gospel." As Witherington[100] has also pointed out, "The choice of words here is to be explained by the fact that Paul thinks the content of his proclamation is being challenged in Galatia. This

---

[95] Longenecker, *Galatians*, 41.

[96] Hendriksen, *Galatians*, 62–63, makes the point that this is a solemn affirmation "with an appeal to God's own presence and omniscience.... He (Paul is filled with a genuine and overpowering consciousness of living 'in the very presence of God.'" This shines through his epistles, e.g., Rom 1:8, 9, 25: 6:17; 7:25; 8:35–39; 9:1, 5; 10:1; 11: 33–36; 15:13, 32; 16:25–27; Eph 1:3ff.; 1:15ff.; 3:14–21.

[97] Witherington, 111, *Grace in Galatia*, 124. See also Moo's discussion of Paul's ministry in Cilicia (Tarsus was a major city) and Syria (in Antioch) making reference to Acts 9:30 and Acts 11:26. Moo, *Galatians*, 111–12.

[98] Moo, *Galatians*, 114.

[99] Hendriksen, *Galatians*, 64.

[100] Witherington, 111, *Grace in Galatia*, 126.

document is intended to argue for that content and against the alternative offered by the agitators."

One can also recognise that at this point we begin to see a shift in Paul's argument from the negative to the positive. He had reasoned emphatically that he had not learned/received his gospel from Jerusalem; now he will move to the positive. The churches in Judaea (vv. 23–24) and next the apostles in Jerusalem (2:1–10) will acknowledge God's acceptance of his mission work. We should note that this content of Paul's gospel is focussed upon the cross (6:14) and the way of blessing is not "by works of the law" but by faith – a word used by Paul 22 times in this short letter. Also, Paul is insistent that "the faith" which must be proclaimed is all about salvation by faith only without works.

Therefore, he was "not known" but "well known." The Judean Christians (the churches of Judea that are said to be "in Christ") "glorified God" for this early mission ministry of Paul, reminding us of Isa 49:3 LXX, God's testimony regarding glory brought to him by his Servant.[101] After "trying" to destroy the church but of course unable to succeed – as many others have tried since – he ended up never "tiring" of preaching this "law-free" gospel of grace.

---

[101] Moo points out that Paul had alluded to the same Servant Song (Isa 49) in v. 15 when writing about his conversion/call (Isa 49:1). Also in Acts 13:47 Paul quotes Isa 49:6 to justify his turning to the Gentiles. "These allusions suggest that Paul generally views his mision to the Gentiles in terms of the prophesies about the Servant in Isaiah." Moo, *Galatians*, 115.

GALATIANS TWO

Gal 2:1–10: Paul's Jerusalem Council or Famine Visit

The way the false teachers tried to undermine Paul's authority was to say that his gospel was different from that of Peter's and indeed from all the other apostles in Jerusalem. They were thus trying to cause a split among the apostles, for this would mean that the apostles were contradicting one another. Of course, such a situation still occurs today when one considers e.g., that "Paulism" is said to be contradictory rather than complimentary to Johannine Theology.

In chapter one, Paul has sought to prove that his gospel was from God and not from man. He made the point, as we noted, that he remained independent of the other apostles, and stressed this by revealing that he only made one visit to Jerusalem in fourteen years and that for fifteen days. In chapter 2, to prove his message was the same as theirs, he stresses that when he eventually did revisit Jerusalem, his gospel was not changed in any way but his ministry and teaching was affirmed and approved by them. As Moo[1] explains, "His sphere of ministry might have differed from that of the Jerusalem apostles, but there was no fundamental difference among Paul and the others over the essence of that gospel." Sadly, there are many scholars today who also will not recognise Paul's authority. They suggest that some of Paul's writings are purely from his own perspective (and therefore from a simply "human" viewpoint), and are not, as Paul would often claim, from God (e.g., 1:11–12; 2 Tim 3:16).

Paul's main aim in setting out his whole argument here is as he states in v. 5, "so that the truth of the gospel might be preserved for you." It was all for the Galatian churches, so that they would not be persuaded by the agitator's gospel-plus-law message. Hendriksen[2] has given a useful summary of 2:1–10. The validity of the gospel as proclaimed by Paul acknowledged by the "pillars" at Jerusalem; the work divided; the poor to be remembered.

In vv. 1–2 Paul recounts, "Then … I went up again" and it was "after fourteen years." The use of ἔπειτα epeita "then" again for the third time is indicating that this happened in a temporal sense just after Paul's time in Syria and Cilicia. There are no gaps here.[3] The fourteen-year period is dated probably from his conversion, not from his first visit.[4] He went with Barnabas, who was a Jew and Titus who was a Greek or an uncircumcised Gentile. There are three important aspects of this visit:

---

[1] Moo, *Galatians*, 118.
[2] Hendriksen, *Galatians*, 69.
[3] See e.g., Fung, *The Epistle to the Galatians*, 85.
[4] Longenecker, *Galatians*, 44–45. See 1:18; see also Witherington, 111, *The Acts of the Apostles: A Socio-Rhetorical Commentary*, 68ff. and his discussion in the Introduction regarding the date of Galatians where he suggests the use of "inclusive reckoning" (n. 44). Also George, *Galatians*, 136. Hendriksen, *Galatians*,

Paul Was Not Summoned

He went "because of a revelation." God had revealed his will to Paul that he should go; it was not because he was ordered to appear by the apostles in Jerusalem. In writing of "a revelation," he is not referring to what happened at his conversion (1:12) – we would then have expected a definite article "the" with this reference.[5] Another possibility was this came through the prophecy of Agabus (Acts 11:27–30) when Paul and Barnabas were sent to bringing relief to Jerusalem. Or did Paul receive another personal revelation similar to his previous visit (see Acts 22:17–21, when he was urged to leave), which would have brought a fresh authorization?[6] The suggested timing is the famine visit which is supported by the reference to the "pillars" requesting them to continue to remember the poor (2:10). It also appears, as we pointed out in the Introduction, that the meeting was a small private affair, not in any sense an official conference (v. 2). However, in the reference to that visit in Acts 11 and 12, Luke does not mention particularly a private meeting. However, it appears there *was* a private meeting leading to a private agreement where both the meeting and the outcome would have remained secret had it not been for the crisis in Galatia brought about by the Judiazers, which meant Paul had to write concerning it, thus making the whole matter public.

Paul came "with Barnabas." He was a Jewish Christian who already had close links with the Jerusalem church (Acts 4:32–37); he had first introduced the apostle to them in the past (Acts 9:26–29) and also had brought him to Antioch where they served together for the full year (Acts 11:22–29). He was a good man, "a conciliatory figure"[7] or a "son of encouragement" as his name means, a Levite from Cyprus (Acts 4:36). He was "full of the Holy Spirit and of faith" (Acts 11:24).

Titus on the other hand was "a Greek" (v. 3). Has Paul (the singular participle is used) taken the initiative in bringing his younger companion with them to give him more experience and to develop his "communication skills?" Note how he was used by Paul later in relation to the difficulties which developed between Paul and the Corinthian church (2 Cor 2:12f.; 7:5–16). Others have suggested Titus was there as a kind of "test case" or "exhibit A"[8] and suggest that this is implied by the wording of v. 3. But it is possible to maintain that his presence there was providential as it later turned out, with "no importance … attached to it at the time but which proved a helpful precedent in the light of later events."[9] George[10] makes the point that if this visit was bringing famine relief to the Christians in Judaea "it would be perfectly

---

as was noted in the Introduction adopts a different view, namely, the Gal 2 trip is to be identified with that of Acts 15. He set out the arguments for and against this understanding in 71–73.

[5] J.D.G. Dunn, *The Epistle to the Galatians*, Black's New Testament Commentaries (London: A&C Black, 1993), 91.

[6] Fung, *The Epistle to the Galatians*, 86.

[7] Dunn, *The Epistle to the Galatians*, 89.

[8] Witherington, 111, *Grace in Galatia*, 132. See also Moo, *Galatians*, 123, who thinks it possible that Titus was brought to force the issue of Paul's law-free gospel.

[9] Bruce, *The Epistle to the Galatians*, 111.

[10] George, *Galatians*, 141.

natural for a Gentile member of the church in Antioch to be sent along as an expression of solidarity between the predominately Gentile church in Syria and the largely Jewish mother church in Jerusalem." Bruce[11] also points out that Ἕλλην *hellēn* in the NT always means a Greek of Gentile origin and not a Greek-speaking Jew. So, for Worthington,[12] Titus is not even a Greek God-fearer, but a convert from paganism – in fact converted through Paul (Titus 1:4). So Paul's two colleagues were "a microcosmic expression of the power of the gospel to break down the barriers that had separated Jews and Gentiles and to create a new unity in Christ – a unity that transcends the ethnic, cultural and social divisions in the world."[13]

When in Jerusalem for the famine relief Paul "set before them" privately the gospel that he was proclaiming (the present tense implies he was still preaching it at that time) among the Gentiles. This "gospel" is summed up in 3:1 "Jesus Christ … as crucified," the object of faith for both Jews and Gentiles (2:16). We must ask who is in view here in the use of the pronoun αὐτοῖς *autois* "them?" Is it the leaders or the whole community? Those who interpret the Jerusalem visit in 2:1 as the Acts 15 Jerusalem Council visit, rather than the famine visit normally would suggest two groups are referred to here, the leaders and then the whole church. The view that we have a smaller and a larger group is suggested by Dunn and Longenecker,[14] although the latter also is persuaded that the visit is the famine visit. Bruce[15] also interprets 2:1–2 as referring to the famine visit, but when he discusses the "false brethren" in vv. 4–5 who infiltrated, he in fact suggests that the reference is to what happened in Acts 15:1, 24, the arrival of the men from Judea *in Antioch* without any mandate from James. Bruce's opinion is then that the reference is to the leaders only, not the whole church – they are named in v. 9, James, Cephas and John.[16] This is a view which should not be quickly dismissed.

What does Paul mean when he writes that he "set before" them his message? The only other use of the Greek verb found here is in Acts 25:14, where Felix "communicated" to King Agrippa the information concerning the prisoner Paul. This is the normal understanding of the verb and so we can say that it does not convey in any sense that somehow Paul was involved in some form of negotiation or authorization concerning the gospel (see v. 5). It was more an act of courtesy and fellowship.[17] He met them "privately," not because as has been suggested these men were in hiding, or even that they could work out a way of making some kind of a proposal that would satisfy the larger body. It is simply that these were the leaders of the church in Jerusalem and it would be normal to report to them of the mighty work God was doing among the Gentiles. Of them he writes "before those who seemed

---

[11] Bruce, *The Epistle to the Galatians*, 111.

[12] Witherington, 111, *Grace in Galatia*, 132.

[13] G. W. Hansen, *Galatians*, The IVP New Testament Commentary Series (Leicester, England: InterVarsity Press, 1994), 54.

[14] Dunn, *The Epistle to the Galatians*, 89; Longenecker, Galatians, 47.

[15] Bruce, *The Epistle to the Galatians*, 115–17.

[16] See also Fung, *The Epistle to the Galatians*, 88–89, who takes this view and advocates a private meeting with the Jerusalem leaders.

[17] Dunn, *The Epistle to the Galatians*, 92; McDonald, *Freedom in Faith*, 40.

influential." In v. 6 there is a similar reference. Bruce[18] accepts that Paul is speaking positively, not negatively. He is not saying they only *seemed* to be leaders but is using the phrase as Josephus "those who seemed to excel" of men highly regarded (and rightly so) in the community (*War* 3.453; 4.141, 159).

He writes using athletic imagery (see also 4:4; 1 Cor 9:24; Phil 2:16; 3:14; 2 Tim 2:5; 4:7; Heb 12:1) "in order to make sure I was not running (present tense) or had run (past tense) in vain." Not that he himself had any misgivings about this; he knew his gospel was the revelation of God; rather, he sought to avoid the work of 14 years being rendered fruitless by the success of the Judaizers. Is it possible that his converts from his law-free gospel would be rejected and the years of fruitful labour to come preaching the same message, which he could never alter, would be seen as producing nothing of value for the kingdom of God? Would the result not be the existence of two different "world" churches out of communion with each other? That Paul valued the unity of the church is seen in his efforts to bring the Gentile collection to Jerusalem. While he "strongly asserted his independence of Jerusalem, he desired no dissociation from Jerusalem."[19]

His Companions – Titus Was Not Compelled

This occasion turned out to be a significant one in the history of the church. Paul tells us that his Gentile companion was not compelled to be circumcised (vv. 3–5). This statement must surely be understood to mean exactly this – not that Titus was not *compelled* to be circumcised but did so voluntarily[20] or through the advice of Paul or others in Jerusalem or Antioch. Would this suggestion not surely contradict what Paul actually wrote in the context i.e., vv. 5–9 that his gospel for the uncircumcised was recognised? Bruce[21] states, "How the circumcision of a Gentile Christian could have been supposed by any one, especially by Paul, to help to maintain the gospel of free grace for Gentile Christians in general, passes understanding."

It is clear from v. 4 that at some point and *somewhere* (see below) pressure was exerted upon them for Titus to be circumcised. This pressure came from "false brothers," regarded at this time as "brothers" by the Jerusalem leadership but actually, in Paul's judgment, in reality, only Jews/Judaizers and no more. They were intruders with no business to be in the fellowship, who had slipped in,[22] "that they might bring us into slavery." They would view the increasing blessing and recruitment of Gentiles with suspicion and were pressing for the maintenance of the movement's distinctive Jewishness, expressed by submission to circumcision with all

---

[18] Bruce, *The Epistle to the Galatians*, 109.

[19] Fung, *The Epistle to the Galatians*, 90.

[20] So G.S. Duncan, *The Epistle to the Galatians* (New York: Harper, 1934), 41–44.

[21] Bruce, *The Epistle to the Galatians*, 113. Dunn also makes the point that such a concession would have "wholly undermined Paul's argument," Dunn, *The Epistle to the Galatians*, 96.

[22] Note Paul's use of the same verb in Rom 5:20 of the advent of the law. Martyn translates "the law came in by a side door." J. L. Martyn, *Galatians: A New Translation with Introduction and Commentary*, Vol. 33A (New York: Doubleday, 1977), 196 n. 10.

that this implied. But when did this happen? As we noted earlier, Bruce[23] suggests that this infiltration took place later, not in Jerusalem but in Antioch – see Acts 15:1, 24. This is understandable as Antioch was the "home" of Gentile Christianity at the beginning.

Paul saw the issue clearly; it was not a matter of circumcision or uncircumcision but of freedom (through grace) or bondage. The Christian's acceptance depended upon God's grace on the basis of the cross, a salvation received through Christ alone, involving regeneration, justification (the opposite of condemnation), a righteousness which is not our own and the power of the Holy Spirit to give us deliverance from the flesh. To introduce the works of the law and make our salvation depend upon obedience to rules and regulations was to bring the individual again into bondage. The issue really was vital, as was mentioned earlier, that "the truth of the gospel might be preserved for you." It was the truth which was at stake. They had previously responded to the truth as Paul preached to them; now they must continue in it. The mention of the concept of "slavery" here would be in preparation for the fuller discussion of this issue on the following chapters of the letter. Note that for Hendriksen,[24] "The word (slavery) is none too strong, for the demands of the law constituted an unbearable yoke." See later Peter in Acts 15:10; but now here in 2:4; 5:1 by Paul himself.

Note also how Witherington[25] points out that the concept of "freedom" is deeply significant in the Epistle, in fact it could be taken as "the theme of this entire act of persuasion." The noun "freedom" is found in 2:4; 5:1, 5:13 (twice); also note the adjectival form in 3:28; 4:22, 23, 26, 30, 31 and the verb in 5:1. Moo[26] also understands the concept of freedom as "an important summary of the view for which Paul is fighting in the letter." Therefore, it is, as has been stated, the cross which has brought us out from under the yoke of the law into this freedom, i.e., to this certainty of our acceptance before God, and to a life lived in the Spirit's power. We should recall the teaching even of 1:4 – Christ gave himself for our sins (later Paul will show that no one can keep the law perfectly) to deliver us from the present evil age (even the law is part of that – see also the full discussion in 4:3, 9). But we also now enjoy in Christ blessings of the new age already![27]

Paul says that to them – the Judaizers – "we did not yield in submission even for a moment." We should note the textual problem here. In the Western Text, a number of the Latin Fathers e.g., Tertullian and Irenaeus in the translation οἷς οὐδέ *hois oude*

---

[23] Bruce, *The Epistle to the Galatians*, 115.

[24] Hendriksen, *Galatians*, 80.

[25] Witherington, 111, *Grace in Galatia*, 137.

[26] Moo, *Galatians*, 129.

[27] Moo also refers to W. Coppings, *The Interpretation of Freedom in the Letters of Paul*, Wissenschaftliche Untersuchungen zum Neuen Testament 261. Tübingen: Mohr Siebeck, 2009, 93–103 and S.F. Jones, *"Freiheit" in den Briefen des Apostels Paulus: Eine historische, exegetische, und religionsgeschichtliche Studie*, Göttinger theologischer Arbeiten, 34. Göttingen: Vandenhoeck & Ruprecht, 1987, who consider that the freedom Paul has in mind is "comprehensive," and includes this freedom from "the present evil age," Moo, *Galatians*, 129, n. 15.

have been omitted. This would make Paul say the exact opposite, i.e., "because of false brethren ... we yielded in submission for a moment" – as a conciliatory gesture. But all the Greek uncial MSS except D˟ include these words, as does p46, all in the versions but d, e and all the Greek Fathers except Irenaeus in translation.[28] So accepting the longer reading, Paul says that he does *not* yield in submission "for a moment" (literally ὥραν *hōran* "hour," but meaning in this verse and most others where it appears the smallest real unit of time).[29] There is strong emotion in this paragraph – the grammar is "wrecked."[30] So for Martyn "it is inconceivable"[31] that having strongly defended the gospel without circumcision he would yield even momentarily for this to happen to his young Gentile colleague. Titus was not compelled. For Paul, what was at stake was "the truth of the gospel" (see also 2:14; 5:7). This gospel of justification by faith alone, in Christ alone, apart from works but by the regenerating and empowering of the Holy Spirit – all through the cross – which Paul will shortly affirm (2:16; 3:2–5; 4:29; 5:16–26), must be preserved at all costs. They had accepted this gospel of grace when he first came to them; they must not now let it go.

Excursus: The Coming of the False Brethren

It is important to explain more fully the order and timing of these events. Most scholars will suggest that this infiltration of false brethren took place in Jerusalem during the private session Paul and Barnabas had with the leaders of the church. These men were able to slip in secretly and demand that Titus who had travelled to Jerusalem with Paul must be circumcised! It can be maintained that this secret spying would fit very well with the coming of men from Judaea *to Antioch* – without any mandate from the Jerusalem leaders – who infiltrated into the church to spy out their liberty and then proceeded to insist on the circumcision of all the male Gentile converts (Acts 15:1, 24). Paul's visit to Jerusalem in Gal 2:1 (the famine visit) will then have taken place earlier and Titus was with him along with Barnabas. No pressure was brought to bear upon them for Titus to be circumcised; the issue did not even arise. The issue of circumcision only arose later when the false brethren came to Antioch and Paul and his colleagues would not move an inch on this. There was not, nor could there ever be, any concession on their demand. But the "dissention" meant that Paul, Barnabas and others had to go again to Jerusalem to discuss the whole matter (Acts 15:2–35).

---

[28] Bruce M. Metzger, *A Textual Commentary on the Greek New Testament*, 2nd Ed. (New York: United Bible Societies, 1994), 591–92.

[29] Dunn, *The Epistle to the Galatians*, 86 n. 2. See e.g., Matt 8:13; 9:22; 15:28; Luke 2:38; John 4:53; Acts 16:18; 22:13; Rev 11:13. Phillips translates it not "an inch," J. B. Philipps, *The New Testament in Modern English* (New York: Macmillan, 1958).

[30] Lightfoot, St. Paul's Epistle to the Galatians, 106.

[31] Martyn, *Galatians*, 197.

Such an understanding of the verses means that vv. 4–5 are a parenthesis. Orchard[32] explains that as Paul is dictating his letter to the Galatians, who were also being troubled by Judaizers at the same time as Acts 15:1, he remembers the earlier events with Titus.

It suddenly struck him as a forcible argument with which to refute the Judaizers of Galatia that the fact that the Apostles did nothing about the Gentile Titus ... on that occasion showed that they agreed with him in recognising "the freedom of the Gentiles" from the burden of the Mosaic law. And so forsaking all of a sudden the train of thought he has pursued in verses 1 and 2, he breaks in with a new debating point against his Judaizing opponents, for all the world as if he were afraid he would forget it if he did not set it down there and then.

This identification of the "false brothers" with the men from Judaea in Acts 15:1 is supported by Bruce and others such as Weiss, Lietzmann, Schlier, Oepke, Hahn. Although, unlike Bruce, these scholars identify the visit of Gal 2:1f. as the Jerusalem Council of Acts 15.[33]

It is clear that Paul gives no ground to these men when they came to Antioch in Acts 15:1 – and this is the position he now adopts – being consistent for the sake of the truth of the gospel – with the problems now among the churches in Galatia. It is therefore suggested that not only in Antioch were the Judaizers active, but as we have explained above and in the Introduction, also in south Galatia. When Paul got news of what was happening there, he dictated this letter *before* the Council of Acts 15:6ff.

Finally, one can note Hansen's discussion of Paul's Jerusalem visits. He argues that if Gal 2:1–10 relates to Acts 11:27–30 rather than Acts 15:1–20, then there were two conferences in Jerusalem and most scholars think it "highly unlikely that there were two conferences in quick succession in which the same people debated the same issue with the same outcome. This duplication of conferences is unnecessary."[34] But should we really consider Gal 2:1–10 as a conference at all? The passage is plain. Having taken the famine relief with Barnabas and Titus, Paul had opportunity to meet the three "pillars." Privately he was able to share with them his ongoing preaching among the Gentiles. However, the meeting was a private meeting with three individuals, however influential, and no more. It was not a first conference. In fact, we can even find support for this position in Martyn[35] who considers that the visit of Galatians 2 is about the Jerusalem Counsel of Acts 15 which he suggests is in fact "a formal conference between the churches in Jerusalem and Antioch as negotiating parties." He has to admit that Paul's repeated use of verbs in the first person singular

---

[32] B. Orchard, "A New Solution to the Galatians Problem," *BJRL* 28 (1944), 165–66; "The Ellipsis between Galatians 2:3 and 2:4," *Bib 54* (1973) 469–81.

[33] Bruce, *The Epistle to the Galatians*, 115; see Fung, *The Epistle to the Galatians*, 94, who follows Bruce here and also as was noted earlier affirms that the Gal 2 visit should be identified with the Famine Visit of Acts 11. Moo considers that the episode with Titus likely took place during the Jerusalem famine visit and is "integral" to the passage, as his young colleague is mentioned already in v. 1, Moo, *Galatians*, 127.

[34] Hansen, *Galatians*, 20.

[35] Martyn, *Galatians*, 208.

"suggests no such thing." Paul is always referring to himself and Barnabas! Does this not point to a "private meeting" rather than a huge conference? *That one conference still lay ahead as Paul wrote Galatians and related in these opening verses of Gal 2 the famine visit to Jerusalem.*

* * *

His Gospel Was Not Changed

This gospel was now laid before the other apostles, even though this was not his main reason for going to Jerusalem. His Gentile gospel was not contradicted or modified in any way (vv. 6–10) and Paul was accepted. The Jerusalem apostles are identified in v. 9. In the other verses in the paragraph Paul uses indirect expressions to describe them. As was pointed out, he was not being derogatory – he has made clear that they were apostles before him (1:17), they were "men of repute" (vv. 2, 6, 9), but he probably knew that the Judaizers were exaggerating the status of the Jerusalem apostles at the expense of his own. Paul hints in v. 6 at the extravagant claims which were being made. Hendriksen[36] points out the break in grammatical sequence (the anacoluthon or interruption) here – in fact Paul interrupts himself! This "unfair comparison" of Paul with the Jerusalem leaders "as if his gospel was definitely inferior" leads him to add his own estimate, "not out of disrespect for *them*, but from disapproval of *the comparison*." His problem was not with the Jerusalem pillars but with those who were flattering or exalting them. For Paul, God (the word is in an emphatic position) does not recognise or regard such external distinctions as wealth, power, rank, or race. Literally, he does not "accept the face" – see for this idea Luke 20:21; Acts 10:34; Rom 2:11; Eph 6:9; James 2:1; in the OT, Lev 19:15; Deut 1:17; 16:19; 2 Chron 19:7; Job 13:10; Ps 81:2; Prov 18:5; Mal 2:9. Human reputations do not influence a man's standing in the sight of God. It could be it was their acquaintance with the earthly Jesus that is in mind, as Peter and John were disciples close to Jesus and James was his earthly brother; but Paul had a personal encounter with the risen Christ and was commissioned by him on the Damascus Road, which was the only prerequisite and sufficient qualification for apostleship (1:1; 1 Cor 9:1; 2 Cor 11:5; 12:11f.).

Note v. 7, "on the contrary" affirming that they found themselves in total agreement with Paul's ministry and message. "They added nothing to me," with the Greek emphatic pronoun ἐμοι *emoi* "to me" first in the sentence, reminding us again of his God revealed message and independence from Jerusalem. They had contributed nothing to Paul, either to his apostleship or his message.[37] They did not find his gospel defective or made any attempt to add circumcision to it; they changed nothing. As Hendriksen[38] explains, "James, Cephas, and John recognise *God's* hand when

---

[36] Hendriksen, *Galatians*, 81.

[37] Dunn, *The Epistle to the Galatians*, 104.

[38] Hendriksen, *Galatians*, 69. Moo highlights two adverbial participles "seeing" v. 7 and "knowing" v9 and suggests that the aorist form "may suggest an inceptive idea ...'came to recognise' these key facts about Paul's ministry," Moo, *Galatians*, 134.

they see it!" It is "the gospel which I preach" (present tense), v. 2 as he writes, he is continuing to preach. Paul explains in vv. 7–8 that the "pillars"[39] recognised that the gospel had been "entrusted" – the verb is in the perfect tense (with the force of a pluperfect) and indicates a commission already given which is ongoing and permanent – actually to both Peter and Paul. Hendriksen[40] notes that "It is clear that equal honor is accorded to Paul and Peter." Note there are not two gospels (Gal 1:6–7) but two "hearers" of the one message. In fact, Peter and Paul are both obligated to make the message known – as we also are.

When v. 7 speaks of the "gospel to the circumcised" it means for the Jews, not in any sense a message of or which *includes* circumcision. Bruce[41] comments, "There was of course no reason why circumcision should figure at all in any preaching of the gospel to Jews." *Both men* had a serious responsibility regarding the message of the cross, salvation by grace through faith, without works. Peter had sought to evangelise the Jew (on one occasion, Gentiles in the house of Cornelius, Acts 10:1–11:18); Paul had been effective to a certain extent among Jews, but God had made it plain that his mission was to Gentiles (Acts 9:15, 26–28; 22:17–21). This was "the grace that was given to me," either his apostleship to the Gentiles (1:15–16; Rom 1:5) or grace in ministry (Rom 12:3; 15:15; 1 Cor 3:10; Eph 3:2, 7). So as Witherington[42] explains, "Paul did not take this agreement to mean that he would never preach to Jews, or that Peter would never address Gentiles. We are speaking of the major focus and purpose of their respective ministries."

However, the point is that there is only ONE gospel – there is no contradiction among the apostles in the NT, whether Peter, Paul or John. As Stott[43] insists, certainly there can be differences in *style*, inspiration did not obliterate personality, *emphasis*, they were called to preach and write to different audiences. But there is "only one gospel, the apostolic faith, a recognisable body of doctrine taught by the apostles of Jesus

---

[39] The Greek is στυλοι *stuloi* used literally of the main supporting columns in a building or temple (1 Kings 7:15–22; 2 Chron 3:15–17 LXX). See also the figurative sense in Exod 13:21–22; 1 Tim 3:15; Rev 3:12; 10:1. These were the main leaders of the Jerusalem church, who must uphold the gospel, engage in a ministry of support and hold the church together. Also what of Barrett's suggestion that we do not forget the "eschatological," that they are the basis of the new people of God? C.K. Barrett, "Paul and the 'Pillar' Apostles," *Studia Paulina*, FS Johannis de Zwaan, ed. J.N. Sevenster and W.C. Unnik (Haarlem: Bohn, 1953), 1–19. Or as Witherington, 111, *Grace in Galatia*, 143, "holding up and holding together the people of God being now renewed and restored in Christ." Moo mentions the Jewish tradition of the three patriarchs through whom God established the world and the world covenant community and quotes Aus, "God was thought of by Jewish Christians as having 'established the world' anew, the new covenant community," R.D. Aus, "Three Pillars and Three Patriarchs: a Proposal concerning Gal 2:9," *Zeitschrift für die neutestamentliche Wissenschaft und die Kunde der älteren Kirche*, 70 (1979), 256–57. See Moo, *Galatians*, 137. Interestingly along with Paul (and his epistles) these three in sequence make up the traditional order of the General letters of the NT canon, documenting a common testimony. See D. Lührmann, "Gal 2:9 und die katholischen Briefe. Bemerkungen zum Kanon und zur regula fidei," *ZNW* 72 (1981), 65–87.
[40] Hendriksen, *Galatians*, 83.
[41] Bruce, *The Epistle to the Galatians*, 120.
[42] Witherington, 111, *Grace in Galatia*, 141. Hendriksen, *Galatians*, 85, explains that this division of labour "must be interpreted in general terms."
[43] Stott, *The One Way: The Message of Galatians*, 47.

Christ and preserved for us in the New Testament." 1 Cor 15:11 states, "Whether then it was I or they, so we peach and so you believed." We must never give up the gospel, the message of the cross. Both Peter and Paul were "entrusted" with this message (see Rom 3:2; 1 Cor 9:17; 1 Thess 2:4; 1 Tim 1:11; Titus 1:3). God "worked" – used often of "effective divine action (Mark 6:14; 1 Cor 12:6, 11; Gal 3:5; Eph 1:11, 20; Phil 2:13; Col 1:29; 1 Thess 2:13) ... a divine 'energizing,'" as Dunn[44] observes. God worked "in" or "through" both Peter and Paul. Moo[45] prefers here the instrumental dative, "through" Peter and Paul and suggests that Paul portrays Peter and himself as "instruments" in the hand of God. The acceptance of both their ministries was evident among other things by their mutual effectiveness.

The pillars gave to him "the right hand of fellowship," signifying agreement, confirmation (cf. 2 Kings. 10:15; Ezra 10:19; Ezek 17:18). In *Antiquities* xviii.328–9 Josephus states "No one would ever prove false when he had given his right hand, nor would anyone hesitate to trust one that he suspected might harm him, once he had received that assurance of safety." The description of "fellowship" here strengthens the bonds of unity. As McDonald[46] states, "there is no suggestion of subjection; but rather a demonstration of fellowship." For Moo,[47] Paul's ministry and Peter's ministry are put "on equal footings."

George[48] here discusses the whole question of cooperation and the truth of the gospel. His insights are important for any mission or evangelical cooperation today:

> Paul could not work together with the false brothers, even though they claimed to be fellow Christians, because their theological position was antithetical to the gospel message itself. However, Paul was eager to work closely together with other Christian leaders who shared with him a common commitment to the good news of salvation through Jesus Christ.

Hendriksen[49] also sees the importance of recognising cooperation not just with regard to the gospel but concerning the NT writings. They do not give us:

> Conflicting theologies – the theology of John, the theology of Paul, etc. – but a harmonious, beautifully variegated unit. It is remarkable that the five men, whose handclasp is here described, produced, between them, no less than twenty-one of the twenty-seven New Testament books!

Paul's ministry included both an evangelistic thrust but also an aspect of social care – holistic only in the sense that it was concerned for the needs of the believers. We note

---

[44] Dunn, *The Epistle to the Galatians*, 106. Remember 1 Cor 2:4 "my speech and my message were not in plausable words of wisdom, but in demonstration of the Spirit and of power."
[45] Moo, *Galatians*, 135.
[46] McDonald, *Freedom in Faith*, 48.
[47] Moo, *Galatians*, 135.
[48] George, *Galatians*, 167.
[49] Hendriksen, *Galatians*, 86.

that while "the pillars" introduced no stipulation regarding Paul's gospel preaching, they simply asked him "only" (the placing of the adverb first gives their direction a special emphasis) to "remember the poor."[50] In this context the reference will likely not be to the poor generally, or certainly not spiritually but to the poor in the Christian community in Jerusalem, no doubt deeply affected by the famine in around AD 47 and the reason for the visit (Acts 11:27–30). The appeal was that their care of them would be continued. Paul in the future would initiate the collection for the poor saints in Jerusalem to which he refers in 1 Cor 16:1; 2 Cor 8:4; 9:1; Rom 15:26.[51] Such care was not in any sense some form of imposed tribute or suggested "temple tax" but the payment of a spiritual debt (Rom 15:27). The use of the aorist ἐσπούδασα *espoudasa* "I was eager" means that the reference is not simply about all future assistance but will include the relief he has just brought to Jerusalem. Paul is pointing out not just that he will adopt this policy in his future ministry but was already doing so during the present visit – the famine relief brought in AD 48. For Moo,[52] the verb expresses indefinite past time.

Concern for the poor was an important principle within the Jewish law and covenant (Lev 19:9–10; 23:22; 25:35–56; Deut 24:10–22; Ps 10:2, 9;12:5;14:6; Isa 3:14–15; 10:1–2; 58:6–7; Amos 8:4–6). Such a principle of compassion and care would also be natural for the new people of God. Therefore, we should not perceive this request as a concession wrung from Paul, while he would not budge on circumcision, for it would be inconsistent with the statement that they "added nothing to me."

One should note Fung[53] here:

> From the perspective of Paul's apologetic interests in this letter, the Jerusalem agreement meant that he owed neither his gospel nor his apostolic commission to the Jerusalem authorities, since he brought both with him to the meeting.

He had already received both his gospel and his apostleship from the risen Lord. The meeting with the Jerusalem leaders confirmed that his gospel and calling as an apostle were already his before he had come to Jerusalem. Finally, one should note, in discussing Paul's visits to Jerusalem how Witherington[54] affirms:

Both the reference to remembering the poor, and the reference to going up by a revelation better suits the account found in Acts 11.27–30 than that in Acts 15 which says nothing about action in response to a revelation and nothing about remembering the Jerusalem poor.

---

[50] A clear pointer to the fact that the timing of this meeting was earlier than the Jerusalem Council – here the stipulation was "only" the poor; in Acts 15:23–29 we have rather the apostolic decrees.
[51] Hendriksen, *Galatians*, 86, includes the reference in Acts 24:17 where Paul speaks of one of his chief aims in coming to Jerusalem then was "to bring alms to my nation."
[52] Moo, *Galatians*, 138.
[53] Fung, *The Epistle to the Galatians*, 101.
[54] Witherington, 111, *Grace in Galatia*, 147.

2:11–21: Peter and Paul in Antioch

This passage gives us one of the most dramatic episodes in the NT. Peter had given Paul the right hand of fellowship in Jerusalem (2:9), but what about this moment in Antioch? It seems likely that at some point Peter would visit Antioch. Is this the "another place" mentioned in Acts 12:17 when he was miraculously released from prison and Herod's evil intentions? There were many Jews to be evangelised in the large Jewish colony in the city. Witherington[55] reveals that Antioch and its environs was "where the largest group of Jews in the Eastern end of the Empire outside of Palestine were to be found." Here Peter would continue his "ministry to the circumcision." Witherington[56] can postulate that this may very well be the time when Paul was gone from Antioch – possibly the time of the first missionary journey of Acts 13–14. Paul evangelised in Galatia for a considerable time and then returned to Antioch where having "gathered the church together," he reported, "all that God had done" in opening a door of faith to the Gentiles. Luke then tells us, "they remained no little time with the disciples" (Acts 14:27–28). It appears that it was during this stay that we see the developing situation where the men from James influence Peter to slowly withdraw from fellowship with the Gentile converts. Barnabas,[57] on his return from the first missionary trip, follows that lead. Paul also writes now to the Galatians of the time "when Cephas came to Antioch" (2:11). This will be fresh in his mind, for he has to write to the churches in Galatia of their own turning to another gospel *after* Peter's withdrawal and shortly *before* the Jerusalem council.

Bruce[58] also claims this incident can be dated[59] in the period after the famine visit of Acts 11 and following the return of Paul and Barnabas from their missionary activity in Cyprus and south Galatia (Acts 14:26–28). It makes clear the need for a decision as to how Jewish and Gentile Christians could share fellowship. The forthcoming council would appeal to Gentiles to be sensitive to the Jewish food restrictions (eating the flesh from which the blood had not been drained) and relations between the sexes as set out in Acts 15:20, 29. Such food restrictions for Jews were given in the law in Lev 3:17; 7:26–27; 17:10–14. In Dan 1:3–16; Macc. 1:62–63 there is a record of

---

[55] Witherington 111, *Grace in Galatia*, 150. Also, his *The Acts of the Apostles*, 360ff.

[56] Witherington 111, *Grace in Galatia*, 150.

[57] Barnabas, as we know already had close ties with the Jerusalem church. In Acts 11:22 he was specially sent to Antioch, to watch over the development of the work and to endeavour to see it develop in fellowship with Jerusalem.

[58] Bruce, *The Epistle to the Galatians*, 130. See also George, *Galatians*, 169 – 173, where he broadly reconstructs the sequence of events as Bruce. Hendriksen, *Galatians*, 90, as we noted earlier, because of his understanding of 2:1–10 as the Jerusalem council visit of Acts 15, will have to place this incident later. But it is difficult to accept that the Paul-verses-Peter incident "immediately follows" the conference, as Hendriksen proposes. How could such a complete change of direction happen when we know the role Peter had in the council (Acts 15:7–11) and the decision reached (Acts 15:19–21)? The very letter from the council was read in Antioch where "they rejoiced because of its encouragement," Acts 15:31. Is it not more logical to understand this incident at Antioch as one of the reasons why such discussions in Acts 15 had to take place?

[59] Witherington, 111, *Grace in Galatia*, 118 makes the point that it is "natural" following the three uses of "then" in 1:18, 21; 2:1 to understand ὅτε δὲ *hoti de* "but when" in 2:12 as telling of further developments taking place after the sequence of the three events, and not before.

those who were willing to die rather than defile themselves and profane the covenant. The Acts 15 conference would make clear that circumcision was not required of the Gentile believers.

A further comment about how those who seek to identify Gal 2 with the Acts 15 council run up against many problems. How could Peter change so quickly from his stance at the Jerusalem Council if this incident follows it? Dunn[60] has to suggest the possibilities that: (1) there were misunderstandings among the parties as to what was agreed; (2) there was a shift in power in the church in Jerusalem; (3) there was a change in the political situation, with more zealous Jews including believers having greater influence; (4) James had simply gone back on the Jerusalem agreement. How much simpler to understand that such a council became necessary because of problems like this arising *before* it.

Moo[61] adds that this section will conclude that part of the letter written in first-person narrative style. Paul's interest throughout the whole has been especially in the gospel. The phrase "the truth of the gospel" occurs in 2:5 and again in 2:14; "the phrase binds together the two narratives in 2:1–14." This is what Paul is contending for, the law-free gospel – through the cross. Today we need to face the challenge of Jude 1:3, "I found it necessary to write appealing to you to contend for the faith that was once for all delivered to the saints." The gospel message – in fact, many aspects of the faith have been lost from many pulpits.

Moo[62] also agrees with placing this incident after the famine visit of Paul to Jerusalem in Acts 11:27–30, "sometime between that visit and the writing of Galatians just before the Jerusalem Council of Acts 15." As Witherington (n. 59), maintains, "Moreover, ὅτε δέ, "but when") while not as explicit as Paul's earlier transitions still suggests that this narrative follows the one before it chronologically," and takes place "shortly after Paul and Barnabas have returned from their first missionary journey." We note v. 14 "When I saw," suggesting that Paul has discovered a new state of affairs after his absence and return to the city of Antioch.

How Peter Acted

It appears that Peter did not deny the gospel of grace in his teaching but his conduct put this in question – at least that is what is implied by his actions. In vv. 11–13 Paul explains that at first Peter "was eating with the Gentiles" – the imperfect shows it to be a regular practice. While the text states "with the Gentiles," it surely means Gentile Christians, many of them recent converts. He enjoyed table-fellowship with them, and some would suggest that it is likely that such meals would include as an

---

[60] Dunn, *The Epistle to the Galatians*, 122–24.
[61] Moo, *Galatians*, 141.
[62] Moo, *Galatians*, 141–42.

integral part, the Lord's supper (1 Cor 11:20–21).[63] Hendriksen[64] is one who sees here in Galatians the fellowship meal or the *agapē* feast of the early Christians. Food normally consumed at home would be brought on this occasion and the possible dangers of damage to the fellowship among believers is set out in 1 Cor 11:17–24.

In Corinth there was separation according to wealth, the rich separating from the poor; in Antioch the segregation which threatened was of an ethnic character, the Jewish Christians separating from their Gentile brothers in the faith.

Peter's initial actions remind us of what we know about him from the four Gospels. In the Acts of the Apostles he goes to Caesarea, directed by God to the house of Cornelius, shares fellowship with him (God showed him in a vision that all kinds of food could be eaten) and accepts his baptism and the others upon whom the Spirit fell (Acts 10:28–48; 11:3). However, in Antioch, when certain Jewish men arrived "from James" (2:12), Peter's actions changed. Witherington[65] explains why those he describes as "Torah-observant Jewish Christians" of the church in Jerusalem would be disturbed at this type of behaviour by Peter.

The Jerusalem church had recognised that God had set him apart for missionary work among Jews, and here he was fraternising with Gentiles over meals which would cause many of those in his target audience to raise questions about his Jewishness. From the point of view of these members of the Jerusalem church, Peter was acting in conflict to the character of his calling.

We can assume that these visitors claimed that it was improper and unwise for Jewish Christians to eat with Gentile Christians until they were circumcised. One recalls Jewett's[66] explanation as to why this pressure was being brought to bear upon the brothers:

> Jewish Christians in Judea were stimulated by Zealotic pressure into a nomistic campaign among their fellow Christians in the late 40s and early 50s. Their goal was to avert the suspicion that they were in communion with lawless Gentiles. It appears that the Judean Christians convinced themselves that circumcision of Gentile Christians would thwart Zealot reprisals.

Note how Paul also tells us in fact that Peter's withdrawal from his former fellowship with the Antiochan Gentile believers was because of fear of the "circumcision party" (v. 12). This "party" for Longenecker[67] would be the Jews in Jerusalem. It has been

---

[63] Others question whether the reference is likely to refer to the Lord's supper exclusively or even primarily, as the original verb is quite general, as is the reference to "live … like a Jew." Fung, *The Epistle to the Galatians*, 106.

[64] Hendriksen, *Galatians*, 90.

[65] Witherington, 111, *Grace in Galatia*, 152.

[66] See Introduction, note 13, Jewett, "The Agitators and the Galatian Congregation," 205. See Moo, *Galatians*, 148.

[67] Longenecker, *Galatians*, 73.

pointed out that the noun ἡ περιτομή *hē peritomē* in the preceding verses (vv. 7–9) is used three times to refer simply to Jews, not the Judaizers or still less Jewish Christians. This is how the word is used elsewhere in Paul's other letters (Rom 3:30; 4:9, 12; 15:8; Col 3:11; 4:11). So Longenecker[68] simply refers to (and translates) Peter's fear of "the circumcision party" as his fear of "the Jews."

Witherington,[69] who makes reference to Jewett's[70] proposal, also notes the record in Josephus (*War* 2, 24–227; *Ant.* 20.112) of the killing of thousands of Jews in the spring of AD 49 by Jewish Zealots and the reference by Paul in 1 Thess 2:14–16 of the persecution of Christians in Judea. He concludes that we cannot be certain if Peter's fear was of Zealots, or zealotic Jewish Christians who would warn of angry Jews causing major trouble for the church in Jerusalem. He takes the reference to the circumcision party as Longenecker, but then makes the further point, "I think, however, it was indeed Torah-true Jewish Christians who raised the spectre of persecuting Jews, namely the ones who came from James." Therefore, for him, the groups are different, while related, both seeking the circumcision of the Gentile converts.

Moo,[71] after a discussion of the various possibilities, takes practically the same position. "The envoys from James were probably sent to investigate and convey concern about the degree to which Jewish believers were associating with Gentiles." Moo also discusses the fear of Peter – and James – concerning "the circumcision." It involved:

> How Jews in Jerusalem would perceive this new messianic movement (that is explicitly a concern that James expresses on a later occasion [Acts 21:20–24]). The envoys from James would, on this reading of the situation, have urged Peter and the other Jewish Christians in Antioch to refrain from close contact with Gentiles, *out of fear that their behavior would bring disrepute to Christians in Jerusalem* and elsewhere. [italics mine]

Therefore, this advice to encourage withdrawal from Gentile Christians in Antioch was given to actually facilitate Jewish evangelism! See below what Paul thought of that! So, Moo sees also two groups here referred to – Jewish Christians "from James" and Jews back in Jerusalem.

One can note that in Acts 11:1–18 "the apostles and brothers ... throughout Judea" heard how the Gentiles also had "received the word of God" in Cornelius' house. When Peter went back to Jerusalem we are told "the circumcision party criticized him, saying, 'You went to uncircumcised men and ate with them.'" When everything was explained to them, "they fell silent. And they glorified God" (11:18). It appears that the same term ("the circumcision party") is being used here in Acts most likely

---

[68] Longenecker, *Galatians*, 74.
[69] Witherington, 111, *Grace in Galatia*, 156.
[70] See note 219 and Introduction, note 13.
[71] Moo, *Galatians*, 147–49.

not of Jews only but of Jewish Christians – zealous of Jewish traditions – who now rejoiced at what God had done in Caesarea. Was it a similar group of professing Jewish Christians who had arrived now in Antioch, with the same concerns about Peter's fellowship with Gentiles while they were still uncircumcised – as Witherington and Moo have suggested? The only point to note is Moo's suggestion that it was the Jews back in Jerusalem whom both Peter and also James and this group were concerned about.

It seems clear that it was Judaizers who were also troubling the churches in Galatia – hence this concerned letter from Paul to them sent around this time, before he went to the Jerusalem Council. As we noted earlier in the Introduction, Paul may not have had a great deal of information about these agitators – note "whoever he is" (5:10). But certainly, Paul knows that they were not just stopping at "fellowship." Circumcising was necessary for inclusion among the people of God. One can say that the circumstances in Antioch from where he was sending the letter were providential. What had happened with Peter served as a ready example of the problems that were affecting the Gentile believers in the Galatian churches. Paul can compare how he stood against Peter, Barnabas and the others, who withdrew their fellowship from the Gentile believers, with how the Galatian believers *receiving his letter* can now oppose the Judaizers who were seeking to persuade them to turn away from the gospel and accept circumcision, as if they were not already children of Abraham, or Spirit-born children of promise by faith.

Peter's action at this time was to now gradually withdraw and separate himself[72] from his Gentile Christian brothers. How could he forget what happened at Joppa i.e., the vision of the great sheet (Acts 10:10–15) and his defence in Jerusalem of his eating in the house of Cornelius (Acts 11:1–18)? Other Jews including Barnabas were influenced. Paul's companion could not bring himself to be seen as standing against the Jerusalem church. So with regard to the others at Antioch, who "acted hypocritically" we learn that even Barnabas was carried away[73] or "led astray by their hypocrisy."[74] The word "hypocrisy" is ὑπόκριτης *hupokritēs* which means taking the role of an actor, as on the stage. As Witherington[75] explains, "one appears and outwardly acts one way, but in fact believes another." Or Hendriksen,[76] Peter was "acting contrary to his inner convictions … just as an actor conceals his real face under a mask." Therefore, Peter and the rest were not acting from theological conviction but expediency. To be leaders in the early church, as both Peter and also Barnabas were, it was vitally important to remain true to one's theological convictions and for this to be demonstrated publically. In v. 13 others of course sadly followed their example as has often been the case today.

---

[72] The verbs are imperfect again
[73] See 2 Peter 3:17, where the same verb warns of being "carried away with the error of lawless people."
[74] The verb συναπάγω *sunapagō* "was *led astray*" signifies an irrational element in Barnabas's emotional action as the others became agents of this. But Paul is more reserved about the action of Barnabas – it is by *their* hypocrisy.
[75] Witherington, 111, *Grace in Galatia*, 156.
[76] Hendriksen, *Galatians*, 94.

Surprisingly, for Longenecker[77] it appears that in a sense Peter can be excused somewhat for his actions as his motives were right! "In such a scenario, Cephas was, in fact, attempting to avert a break between the Jerusalem church and the community of believers at Antioch, even though Paul interpreted his action as doing just the opposite." But it can be maintained that whatever his love for the Jerusalem church was, the action in refusing fellowship with Gentile converts in Antioch (and of course with other Gentile churches elsewhere in the future) could never be excused.

So, Peter still believed the gospel and had not apparently changed his position. But his actions (drawing back little by little), undertaken because of appearance not from true conviction, influenced others and negated the fellowship that had been evident among the Jewish and Gentile Christians.[78]

Who Peter Faced

"But when I saw...." The strong adversative ἀλλά *alla* "but" signifies a direct contrast. Moo[79] suggests from these words "when I saw" that Paul was away from Antioch when the delegation from James arrived. If this is the case then Peter must also have been gradually withdrawing his fellowship at that time. So, the fact is that Paul was presented with a "fait accompli."

Things were going in the opposite direction[80] from where they should have been going i.e., "their conduct was not in step with the truth of the gospel" which eventually led Paul to withstand Peter to the face publicly (vv. 14–16). Peter's actions were public and so was the rebuke (1 Tim 5:20); there was no private meeting with some smuggled in. Moo[81] suggests, "The reference is probably to a public meeting of the Christians in Antioch, perhaps called at Paul's request to hash out this issue in particular."

Paul writes "he (Peter) stood condemned" – probably the meaning for most commentators is just *self*-condemned by his own actions i.e., in the wrong. But serious issues were at stake. For Dunn[82] the abruptness of the language and depth of feeling is not concealed in these verses. Important matters were involved. The reference to opposing Peter to the face (see other instances Deut 7:24, 9:2, 11:25; Josh. 1:5) suggest the incident was "of epochal significance" – because of the "truth of the gospel" (v. 14, also v. 5). It seems clear that to give in to circumcise Titus or to accept Peter's rejection of fellowship with the Gentile believers, with Barnabas and

---

[77] Longenecker, *Galatians*, 74.
[78] Witherington also in a footnote refers to the actions of Peter, Barnabas and others as "impersonation" i.e., playing a part when you have other convictions. He still considers that they hold to the same beliefs as Paul does. Witherington, 111, *Grace in Galatia*, 169, n. 1.
[79] Moo, *Galatians*, 149.
[80] Hendriksen, *Galatians*, 95, translates the Greek verb found only here in the NT "they were not pursuing a straight course in accordance with the truth of the gospel." He in fact suggests that the implication was that they were "pulling farther and farther apart" from gospel truth.
[81] Moo, *Galatians*, 150.
[82] Dunn, *The Epistle to the Galatians*, 117.

the other Jewish Christians, was taken by Paul as having the utmost gravity because as v16 will affirm, both actions violate the foundational truth that gospel blessings i.e., here justification, is by faith alone in Jesus Christ. The gospel states that we are accepted by sheer grace, not through any works of ours. Salvation as Paul goes on to expound is by grace alone, through faith alone, because of the cross, resulting in the acceptance of all, Gentile or Jew.

Peter's behaviour was contradicting this, for he had been actually living "like a Gentile and not like a Jew" (2:14) in Antioch and no doubt in other Gentile communities from time to time. Yet now he was forcing[83] the Gentiles to live like Jews. Just as Paul told the Galatians in his letter how he had to take a stand against the pressures of the "false brothers," so Peter ought to have stood against the pressure by the Jewish visitors from James. As Longenecker[84] has pointed out, "that theologically based call for Gentile Christians to practice a Jewish lifestyle was tantamount to a denial of the Christian gospel."

This interpretation is important because of how the incident was understood in the Patristic period with Jerome and Augustine and the positions taken later by Luther and Calvin.[85] Jerome was persuaded by Origen that the apostle Peter actually pretended to compromise his true convictions so that Paul would be able then to clearly affirm the true teaching concerning justification. Erasmus then followed this understanding which was based on a doubtful rendering of κατα προσωπον *kata prosōpon*; rather than translating "I opposed him to the face" the translation was "I opposed him to outward appearances," i.e., "I appeared to or made a show of opposing him" – so that the true gospel might be articulated. Augustine resolutely disagreed with Jerome – Paul would not have been part of any such deception as he had already put himself under oath (1:20). At the time of the reformation the differences became fixed, as Luther and Calvin followed Augustine and Erasmus and Roman Catholic commentators followed Jerome.

The problem is really that someone like Peter, who came to be regarded in Catholicism as the first pope, the head of Christ's church on earth, could err so seriously. Protestant theologians, following the Reformation made much of this incident affirming that popes, church councils could be wrong; Holy Scripture *sola scriptura* was the only authority to which one could appeal. Luther[86] maintains concerning Peter:

---

[83] The verb ἀναγκάζεις *anagkazeis* "force" or "compel" used also in 2:3 is intentionally setting up the contrast. Titus was not "compelled" – why should they?

[84] Longenecker, *Galatians*, 80.

[85] See summary in George, *Galatians*, 184–86.

[86] Luther, *A Commentary on St. Paul's Epistle to the Galatians*, 116. Luther ponts out that all committ sin whether OT prophets, Nathan (2 Sam. 7:3, when he "in his own spirit" proposed that David, the man of war, build the temple), even the Apostles, who misunderstand the nature of the kingdom; again Peter, when he is slow to take the gospel to the Gentiles, even to Cornelius and needed a vision (Acts 10:9ff.).

And in this matter he did not only err, but also committed a great sin, and if Paul had not resisted him, all the Gentiles which did believe, had been constrained to receive circumcision and to keep the law. The believing Jews had been confirmed in their opinion: to wit, that the observation of these things were necessary for salvation; and by this means they had received again the law instead of the Gospel, Moses instead of Christ. And of all this great enormity and horrible sin, Peter by his dissimulation had been the only occasion.

Calvin actually expressed the view that Paul's rebuke of Peter was a matter of church discipline – a public rebuke as 1 Tim 5:20, something which should be carried out with regard to any elder.[87] This failure on the part of Peter was another demonstration that in us there is no righteousness – our only righteousness is the righteousness of God received by grace – as Gal 3:6–9 will show, we are children of Abraham by faith and like him have been given this righteousness.

What Peter Forgot

"We ourselves" (v. 15). Paul reminds him of the gospel which they both knew and held in common. On this matter there was no difference between them. They were agreed that God accepts the sinner through faith in Christ because of what he had accomplished at the cross. If God justifies sinners, Jews and Gentiles, on the same terms and puts no difference between them, Paul asks how one can withhold fellowship from Gentile believers until they are circumcised? If God receives them into his fellowship, why shall we deny them ours? Peter no longer observed the Jewish food regulations and why should he compel others then to live like Jews? Witherington[88] explains that Peter was leaving the Gentiles no choice if they wanted fellowship with other Jewish Christians – they must Judaize! "Paul's objection to this is fundamental because he does not see Christianity as simply a subset of early Judaism. He sees it as involving the creation of a new eschatological community."

Both Jews and Gentiles are Justified by Faith 2:15–21

It is difficult to decide where Paul's rebuke of Peter ends and the general exposition begins. Hendriksen[89] notes the change in pronouns from the singular συ *su* "you" to the plural Ἡμεις *Hēmeis* "we" in v. 15. He still considers that Peter is never absent from Paul's mind but the attention is now shifting to the entire group. We can take vv. 15–16 as one sentence introducing the presentation of justification by faith as

---

[87] J. Calvin CNTC 11.33 in George, *Galatians*, 186.

[88] Witherington, 111, *Grace in Galatia*, 159.

[89] Hendriksen, *Galatians*, 96. Betz, *Galatians*, 114, takes vv. 15–21 as the *propositio* of Galatians following the statement of the facts in the opening *narratio*. The *probatio* of 3:1–4:11 has the proofs or arguments introduced in vv. 15–21. This is the reason for Betz for the compressed language of these verses. See also Witherington, 111, *Grace in Galatia*, 170. Certainly, it seems clear that the summary here in these verses will be reasoned out at length in the next two chapters. Is Paul addressing Peter personally, but also the Galatians substantially? We can add also all who will take time to read the letter.

Paul reminds Peter of what they both believed and preached. Of course, the teaching would also be for all in the public meeting. We do not learn from Paul of any response from Peter here or that the situation had been put right in the local context – at least by the time Paul sent this letter to the Galatians. However, the point of including and rehearsing this incident is because of the fact that something similar was happening in Galatia. All that is recorded here about Paul's response to Peter and the others in Antioch is just what the Galatian churches needed to hear in the letter he sent. Moo[90] quotes I. W. Scott as affirming that Paul's purpose was "to lay the situation in Antioch alongside the situation in Galatia, to see the crises as parallel and the true solution as the same in both cases."

In a short space of time, as we understand, the issue was to arise again in Antioch, as Acts 15:1–2 reveals. But by this time both Barnabas and Peter had come to appreciate the seriousness of their withdrawal of fellowship from the Gentile believers. Again, at the forthcoming Council of Jerusalem, the Christianity of the Gentile believers was seen as not in any sense defective or less than complete (Acts 15:6–21). Circumcision was not imposed, encouragement expressed and suggestions given as to how social contact could be deepened between Jewish and Gentile believers (Acts 15:23–29).

As we have stated, vv. 15– 21 are critical verses for the whole of the letter.[91] They function as a kind of central affirmation for the argument. Moo[92] makes the point that in writing to the Galatian churches, "Paul continues to quote his speech at Antioch right up through the end of verse 21." The "key paragraph" which looks back to the Antioch incident, "also looks ahead to the argument that Paul will be making to the Galatians. Key words that are central to that argument are first introduced here."

In spite of the fact that these verses at first reading seem to be straightforward – having a standing of acceptance with God for men is through grace, and by faith in Christ because of the cross – they will require careful treatment because of the various false understandings that has been proposed concerning their interpretation. The methodology I shall use here is to first present my own interpretation and then provide a brief but reasonably detailed history of how these themes have been interpreted over the past 40 years or so by various scholars. During those decades, some scholars have suggested that there has been a paradigm shift in Pauline studies. While we agree that interpreting Paul has been a major focus, I take the view of other commentators like Stott, Cranfield, Carson and Piper who challenge many of the elements of the proposed "New Perspective" on Paul.

---

[90] I.W. Scott, *Implicit Epistemology in the Letters of Paul: Story, Experience and the Spirit*, Wissenschaftliche Untersuchungen zum Neuen Testament 205 (Tübingen: Mohr Siebeck), 180 in Moo, *Galatians*, 154.

[91] With regard to the structure of these verses Longenecker, *Galatians*, 82, explains that the argument is set out first negatively (vv. 17–18) and then positively (vv. 19–20), summed up in the statement "Christ lives in me." In v. 21 the whole argument is brought to a conclusion i.e., "his [Paul's] gospel does not nullify the grace of God, but focuses on 'Christ crucified' for righteousness."

[92] Moo, *Galatians*, 153.

That vv. 15–16 provide a kind of summary[93] with the concepts or key terms expanded upon in the following chapters is clear. See "righteousness" in 2:21; 3:6, 21; 5:5; "justify" 2:16 (x3), 17; 3:8, 11, 24; 5:4; "law" 2:16 (x3), 19 (x2), 21; 3:2, 5, 10 (x2), 11, 12, 13, 17, 18, 19, 21(x3), 23, 24; 4:4, 5, 21(x2); 5:3, 4, 14, 18, 23; 6:2, 13. Also "works" 2:16 (x3); 3:2, 5, 10; 5:19; 6:4; "faith" 2:16 (x2), 19 (x2), 21; 3:2, 5, 10 (x2), 11, 12, 13, 17, 18, 19, 21(x3), 23, 24; 4:4, 5, 21 (x2); 5:3, 4, 14, 18, 23; 6:2, 13. Finally "to live" 2:14, 19, 20 (x2); 3:11, 12; 5:25. So the key terms are introduced. Here we find "the truths in embryo."[94]

The People Named

The "We" of v. 15 is emphatic in the text – "we" Jews as distinct from the others who are Gentiles. Here the important statement is that they all as Jews have something which they hold in common.

Paul refers to "Jews by birth and not Gentile sinners." The meaning is not that the Jews were righteous but rather that Gentiles were outside the covenant (e.g., Eph 2:12) and so seen as sinners in the general sense of the term. This was demonstrated to Jews by the general level of pagan morality (see Luke 24:7; Acts 2:23; for Gentile believers before conversion, 1 Cor 6v:9–11; 1 Thess 1:9–10). This statement may be a quotation from the vocabulary of law-abiding Jews – almost a synonym for Gentiles (Isa 14:5; 1 Macc. 2:44; *Pss. Sol.* 1.1, 2.1; Matt 26:45; Luke 6:32–33). So here, Paul is clearly writing from the perspective of a typical Jew. For Fung,[95] "the two nouns (Gentile, sinner) are synonymous and form a single concept." But we must not miss the intention of v. 15, to highlight the birth privilege of Jews compared to Gentiles. Yet v. 16 will show that the trap laid in v. 15 is now sprung. As Moo[96] explains, "The gospel reveals that all people are 'sinners' and therefore *equally in need* of finding justification in Christ." [Italics mine]

Bruce,[97] notes the use of "person" lit. ἄνθρωπος *anthrōpos* "man" in v. 16 which makes the point that Jews as well as Gentiles now stand before God as human beings, neither privileged Jew nor underprivileged Gentile.[98] Witherington[99] can refer to a text like 2 Macc. 6.12–17 where the sinfulness of the Gentiles and Jews are compared. The Gentiles will suffer destruction for their sin; the Jews receive discipline. But "God takes Jewish sinfulness as seriously as Gentile sinfulness ... (cf. Gal 5. 17–21; 1 Thess 2:14–16)." Moo[100] also explains that Paul is affirming that

---

[93] Fung, *The Epistle to the Galatians*, 112 finds here "a single, overloaded sentence ... aptly described as 'Paul's doctrine of Justification in a nutshell.'"
[94] See W. M. Ramsay, *A Historical Commentary on St. Paul's Commentary to the Galatians* (Grand Rapids: Baker, reprint 1979), 306 in Witherington, 111, *Grace in Galatia*, 171, n. 5.
[95] Fung, *The Epistle to the Galatians*, 113.
[96] Moo, *Galatians*, 156.
[97] Bruce, *The Epistle to the Galatians*, 137.
[98] See also Longenecker, *Galatians*, 82, for whom ἄνθρωπος *anthrōpos* "man" is clearly indefinite, meaning "a person," "anyone," or "someone." as we find it in 1:10, 11, 12; 2:6; 3:15; 5:3; 6:1, 7.
[99] Witherington, 111, *Grace in Galatia*, 173.
[100] Moo, *Galatians*, 157.

these statements are not about Gentiles being included with Jews in the people of God, the point is rather that Jews are included with Gentiles in the whole mass of sinful humanity; the term *anthrōpos* means "people in general." Therefore, v. 16 is affirming that no works of the law can justify, for they, the Jews, cannot keep the law perfectly. He quotes Ps 143:2 "for no one living is righteous before you" (v. 16b), which we will discuss later. As Paul will continue to stress in the letter (e.g., 3:10–13, 19, 21–22; 5:3), all are sinners and through the cross on the basis of faith, God in his grace can accept both. Paul will affirm through the cross and by faith alone sinners, Jews and Gentiles, can find regeneration, justification and more – spiritual transformation in Christ (2:20; 5:16–26). We also ought to note that this emphasis here is so important because there are certain Jewish commentators who in studying Paul now suggest that only the Gentiles and not the Jews were in need of salvation.[101]

The Terms Employed

We note v. 16 has the verb "justified" 3 times, 1 in v. 17 and the noun "justification" is used again in v. 21. It is predominantly Paul's word, occurring for the first time in his letters in the NT[102] (8 in Galatians, 2 in 1 Corinthians, 15 in Romans, and 2 in the Pastoral Epistles). It is a forensic term, a word which involves acquittal in the law court. When applied to salvation, the meaning is that your guilt and condemnation before God is removed and it is affirmed that you are given a standing of acceptance, because God imputes to you the righteousness of Christ on the basis of the cross. We need to be clear about this. Catholicism protests against this "forensic" understanding of justification, emphasising the infusion of God's grace rather than imputation. But to be justified does not mean "to make righteous" but "to declare righteous." Remember how Paul refers to God in Rom 3:26 as the one who "shows his righteousness at the present time, so that he might be just and the justifier." Now God cannot be "made righteous" but he can be recognised as righteous because of actions which are in keeping with his intrinsic holy character. In justifying God imputes his own righteousness to us, giving us a perfect standing of acceptance.

However, we must also understand the eschatological nature of justification. In Jewish apocalyptic there was the understanding that in the age to come, in a future judgment, God would finally vindicate his people, put right all the wrongs and give his final verdict upon all men. But while the NT and Paul still affirms the final judgment, the fact has become clear that God has already stepped into this age[103] in

---

[101] We need to remember e.g., Rom 1:16–17 "the gospel, for it is the power of God for salvation to *everyone who believes, to the Jew first and also to the Greek"*; also 9:1 "My heart's desire and prayer to God for them (Israel) is *that they may be saved"*; Rom 3:29–30 states Jews also need to be justified; Rom 10:13 "whoever will call upon the name of the Lord *will be saved.*" For this suggestion about *Gentiles only,* see the review of Pamela Eisenbaum, *Paul was not a Christian: the Original Message of a Misunderstood Apostle* (New York: HarperOne, 2009) in www.denverseminary.edu by J.D. Kim. Accessed May 2017. Also e.g., M.D. Nanos, "Paul and Judaism: Why Not Paul's Judaism?" 117–60 in *Paul Unbound: Other Perspectives on the Apostle*, Ed. M.D. Given (Peabody, MA: Hendrickson), 2010.
[102] The fact that the theme is not in most of Paul's letters is simply because they were "occasional" writings, dealing directly with the issues that arose in different local churches.
[103] See the fuller discussion of "this present evil age" and the age to come in 1:4.

the person of his Son. As a result and through the cross, God's blessing of the gift of regeneration and eternal life, the indwelling Holy Spirit *and* justification have been imparted to all who come to repentance and put their faith in a crucified but now risen and returning Saviour. Therefore, the end time verdict has been pronounced upon the man of faith in the present, e.g., Rom 5:9, "being *now* justified."[104]

So here for the first time in the epistle this important word justification occurs, a word which is central to its message (2:16–17; 3:8, 11, 24; 5:4) central to the gospel of Paul and central to Christianity itself. Hendriksen[105] compares the doctrine of justification and that of sanctification. The first is a matter of *imputation* (reckoning, charging). The sinner's guilt is imputed to Christ; the latter's righteousness is imputed to the sinner (Gen 15:6; Ps 32:1–2; Isa 53:4–6; Jer 23:6; Rom 5:18–19). Sanctification is rather a matter of *transformation* (2 Cor 3:17–18).

In justification the Father takes the lead (Rom 8:33); in sanctification the Holy Spirit does (11 Thess 2:13). The first is a "once for all" verdict, the second a life-long process. The Judge (who justifies) now turns to that free man and adopts him as his son and even imparts his own Spirit to him (Rom 8:15; Gal 4:5, 6) … out of gratitude, this justified person, through the enabling power of the Spirit, begins to fight against his sins and to abound in good works to the glory of his Judge-Father.

There is another important term which needs further discussion because of the opinions of certain scholars. As we will see, it is a crucial part of a whole area of debate on the subject of the New Perspective. The text says, "a person is not justified by works of the law." The phrase ἐργων νομου *ergōn nomou* "works of the law" means in this commentary the sum total of God's commandments, not just *boundary markers*, as we will now seek to comment upon in the following pages.

It can be maintained that contrary to the views of some scholars, "the works of the law" are the acts done in obedience to the law. As Bruce[106] pointed out, the works of the law are *the actions* prescribed by the law; this remains an important insight in light of recent understanding. Witherington[107] also takes the same position. Various texts in Galatians refer to the law *as a whole* e.g., 5:3, 14. Witherington comments:

---

[104] Also note Moo's undrestanding. The agitators probably adopted the usual Jewish view – justification tied to the last judgment depending upon how one has performed in keeping "the works of the law" while for Paul it was a matter of faith in Christ – a blessing available through the cross. Therefore, he suggests that the tenses used for this concept, present, aorist, future are not particularly significant. Moo, *Galatians*, 162. One can accept that there will be a final confirmation and demonstration of the believer's justification in the final judgment, but this must never rule out the teaching of the NT regarding its present possession. Passages like Matt 25:31–46; James 2:14–26; Rev 20:11–15 refer *not* to final salvation by good actions or works but salvation *by faith evidenced through works.* Also, it can be maintained that one can never become "unjustified."

[105] Hendriksen, *Galatians*, 98.

[106] Bruce, *The Epistle to the Galatians*, 137.

[107] Witherington, 111, *Grace in Galatia*, 177.

In other words Paul connects the ritual law, including the distinctive boundary rituals to the rest of the law and says that the one entails the other.... We must thus conclude that by "works of the law" Paul means actions performed in obedience to the law, or more specifically acts performed in response to any and all the commandments of the law. He is not simply concerned with specific laws, nor with the social function and effect of the law separating Jews from Gentiles.

This is a crucial viewpoint as we will see when the full treatment of these things takes place. Moo[108] also recognises the importance of discussing the meaning of the phrase "works of the law" (see Galatians 2:16 [3x]; 3:2, 5, 10 and Romans 3:20, 28). He proposes:

> The genitive in the phrase could be subjective, "works prescribed by the law"; but it perhaps more likely is objective, "works done in obedience to the law." Thus the phrase semantically matches phrases such as "doing the law" (Rom 2:14, 25, 27; Gal 3:10; 5:3; 6:13; cf. Rom 10:5 and Gal 3:12 [Lev 18:5]) or "doers of the law" (Rom 2:13 ESV).

He also makes the point which will be emphasised later in Galatians:

> Why then, can't "works of the law" justify? Because they are *torah* works: insisting on them is effectively to turn back the clock in salvation history, to a time before Messiah came and when the Gentiles were excluded from the kingdom.... Salvation history surely is crucial to Paul's argument in Galatians: it is partly because the era of the law is over that its "works" cannot justify.[109]

Note that the three-fold repetition here of the phrase "the works of the law" is striking. Paul emphasises that it is not by or through works of the law[110] but "through faith in Jesus Christ, so we also have believed in Christ Jesus." Every individual "person," either privileged Jew or underprivileged Gentile can be justified – but only by grace (v. 21 "the grace of God" is foundational to all of this passage and in fact, throughout the whole of the letter) and on the basis of faith can God accept both.

We have quoted a few scholars i.e., Bruce, Witherington and Moo concerning this subject. In the following Excursus a brief summary is given of the recent history of interpretation concerning the nature of Second Temple Judaism, the phrase "works of the law" and broader issues surrounding these themes. This will follow our own understanding.

---

[108] Moo, *Galatians*, 158.

[109] Moo, *Galatians*, 158–59.

[110] The preposition ἐκ *ek* will have an insturmental force – not "by" but "through" and ἐὰν μή *ean mē* best understood as "but" as with most English translations – "an antithetical relationship," Moo, *Galatians*, 162.

Excursus: The Nature of Second Temple Judaism, the "Works of the Law" and "Righteousness"

The statement here by Paul that we are "not justified by works of the law" has led to prolonged discussion among commentators in the West and has produced interpretations which have deeply divided scholarship across many of the disciplines. This book, as was mentioned above, maintains that "works of the law" is a phrase which *does not* mean only the "national badges" or the "boundary" or "identity" markers of Judaism, taking on circumcision, Jewish feasts and observing the Sabbath i.e., living like a Jew. Nor does "justified, not by works of the law" simply imply that the gospel is for Gentile as well as Jew. The "works of the law" should still be understood as merit-earning works or endeavouring to find favour with God by means of works, or actions as in NIV, by "observing the law." I will take time to first, briefly outline my own understanding of the law in Paul, particularly in the Galatian and Roman letters, and secondly I will concisely summarise the history of the interpretation of these wider issues in the last 40 years or so, making mention of reputed commentators like Stott, Cranfield, Carson and Piper as they respond to interpretations of this theme by scholars with whom they – and I! – disagree. Firstly, then, I submit my own understanding.

The Word "Law" in Paul

Paul uses the word "law" (νομος *nomos*) 119 times in his letters in various ways; it is found on 32 occasions in Galatians. He can use it of a principle of action (Rom 3:27; 7:23; 8:2). Again, it can refer to the whole of the Old Testament, the Scriptures (Gal 3:22; Rom 3:10f.; 1 Cor 14:21, quoting Isa 28:11), or the Pentateuch (Gal 4:21). But most of the time he means the Mosaic law contained in the Pentateuch (1 Cor 9:9; Rom 7:22, 25; 8:7).[111] It should be noted that there are no occasions where Paul draws a clear distinction between the ceremonial and moral law.

Paul's Estimate of the Law

It is explicitly called God's law in Rom 7:22, 25, 8:7. As God's law it is "holy, righteous and good" (Rom 7:12); it is "spiritual" (Rom 7:14) and its commandment was intended unto "life" (Rom 7:10). There is no moral defect in the law (Rom 7:7); as it had a divine origin (Gal 3:19). Possessing the law is reckoned as one of the great privileges of Israel (Rom 9:4). It is not an inferior or false revelation of God's will, but in it the Jewish people have "the embodiment of knowledge and truth" (Rom 2:20). Yet in spite of what we have seen we shall soon discover a very negative estimate of the law in Paul and the absolute rejection of it as a means of salvation.

---

[111] In 1 Cor 9:21 and also here in Gal 6:2 he speaks of the "law of Christ." These references need to be explained further at the appropriate time. See 5:14, 18 and the Excursus of 6:2.

We should note that in Galatians as Moo[112] explains, the law is given a consistently negative portrayal because of the polemical situation Paul was facing in the letter.

In Rom 8:3 Paul explains that the law was "weakened by the flesh," our sinful fallen nature, and could not give us the power to live to please God. Or as Witherington[113] clarifies, in Gal 3:23–4:7 the law imprisons those under it. The law is a temporary expedient until "the fullness of time" came and is incapable of giving life, impotent of giving the power or ability to keep God's commandments. He states:

> It must be borne in mind that the Ten Commandments and the Shema were at the very heart of the law, something of which Paul is well aware, and yet Paul was willing to place the law in the categories of a ministry of death and a form of fleeting and fading glory *while talking about those very ten commandments* (2 Cor 3).

Silva[114] also takes the same view. He first points out that Paul's understanding of the law is related to his eschatological perspective – see 1:4 where believers are "new age" people. He sets out what he sees as the "eschatological undercurrents" of the letter in the following passages: 1:1 (reference to the resurrection); 1:4; 1:12, 16; 2:2; 2:16; 2:19–20; 3:2–5; 3:8, 14, 16; 3:19–4:7; 4:25–27; 5:1, 13–14; 5:5–6; 5:16–26; 6:8. He sees the law (the Mosaic economy as a whole) representing "the old existence" and "the new life made possible by Christ's crucifixion." The antinomy is spelled out in chapter 3 where he considers that Paul unmistakably "locates the Judaizer's message in a bygone stage of redemptive history ... *the mode of existence based on the works of the law is eschatologically obsolete*" [italics his]. Verses like 3:19 "until the coming of the seed," 3:25 "we are no longer under a guardian," 4:1 "until the time set by the father," leave "no room for ambiguity." The end of the period is identified with "the coming of faith" (3:23, 25) and "the fullness of time" (4:4). When we reach 6:13–17, and particularly vv. 14–15, we will, according to Silva, note that Paul's criticism of the Judaizers is their failure to recognise the eschatological significance of the crucifixion over against remaining in the old world of circumcision.

When we come to 5:16ff. – our life in the Holy Spirit – we will see how Paul explains that in this age of fulfilment, believers, born of the Spirit are now empowered by the Spirit. Later he explains this in the letter to the Romans, "in order that the righteous requirements of the law might be fulfilled in us, who walk not according to the flesh but according to the Spirit" (Rom 8:4). As Galatians puts it, we can produce the positive "fruit of the Spirit" (Gal 5:23). Then in 6:2 Paul can write of fulfilling "the law of Christ." This law of Christ does refer in part to the example of Christ, but includes the teachings of Christ, the various portions of the OT which are reaffirmed

---

[112] Moo, *Galatians*, 36.
[113] Witherington, 111, *Grace in Galatia*, 343.
[114] Silva, *Explorations in Exegetical Method: Galatians as a Test Case*, 169–86. Moo makes the same point stressing on four occasions that believers are no longer "under the law," 3:23; 4:4–5, 21; 5:18, Moo, *Galatians*, 36–37.

in his ministry and also in the teachings of Paul; in fact, throughout the whole of the NT – all basically a pattern to be emulated in the power of the Holy Spirit. As Witherington[115] has maintained:

> Paul's letter to the Galatians is … a salvation historical document about recognising what time it is, and what covenant God's people are and are not under. The law of Christ is not the Mosaic law in a new guise. It is the new eschatological dictums appropriate for those living as new creatures albeit in an already and not yet situation.

So, to emphasise this point again, this "law of Christ" provides the example, the guidance, and the Holy Spirit provides the power. More on that later; sufficient to say for now, as Moo[116] notes, that however the Judiazers may seek to persuade the believers in Galatia to put themselves under the law of Moses, "the Spirit, introduced into the Galatians' lives by their faith in Christ, provides all the guidance and power necessary to fulfil God's law (5:18, 23)."

The Law in Judaism

The traditional viewpoint of the Judaism of Paul's day has been to see it as largely legalistic with a perverted understanding of the role of the law. Scholars would point out that when the law was first given it was not with the purpose of achieving a right relationship with God by means of obedience. Israel already had a relationship with God by means of his election of them and their redemption from Egypt. The context of the law was the covenant and this was instituted by the gracious act of God. As Ladd[117] explained, the law did not constitute them God's people but provided Israel with a standard through which the covenant relationship could be preserved. The problem was that, following the exile, the law came to occupy a primary position and keeping it was of vital importance, in the light of God's past judgment on the nation for their disobedience. The observance of the law became the basis of God's verdict on the individual and that which determined his fate in the world of the hereafter; in fact, it had reached the position of intermediary between God and man.

Many scholars – not of course New Perspective scholars – maintain that the law was therefore viewed as the unique means to acquire for oneself merit, reward or righteousness before God and the instrument given by God to subjugate the evil impulses within. It is claimed that it is this Jewish legalistic perversion which treats the law as a means of earning one's own salvation or acquiring favour with God by good works against which Paul contends. As we noted, this understanding has been denied in the past decades by a number of Western scholars whose influence has been far-reaching. These and related issues can be mentioned briefly and a summary of the responses which present the main points of disagreement.

---

[115] Witherington, 111, *Grace in Galatia*, 345.
[116] Moo, *Galatians*, 38.
[117] G.E. Ladd, *Theology of the New Testament*, Rev ed. (Grand Rapids, Michigan: Eerdmans Publishing Company, 1993), 540.

Stott, Carson and Neusner in Response to Sanders on the Nature of Palestinian Judaism

A major challenge to the above standard interpretation in the past decades which we must mention is that of E. P. Sanders.[118] It was his approach that became known as the New Perspective on Paul. Sanders was not willing to accept the nature of Palestinian Judaism as a legalistic works-righteousness religion. This view he considered totally a mistake "based on a massive perversion and misunderstanding of the material,"[119] i.e., the apocalyptic literature and that from Qumran. He preferred to call it "covenantal nomism" involving first God's election of his people and then the giving of the law. Judaism was more devotional than many scholars allowed. For many, this was a major paradigm shift in Pauline studies. But this proposal has been challenged. Our summary of the history of this challenge from some conservative commentators will begin with Stott, whose writings are widely available.

Stott[120] elaborates on Sanders' position in his commentary on Romans, where he includes a section in the Preliminary Essay "New challenges to old traditions"; here he assesses his claims. We include a few points.

Firstly, Stott agrees that the evidence is plain that the language of "weighing," i.e., of "balancing merits against demerits" does not occur in the literature of Palestinian Judaism. However, Stott claims, does the absence of this imagery prove the absence of the concept of acceptance by merit? Paul was not mistaken in describing some Jews as "pursuing" righteousness but not attaining it (9:30ff.), and again, as trying to be "justified by the law" (Gal 5:4).

Secondly, Sanders writes of God's grace in the election of his people. But what of this grace when it is not just about "getting in" but "staying in?" He maintains:

> The conception is that God acts, that Israel accepts the action as being for them, that God gives commandments, that Israel agrees to obey the commandments, and that continuing to accept the commandment demonstrates that one is "in" while refusing to obey indicates that one is "out."[121]

---

[118] E. P. Sanders, *Paul and Palestinian Judaism: A Comparison of Patterns of Religion* (London: SCM 1977); see also *Paul, the Law and the Jewish People* (Philadelphia: Fortress, 1983). We should note that before Sanders another influential reappraisal of Second Temple Judaism was carried out by Stendahl who proposed that Luther had read Paul incorrectly through the lens of his own struggles with medieval Catholicism. K. Stendahl, "The Apostle Paul and the Introspective Conscience of the West," *Harvard Theological Review*, 56, no 3 (July, 1963), 199–215.

[119] Sanders, *Paul and Palestinian Judaism*, 59.

[120] J. Stott, "New challenges to old traditions" in *The Message of Romans*, The Bible Speaks Today (Leicester: Inter-Varsity Press, 1994) 24–31. In Romanian *Epistola lui Pavel catre romani* (Cluj Napoca: Logos, 2000).

[121] Sanders, *Paul and Palestinian Judaism*, 237.

Stott makes the point that in the Old Testament itself God is seen to take the initiative in his grace to establish his covenant with Israel. There could be no question of "deserving" or "earning" one's membership. Yet Sanders[122] claims that "the theme of reward and punishment is ubiquitous in the Tannaitic literature," especially with regard to gaining life in the world to come. Does this not mean that human merit, while not the basis (in Judaism) of entering the covenant, was yet the basis of remaining in it? Stott[123] insists:

> Paul would have been vehement in his rejection of this. To him "getting in" and "staying in" are both by grace alone. Not only have we been justified by grace through faith (5:1), but we continue to stand in this grace into which we have been granted access by faith (5:2).

Thirdly, Stott points out that Sanders conceded that 4 Ezra was an exception to his argument about the nature of Second Temple Judaism. He writes of this apocryphal work, "one sees how Judaism works when it actually does become a religion of individual self-righteousness ... 'covenantal nomism' has collapsed. All that is left is legalistic perfectionism."[124] But for Stott, if this one literary example survived, there may have been others which did not survive. There is the possibility that this "lapse into legalism" may have been more widespread than Sanders admits. Stott points out that Sanders has been criticized for not fully recognising the complexity of first-century Judaism, with serious questions asked about how he presents Judaism as "a single, unitary, harmonious; and linear development."[125] Stott quotes Hengel[126] as one example of those who stress this point. He explains that "in contrast to the progressive 'unification' of Palestinian Judaism under the leadership of the rabbinic scribes after AD 70, the spiritual face of Jerusalem before its destruction was a markedly 'pluralistic' one." After listing nine different groups he states: "perhaps there was no such thing as this one Palestinian Judaism with the one binding view of the law."[127]

Fourthly, Stott points out that the thesis presented by Sanders and other scholars rests on the meticulous examination of the relevant literature. Stott claims that it is well known that popular religion may very well be different from the official literature of its leaders. This possible distinction results in this comment by Sanders[128]:

> The possibility cannot be completely excluded that there were Jews accurately hit by the polemic of Matthew 23.... Human nature being what it

---

[122] Sanders, *Paul and Palestinian Judaism*, 117.

[123] Stott, The Message of Romans, 27.

[124] Sanders, *Paul and Palestinian Judaism*, 409.

[125] J. Neusner and B. Chilton, "Uncleanness: a Moral or an Ontological Category" in Bulletin for Biblical Research, 1 (1991), 64 in Stott, *The Message of Romans*, 27.

[126] M. Hengel, *A Pre-Christian Paul*, in collaboration with Ronald Deines (London: SCM and Philadelphia: Trinity Press International, 1991), 44, in Stott, *The Message of Romans*, 27–28.

[127] Hengel, A Pre-Christian Paul, xi, in Stott, *The Message of Romans*, 28.

[128] Sanders, *Paul and Palestinian Judaism*, 426, in Stott, *The Message of Romans*, 28.

is, one supposes that there were some such. One must say, however, that the surviving Jewish literature does not reveal them.

Stott draws a parallel with Anglicanism. The Book of Common Prayer and the Thirty-Nine Articles, i.e., the official literature of the church, insist that "we are accounted righteous before God only for the merit of our Lord and Saviour Jesus Christ by faith, and not for our own works or deservings." (Article XI). Again, in The Prayer of Humble Access in the Holy Communion Service, we are reminded that we may not "presume" to approach God "trusting in our own righteousness." The literature is clear. But Stott acknowledges that one has to admit "that the actual faith of many Anglicans remains one of works-righteousness."[129]

Fifthly, Stott makes clear that Paul had a horror of boasting. This traditionally has been taken as a rejection of self-righteousness. We boast in Christ and his cross, not in ourselves or each other. Sanders, however, maintains that Paul's antipathy to Jewish boasting (Rom 3 27ff.; 4:1ff.) was directed against pride in their favoured status (2:17; 23). This would be incompatible with the equal standing of Jews and Gentiles in Christ; for Sanders, it was not against pride in their merit, which would be in contrast to humility before God. Stott questions if this distinction can be maintained as neatly as Sanders suggests. Paul seems to bring them together in Phil 3:3–9, where there is a contrast between "glorying in Christ Jesus" with "putting confidence in the flesh." The context reveals that in "the flesh" – what Stott calls "our unredeemed self-centredness" – is a concept in which Paul includes both his status as "a Hebrew of Hebrews" and his obedience to the law. "In regard to the law, a Pharisee ... as for legalistic righteousness [that is, external conformity to the requirements of the law] faultless."

In other words, the boasting which Paul had himself renounced, and now condemned, was a self-righteousness compounded of both status-righteousness and works-righteousness, In addition, the apostle twice writes of a righteousness which can be described as our "own" either because we think we "have" it or because we are seeking to "establish" it. Both passages indicate that this righteousness of our own (i.e. self-righteousness) is based on law-obedience, and that those who "pursue" it thereby indicate that they are unwilling to "submit" to God's righteousness. In Romans 4:4–5 Paul also makes a sharp contrast between "working" and "trusting," and so between a "wage" and a "gift."[130]

Finally, Stott is grateful for Sanders' reference, already quoted, to "human nature being what it is." Stott[131] explains that our fallen human nature is incurably self-centred, and pride is the elemental human sin, in whatever form it is manifested, self-importance, self-confidence, self-assertion or self-righteousness. For human beings, often their religion can end up serving themselves instead of being the means for the selfless adoration of God. Their worship exercises become the means by which they

---

[129] Stott, *The Message of Romans*, 28.
[130] Stott, *The Message of Romans*, 29.
[131] Stott, *The Message of Romans*, 29.

would presume to approach God and to attempt to establish a claim on him. In Stott's understanding the ethnic religions all seem to degenerate thus, even Christianity. He claims:

> In spite of the learned literary researches of E. P. Sanders, therefore, I cannot myself believe that Judaism is the one exception to this degenerative principle; being free from all taint of self-righteousness. As I have read and pondered his books, I have kept asking myself whether perhaps he knows more about Palestinian Judaism than he does about the human heart.[132]

Certainly, Jesus included "arrogance" among the evils to which our hearts are prone. He often in his teaching highlighted self-righteousness. Stott recalls as an example the parable of the Pharisee and the tax-collector where Jesus emphasized divine mercy, not human merit, as the means of justification by faith. Again, in the parable of the labourers in the vineyard he challenged the mentality of those who demand payment and resent grace, and he presented little children as examples of the humble spirit which can receive the kingdom as a free, unmerited gift. Finally, Paul was aware of the subtle pride of his own heart, and so he could find it in others, even under a cloak of religion.

It is important to move on from this earlier treatment of the claims of Sanders regarding the nature of Palestinian Judaism to other scholars who have examined the literature of Second Temple Judaism. Consideration should be given to D. A. Carson's[133] treatment of this theme; the work contains the findings of fourteen scholars as they reviewed the vast literature regarding the subject. The question asked of the survey was whether or not covenantal nomism served as an acceptable label for an overarching pattern of the religion of Judaism.

Carson[134] makes the point that the variations found within the literature as it reflects patterns of belief and religion are "too diverse to subsume under one label" and covenantal nomism is too restrictive a pattern to describe the literature. Sanders has been over selective of the material to support his claims. He concludes, "it is not that Sanders is wrong everywhere, but he is wrong when he tries to establish that this category is right everywhere."[135]

Further consideration should be given to the assessment of the Jewish scholar Neusner[136] who also examines Sanders' contribution. He pays particular attention to

---

[132] Stott, *The Message of Romans*, 29.

[133] D.A. Carson, T. O'Brien and M. Seifrid, eds. *Justification and Variegated Nomism: The Complexities of Second Temple Judaism*, vol. 1 (Grand Rapids, Michigan: Baker Academic 2001); *Justification and Variegated Nomism: The Paradoxes of Paul*, vol. 2 (Grand Rapids, Michigan: Baker Academic 2004).

[134] Carson, O'Brien and Seifrid, *Justification and Variegated Nomism*: vol 1, 5.

[135] Carson, O'Brien and Selfrid, *Justification and Variegated Nomism*: vol 1, 543.

[136] J Neusner, "Introduction: 'The Four Approaches to the Description of Ancient Judaism(s): Nominalist, Harmonistic, Theological and Historical,'" in Alan Jeffery-Avery Peck and J Neusner, *Judaism in Late Antiquity: Death, Life-after-Death, Resurrection & The World to Come in the Judaisms of Antiquity* (Leiden; Boston; Köln: Brill, 2000), 28–29.

his handling of the Mishna and other rabbinic sources which he suggests are "profoundly flawed" in that the Pauline-Lutheran questions he brings to it are not the source's central concerns. He explains that Sanders quotes all the documents equally with no attempt at differentiation among them. For Neusner, Sanders seems to have culled sayings from the diverse sources he has chosen, written them down on cards, organising them around his critical categories. He has then constructed his paragraphs and sections by flipping through these cards and adding his comments. So, there is no context in which a given saying is important in its own setting, in its own document:

> The diverse rabbinic documents require study in and on their own terms. (Sanders') claim to have presented an account of "the Rabbis" and their opinions is not demonstrated and not even very well argued ... (He) has not shown how systematic comparison is possible when, in point of fact, the issues of one document, or of one system of which a document is a part, are simply not the same as the issues of some other document or system; he is oblivious to all documentary variations and differences of opinion.

Looking at the situation generally, one important comment by Witherington[137] should be remembered:

> Even with all the diversity that was tolerated in early Judaism and even with all the movements and parties, no truly Jewish group, whether we think of the Pharisees, or Sadducees, or Qumranites, or even the Samaritans, was prepared to say in the first century that observance of the Mosaic law was no longer obligatory for God's people.

The early insights of Guthrie are also worthy of consideration before leaving this subject.[138] He saw two different approaches in contemporary Judaism, one strictly legalistic, i.e., faithful adherence to the tenets of the law with an emphasis on what man can do, and the other concentrated more on trust in God, beginning from God's doings rather than man. Guthrie comments; "Both regarded the law as the main means by which man could approach God." The question as to what makes the difference, as Stott suggests, is attitude i.e., the human heart. Was a particular individual in the first century, like the self-righteous Pharisee in the parable, confident that he was "not like other men?" Or rather, as the tax collector who stood at a distance crying out for mercy (literally "O God on the ground of the sacrifice be propitiated to me the sinner!"), who "went down to his house justified, rather than the other" (Luke 19:9–14)? In other words, was their confidence in themselves or in God's provision of sacrifice?

---

[137] Witherington, 111, *Grace in Galatia*, 112.
[138] D. Guthrie, *New Testament Theology* (Leicester: Inter-varsity Press, 1981), 689.

Cranfield in Response to Dunn

James Dunn is another eminent scholar associated with New Perspective ideas. We must focus particularly on his views as to what Paul means by "the works of the law." For Dunn,[139] we should consider his 1982 Manson Memorial Lecture, "The New Perspective on Paul," and his New Testament Studies article, "Works of the Law and the Curse of the Law." He maintains that Gal 2:16; 3:2, 5, 10 explain "works" as not means to earn God's favour, but *badges* which mark Jews out from others, e.g., circumcision, food laws.

Cranfield[140] responds to Dunn's interpretation when he discusses Dunn's[141] understanding of the phrase ἔργα νομου *erga nomou*, "works of the law." Whilst Cranfield acknowledges the value of Dunn's commentary, he does not accept his understanding of "the works of the law." He notes that the phrase ἔργα νομου *erga nomou* occurs three times in Romans (inc. 9:32) and six times in Galatians. Also τὸ ἔργον του νομου *to ergon tou nomou* is in Romans once, and these words are common in the NT.

Cranfield examines Galatians first, and admits that there are many references to circumcision (also once, special days, food laws) in the epistle, "which might seem to be some support" for taking Dunn's ἔργα νομου *erga nomou* in a restricted sense. But it is easier to understand the texts when they are read in what is their natural or general sense as a Greek phrase, meaning "doing" the works required by the law or "obedience to the law." Again, should Christ's death which delivers from the curse (3:13) be understood as Dunn suggests, simply as removing "the curse of a wrong understanding of the law?" Or is Christ's death just to remove the boundaries? For Cranfield[142] surely Gal 2:20 "the Son of God giving himself for me" means more than this.

Regarding Dunn's commentary on Romans, Cranfield discusses Rom 3:20. Dunn takes ἔργα νομου *erga nomou* again simply as a reference to boundary markers. Cranfield rejects this interpretation for the following reasons:

1 It fails to take account of the whole argument from 1:18, which surely leads up to the conclusion expressed in 3:20a and restated in 3:23. It is not just about Jewish

---

[139] Printed in J.D.G. Dunn, "The New Perspective on Paul," *Bulletin of the John Rylands Library*, 65 (1983), 95–122; Reprinted in Dunn's *Jesus, Paul and the Law: Studies in Mark and Galatians* (Louisville: Westminster John Knox, 1990), 183–214. "Works of the Law and the Curse of the Law" NTS 31 (1985), 523–42. Dunn also in *Galatians*, 136 describes "works of the law" as "boundary issues" which reflect the distinctiveness of Jew from Gentile. This is later than Cranfield's assessment (to follow).

[140] C.E.B. Cranfield, "'The Works of the Law' in the Epistle to the Romans," in *On Romans and Other New Testament Essays* (Edinburgh: T&T Clark, 1998), 1–14. Cranfield was Dunn's professor whilst a student at Durham.

[141] J.D.G. Dunn, "The New Perspective on Paul," in *Romans* (Dallas: Word, 1988), lxiii – lxxii.

[142] Cranfield, "'The Works of the Law' in the Epistle to the Romans," 4.

pride in the law, especially circumcision. Paul is stating all are under judgment, even the Jews who might consider themselves superior.

2 It is ruled out by the latter part of 3:20 – ignored by Dunn. This statement that the law actually shows up human sinfulness, supports what is said in the first part of the verse, *if* the first part, "the works of the law" means obedience to the law.

3 The statement should be linked to 2:15 "the work which the law requires" and there it is impossible for it to have Dunn's restricted sense. He finds here the fulfilment of Jer 31:33, God writing the law upon the heart and accepts that it may refer to pagan Gentiles.

4 The restriction is further called into question by the expressions concerning the law in 2:13, 14, 25, 26, 27; 7:25; 8:4; 13:8. In none of these occurrences is it feasible to see a reference to circumcision etc., Dunn's restricted sense of ἔργα νομου *erga nomou*. "In 2:25 circumcision is explicitly contrasted with practising the law."[143]

5 It must be questioned also when the words occur separately. In 7 out of the 10 occurrences of "works" (others later) it does not refer to things like circumcision, etc. In the over 70 occurrences of "law" it is not possible to get away from the main ethical sense: it cannot be understood as simply identity markers distinguishing Jews from Gentiles.

6 His teaching in Rom 14:1–15:13 would not be expressed as it is if he was as much preoccupied with Jewish reliance on circumcision and the observance of the food laws as Dunn seems to think.

The meaning of 3:20 is surely, as others have long recognised, that justification before God on the ground of one's obedience is not a possibility for fallen human beings, since none of them is righteous and the effect of the law is to show up their sin and themselves as sinners.[144]

Cranfield refers to 3:27–31, which Dunn calls "The Consequences for the Self-Understanding of the Jewish People." How could Paul after vv. 21–26, which repeat the conclusion to the whole argument of 1:18–3:20 (all sinned, redemption, God's costly forgiveness) simply deal with Jewish self-understanding? It is the self-understanding of human beings – not just Jewish boasting but all human boasting before God. The phrase ἔργα νομου *erga nomou* must have the same sense as 3:20 i.e., if any are justified it must be without having obeyed the law, since all are sinners. Jew and Gentile are accepted by faith through grace which is undeserved.

---

[143] Cranfield, "'The Works of the Law' in the Epistle to the Romans," 7.
[144] Cranfield, "'The Works of the Law' in the Epistle to the Romans," 8.

What of the use of the single word "works" then? It is also used in Rom 4:2 which Dunn wants to take in the restricted sense – typical national confidence, rather than as a more generalized statement which makes better sense. Also:

1 The statement "he who justifies the ungodly" in v. 5 strongly suggests that Abraham's lack of works is thought of as having a moral content.

2 The quotation from Ps 32 in vv. 7–8 supports taking "works" in a general sense – justified apart from "works."

3 In vv. 14–15 again the general sense is required – justification by the law is not open since all are sinners and cannot fulfil its requirements.

4 The position of chapter 4 in the overall argument of the letter requires the general sense – if what was affirmed about 3:20 and 28 is accepted.

5 Again, Dunn interprets 9:11–12 as suggesting that Israel's election was not based on "works of the law" in the restricted sense since it happened before he was born. Yet it should be noted that even the reference "because of works" being linked with the phrase "neither having done anything good or bad" would mean the reference has a general sense – the works referred to must have a moral content.

6 Also 9:32. Paul explains why Israel, which was pursuing the law of righteousness did not attain it, because they pursued it not on the basis of faith but on the basis of works. Dunn again suggests that rather than the notion that one might so fulfil the law's demand as to put God in our debt (righteousness on the basis of our deserving through our works), the meaning of the word is more how they defined righteousness – the certain acts which mark off Jews from Gentiles. When Paul then writes of "their own righteousness" in 10:3 Dunn suggests that it is not meant to be interpreted as righteousness attained by their own efforts but as peculiar to them to the exclusion of the Gentiles. But righteousness should be the same in all the passage. In 10:3 there is surely a contrast intended between God's righteousness and our own. There is a status of righteousness before God which is his gift and a status men attempt to earn by themselves. For Cranfield, 10:3 supports this understanding.

7 Finally 11:6. Again Dunn suggests "national customs and ritual acts." He is naturally unhappy with the Jerusalem Bible's rendering of "works" as "good actions." Cranfield[145] also explains:

In 11.2b–10 Paul is concerned to make the point that not all of Israel is unbelieving. As in Elijah's time there were the mysterious seven thousand ... so now too there is a remnant – the Jewish Christians. And, as it was in Elijah's day, so now also it is by God's election of grace that a remnant exists. And, if it is by grace that a remnant consisting of the Jewish Christians exists, then it is not on the ground of their ἔργα

---

[145] Cranfield, "'The Works of the Law' in the Epistle to the Romans," 12.

(works).... In this context then a statement that the present remnant's existence stems from God's grace and not from the remnant's works in the sense of their having obeyed the law makes good sense, as it suggests there is hope for still unbelieving Israel which also lacks works in this sense; but a statement that the remnant's existence stems from God's grace and not from its works in the sense of loyalty to circumcision, food laws etc., does not in the context make such good sense, since unbelieving Israel has such works in abundance. It this context one would expect ἔργα (works) to denote something which both the members of the remnant and also unbelieving Israel alike lack.

So, Cranfield accepts that the explanation of the "works of the law" which Dunn generally rejects is after all sound. It really refers to *obedience* to the law.

George[146] also makes the point that while it is true that circumcision and to a lesser extent Sabbath keeping and food laws were prominent features of the crisis in the Galatian churches, the phrase "the works of the law" cannot be restricted to these three issues. "As he would later tell the Galatians, circumcision implies an obligation to obey the whole law, and, moreover, the curse of the law will fall with equal weight on everyone who does not persevere in all of the commandments of the law (5:3; 3:10)." Therefore, the phrase will refer to commandments given by God in the Mosaic legislation, ceremonial and moral – not just Jewish badges.

Dunn was one of the original thinkers in New Perspective ideas, advocating that works of the law were restricted to circumcision, food laws, and Sabbath in his earlier material. However, after coming under the sustained scrutiny of the academic community, he has clarified that he is willing to acknowledge the broader scope of the phrase. As Peter T. O'Brien[147] notes:

> In response to criticisms of his initial presentation, Dunn clarified several earlier emphases. He concluded that "works of the law"... refers to all the law requires of the devout Jew, the "deeds" which the law makes obligatory.

Likewise David E. Aune[148] states:

> Dunn has been widely criticized for restricting the meaning of "works of the law" to markers of Jewish identity. Some of his critics (e. g. Douglas Moo) have proposed that "works of the law" to mean "deeds done in obedience to the law of Moses," implicitly rejecting Dunn's distinction. Dunn's earlier restriction of "works of the law" to mean markers of Jewish identity (Sabbath observance, food laws, circumcision) was subsequently broadened

---

[146] George, *Galatians*, 195.
[147] Peter T. O'Brien, "Was Paul a Covenantal Nomist?" D. A. Carson, Mark Seifrid, Peter T. O'Brien, eds, *Justification and Variegated Nomism*, Vol. 2 , 278.
[148] David E. Aune, *Rereading Paul Together: Protestant and Catholic Perspectives on Justification* (Grand Rapids: Baker Academic, 2006), 210.

to mean "what the law required of Israel as God's people," that is, "the deeds" that the law makes obligatory.

That this appears to be the case is evidenced by the fact that in his later 1998 work *The Theology of Paul the Apostle* he concluded that works of the law refer more broadly, as Aune and others have noted, to "what the law required of Israel as God's people"[149] i.e., covenantal nomism as a whole. Most scholars in assessing Dunn's position understand that he is advocating the "social function" of the law i.e., its nationalistic exclusivism,[150] or the separation of the nation as they seek to follow the covenantal requirements, circumcision, feasts, days. In reality, it appears that he has not moved very far from "New Perspective" ideas.

Wright with Eveson and Piper

N. T. Wright is the third influential scholar whose treatment of these themes show sympathy with Dunn's position. His writings are quite prolific; here we must concentrate on what he has affirmed concerning justification – since this is Paul's theme in 2:16. He[151] writes:

> "Justification" in the first century was not about how someone might establish a relationship with God. It was about God's eschatological definition, both future and present, of who was, in fact a member of his people ... in standard theological language, it wasn't about soteriology as about ecclesiology; not so much about salvation as about the church.

Again, in presenting his own thinking regarding Paul's response here to Peter:[152]

> His (Paul's) polemic against "works of the law" is not directed against those who earn covenant membership through keeping the Jewish law (such people do not seem to have existed in the 1st century) but against those who sought to demonstrate their membership in the covenant through obeying the Jewish law.

Regarding "righteousness" Wright[153] claims, "To have 'righteousness' meant to belong to the covenant." He considers that when Paul writes of those who "are ignorant of God's righteousness" he means that they are ignorant of how God is fulfilling his covenant and are seeking to establish a righteousness of their own (i.e., a

---

[149] James D. G. Dunn, *The Theology of Paul the Apostle* (Grand Rapids: Wm. B. Eerdmans, 1998), 355.

[150] For example, A. H. Wakefield, "Summary and Analysis of Recent Scholarship: Paul and the Law," in *Where to Live: The Hermeneutical Significance of Paul's Citations from Scripture in Galatians 3:1–14* (Leiden: Brill Boston: Society of Biblical Literature, 2003), 31. Also F. Thiemann, "Paul, the Law & Judaism: The Creation & Collapse of a Theological Consensus," *Paul and the Law: A Contextual Approach* (Downers Grove Illinois: InterVarsity Press, 1994) 42.

[151] N.T. Wright, *What St. Paul Really Said: Was Paul of Tarsus the Real Founder of Christianity?* (Grand Rapids: Eerdmans, 1997), 120.

[152] N. T. Wright, "Justification," *New Dictionary of Theology,* 1998, 360.

[153] Wright, "Righteousness," *New Dictionary of Theology,* 591.

covenant membership for Jews alone), whereas in God's plan Christ offers covenant membership to all who believe the gospel (Rom 10:3–4). His views seem to have remained much the same in his more recent treatment of this theme in Galatians 2. Wright[154] affirms:

> For Paul, "justification," whatever else it included, always had in mind God's declaration of membership, and that this always referred specifically to the coming together of Jews and Gentiles in faithful membership of the Christian family.

For Wright, being justified is about covenant membership of the people of God – although Wright does say "whatever else is included," which is a little vague. However, it appears that other things are actually being excluded or are seen of very little significance when Paul uses this word or speaks of "righteousness."

We can acknowledge that there are many aspects to the salvation God has so graciously given us through faith in Christ. Galatians itself will teach us this. We will read that we are Spirit-born, part of the true family of faith, sharing Abraham's faith adopted as sons and heirs. But we must not lose sight of the forensic nature of justification affirmed here. For me, justification is not so much focussed on ecclesiology (covenant membership) as upon soteriology. It is about our guilt as sinners, for whether we are Jew or Gentile, we are condemned by a broken law and may be acquitted, declared righteous in God's sight, only because of the righteousness of Christ imputed to us. So, in the final analysis, justification is not about membership in the covenant community – it is about our legal standing before God. Justification is set over against condemnation, against the wrath of God and peace with God in Rom 5:1, 9; 8:33–34. Again, Rom 5:18 speaks of "condemnation for all men" and through the cross "justification for all men," in Christ. Rom 4:7–8 citing Ps. 32:1–2 refers to the non-imputation of sin to David on the one hand and the imputation of righteousness on the other.

In keeping with the above, Eveson[155] highlights a number of difficulties with Wright's approach. It appears that justification is presented, as has been suggested, more in the context of the church than salvation; more in relational than judicial terms and there is no place for the doctrine of imputation. The evangelical significance of the death of Christ is actually marginalized and it is no longer seen as the article by which the church stands or falls.

The writings of scholars such as Sanders and more particularly Dunn and Wright have wide acceptance and influence today. Their views of the nature of first century

---

[154] N.T. Wright, *Justification: God's Plan and Paul's Vision* (Downers Grove, Ill: IVP Academic, 2009), 116.

[155] Eveson, "Justification: Is Wright Right?" in www.the-highway.com/justification. See also *The Great Exchange: Justification by Faith Alone in the Light of Recent Thought (Facing the Issue)* (Leominster, UK: Day One Publications, 1996).

Judaism, "the works of the law" and justification have been enthusiastically received – but not by all.

A well-known example of critique of Wright's contribution in this area is the response of John Piper,[156] who presents eight aspects of the teaching in N.T. Wright's publications concerning his understanding of these crucial issues. Piper first includes various quotations from Wright's publications to ensure that he was representing his teaching correctly. A brief summary can be set out as follows:

1 That the word "gospel" does not mean for Paul "how to get saved." Piper responds briefly in the Introduction with 1 Cor 15:1–2 and then in Ch. 5, notes again e.g., Acts 13:26 – the message brought for God to those at Antioch is "the message of salvation."

2 That justification is not about how you become a Christian. Piper responds to Wright who considers that justification is about membership. Piper considers it is more about relationship and "peace with God," Rom 5:1.

3 Justification is not the gospel. Yet Piper can point to Acts 18:38–39 where Paul actually uses this term in the synagogue at Antioch as he comes to the climax of his gospel message.

4 That we are not justified by believing in justification. Piper can make the point that while it is true that someone can be saved without being taught in specific detail about the doctrine of justification – or any other doctrine e.g., regeneration, propitiation, yet when he hears about them if he will not trust Christ for any one of them, there has to be a serious question mark over his salvation. Therefore, it could be misleading to simply say that we are not saved by believing in justification by faith.

5 That the imputation of God's righteousness does not make sense. Piper does not accept that. The believer is "in" Christ who has fulfilled the moral law and accumulated a righteous status, and this is basically what the reformers meant by imputation.

6 That future justification is on the basis of the complete life lived. Is this not a salvation by works? Piper doubts that Wright means that the life of the believer is the evidence of faith.

7 That Judaism was not about "legalistic self-righteousness." Piper explains that when Wright assessed the Qumran document 4QMMT, he could not find the self-righteousness and legalism said to characterise the Jews of Paul's day. Piper does not

---

[156] J. Piper, *The Future of Justification: A Response to N.T. Wright* (Wheaton Ill: Crossway Books, 2007). This book is available to download free.

accept this judgment and responds in Ch. 9–10. (See also the treatment of the subject of Second Temple Judaism earlier in this chapter). He also maintains:

> More importantly, I will try to dig out the implications of the fact that a common root of self-righteousness lives beneath both overt legalism and Jewish ethnocentrism. Something was *damnable* in the Galatian controversy (Gal 1:8–9). If it was ethnocentrism, it is hard to believe that the hell-bound ethnocentrists were 'keeping the law out of gratitude, as a proper response to grace.'

8 That God's righteousness is the same as his covenant faithfulness to Israel. Piper queries Wright's understanding of this, especially his treatment of 2 Cor 5:21. "For our sake he made him to be sin who knew no sin, so that in him we might become *the righteousness of God.*" He is amazed that Wright can read this as affirming that believers actually "become" the covenant faithfulness of God.

After careful reading of Wright and, as noted, personal correspondence with him to be sure that he has understood his proposals, Piper[157] expressed his opinion:

> I am not optimistic that the biblical doctrine of justification will flourish where N. T. Wright's portrayal holds sway. I do not see his vision as a compelling retelling of what Saint Paul really said. And I think, as it stands now, it will bring great confusion to the church at a point where she desperately needs clarity. I don't think this confusion is the necessary dust that must settle when great new discoveries have been made. Instead, if I read the situation correctly, the confusion is owing to the ambiguities in Wright's own expressions, and to the fact that, unlike his treatment of some subjects, his paradigm for justification does not fit well with the ordinary reading of many texts and leaves many ordinary folk not with the rewarding "ah-ha" experience of illumination, but with a paralyzing sense of perplexity.

I would argue that such expressions of concern about the New Perspective must be carefully weighed and not ignored. It is my opinion that the gospel of good news of justification (involving removal of guilt, righteousness imputed), must not be lost from our understanding of Paul's theology.

Aune[158] has brought some valuable insights into the discussion on Paul's response to the Judaizers troubling the Galatians. Moo defines "the works of the law" as "works done in obedience to the law"[159] and also mentions Dunn's[160] later clarification of his views i.e., the phrase works of the law "simply denotes doing what the law requires."

---

[157] Piper, *The Future of Justification,* 24.
[158] Moo, *Galatians,* 157–61.
[159] Moo, *Galatians,* 175.
[160] J.D.G. Dunn, *Christianity in the Making,* Vol. 2 *Beginning from Jerusalem* (Grand Rapids: Eerdmans, 2009), 475.

Moo focusses upon 2:15–16 setting out his own particular interpretation of these verses which he sees as crucial for any understanding of Paul. Similar to our exegesis in these pages, he explains that in Paul's use of "we" in v. 16 he is referring to himself, Peter and the other Jewish believers, even the agitators who did not question the need for faith in Christ for justification. "What was in dispute was whether 'works of the law' needed to be *added* [italics his] to Christ faith for justification." Also, the real force of the argument is not how Gentiles can be included with Jews in the people of God but how *Jews – who were also sinners* like the rest of humanity could be included! It is implied that their obedience to "the works of the law" including covenant stipulations cannot put them right with God; only faith in Christ alone and grace can do this.[161]

In this discussion Moo makes further important points which are related to the above. He sees first of all a distinction between the Reformation tradition and the new perspective's understanding of the situation. Moo[162] claims:

> The Reformers thought that "works of the law" could not justify because they were "works" and therefore suffered from the problem of all human works: sinful humans could not perform enough works well enough to be justified. However, many contemporary interpreters insist that the problem is not with "works" but with "law".... The people to whom Paul was responding were not "legalists" in the sense of people insisting on doing works to become saved; they were "nomists" insisting that faith in Christ had to be combined with law obedience in order to secure ultimate salvation.

It almost appears that Moo is aligning himself with new perspective scholars, particularly Dunn, who identified those elements in the law which would distinguish Jews from Gentiles e.g., circumcision, food laws, feasts and these are the issues that Galatians highlights. But two points need to be clarified.

Firstly, we ought not to forget our own earlier identification of the nature of Palestinian Judaism in the first century as generally merit earning, seeking by a works righteousness to find acceptance with God – see Luke 18:9–14; Rom 10:1–10, also Stott, Cranfield and Carson. Therefore, in Galatians 2 "works of the law" must also include this understanding.

Secondly, Moo himself continues in his discussion of these issues to show why he is not ready to accept the classic new perspective reading as adequate treatment of these verses. His arguments can be summarized as follows: (1) the salvation history reflected in Galatians affirms that the era of the law is over; and (2) in Galatians at several points "works" must have the more fundamental meaning of "human-oriented accomplishment" – see 3:10–12 and, in the 2:16 quotation from Ps 142:2, "Do not

---

[161] We remember the earlier discussion by Bruce of Paul's use of ἄνθρωπος *anthrōpos* "man" or "person" in v. 16 suggesting that both Jews and Gentiles now stand before God as human beings, neither privileged Jew nor underprivileged Gentile – simply sinners.
[162] Moo, *Galatians*, 159.

bring your servant into judgment, for no one living is righteous before you." He notes Paul's use of *sarx* (flesh) in this quotation to emphasise the frailty and weakness of human beings. "Thus Paul suggests that it is partly *because* human beings are flesh that they cannot fulfil the law and so be justified." Moo[163] also earlier in his Introduction to *Galatians* has highlighted the fact that Paul's polemic against "works of the law" may rightly be viewed as a polemic against works in general for two reasons.

Firstly, because the failure of Israel clearly set out in e.g., Deut 31:14–29 and Dan 9:11 reveals that "innate human failure to remain consistently oriented toward God and his law" was "remedied only by God's own new work in the human heart, replacing the 'heart of stone' with a 'heart of flesh' and sending his Spirit to enable his people to produce the obedience he expects (Ezek 36:24–28) ... a viewpoint which Paul takes over in his other letters." The answer to the failure to do all the law requires (3:10; 5:3) Moo[164] suggests is the sacrifice of Christ (see 1:4; 3:1, 13) – Paul ignores OT provisions in favour of the sufficiency of the cross.

The second reason is "the way he introduces 'grace' into his argument." While the word appears only seven times in Galatians (1:3, 6, 15; 2:9, 21; 5:4; 6:18), it is "nevertheless a fundamental issue" (which) "summarizes the argument of the letter."

These two arguments suggest that for Moo,[165] "Paul's polemic against the law in Galatians rests, to some extent, on a pessimistic anthropology." For such reasons as these, in addition to the arguments reflected above concerning the phrase "the works of the law" and the nature of Second Temple Judaism, I do not interpret these verses in the way new perspective scholars have.

One basic point should be remembered. Paul's affirmations concerning justification apart from the works of the law stem from his Damascus Road experience and the light that burst in upon him there, concerning the significance of Christ's death and resurrection and his own justification. Ladd[166] explains:

> In writing as he does about the law Paul is writing from a distinctly Christian viewpoint. His experience of justification through faith in Christ and the subsequent conflict with the Judaizers led him to insights he could not have held as a Jew and a fundamental reinterpretation of the role of the law in redemption history.

* * *

---

[163] Moo, *Galatians*, 30–31.

[164] Moo, *Galatians*, 29.

[165] Moo, *Galatians*, 31. See also 176 where Moo proposes that it was this "human incapacity" and "human captivity" to sin e.g., the inability to keep the law which means that "the Reformers, we think, were entirely justified in viewing Paul's phrase 'the works of the law' as a synecdoche for the more general category 'works.'"

[166] Ladd, *Theology of the New Testament*, 539.

The Way Revealed

In addition to what has already been highlighted concerning v. 16, there are also the following points to be made. "We know" Paul reminds Peter, "that a person is not justified by works of the law." The Judaizers professed to believe in Jesus but wanted everybody to follow Moses, not only the moral commands, but the ceremonial law as well. This religion, because it is based on self-effort, self-achievement can be said to be the religion of the man in the street[167] – or the man in the pew! It is popular because it is flattering – we can accomplish our own salvation. However, see v. 16b, for we cannot keep the law perfectly. Here in the first part of the verse this statement anticipates the amplified quotation of Ps 143:2 in the second part.

It is hard to find a more forceful statement of the way of justification than what we find here in v. 16. It is insisted upon by the two leading apostles, Peter and Paul *and* confirmed by the OT scriptures in this Psalm.

Note also the phrase "through faith in Jesus Christ," taken as Bruce[168] affirms, as objective genitive (i.e. our faith in Christ) rather than subjective (i.e. through the faithfulness of Jesus Christ). Dunn is happier to understand the phrase as a reference to *our* faith rather than Christ's faithfulness in going the way of the cross, or a covenant faithfulness which made good the unfaithfulness of Israel. Note that the Greek πιστις *pistis* can really mean either "faith" or "faithfulness." The next clause, in v. 16 "so we also have believed in Christ Jesus," which is a deliberate repetition for the sake of emphasis, supports Dunn's understanding and there are other reasons for the normal use:

> "Faith" = "belief or trust in" as a religious term was familiar in the Hellenistic world.... One would expect phrases using the verb to function as equivalent alternatives to phrases using the noun. This is just what we do find here (the next clause) and in iii. 6–9, 22.... Both here in Galatians and in Romans the issue addressed is how someone is "justified." His key text is Gen xv.6 (Gal iii.6; Rom iv.3) ... Abraham was justified by his faith. Gal ii.16 is most obviously heard as sounding the first note of that theme.[169]

Fung[170] also affirms that by the clause which follows "so we have believed in Christ Jesus" other interpretations "flounder" and "put beyond reasonable doubt that the *Christou Iēsou* is to be construed as objective genitive, expressing the object in whom the faith is reposed." It appears also that the objective sense is how Chrysostom and the other Greek Fathers understood it.[171] George can affirm with Dunn that while the faithfulness of Christ is a prominent theme in Paul's theology what is being

---

[167] Stott, *The One Way: The Message of Galatians*, 62.
[168] Bruce, *The Epistle to the Galatians*, 139.
[169] Dunn, *The Epistle to the Galatians*, 138–39.
[170] Fung, *The Epistle to the Galatians*, 115.
[171] R.A.Harrisville 111., "Πίστος Χπιστοῦ: Witness of the Fathers" *Novum Testamentum* 36 (1994), 233–41.

contrasted in Galatians requires that faith here be understood as "the necessary human response to what God has objectively accomplished in the cross of Christ ... we are justified 'by' faith (*dia* plus the genitive), not 'on account of' faith (*dia* plus the accusative)."[172] Again, Bultmann[173] claims that this phrase is equivalent to believing that he died and rose – see v. 20.

The contribution of Moo, must again be considered.[174] He sets out the alternative interpretations. Namely, the subjective – faith *in* Jesus Christ, the traditional, which was also the Reformation tradition. "Paul was seen to be enunciating a critical distinction between human doing (the works of the law) and human believing when it came to justification," which he sees as an "anthropologically focused contrast." He explains the subjective interpretation: (1) matches Paul's custom of using the cognate verb to refer to human believing (and never to Christ's "believing"); (2) it fits with the two critical OT texts he cites to buttress his emphasis on πίστις (Gen 15:6 and Hab 2:4); and (3) it better fits in the respective contexts where the phrase occurs. In the case of Gal 2:16, there is the key and programmatic link between πίστις and justification again in Gal 3, where Paul cites Abraham "believing for righteousness" (v. 6).

Christ was the only one who kept the law perfectly. On the cross Christ suffered for our disobedience, for both Jew and Gentile. We must believe in Jesus Christ, in the sense not just that we must believe in his existence and that he died on the cross, but we must put our trust in him. He spells it out again that justification cannot be by the works of the law and this leads to the paraphrase of Psalm 143 which must have been a habitual Scriptural proof-text.

Paul stresses, "a person is not justified by works of the law, but through faith in Jesus Christ ... because by works of the law no one will be justified." He says it twice that justification cannot be by the works of the law. As Paul will show later, the law only condemns us; we cannot keep it (3:10–14, 19, 21–22; 4:4–5; also Rom 3:20). So here, as we noted, he actually quotes the OT (Ps 143:2) to back up his teaching and claims that this is also the conviction of the two leading preachers, one to the Jews and the other to the Gentiles. Ps 143:2 states "for no one living is righteous before you," and as we also noted earlier in the Excursus the clear emphasis must be the inability of man to be right before God i.e., his sinfulness. In this quotation from the Psalm, Moo

---

[172] George, *Galatians*, 197.

[173] R. Bultmann, *TDNT* VI eds. G. Kittel, G. Friedrich, trs. Geoffrey W. Bromiley, Grand Rapids, Michigan; Wm. B. Ferdmans Publishing Co. (1969), 203.

[174] Moo, *Galatians*, 41–48; 160–63. Note also that Moo highlights the statement "[we] have believed *in* Christ Jesus." He explains that the preposition εἰς *eis* used with believe, while virtually unknown before the NT, is common in the writings of John, almost always with Christ as the object. While it has a "cognitive element – a 'believing that' certain things are true" it is "much more, involving both trust and commitment," 163.

also noted how Paul omits the phrase "before you" and adds the clause "by works of the law."[175]

One can emphasise that Paul's teaching here is surely contrary to any doctrine of merit, the idea advocated by some that the just (said to be in this state by baptism) can hope for eternal reward in return for their good works, done either *before or after* their supposed regeneration.[176] One is reminded of Luther's response to this teaching when he affirmed:

> That a man do acknowledge himself by the law, to be a sinner, and that it is impossible for him to do any good work.... The first part of Christianity is the preaching of repentance, and the knowledge of ourselves.... The second part is: if thou wilt be saved, thou must not seek salvation by works; for God hath sent his only begotten Son into the world, that we might live through him.... For God hath revealed unto us by his Word, that he will be unto us a merciful father, and without our deserts (seeing we can deserve nothing) will freely give us remission of sins, righteousness and life everlasting, for Christ his Son's sake.

If the way is through faith in Christ; it is through faith in Christ crucified, v. 20. It is his death for us – he "gave himself for me" which delivers us from condemnation by the law and allows God to accept those who in believing the good news, depend, not upon themselves but upon Jesus Christ and his death for them. This is what it means to "glory" in the cross.

The Objection Lodged

In considering v. 17, critics argue that forensic justification by faith[177] weakens our sense of responsibility to live a holy life. If God justifies by faith, apart from works, can we not live as we like?[178] So here the objection is: if we are "in Christ" and justified apart from the law, free to live without restriction, do we not make Christ (in

---

[175] Moo again mentions how Paul uses πᾶσα σάρξ *pasa sarx* for πᾶς ζῶν *pas zōn*, which is the LXX translation. This phrase can mean "all mankind" but Moo will translate "human beings as *flesh*" and suggest this as Paul's way of implying man's weakness and frailty i.e., his sinfulness, 159.

[176] See comments by Luther, *A Commentary on St. Paul's Epistle to the Galatians*, 131–32. Luther was responding to "the Schoolmen," the theologians of the Middle Ages. He rejected their teaching that a good work before grace (proposed by them to be imparted through infant baptism) might obtain the grace of congruence, *"meritum de congruo"*; also the teaching that when grace is obtained "the work following deserveth everlasting life of due debt and worthiness" called *"meritum de condigno."* But whether it involves merit-earning works in the Middle Ages or the modern day surely Paul's teaching is arguing against both, as he also did with the Judaizers.

[177] Fung, *The Epistle to the Galatians*, 119, explains that when Paul writes about being "justified in Christ" the phrase seems to be a counter formula to 3:11; 5:4 "justified by the law."

[178] Note that later in 5:13–26 Paul will focus upon the libertinism of the Galatian Christians. He will reveal that holiness can be realised by remembering that, through God's gracious initiative in regeneration and justification, every believer has the gift of the Holy Spirit (3:2) and endeavouring to live in his power and following his leading (5:22–25) is what Paul directs as far as godliness is concerned.

that case) the agent or author of sin?[179] Note Paul's emphatic denial of this μὴ γένοιτο *mē genoito*, "God forbid!"[180] The apostle affirms in v. 18 that if he builds again what he destroyed,[181] he is a transgressor! Or, if he turns back to the way of works and to the law, he will be left still, or have made himself a sinner, for he is unable to fully keep that law. Note that Paul uses "I" here. He is making a reference to the individual and implying that this is just the position that Peter and each individual in vv. 12–13 have put themselves in. Peter and the others had built up what they formally destroyed (cf. Eph 2:14). Fung[182] explains that if Peter and the others upheld again the ordinances of the law as a necessary condition for justification, "then they were thereby submitting themselves afresh to the dominion of the law and were bound to become transgressors of it (cf. 5:2; 2:16)."

The Truth Expressed

Paul will go on to write of dying and rising to life again in union with Christ. He is reminding us that it is Christ's death and resurrection in which we share. The phrase "through the law" (its place in the Greek suggests emphasis) is affirming that through the law's authority, its demand of death for me because of sin, "I died to the law" (meaning its condemnation, because the law's demand of death was satisfied for me in the death of Christ) and now I "live to God." Paul – for, as we noted, puts the case in the first person singular – no longer lives under the jurisdiction of the law; he has been released from its dominion through his death in Christ and he has entered into new life. As Longenecker[183] explains it:

> Christ's death on the cross and our spiritual identification with his death effects freedom from the jurisdiction of the Mosaic law ... the Christian's focus is to be on Christ who lives within us and to whom we look for direction in life.

We must of course recognise that Paul as he uses the emphatic ἐγώ *ego* "I" is speaking in a paradigmatic sense; while he is referring to personal experience, for Moo,[184] the statement is true of all believers. It includes all those who have exercised

---

[179] Bruce, *The Epistle to the Galatians*, 141. Paul is surely talking about sin in a general sense, not as Dunn, a reference to Peter eating with Gentiles perceived by "traditionalist" Jewish Christians to be sin; also the suggestion that Christ could be accused of sin since he accepted those who believe. Dunn, *The Epistle to the Galatians*, 141. Also, not as Witherington 111, *Grace in Galatia*, 185, who suggests that Paul is thinking of those who by trying to re-establish the law are actually sinning against the finished work of Christ. Paul's argument is broader than this.

[180] Paul often in his letters uses this phrase, the negative μὴ *mē* with the optative γένοιτο, *genoito*, 3:21; 6:14 (just as an absolute contrast); Rom 3:4, 6, 31; 6:2, 15; 7v7, 13; 9:14; 11:1, 11; 1 Cor 6:15.

[181] Longenecker, *Galatians*, 90–91, reminds us that when Paul uses the phrase "the things he destroyed/annulled, the aorist tense as a historical aorist points to a past once-for-all act, the time of his conversion when he ceased to rely on the Mosaic law ... but turned to Christ for both acceptance before God and the pattern for living."

[182] Fung, *The Epistle to the Galatians*, 122.

[183] Longenecker, *Galatians*, 91.

[184] Moo, *Galatians*, 168.

the same "faith" in the Son of God by an act of personal trust. This applies to everything that he now is writing in vv. 18–21.

Paul's life could be divided into chapters of a book.

1. The Chapter Which Concerns the Former "I" – His Former Life

As we noted, v. 18 explains that if Paul builds again the things he once destroyed, if he reverts again to life under the law, he makes himself a transgressor. He cannot keep the law – see v. 16; so, he is condemned as a transgressor. See also Paul's later teaching about this in Rom 7:13.

2. The Chapter Which Concerns the Old "I" – His Sinful Life

We need to see the significance of Paul's statements "The Son of God who loved me and gave himself for me"; "I died to the law"; "I have been crucified with Christ." In the Greek text the phrase "crucified with Christ" is placed in the great majority of editions actually at the end of v. 19. It is the Christ who died and rose again who is the answer here for the sinful old life which brought Paul under condemnation and who brings him into a new life.

Paul writes of "the Son of God." There is a variant reading "God and Christ" which has support in p46 B, D* G and a few Latin MSS; the textual reading is found in א A and C, plus almost all versions and patristic witnesses and suits best the context. Paul can state that this one both "loved" and "gave" himself "for me." Both verbs are aorists pointing back to the cross, the historic event of Calvary. Christ "gave up himself" – the word is παραδιδομι *paradidomi* which resonates with the Suffering Servant of Isaiah 53:6, 12. His sufferings were in love "for me." The whole statement is "radically personalised" and reflects Paul's wonder at what Christ did for him; the idea is that Christ died not only "for me" but for "even me."[185]

In order to cause his own to live, Christ had to subject himself to the power and curse of the law (see 4:4 "born under the law") and although he was not condemned by the law himself – he kept it perfectly – he surrendered himself to its curse for his own (3:13).

In the use of συν *sun* in συνεσταύρωμαι *sunestaurōmai* "crucified *with*" we see our identification with Christ in his crucifixion – not physically of course, but spiritually.[186] Here we also have the perfect tense used, where Paul is referring to

---

[185] Dunn, *The Epistle to the Galatians*, 147.
[186] Note that crucifixion with Christ is not what Paul means by justification as Gorman suggests. They may both be here in this passage but are not to be merged. They are different blessings through the cross – in fact justification can be seen as part of conversion, while co-crucifixion surely happened in the first century! See M.J. Gorman, *Inhabiting the Cruciform God: Kenosis, Justification, and Theosis in Paul's Narrative Soteriology* (Grand Rapids, Michigan: William B. Eerdmans, 2009) 40–104.

something that once took place and has not lost its power since. We are in a state of being crucified (cf. Rom 6:6). Note therefore that this is not about Paul presently crucifying the flesh – that is Gal 5:24; this is the actual event of Calvary. This is something which happened TO us from then, not done BY us now.

The apostle claims that all believers were included in that dying. Paul saw himself so connected with Christ that when the Son of God was crucified, *he* was crucified with him. As Christ is crucified he endures the curse and Paul and also every Christian endured it. This is the real meaning of substitution. So, Paul could state through the law (facing up to its demands, and his guilt under it), he is dead to the law – through the death of Christ he is delivered from the law's condemnation. The old sinful "I," the sinful life, is gone, dealt with at the cross. To emphasise this point, we are now free from its condemnation. Witherington[187] explains Paul's statement:

It was Christ himself, taking on the curse of the law who died to the law for all, through the execution of the law's curse upon him. Inasmuch as Paul or any Christian was crucified "with" Christ on that occasion (Christ being both representative and corporate head of his group of followers), he or any Christian also as a result died to the law. This meant that they are no longer under the law's jurisdiction, no longer obligated to keep the law, no longer under the law's power, free from the law's curse and its demands.

3. The Chapter Which Concerns the Present "I" – The New Life Lived "By" or "In" Faith

Paul firstly explains this life liberated from the condemnation which comes through sin, in v. 19, as living unto God i.e., a new life *before* and *with* God. Longenecker[188] states, "In Pauline usage, 'to die to' something is to cease to have any further relation to it (cf. Rom 6:2, 10–11; 7:2–6). Conversely, 'to live to' someone means to have a personal unrestricted relationship with that one (cf. Rom 6:10–11; 14:7–8; 2 Cor 5:15)." In v. 20 he continues to describe it thus: "I have been crucified with Christ (as we have explained). It is no longer I who live, but Christ who lives in me." The old Paul had "died" in Christ, but now he goes on living! The life he now lives has come to him by faith in the Son of God who died for him. This involves the personal appropriation of what Christ has done for him. And now it is no longer the old Paul who "lives"; he lives a new life, a life lived in fellowship with Christ; in fact, it is Christ who is really living in him, as we noted, by means of his Spirit. He lives this new life, this life "in the flesh," meaning his "present, bodily life … an instance of the non-theological use of σάρξ *sarx* ("flesh") in Paul"[189], through faith in him, the risen Christ. Moo[190] explains, "'I no longer live' means that the 'old I,' the 'I'

---

[187] Witherington 111, *Grace in Galatia*, 189.

[188] Longenecker, *Galatians*, 91.

[189] Fung, *The Epistle to the Galatians*, 124. f/n. 124.

[190] Moo, *Galatians*, 171.

enslaved to sin and the law, has been done away with, to be replaced by a new 'I' whose existence is determined by the indwelling Christ."

Once again, this reference to "by faith" here is not about the faithfulness of Christ; it is Paul's personal faith. The word "faith" is put first before the verb for emphasis. His present life flows from faith/communion with Christ and can be a Spirit enabled life, so different from the old life. In fact, Christians are now, as Witherington[191] affirms, "part of the eschatological new creation. They are now under a new mandate, namely the law of Christ, which meant first and foremost following the example of Christ." This will become clearer in 6:2, 15.

Paul's teaching here in v. 20 is not some teaching about Christian perfectionism and that the fallen nature has been eradicated, as we will later see in 5:13–24. We will still be in a battle. Yet we are "born according to the Spirit" (3:29), not only freed from condemnation and justified, but have Christ within and, having the power of the Holy Spirit, we are enabled to walk in holiness. Here Paul explains that we have a life which is consciously Christ-orientated. Faith is not just something which happened back then at the moment of conversion; it leads to a daily experience of communion with and help from the Christ who died and rose again to deliver us. Here we have again how we "glory in the cross."

At Easter-time (and throughout the year) we can best affirm to others the fact of the resurrection not by going over the proofs etc., but demonstrating the reality that Christ is risen by living in fellowship with him and experiencing his power each day through the Holy Spirit living in us.

Therefore, Paul lives "in the flesh"; but he lives "by faith." The new life is a "faith-life." First of all, we noted Christ giving himself "for me" – he dealt with the past, the old sinful life; now he lives "in me" – he gives a completely new life as we walk in fellowship with him. Christ living in us brings us new desires for holiness, for God, for heaven. It is not that we cannot sin again; but we do not want to. By Christ's power we can live differently from the old life. This becomes an increasing emphasis in Galatians chapters 3–6 – but expressed more as through the power of the Holy Spirit; believers are in Christ, a new creation, regenerated, empowered, enabled to "walk in the Spirit" reflecting a Christian lifestyle in all their relationships with others in the church communities.

Note how Bruce[192] refers to Tannehill, who understands Paul's wording in the light of the law's relation to Christ. In 3:13 we will learn that Christ bore the curse of the law and exhausted its penalty on his people's behalf: in this sense Christ died "through the law," and the believer's death to the law is also "through the law" because he died in Christ's death, as Paul affirms here. We share his death to the old order. As Romans 6:6 explains, "our old self" – the person we formally were – "was crucified

---

[191] Witherington 111, *Grace in Galatia*, 189.
[192] See R. C. Tannehill, *Dying and Rising with Christ*, BZNW, 32, Berlin 1967, 59, in Bruce, *The Epistle to the Galatians*, 143.

with him." Christ now lives in me – or as we pointed out, the Spirit – it makes little difference how Paul expresses it – see 3:26–29; 4:6; 5:16–25. Here, again is how we glory in the cross. This is why we are no longer free to live as we please. Our faith-union with Christ links us with him in his death and resurrection in which we have come to share. Therefore, we are dead to the law and live to God a life of holiness. This faith-union is not a momentary thing, it is perpetual. "Christ … gave himself for me … Christ lives in me." Finished with the old, as we live in this mortal body, he gives me new desires for holiness and for a life of holiness living with God, knowing the enabling power of the Spirit. We could never revert to the old life if we grasp these truths.

Finally, in v. 21 as they tried to overthrow his argument, now he overthrows theirs. "I do not" – "I will not" (NEB), "nullify the grace of God." Stott[193] explains that:

> The two foundation planks of the Christian faith are the death of Christ and the grace of God. The Christian gospel is the gospel of the grace of God. The Christian faith is faith in Christ crucified. So if anyone insists that justification is by works, and that he can earn his salvation by his own efforts, he is undermining the foundations of the Christian faith. He is nullifying the grace of God (because if salvation is by works, it is not by grace) and he is making the death of Christ and faith in that death superfluous (because if salvation is our own work then Christ's work was unnecessary).

The question remains, why did Christ die? Self-trust is an insult both to the grace of God and to the cross of Christ, for it declares that both are unnecessary. Christ died "for nothing!" The accusative δωρεά *dōrea* "gift" here is used adverbially to mean "for no purpose" or as above, "for nothing." It has this use only here in the NT. As George[194] affirms:

> If we add works of the law to the sacrifice of the cross, then indeed we make a mockery of Jesus' death just as the soldiers who spat upon him, the thieves who hurled insults at him, and the rabble who shouted, "Come down from the cross."

As Longenecker[195] affirms, acceptance "through the law" and "Christ crucified" are "uncomplementary." Witherington[196] has also explained, "Paul's implication is that there are those who are annulling the grace of God by insisting on Christians, in particular Gentiles in this case, keeping the Mosaic law." We glory rather in the cross. It is also important to see how Paul connects grace and righteousness here in this verse directly to the death of Christ – it is through the cross that these blessings come to us. Note how Paul has now taught the fact that, if we are "in Christ", we are

---

[193] Stott, *The One Way: The Message of Galatians*, 66.
[194] George, *Galatians*, 201.
[195] Longenecker, *Galatians*, 95.
[196] Witherington 111, *Grace in Galatia*, 192.

more than justified; we have actually died and risen in him to a new life. Paul's affirmations, as we noted earlier, have set out the stark contrast between first, the anthropological – the doing of the law versus the believing in Christ who has done everything, and second, the salvation-historical – the Torah and the era it covers versus the death of Christ and the new age. As Moo[197] makes clear:

> We should not overlook how shocking is the claim – particularly for first-century Jewish ears – that Paul makes here: he could only truly live "for God" by dying to the law that God himself gave to his people! But this claim is part and parcel of the radical antinomies that Paul works with throughout Galatians, as he tries to persuade the Galatians to understand the epochal shift of focus that the cross of Christ has introduced into salvation history.

Paul has now completed what some see as simply the long autobiographical narrative section of his letter. Others who find the prevailing influence of rhetoric in Galatians will suggest that here we have his opening "defence," or, as in deliberative rhetoric, the appeal to example. Witherington[198] explains, "Paul's rhetorical strategy in the *narratio* is to present himself as a positive example for the Galatians to follow, and others as negative examples."

In the letter he has affirmed that rather than any influence from the leaders at Jerusalem, he had received his calling as apostle to the Gentiles and his gospel directly from God. He did not receive the message during his brief time spent with Cephas only; in fact, he had remained independent of Jerusalem, being far away in the regions of Syria and Cilicia. Yet when he met the "pillar" apostles, they acknowledged the true nature of his message, simply recognised his commissioning from God and added nothing. In his meeting in Antioch with Peter, he recognised the crucial nature of his understanding of the truth of the gospel and reaffirmed it plainly – with no qualifications. He needed now to directly address his Galatian converts in the churches, as they were also exposed to the similar threat he had seen developing in Antioch. This he begins to do in chapter 3. The themes affirmed in 2:15–21 must now be developed further; firstly, in chapter 3–4 – particularly justification by faith without the works of the law, being "in Christ," possessing sonship and secondly, the new life of faith in chapter 5–6, lived in the power of the Holy Spirit, following the example of Christ.

---

[197] Moo, *Galatians*, 170.
[198] Witherington 111, *Grace in Galatia*, 93. Paul will be able to return to this appeal to example later in the middle of his argument, 4:12.

GALATIANS THREE

Galatians 3: 1–29 The Foolishness of the Galatians

Betz calls this section of the letter the *probatio,* where usually in ancient speeches the "proofs" are presented. These will determine whether or not the speech as a whole will succeed.[1] Witherington[2] also suggests Paul's use of rhetoric here – but a piece of deliberative rather than forensic rhetoric.

Deliberative rhetoric points out examples, such as that of Abraham or Paul himself (cf. Gal 3:1 to 4:2) and asks the audience to emulate their behaviour. What the rhetor must do is to show his audience that the course of conduct or action he is proposing is or will be beneficial, useful, honourable, and, by contrast, to pursue an alternative course of action or behaviour will bring strife, will be useless, will be foolish (3:1) and the like.

In fact, at 3:6–4:11 Paul seems to be using more Jewish exegetical methods, with arguments based upon Scripture, rather than rhetorical method. However we identify the text, it is clear that Paul now moves on to present the positive arguments to support his God revealed doctrine. He will appeal to the Galatians' own experiences, which did not involve submission to circumcision, good works or observing special days, but knowing by grace the possession of the Holy Spirit, i.e., the moving of that Spirit, bringing them to faith as they heard the gospel and coming upon them in power, working miracles (3:3–5). Witherington[3] explains, "Unless they are prepared to renounce their own experiences of God, they must listen to Paul's arguments about what conclusions they should draw on the basis of those experiences." Also, he will bring them to Scripture in support of his arguments. Yet Paul will begin with, as Witherington[4] also highlights (in keeping with his own understanding of Paul's use of rhetorical elements), "his own 'pathos'-filled presentation of Christ crucified."

Paul had focused in 1:9 upon the situation in Galatia and in 2:5 referred to the Galatians themselves. But in other verses he had been stressing his own apostleship "through Jesus Christ and God the Father" (1:1) and defending the "truth of the gospel." i.e., that his message was of divine origin. Now he returns to address the church communities. Longenecker[5] points out that addressing readers directly is quite common in the letters of Paul. Moo[6] suggests that the direct address to the Galatians in 3:1 signifies a shift and new movement in the apostle's appeal to them, with second person plurals being used at critical places (3:1–6, 26–29; 4:6–20, 21; 4:28–5:4; 5:7–10). In fact, this second major part of the letter is "framed by two passages

---

[1] Betz, *Galatians: A Commentary on Paul's Letter to the Churches in Galatia*, 128.
[2] Witherington, 111, *Grace in Galatia*, 198.
[3] Witherington, 111, *Grace in Galatia*, 199.
[4] Witherington, 111, *Grace in Galatia*, 200.
[5] Longenecker, *Galatians*, 100.
[6] Moo, *Galatians*, 177.

of rebuke and exhortation (3:1–6; 5:1–12)." The main point to notice is that Paul having set out the truth of the gospel in 2:15–21, noted earlier, now sets out his defence of that gospel. As mentioned above, he begins with the fundamental challenge – surely it was not by means of "the works of the law" that they experienced the coming of the Holy Spirit into their lives (3:2, 5)? Why then should they now consider submitting to circumcision and law-keeping in their future walk with God? The chapter will also make clear that God has included Gentiles in the blessing of justification.[7] In addition, both Jews and Gentiles are by faith children of Abraham and actually "in Christ." As Moo explains:

Since Christ is himself *the* "seed" of Abraham (3:16), one becomes Abraham's child by becoming integrated with Christ (3: 7, 29). In the period inaugurated by Christ's coming into the world, the "fullness of the time" (4:4 AT), God's people are defined in terms of Christ, and Christ alone (esp. 3:26–29). And as belonging to Christ is the only entry into God's people and the righteous verdict pronounced over God's people, so that entry into Christ is by faith alone. The great Reformation slogans of "Christ alone" (*Christus solus*) and "by faith alone" (*sola fide*) find solid scriptural basis in this central section of Galatians.

The chapter actually begins with a rebuke; in fact, with a tone typical of a Hellenistic letter of rebuke.[8] "O foolish Galatians!" v. 1. Ὦ "*Ho*" here is emphatic and while there is an aggressive tone, the particle expresses the emotion of pain and deep concern. Sometimes as we earlier noted in this letter Paul can call them "brothers" (1:11; 4:12, 28, 31; 5:11, 13; 6:1, 18), "children" (4:19); here he accuses the Galatians of being "foolish." George[9] makes the point that at times there is need for plain speaking rather than mild criticism. "He confronted the Galatians with their folly so that by this means he might win them back to the truth they were in danger of forsaking." He maintains that the adjective "foolish" does not indicate a low intelligence – Paul's arguments throughout the letter presuppose a high level of comprehension; the problem was lack of spiritual discernment. They had been *led* astray. The fact was that they were turning their eyes away from the cross, from faith in Christ to seek salvation by works of the law. Hendriksen[10] stresses what the Galatians had done. "And is not everyone foolish who barters the truth of God for the lie of Satan, peace for unrest, assurance for doubt, joy for fear and freedom for bondage?"

There are five rhetorical questions in vv. 1–5. In the first, as we noted, Paul queries if this foolishness was not only a kind of spiritual treason (1:6), but also so senseless that perhaps some sorcerer had "bewitched" them or had been "casting a spell" (JBP) over them. Firstly it must be asked; "Who bewitched you?" Paul uses τις *tis*, singular. Is this Satan, or one unknown individual who had greatly influenced the believers? For many commentators, the apostle detects the activity of the deceiving spirit. One

---

[7] Paul has been making clear already (see 2:16) that *both* Jews and Gentiles *need* and *can* receive the blessing by faith.

[8] Longenecker, *Galatians*, 97. Note that this is the second rebuke of the Galatian churches – see 1:6–10.

[9] George, *Galatians*, 206.

[10] Hendriksen, *Galatians*, 111.

remembers again Paul's warning to the Corinthians, "as the serpent deceived Eve by his cunning, your thoughts will be led astray from a sincere and pure devotion to Christ" (2 Cor 11:3). See also 1 Tim 4:1 "Now the Spirit expressly says that in later times some will depart from the faith by devoting themselves to deceitful spirits and teachings of demons." These doctrines were of course delivered by the false teachers of Ephesus and the situation is something similar in south Galatia. Some commentators, because of Paul's use of the term "bewitched" make much of the concept of "the evil eye"[11] but as Hendriksen[12] maintains:

> Paul was probably not thinking about the sorcerer who had brought the Galatians under the baleful influence of his evil eye, but rather of the Judaizer who had cast a spell upon them *not* by means of his eyes but by means of his *words, his teaching*; specifically, by telling them that faith in Christ must be *supplemented* by Mosaic ritualism.

For him, as we saw already, this was truly "the lie of Satan." Witherington[13] suggests that Paul is writing polemically but metaphorically of the false teaching. But we must not lose sight of who was behind it! Remember Jesus' rebuke of Peter in Mark 8:33 "Get behind me, Satan!"

Paul continues to give a number of reasons why their action was such a "foolish" thing to do. These can be set out as follows:

Because of the Gospel v. 1

We noted how Paul began with what Witherington[14] described as a "pathos-filled presentation" of the preaching of the cross when he first was with the Galatians. How could this happen when Christ had been set before them publicly as crucified? McDonald[15] stresses that Christ was indeed "placarded" – Paul uses a word which was commonly used of public notices and proclamations. "As on a notice board written in large capitals so that none could miss it, Paul had set before their eyes Christ as crucified." Christ crucified was so vividly presented to the listeners in Galatia that they could almost in effect see him suffering upon the cross. Moo[16] suggests that "the agitators may be trying to persuade the Galatians by means of the

---

[11] In the ancient world there was the idea that some people, animals or gods have the power to cast an evil spell over someone by fixing their eyes upon them. See early Jewish literature (Sir. 14.6, 8; Wis. 4.2).
[12] Hendriksen, *Galatians*, 112.
[13] Witherington 111, *Grace in Galatia*, 202–04, also discusses whether the Galatians have been deceived by magicians or sorcerers. Did someone cast a spell over them? He mentions Luther's reference to 5:20, where the works of the flesh include the activity of witches, *A Commentary on St. Paul's Epistle to the Galatians*, 520. He acknowledges that some scholars have written about the characteristics of a society where witchcraft was strong. He however, as we note, is inclined to think Paul is writing metaphorically. It can be noted that it appears while Satan is the true origin of the teaching, it was the agitators who were the instruments.
[14] Witherington 111, *Grace in Galatia*, 200.
[15] McDonald, *Freedom in Faith*, 66.
[16] Moo, *Galatians*, 202.

demonic device of the 'evil eye'; but the Galatians, who had seen Christ's cross with their own eyes, should know better." Dunn[17] reminds us that it is important to grasp here the fact "that Paul could sum up his preaching of the gospel precisely as a preaching of the cross." Here is the gospel – not a general instruction about the Jesus of history but the specific proclamation of the cross, 1 Cor 1:23; 2:2.[18] How far we have departed from this today?

The force of the perfect tense of the participle "crucified" is that Christ's work was completed on the cross and that the blessings of Christ's death are still available and it is possible for us to experience them. Stott[19] maintains, "The gospel is not good advice to men but the good news about Christ; not an invitation to us to do anything, but a declaration of what God has done; not a demand, but an offer." If they had grasped that Christ had done everything for them on the cross, they would have realised that all that was needed was to trust in what he had done. There was no need to think that what had been accomplished was to be supplemented in some way. For the agitators, who were still among them, to affirm that circumcision and the works of the law were necessary was an offence to his finished work. Moo[20] affirms, "When truly appreciated, the cross of Christ, *the* manifestation of God's wisdom, power, and grace, should rule out of court the kind of human-oriented law program that the agitators were perpetuating." But the Galatians could not resist the spell of those who were bewitching them. Their foolishness was also evident for other reasons.

Because of the Spirit/Their Own Experience vv. 2–5

Paul introduces further rhetorical questions which challenge them about their experience of the Holy Spirit, initially as to how the Christian life begins and their continued experience of the Spirit. It is clear that their conversion did not involve in any sense "the works of the law" (2:16; 3:2–5). As Witherington[21] points out, v. 2 reads literally, "From works of the law did you receive the Spirit?" The emphasis here is certainly on "works of the law" as the phrase is placed first in the sentence. He reminds them that their salvation was not through law-keeping, works of any kind; not "doing" but "hearing" with faith.

To repeat, what Paul is affirming is that it was not through any works of the law but, as we will see, through God's initiative of grace – his work through the Holy Spirit bringing them to faith that they were justified. As we noted earlier, the first advent of Christ has brought about the possibility of the blessings of the new age bring experienced already in this present age. These blessings included – as well as

---

[17] Dunn, *The Epistle to the Galatians*, 152.

[18] True preaching involves not just calling people to "Come to Jesus" but preaching the cross. It is the cross that emphasises the awful nature of our sin before a holy God – his Son must come to take that sin upon himself – and the fact that it is the work of Christ which is all-sufficient – all that needs to be done for our salvation has been done once and for all e.g., Heb 9:25–28.

[19] Stott, *The One Way* 70.

[20] Moo, *Galatians*, 182.

[21] Witherington, 111, *Grace in Galatia*, 210.

justification – the fulfilment of OT promises concerning the Holy Spirit (Ezek 36:25–27; Joel 2:28–32; Acts 2:17–21) Paul now is emphasising that works of the law were not the source of their experience and possession of the Spirit. Rather, the initiative was God's.

Excursus: The Spirit in Galatians

We should note that this is the first reference to the Holy Spirit in the letter. It may appear to be quite late, but it is exactly where we would expect it in Paul's overall argumentation. With regard to many commentaries on Galatians, while they may not have actually ignored the work of the Spirit in their exegesis, they have still not recognised his initial activity, presence and power as they should (cf. 3:2–5; 14; 4:6, 29; 5:5, 16 -18, 22–23, 25; 6:8). Moo[22] comments, "The Spirit, the characteristic gift and mark of the new age of salvation (3:2, 5, 14), has an important, and often underappreciated role in Paul's argument."

It will become clear as the letter proceeds that Paul was challenging the Galatian believers not just to reject a lifestyle of Jewish nomism but to recognise the many blessings that have come to them through the cross. These blessings are available by the grace of God, and regeneration or new creation (6:15) in the Holy Spirit is one of those blessings that leads to a Spirit enabled lifestyle. Having begun in the Holy Spirit (3:3), which takes us back to their conversion, they ought to know what it is to "keep in step with the Spirit" (5:25). As Longenecker[23] has affirmed, the life of the believer is "one that starts, is maintained, and comes to culmination only through dependence on the activity of God's Spirit." We should note that in v. 5 the verb in the statement "he who *supplies* the Spirit to you" is in the present tense – God keeps on supplying the Holy Spirit day by day.

One insight that is important to mention here, is that often the NT uses the phrase about receiving the Holy Spirit when referring to conversion and the evidence of God's acceptance of the individual (3:2, 14; Acts 2:38; 8:17; 10: 47; 19:2). One can note Witherington's[24] discussion concerning the reception of the Holy Spirit as not just "a matter of purely rational conviction, or simply a deduction to be drawn from the fact that they have been baptised" i.e., not something unconscious, but a conscious experience. He agrees with Fee[25] that what Paul has in view here is:

> Unimpeachable evidence … surely referring to some dynamic experiences of the Spirit in Galatia … irrefutable evidence that God has accepted these Gentiles, and has accepted them without their having to submit to the Law of Moses and do "works of the Law."

---

[22] Moo, *Galatians*, 178.

[23] Longenecker, *Galatians*, 104.

[24] Witherington, 111, *Grace in Galatia*, 210–11.

[25] G. D. Fee, *God's Empowering Presence: The Holy Spirit in the Letters of Paul* (Peabody MA: Hendrickson Publishers, 1994), 384ff.

As Ziesler[26] also has stressed:

> For Paul, the indisputable fact that they have the Spirit is proof that they are God's people (cf. Ezek 36.22–27), and his argument is that the law had nothing to do with it. It therefore cannot be a necessary condition for being the people of God.

So here in Galatians the emphasis begins that without circumcision, followed by "the works of the law," these Galatians have become God's people, having initially and graciously been born again of the Holy Spirit and their responsibility is to live the Christian life by his power.

To conclude, in v. 3 Paul reminds them that "having begun by the Spirit." We referred above to Longenecker[27] who noted that the participle is both aorist and temporal and accepted that it cannot refer to anything other than the moment of becoming a Christian. It seems clear from what references we have in Galatians that it is the Holy Spirit who works in our hearts and brings us to faith (4:29; 6:15). However, that same Spirit is then the enabling power in which we are to walk.

To continue with the text, what does the phrase in v. 2 "hearing with faith" signify? Scholarly discussion has given us three main possibilities. In Greek ἀκοή *akoē* was sometimes simply used for *the organ of hearing*; but here this can surely be ruled out. It was also used for *the content* of what was heard, the actual message. We remember Isa 53:1 (LXX), quoted by Paul in Rom 10:16, referring to the gospel. Here in Galatians that message is of course referred to as Christ crucified (3:1). Again, it was possible to use the word for *the act* of hearing. Taking this as the interpretation the emphasis will be that it is, as was suggested above, the Holy Spirit who moves in our hearts i.e., it reminds us of a hearing initiated by that Spirit that involves believing and heeding the word spoken. Witherington[28] writes of:

> The "hearing" that is more than listening but in fact believing and heeding (cf. Rom 1:5) the word spoken (cf. 1 Kgs 22:19–23; Isa 6; Jer 1:11–16; Ezek 1; Amos 7:1–9; 8:1–3; 9:1–4). Jesus himself appears to have emphasised this sort of believing hearing – "let the one who has ears, hear" (Mark 4:9 and passim).

Moo[29] affirms something broadly similar. However, firstly, regarding the Galatians "faith" this interpretation (rather than "the faithfulness of Christ") is best since it is

---

[26] J. Ziesler, *The Epistle to the Galatians* (London: Epworth, 1992), 32.

[27] Longenecker, *Galatians*, 103. See also J.D.G., Dunn, *Baptism in the Holy Spirit* (London: SCM, 1970), 108.

[28] Witherington, 111, *Grace in Galatia*, 213. Hendriksen, *Galatians*, 112, n. 80, also discusses the Greek phrase whether it is to be understood as the "hearing" or listening of faith or does ἀκοή *akoē* refer to the "message," that which is heard. He considers that both are possible and can amount to the same thing, namely, "listening with a believing heart to the gospel message."

[29] Moo, *Galatians*, 183.

confirmed by the reference to follow i.e., Abraham's faith (v. 6). Also, the "hearing" "conveys something of the connotation of the equivalent Hebrew word: faithful receptivity, an 'attentiveness' to the word of God that includes both trust in its content and giver and the disposition to obey." So, he sees here a hearing that "involves" faith, or is accompanied by faith. It is clear that faith is the crucial issue, not "the works of" or "obedience to" the law.

To stress again, Paul reminds them (v. 3) that "having begun by the Spirit" – his is the initiative that effects hearing – and this must clearly go back to the moment they first became Christians. Moo[30] also explains that the aorist participle "having begun" points back to v. 2 and refers to "the inauguration of Christian experience" which Paul claims has taken place "by means of the Spirit," which can be taken as "a dative of means."

Paul then asks, since they "began" through the initiative of the Spirit, how they would be "perfected by the flesh?" This phrase "perfected by the flesh" is a tragic description of what the Judaizers were advocating. We must remember what the cross has achieved for us, Heb 10:14 "By a single offering" he has "perfected" us "for all time." His sacrifice is all we need. The cross gives us a perfect standing before God. Hendriksen[31] stresses:

> What the apostle writes applies not only to the Galatians of his day. It applies equally to those who today are trusting in such things as ritual, the moral life, scientific achievement, intellectual attainment, physical charm, financial resources, political power, doctrinal liberation, or even doctrinal purity. If one bases his hope for this life or the next upon anything apart from Christ he is placing confidence in *flesh*.

Paul by using this phrase "perfected by the flesh" is no doubt also thinking of them submitting to circumcision, the ritual which confirmed one's entrance into the Mosaic covenant (Gen 17:13) and then continuing to seek acceptance by "human effort" (the word "flesh" also implies this here). Paul warns the Galatians from being tempted by the agitators to change to another means to complete their Christian pathway or pilgrimage. We should note with Fung[32] that:

> The faith/works antithesis (2:16–21) is brought into connection with, and indeed given expression through, the new antithesis between the Spirit and the flesh. Having received the Spirit ... by faith, the Galatians have no need to look to fleshly works of the law to bring them perfection. The two principles, Spirit-faith and flesh-works are mutually exclusive.

---

[30] Moo, *Galatians*, 184.
[31] Hendriksen, *Galatians*, 114.
[32] Fung, *The Epistle to the Galatians*, 134.

His next question concerns their suffering (v. 4). "Did you suffer so many things in vain?" For most scholars the verb πάσχω *paschō* here is best taken as it is generally used in the NT i.e., focused on suffering. The word is used elsewhere in this sense 41 times e.g., Luke 22:15; 24:46; Acts 1:3; 3:18; 17:3; 1 Cor 12:26; Heb 1:18; 9:26; 1 Pet 2:20, 23; 3:17, rather than of positive "experiences" of the Spirit. Longenecker[33] however translates, "have you experienced so many things," which allows for these.

Acts 14:2–3, 22 records the hostility that the believers in that region experienced when they confessed Christ. Paul and Barnabas had already experienced it themselves (Acts 13:45, 50; again, 14:2, 5–6, 19). Now there was the temptation in order to avoid persecution, as George[34] explains, to accept circumcision so that they might have appeared just like normal proselytes submitting to the rituals of the synagogue (see 6:12). Yet the context which follows here (3:5) means that the alternative meaning of positive experiences of the Holy Spirit should not be cursorily dismissed. Moo[35] however, favours the sense of "suffering" for the word here, suggesting that it refers to the fact that the continuing ministry of the Spirit among them, "should teach them about the complete adequacy of the Spirit to bring them successfully to the final day of judgment."

Paul is concerned unless his ministry has all been "in vain" – but the conditional clause "if yet" at the end of the verse holds out hope. The situation was not beyond recovery. Those truly regenerate would persevere in faith.

Paul again reminds then in v. 5 that God has given ("supplies" – present tense) to them the Spirit and works miracles among them, not by works of the law but by the means of hearing with faith. This was all a fact of their experience. Is the reference here only to the miracle of their conversion or also to continuing miraculous signs? Moo[36] points out that there are two parallel phrases in the text, "the one who gives you the Spirit" and "the one who works miracles among you." The first will be to their initial conversion and the second to the ongoing experience of the Spirit. Bruce[37] also affirms that ἐν ὑμῖν *en humin* is best understood as "among you." The present participles "supplies" the Spirit and "performs" or "works" miracles, "probably imply that this divine activity still continues." Hendriksen[38] takes a similar position. He examines the two possible translations "within you" or "among you." Either the references will be to *miracles* and *outward charismata* or *inward moral and spiritual endowments*. "There would seem to be good reason that Paul had both of these groups in mind.... Blessings of both kinds have been bestowed – yes, *liberally bestowed* upon the Galatians."

---

[33] Longenecker, *Galatians*, 104. Also Witherington, 111, *Grace in Galatia*, 215.

[34] George, *Galatians*, 213.

[35] Moo, *Galatians*, 186.

[36] Moo, *Galatians*, 187.

[37] Bruce, *The Epistle to the Galatians*, 151.

[38] Hendriksen, *Galatians*, 116.

No doubt there were miraculous signs at the beginning affirming Paul's message and ministry.[39] Most scholars will here see that Paul affirms if God so honoured his preaching at the beginning before those who had troubled them arrived, if his preaching of a law-free gospel had brought them such blessing, what more could they possibly require? So as Witherington[40] explains:

> The Galatians are, however, confused Christians who do not understand the implications of what happened when they the received the Spirit and what they committed themselves to then, and what sort of persons of faith they became when they became Christians. Nor do they grasp the implications of how taking on the duties of the Mosaic law will violate that past.

* * *

Because of the Scriptures vv. 6–14

Paul now focuses on arguments based upon the teaching of the OT Scripture rather than the Galatian's experience. Yet he makes the connection with the latter in v. 14 with a reference to "receiving the promised Spirit through faith." Also there is the linguistic connection in the use of πίστις *pistis* "faith" i.e., now for the faith of Abraham. Hendriksen[41] points out that the likely reason for Paul focussing upon Abraham was "the fact that the opponents were constantly boasting about their descent from Abraham, as if this biological circumstance would give them a higher rating with God (Acts 15:5; Gal 2:3; 5:2; 6:12, 13, 15; Matt 3:9; Luke 3:8; John 8:33, 39, 40, 53)."

Paul appeals to the example of Abraham[42] the greatest of the patriarchs and the "Father" of Israel.[43] We see first the use of καθὼς *kathōs* "just as" it was with Abraham. As Witherington[44] explains, "In short, Paul will compare the faith of the Galatians and what they received when they believed, to the faith of Abraham and what he received when he believed." Paul in fact cites 6 OT passages to show that salvation is by faith. The structure of his argument is manifestly Jewish.

---

[39] See also Rom 15:19; 2 Cor 12:12.

[40] Witherington, 111, *Grace in Galatia*, 102.

[41] Hendriksen, *Galatians*, 119.

[42] Fung, *The Epistle to the Galatians*, 141 n. 23, refers to D. Cohn-Sherbok, "Paul and Rabbinic Exegesis", *SJT* 35 (1982) p 117–132, who claims that Paul's argument reflects the kind of typological approach occasionally taken by the rabbis where "the action of a Biblical personage is presented as an archetypical model," 122f.

[43] Witherington 111, *Grace in Galatia*, 216, explains that deliberative rhetoric often appeals to example, as we noted initially at the beginning of this chapter. Often the hearer or reader would be influenced by the person they respect and admire. He refers among others to Aristotle, *Rhet.* 1.6.29, "all things that those whom they admire, they deliberately choose to do."

[44] Witherington 111, *Grace in Galatia*, 218.

Note that while the Judaizers looked to Moses, Paul here went further back to Abraham[45] and to Genesis 15:6, the first text he quotes. Paul shows in positive arguments that God affirmed Abraham was accepted through faith, vv. 6–9 (more negative in vv. 10–14). God made Abraham a promise which he "placarded" before his eyes (Gen 15:5–6). Despite the apparent impossibility of the promise, Abraham "believed God, and it was counted to him as righteousness."[46] These words are a quotation from Gen 15:6 LXX. The verb λογίζομαι *logizomai* is used by Paul meaning to "account" or "credit" (here but also in Rom 4:3, 5, 9 10, 22; 2 Cor 5:19).

Longenecker points out that the Jews of Paul's day used Gen 15:6 but interpreted it in the context of Abraham's deeds (see the insertion in the Targum of the *Genesis Apocryphon of Qumran Cave 1: A Commentary*.[47] They would refer either to Abraham's actions in rescuing Lot and his family in Gen 14 or to Gen 17:4–14, his acceptance of circumcision, even Gen 26:5, where God speaks to Isaac of his father "who obeyed my voice and kept my charge, my commandments, my statutes, and my laws." So, Second Temple Judaism would focus upon Abraham's obedience.

But Paul's stress is on the fact that Abraham was affirmed as righteous simply because he believed God, his word of promise – by faith alone without righteous deeds or circumcision. As George[48] points out, Paul's real purpose was "to set the Abraham of 'faith alone' over against the Abraham of rabbinic exegesis who was blessed by God because of his meritorious deeds." Again, Fung[49] makes the point that Abraham was considered to stand in a right relationship with God simply because of his faith in God, not some meritorious achievement before God. He quotes James Denny:[50]

> The spiritual attitude of a man, who is conscious that in himself he has no strength, and no hope of a future, and who nevertheless casts himself upon, and lives by, the word of God which assures him of a future, is the necessarily and eternally right attitude of all souls to God. He whose attitude it is, is at bottom right with God.

McDonald[51] makes a useful contribution here: "Abraham's faith was faith in a promise of God which contained the promise of Christ." This we will see in v. 16 and v. 22.

---

[45] Abraham is referred to nineteen times in Paul's letters.

[46] Note Abraham "believed God," not just "believed *in* God." He accepted what God said or rested upon his word.

[47] Longenecker, *Galatians*, 114. There are references to Gen 15v6 in *Targum Pseudo-Jonathan,* also in Philo *Abr. (de Abrahamo)* 262–74, *Praem.* 27 *(praemiis et poenis)* and in the rabbinic Midrashim of *exodus rabbah* 3.12; 23.5.

[48] George, *Galatians*, 217.

[49] Fung, *The Epistle to the Galatians*, 135.

[50] J. Denny, "The Epistle to the Romans" *The Expositor's Greek Testament*, ed. W. R. Nicoll (5 vols.; 1897–1910; reprint, Grand Rapids, 1961), II 621a, in Fung, *The Epistle to the Galatians*, 135.

[51] McDonald, *Freedom in Faith*, 70.

The affirmation of v. 7 is that salvation, blessing, and justification follow as a logical consequence[52] of faith, for "it is those of faith, who are the sons of Abraham." Moo[53] takes the preposition ἐκ *ek* "of" as highlighting people who are "marked by," "characterised by" or "those who depend on" faith; to suggest as a few commentators that the reference would be to either God or Christ's faithfulness does not give enough weight to the connection between v. 6 and v. 7.

Dunn[54] explains concerning "those of faith" that, "the scope is deliberately unrestricted" and the οὗτοι *houtoi* "they" (not expressed in ESV) is "emphatic, ever restrictive, they and not others." As Hendriksen[55] also put it "Those that are *of faith, they alone* but also *all of them* without exception, are sons of Abraham."

It is likely that the Judaizers were promising the Galatian Gentile converts that they would become sons of Abraham by circumcision. Paul counters by saying that they were *already* sons[56] of Abraham by faith. See also 3:16, 29; 4:21–31; 6:16. So McDonald[57] can write of many "faith-sons" and the fact that they are anticipated in the promise made to him. Fung[58] explains, "In contrast to 'the circumcision party' (2:12 RSV *hoi ek peritomēs*) these may be called 'the faith party'; the preposition *ek* in these contrasting expressions designates 'circumcision' (that is, the law) and 'faith' as the characteristic features of the two groups."

Moo[59] highlights the significance of Abraham in the whole unfolding argument of the letter. He notes Paul's many references to him (vv. 8, 14, 16, 17, 18, 19, 21, 22, 29). Moo explains that for the Jews Abraham played a foundational role in salvation history, focusing, as we have seen, especially on his obedience to the law and their "biological" relationship with him (Matt 3:9; Luke 3:8; John 8:39–40). We see how significant Abraham was already in the Galatian Christian communities when Paul can introduce the concept of being "sons of Abraham" without any explanation. He however, stresses Abraham's faith as "the crucial element," as we noted. Again, in vv. 10–12 to come, Paul will argue that "works of the law" or "works" of any kind add nothing to the adequacy of faith as a means of righteousness. Later in the chapter he will affirm:

> That what gives rise to Paul's confidence in the ability of faith "alone" to justify is his insistence that faith brings people into union with Christ (vv. 14; 26–29) [note he is the "seed" of Abraham]. It therefore is Paul's

---

[52] Witherington discusses whether to take "know" as imperative or indicative. "You know" (indicative) is to be preferred with "then" and is a clear reference back to v6 as its logical consequence. Moo on the other hand prefers to understand the imperative, translating it as "understand that" or realize that." Moo, *Galatians*, 197.

[53] Moo, *Galatians*, 197.

[54] Dunn, *The Epistle to the Galatians*, 162–63.

[55] Hendriksen, *Galatians*, 124.

[56] When Paul writes of "sons" of Abraham he no doubt has daughters also in mind – see 3:28.

[57] McDonald, *Freedom in Faith*, 71.

[58] Fung, *The Epistle to the Galatians*, 138.

[59] Moo, *Galatians*, 192–93.

conviction about the utter adequacy of *Christ* that engenders his insistence on the adequacy of *faith.*

The realisation here is that faith in Christ *alone* is of course, faith in Christ *crucified –* see 3:1.

Verse 8 is a crucial statement in respect of the importance of Scripture, "preaching the gospel beforehand to Abraham," and the content of the message, "In you shall all the nations be blessed." The personification of Scripture – Scripture "preaching" (see also 3:22; 4:30; Rom 9:17) for Dunn[60] is "typical of the high view then common of the divine inspiration and authority of the sacred text." Witherington[61] can explain, "Scripture is seen as a written transcript of the living divine word that comes directly from the mind and mouth of God and so can be personified as it is here." We believe that through the inspiration of the Spirit the Scripture can set out God's plan for the inclusion of the Gentiles in the blessing which comes from faith. Bruce points out that the quotation conflates Gen 12:3 and 18:18 and is a kind of midrashic interpretation of these verses, a promise which finds its fulfilment in Christ, "to whom it primarily referred."[62] So in this sense Scripture here preaches the gospel – it is not just a prefiguring of the gospel which is highlighted, but the gospel itself. The word προευηγγελίσατο *proeuēngelisato*, is found only here in the NT. Hays[63] suggests we translate it as "pre-preached" the gospel.

We see God's initiative and purpose at this point; all is bound up with the seed "who is Christ" (v. 16), and this is at the heart of the gospel. As Moo[64] explains, verse 8 carries on the emphasis on faith and "introduces a new idea: that the initial promise to Abraham included, according to Gen 12:3, the Gentiles in its scope." Again, as we will see shortly, "verse 9 draws a conclusion: it is 'those of faith' who receive the blessing of Abraham." The Judaizers were preaching that the Gentiles in the churches in Galatia could through their circumcision become "sons of Abraham" by adoption. Paul was urging them to realise that in believing the gospel about Christ they are justified or counted righteous, *already children of Abraham* in the true sense that matters, because they shared his faith and thus had found acceptance before God.

That the mixed quotation is from Gen 12 and 18 may be significant. The promise is repeated a number of times in Gen 22:7–18; 26:4; 28:14 but as Dunn[65] points out, these link the reaffirmation of the promise to Abraham's obedient faithfulness, rather

---

[60] Dunn, *The Epistle to the Galatians*, 164. Some scholars consider that rather than a view "then common" it is still being maintained, see H. Moore, *The Letters to Timothy and Titus: Missional Texts from a Great Missionary Statesman* (Belfast: Nicholson and Bass, 2016), 254–58.

[61] Witherington 111, *Grace in Galatia*, 227.

[62] Bruce, *The Epistle to the Galatians*, 152.

[63] R. B. Hays, *Echoes of Scripture in the Letters of Paul* (New Haven: Yale University Press, 1989), 105.

[64] Moo, *Galatians*, 195.

[65] Dunn, *The Epistle to the Galatians*, 164–65. Moo seems to adopt a similar view regarding 12:3 and 18:18 as sources, rather than 22:18 and 26:4 where the promise is attached to obedience. He mentions the marginal cross-reference in NA 28 which cites Gen 18:18 as source of the Galatian reference. Moo, *Galatians*, 200.

than his believing trust when he was still without an heir. The affirmation of God's acceptance of Abraham was "prior to and without reference to ... obedience to specific laws," as those mentioned in Gen 26:4–5. George[66] also makes this point. We noted that in Second Temple literature Abraham is presented as the one whose fidelity and obedience merited the favour of God. Sirach (Ecclesiasticus) 44:19–21 goes back to his circumcision in Gen 17; 1 Macc. 2:45–64 has in mind Abraham's testing under ten trials (corresponding to the ten commandments), but especially the ultimate trial in Gen 22 and so gained credit as a righteous man. But Paul has "shifted the point of departure to an earlier event in Abraham's life" and does not mention the circumcision of Gen 17 or the test of faith in Gen 22. He maintains:

> Just as the Galatians had trusted God's word which they heard through Paul's preaching, so also Abraham believed what God said and was counted righteous, just like the Galatians through "the hearing of faith," not by the doing of deeds.

Moo[67] also notes that this righteousness cannot be *covenant* righteousness because of the fact that the covenant was not yet in place until Gen 17. He maintains that Paul uses this central OT statement about Abraham to say to the Galatians in effect, "just as Abraham's full and complete 'rightness' before God came by virtue of his faith – and so he was accepted on that basis before God – so your full and complete 'rightness' before God (in a distinctively forensic sense) comes by virtue of your faith – 'alone'."

Verse 9 provides the conclusion, using ὥστε *hōste* "so." It is not those who rely on the law (vv. 2, 5) but "those who are of faith are blessed along with Abraham, the man of faith."[68] As McDonald[69] states, "The faith-man of the Old Testament and the faith-man of the New are found to be one in declaring the same faith-principle of man's acceptance by God." The reference in v. 8 to τὰ ἔθνη *ta ethnē* will mean that the Gentiles, are the people in focus.[70] Paul as George[71] explains has, "redefined the Abrahamic family." So, as a consequence he calls us to note that, "God has provided one and only one way of salvation for all peoples everywhere, the atoning death of his Son on the cross ... he (Abraham) believed in the Christ who was to come, just as we trust in the One who had already come." Hendriksen[72] also finds "Christ" in the story and in the "gospel" Abraham heard, quoting John 8:56, "Your Father Abraham rejoiced that he would see my day. He saw it and was glad," and Heb 11:13, "These all died in faith, not having received the things promised, but having seen them and

---

[66] George, *Galatians*, 219. See also Moo, *Galatians*, 216, for some comments about Abraham's blessing through obedience and response to trial.

[67] Moo, *Galatians*, 188, 191.

[68] Here one can understand πιστός *pistos* not as "faithful Abraham" (AV, RV) but as the ESV has translated, meaning to believe God, as also the Gentiles do, Bruce, *The Epistle to the Galatians*, 157.

[69] McDonald, *Freedom in Faith*, 71.

[70] Note the earlier discussion of Gen 12:3; 18:18; 22:18; 26:4; see 28:14 – "all the families of the earth."

[71] George, *Galatians*, 226.

[72] Hendriksen, *Galatians*, 122.

greeted them from afar." So Abraham's faith "was the hand that laid hold on God's promise, however dimly apprehended." Luther[73] also made this point:

> All the promises are to be referred to that first promise concerning Christ: "The seed of the woman shall bruise the serpent's head" (Gen iii.15). So did also the prophets understand it and teach it. By this we may see that the faith of the fathers in the Old Testament, and ours now in the New is all one, although they differ in touching their outward objects. Which thing Peter witnesseth in the Acts when he saith: "which neither we nor our fathers were able to bear. But we believe through the grace of our Lord Jesus Christ to be saved even as they did" (Acts xv.10f.): and Paul saith: "Our fathers did all drink of that spiritual rock that followed them, which rock was Christ" (1 Cor x.4); and Christ himself saith: "Abraham rejoiced to see my day, and he saw it and was glad" (John viii.56). Notwithstanding the faith of the fathers was grounded on Christ which was to come, as ours is on Christ which is now come. Abraham in his time was justified by faith in Christ to come, but if he lived at this day, he would be justified by faith in Christ now revealed and present.

So Luther[74] can affirm:

> Hereof it followeth that the blessing and faith of Abraham is the same as ours; that Abraham's Christ is our Christ; that Christ died as well for the sins of Abraham as for ours ... we see that God speaketh to Abraham the patriarch, not of the law nor the things to be done, but of things to be believed; that is to say, that God speaketh unto him of promises which are apprehended by faith.

Longenecker[75] reminds us of the fact Paul wished his Gentile converts to know that "they were in the mind and purpose of God when God gave his covenant to Abraham." They are "blessed along *with* (using συν *sun*) Abraham." Note the present tense – the Gentiles were already sharing the blessing through Paul's mission ministry! Again, the blessing they receive is the blessing affirmed to Abraham i.e., justification.[76] The "blessing" written of here is set in contrast to the curses to follow in v. 10.

Having argued for justification by faith, Paul now presents the negative counterpart. He uses three OT passages to argue against any possibility of justification by the

---

[73] Luther, *A Commentary on St. Paul's Epistle to the Galatians*, 232.

[74] Luther, *A Commentary on St. Paul's Epistle to the Galatians*, 237.

[75] Longenecker, *Galatians*, 114.

[76] It is not just that the Gentiles receive the blessing as Abraham did – through faith, but "in fact they are the objects of blessing already referred to in the original promise to Abraham ... the promise to Abraham was inclusive in scope," Witherington 111, *Grace in Galatia*, 228. Dunn points out that the Hebrew word *barak* has a fullness about it, involving grace and peace, sustaining and causing to prosper – Num 6:24–26. Dunn, *The Epistle to the Galatians*, 165.

works of the law. Hendriksen[77] observes that at this point "Paul's attack against the false doctrine of the Judaizers, by which the Galatians were being influenced, thus increases in intensity and directness." For Moo,[78] the verses focus on the inability of the law to secure the Abrahamic blessing: sonship. In fact, "The contrast in this passage is between 'by faith' (vv. 7–9) and 'not by works of the law' or 'the law' (vv. 10–25) carries forward this same contrast from 2:16 and 3:1–5."

The particular group of people are described as "all who rely on the works of the law" i.e., rely upon their attempted performance of the law for acceptance; they are as we noted, set in contrast to those in v. 7, 9 who are "of faith." At this point Moo[79] makes us aware of a recent interpretation which is actually similar to those in the excursus in Gal 2 on the nature of Second Temple Judaism and "the works of the law." The phrase "all who rely on the works of the law" refers to the people of Israel generally. The Galatians are being warned not to join themselves to Israel by their own "works of the law" since Israel incurred "the curse" of exile because of their unfaithfulness to God's covenant. "Paul's point, then, would be to warn his Galatian readers that, if they try to identify with Israel by taking on the distinctive 'markers' of Judaism, 'the works of the law,' they will themselves fall under the curse that hangs over Israel." For Moo, as argued elsewhere in chapter 2, the phrase "the works of the law" is a common way of referring to "doing" the law, i.e., obeying the law generally, not just identifying with Israel or a reference only to boundary markers. He asks us to note that Paul's reference to Deuteronomy (v. 10) ends with the words "to do them." Again, he picks up this emphasis in v. 12 and in 5:3: "now I testify again to every man who wants to be circumcised that he is obligated *to do the whole law*," [italics mine]. "The critical point in unpacking the logic of this verse, then, is that 'works of the law' at the beginning of the verse and 'doing' at the end refer to the same basic thing." Another reason for preferring the traditional interpretation is that the text chosen – from all the texts that could have been selected concerning the curse that fell on Israel as a nation, Paul selects one that focuses on individuals – "everyone who" and their consistent obedience. "The quotation serves perfectly as a way of reminding the Galatian Christians of a central principle in the law: that blessing and cursing depend on *doing*," [italics mine].

Paul therefore affirms that actually relying on the law places all who seek to "do" it under a curse, for the law has no power to subdue man's sinful tendencies; the situation is clear that those in this group will be under God's judgment because of a failure to live up to his covenant requirements. Hendriksen[80] explains that

---

[77] Hendriksen, *Galatians*, 126.

[78] Moo, *Galatians*, 201.

[79] Moo, *Galatians*, 203–204.

[80] Hendriksen, *Galatians*, 126. He also explains that the law was given so that man, by nature a child of wrath, under the curse "as definitely declared in Deut 27:26; John 3:36; Eph 3:2, might be reminded not only of his unchanged obligation to live in perfect harmony with this law (Lev 19:2), but also his total inability to fulfil this obligation. Thus the law would serve as a custodian to conduct the sinner to Christ. The Judiazers were perverting the true purpose of the law. They were relying on law-works *as a means of salvation*. On that basis they would fail forever and Deut 27:26, when interpreted in that framework, pronounced God's heavy and unmitigated curse upon them."

Deuteronomy 27 sets out the blessing which was to be shouted from Mt. Gerizim and also the curses from Mt. Ebal. All this was happening as Hendricksen suggests, "in a setting of love, the idea being that by means of proclamation of this blessing and curse Israel, tenderly addressed as 'the people of Jehovah thy God' shall live a consecrated life to the glory of their merciful Deliverer."

Deut 27:26 is the final curse of twelve proclaimed by the Levites on Mt. Ebal in the renewal of the Mosaic covenant. The "all" may be imported from the following verse, 28:1, but this just brings out the full sense. Bruce explains the variations with reference to the LXX rendering.[81] The twelfth curse is the most comprehensive with the LXX wording generalised to include the two-fold "all" and the full phrase "all that is written in the book of the law." But there is no intention to misrepresent the sense. A solemn curse is imposed upon "all" who fail to keep "all" the commandments in the book of the law. As Moo[82] explains, "*everything* that is written in the law must be done if the curse is to be avoided."

Paul understands that this failure is true for all men. This is why we cannot be justified before God by works of the law since we fail to keep it. True if we could, as v. 12, states, "the one who does them shall live by them." But no one has ever "done" them perfectly, therefore no one can live by them; we are rather condemned by them. This is why Paul can state in v. 11 "Now[83] it is evident that that no-one is justified before God by the law," which reminds us of 2:16 and the quotation of Ps 143:2 (LXX 142). "By the law" is really a re-statement of "by the works of the law" in 2:16; 3:2, 5, 10. The reference is still to the law of Moses and ἐν νόμῳ *en nomō* will have an instrumental use.[84] The word "justified" is passive – righteousness is bestowed by another, not by one's own achievement, as is also expressed in many references in Galatians and Romans (Gal 2:16, 17; 5:4; Rom 2:13; 3:20, 24, 28; 4:2; 5:1, though active when God is in view, Rom 3:30; 4:5; 8:30).[85] It is clear that no-one can achieve this blessing by law keeping, for faith is the means to justification.[86] Concerning the law Stanley[87] explains:

> Anyone who chooses to abide by the Jewish Torah in order to secure participation in Abraham's blessing is placed in a situation where he or she is threatened instead with a "curse" since the law itself pronounces a curse on everyone who fails to live up to every single one of its requirements.

---

[81] Bruce, *The Epistle to the Galatians*, 158.
[82] Moo, *Galatians*, 202.
[83] Paul continues the argument using δε *de* "but" or as ESV "now." It is best to take the particle as adversative rather than simply a connective.
[84] Moo, *Galatians*, 206.
[85] Longenecker, *Galatians*, 118.
[86] Lightfoot sets out the stark reality, "Having shown by positive proof that justification is by faith, he (Paul) strengthens his position by the negative argument derived from the impossibility of maintaining its opposite, justification by law." Lightfoot, *Saint Paul's Epistle to the Galatians*, 137.
[87] C. Stanley, "'Under a Curse': A Fresh Reading of Galatians 3:10–14" *NTS* 36 (1990), 500.

This reality was also stated earlier by Luther:[88]

> When the Scripture saith that all nations which are of faith are blessed with
> faithful Abraham, it followeth necessarily that all, as well Jews as Gentiles,
> are accursed without faith, or without the faithful Abraham. For seeing the
> promise of blessing for the nations was given to Abraham, there is plainly
> no blessing to be looked for, but only in the promise made unto Abraham,
> now published by the Gospel throughout the whole world. Therefore,
> whatsoever is without the blessing is accursed.

Paul makes clear that what was true for Abraham, was/is also possible for all people.

As Moo[89] explains, "Making the quotation of v. 11b the basis for Paul's assertion in
11a fits the pattern of Pauline assertions of scriptural grounding that we find in this
context (vv. 8, 10, 12, 13)." Paul affirms, quoting Hab 2:4[90], for "the righteous shall
live by faith." Bruce, Longenecker and Witherington discuss the variations in the
wording between the MT, the forms in the LXX and Paul. The most important point
for Bruce[91] here is the fact the vision and vindication of the prophet Habakkuk would
finally be realised in the coming of God for which he must wait in faith – he must
believe in the faithfulness of God[92] and his promise.

> Paul omits the possessive pronoun from his quotation altogether, although it
> would have made little difference to his argument had he included it.... The
> faith by which one becomes righteous in God's sight is faith in God,
> believing acceptance of his promise, such as Abraham showed.

Longenecker[93] also agrees that because Paul does not focus upon the suffix, the issue
has to be here those who have faith like Abraham. He has explained that in bringing
the concepts of being "righteous" and "by faith" beside one another in the word order
of the text he is making this point clear.

---

[88] Luther, *A Commentary on St. Paul's Epistle to the Galatians*, 241.

[89] Moo, *Galatians*, 205.

[90] Fung, *The Epistle to the Galatians*, 143, explains that Paul quotes the Habakkuk statement because it, as Gen 15v6, mentions both being "righteous" and also "faith."

[91] Bruce, *The Epistle to the Galatians*, 161; Hendriksen, *Galatians*, 127–129 makes a similar point. Habakkuk lays aside his questioning of the ways of God's providence to exercise humble trust and quiet confidence in God. "Whether a person trusts in his own *works,* or in his own *reason,* in either case is he not trusting in 'flesh?'"

[92] Silva also affirms as far as Abraham is concerned, "faith involves *waiting* for fulfilment." Silva, *Explorations in Exegetical Method*, 167. Or as McDonald puts it, "Paul sees behind this fidelity to the faith from which it springs," McDonald, *Freedom in Faith*, 74. See also Moo, *Galatians*, 220, who writes of Habakkuk's "deep-seated trust in the Lord and his promises."

[93] Longenecker, *Galatians*, 119; see also Witherington 111, *Grace in Galatia*, 234, who also accepts this approach. Moo suggests that Paul is drawn to the passage because it is as Gen 15:6 connecting "Righteousness" language and faith. Moo, *Galatians*, 207.

Paul continues in v. 12 (as with v. 11, using the adversative δϵ *de*), affirming that the law is not "of faith."[94] Paul then uses ἀλλά *alla* a strong adversative "but," "on the contrary," or "rather," and quotes Lev 18:5, "the one who does them shall live by them." Hendriksen[95] explains that the setting of the quotation from Leviticus "is beautiful and comforting" with assuring references in vv. 2, 4 "I am Jehovah." He suggests that God was saying:

> As your *sovereign God* I have the right to order you to keep my statutes, and as your *faithful and loving God* I will help and strengthen you to observe these statutes out of gratitude. So interpreted, obeying God's law is the believer's joy. Did not the Psalmist exclaim: "O how I love thy law! It is my meditation all the day."

One can then ask what would happen when an Israelite transgressed the law? This was the reason for the sacrifices which were offered in the tabernacle. There was the possibility that the offender could be "forgiven" (e.g., Lev 4:20, 26, 31, 35). By means of the sacrifices, God could continue to dwell among a sinful people. So, it appears that faith in the sacrifice and what it pointed to would preserve the guilty (Lev 1:4; 4:4, 15, 24, 29, 33).

The problem was as Hendriksen[96] explains when one begins to *rely* on law-works, "as if such obedience to law amounts to a ticket of admission into the kingdom of heaven – and that, after all, is the context here in Galatians – he should bear in mind that, *so conceived, law* is the very opposite of faith." He insists that the two cannot be combined. "Leaning on law means leaning on self. Exercising faith means leaning on Christ."

Therefore, the meaning here concerning the law is about relying upon i.e., "obeying" or "living by its commandments," rather than faith. Moo[97] also discusses this statement, which is given in the context of specific commandments concerning sexual relationships.

The series is introduced (vv. 1–5) and concluded (vv. 24–30) by general exhortations to obey the law of God, grounded in warnings about what would happen if the people failed to obey and in promises of what God would do if the people did obey. This context strongly suggests that Lev 18:5 functions as one of the promises of blessing for obedience ... doing is a way of life. In contrast then, to Hab. 2:4, which claims that faith is the means of life, the law, in the words of Lev 18:5, claims that "doing"

---

[94] Literally, the law is not "from faith" – the "dogged repetition of the same phrase ... for the fifth time in six verses (3v7, 8, 9, 11, 12) makes Paul's point," Dunn, *The Epistle to the Galatians*, 175. For Moo we have a contrasting point following the "but" i.e., "a person finds life by faith, *but* the law is not 'of faith.'" He maintains that the NTL translation captures the point well, "The way of faith is very different from the way of law," Moo, *Galatians*, 207–08.

[95] Hendriksen, *Galatians*, 129.

[96] Hendriksen, *Galatians*, 129.

[97] Moo, *Galatians*, 208.

(ὁ ποιήσας *ho poiēsas* the one who does) brings life. Indeed, these two texts are antithetically parallel.

This argument is so important here. Again we are reminded of the discussion in the excursus of chapter 2 concerning the "works of the law." Here we have not just Jewish badges for "doing the law" but the actual *obedience of the law itself* is required. Paul is insisting that faith[98] is the only instrument or means by which justification or life can be attained.

Keeping the law is of course what we are not able to do. The whole Pentateuchal law had 242 positive and 365 prohibitions, but no "flawless person"[99] can be found – hence we fall under the law's curse as v. 10 (quoting Deut 27:26) has already stated. This is why Paul affirms that for sinners – which all men are – there is an answer in Christ's redemption (v. 13). One should recall that the curse was affirmed at the end of a covenant renewal ceremony – so Christ himself is the one who bears the penalty for the covenant breaker![100] There is emphasis here with the introduction again of the word "Christ." As Fung[101] also explains, "Paul presents Christ as the deliverer from the curse of the law and the one who obtains the blessing of Abraham for believers." He and he only accomplished this for us. Paul has now finally introduced Christ and his cross into his first major argument.

The way of deliverance is by the cross – here the aorist tense of "redeem" points to this work (see already, 1:3–5; 2:20–21; also 4:5; 6:14). When we could not escape from the curse ourselves, we can be delivered by what he has done for us. Christ became a curse for us.[102] For Moo[103] the word "probably conjures the widespread ancient practice of manumission, whereby slaves could purchase their freedom." When we could not do this Christ redeemed us!

Paul uses ἡμᾶς *hēmas* "us" of those redeemed. Surely NOT just Jews under a curse are in view here, but also the pronoun will include Gentiles, contra Witherington.[104]

---

[98] To return to Moo again. He can affirm, "The Reformers, therefore, were entirely justified to find in Paul's argument here a fundamental and universally valid principle about the exclusive value of believing verses doing." Moo, *Galatians*, 210.

[99] George, *Galatians*, 235.

[100] Bruce, *The Epistle to the Galatians*, 164.

[101] Fung, *The Epistle to the Galatians*, 147.

[102] Not all will accept how Dunn in his 1995 commentary explained these verses here, particularly about the curse. He refers to the Jews in their understanding of "the works of the law" as *boundary markers* who were convinced of "the restrictiveness of covenant grace on the exclusion of Gentiles." They are under the curse i.e., they effectively put themselves *outside* the covenant. So, for Dunn, those Jews who had confidence in their favoured status are "under a curse" because of a wrong "attitude" (172) or "a fatal misunderstanding" (178). But note Deut 28:15–68 outlines the fearful judgments of being cursed, not just "effective exclusion from the covenant and its blessings." Again, is the death of Christ who "redeemed us from the curse of the law" only about delivering us from misunderstanding or ignorance of the grace of God? The cross or Christ's redemption, with the horror of his separation from God (for Dunn he reaches the same place of those Jews *outside* the covenant) is surely because of much more and accomplished so much more than this. Dunn, *The Epistle to the Galatians*, 170–81.

[103] Moo, *Galatians*, 210.

[104] Witherington 111, *Grace in Galatia*, 236–38.

Fung[105] insists that the "we" of v. 14b will pick up the "us" of v. 13a. So, Gentiles are clearly in focus also as the sentence continues into the next verse, v. 14. How can the blessing of Abraham "come to" the Gentiles and they receive the "promised Spirit" if Christ has not become a curse for them first? See also Rom 2:14–16 where we are informed that the Gentiles have the law "written on their hearts." As Bruce[106] maintains, "they too are in principle liable to 'the curse of the law.'"

We should also note Wright's[107] view of the curse. The Deuteronomy curses have come to pass in the history of the Jewish people from the exodus to the exile. Jesus the messiah on the cross took upon himself the curse that was Israel's as their representative and exhausted it. However, George[108] is certain that deeper truths are to be found here. What happened outside the gates of Jerusalem just a few decades before Paul wrote Galatians was not merely another episode in the history of Israel. It was an event of universal human and cosmic, significance.

While Paul posed the problem, as he had to, in Jewish terms of blessing and curse, law and faith, it is clear from Abraham on that God's dealing with Israel had paradigmatic meaning for all peoples everywhere. As Paul argued in Rom 1–3, both Jews and Gentiles are "under the law," albeit in very different ways. Thus when Paul spoke of the curse of the law he was not thinking merely of Jews, anymore than when he showed how one becomes a true child of Abraham through faith he had only Gentiles in mind … not merely Jewish Christians but instead all the children of God, Jews and Gentiles, slaves and freed ones, males and females, who are Abraham's seed and heirs according to the promise because they belong to Christ through faith (3:26–29).

One question we can pose. Should we not then consider that Paul was thinking as he wrote in 3:13 of "the Israel of God" (6:16), which of course was a company made up of more than Jews only? Moo[109] also, in responding to Wright and those in mind in v. 13 can affirm:

> Paul's purpose is to warn the Gentile Christians in Galatia about their depending on their doing of the law for their justification (v. 10). It therefore makes slightly better sense to think that Paul assures them in verse 13 that they have themselves been definitely rescued … from the curse that stands over all human beings by virtue of their failure to meet the demands of God, expressed in its clearest form in the law of Moses…. From that plight God

---

[105] Fung, *The Epistle to the Galatians*, 140.
[106] Bruce, *The Epistle to the Galatians*, 167.
[107] Wright, Climax of the Covenant: Christ and the Law in Pauline Theology (Minneapolis: Fortress, 1991), 144–56.
[108] George, *Galatians*, 213. See also R.Y.K. Fung, "Cursed, Accursed, Anathema," in *Dictionary of Paul and His letters*, G.F. Hawthorne and R. Martin eds. (Downers Grove: Intervarsity, 1993), 199, who states, "the first person pronouns are most naturally understood as referring to both Jews and Gentiles." In 3:22 we see that the Scripture affirms that all are "imprisoned" under sin.
[109] Moo, *Galatians*, 213.

has redeemed both Jew and Gentile by means of his son's identification with that plight.

Now regarding this redemption through the cross, Paul again adds scriptural confirmation by quoting Deut 21:23, which shares the common word in the LXX ("cursed") with Deut 27. Here every criminal under Mosaic legislation, executed by stoning was then fixed to a stake or "hanged on a tree" exposed before all as a symbol of divine rejection. It was an outward sign that the man himself was cursed by God. So, the cross was a sign that Jesus had died under the divine curse, the exchange curse. The law looked for obedience which they could not give but salvation is by faith in what Christ has done for us. McDonald[110] explains:

> Here, the idea is of redemption from law's slavery to become free men in Christ…. In the term "redeemed" there is the idea of the "cost." Christ did not accomplish our redemption easily and at little personal loss. Rather, it involved Him in the infinite condescension of His incarnation and the immeasurable suffering of His atonement … He has become Himself the very thing the law made us – a "curse"… In 2 Cor 5:21 it is stated, by the same apostle, that He became "sin for us," but certainly not a "sinner"; here it is stated that HE became a "curse" for us, but certainly not Himself "accursed."

Paul uses two ἵνα *hina* clauses, "in order that" which bring together the two previous themes of the chapter, both accomplished through the cross – "in Christ Jesus" (v. 14). Through our faith in him the blessing of Abraham[111] comes to us *and* we receive the promised Holy Spirit who transforms our lives – here "two parts of the one whole."[112] Hendriksen[113] also comments, "The two purpose clauses are co-ordinate." Paul emphasises that "the Gentiles" are included in these blessings by putting the phrase first in its clause. Moo[114] makes the point regarding the Spirit that, "the evident presence of God's Holy Spirit in power among the believers constitutes clear evidence that the 'last days' have dawned (Acts 1:4; 2:33, 39)." He also explains that verse 14 "weaves together many of the key ideas from verses 1–14, functioning therefore as a conclusion not only to verses 10–14 but also, to some extent, verses 1–14." Referring to the two purpose clauses he explains that they:

---

[110] McDonald, *Freedom in Faith*, 75.

[111] Moo explains that "the blessing of Abraham" is a general way of referring back to the blessing associated with Abraham. "This blessing, as verse 8 reveals, is specifically interpreted by Paul in this context in terms of justification," Moo, *Galatians*, 215.

[112] Dunn, *The Epistle to the Galatians*, 179. George also affirms that the declarative aspect of justification in Gal 3 "can never be divorced from the new life in the Spirit with which Paul began his appeal." George, *Galatians*, 234. Yet we should note, as Moo points out, that while Paul understands that justification and the Spirit as "closely related" it does not mean that righteousness "includes the transforming work of God's Spirit." The Spirit functions in 3:1–5 as "confirmation" that the believers are now in relationship with God. Moo, *Galatians*, 188. We are therefore thinking of forensic righteousness here as in 2:16.

[113] Hendriksen, *Galatians*, 131.

[114] Moo, *Galatians*, 214–16. The references to the Holy Spirit in chapter 3, particularly here at the climax of the section anticipate what is to come in the role of the Spirit in 5:16–26; 6:1–10.

Bring to a climax two of the key themes of 3:1–9: the extension of the blessing of Abraham to the Gentiles (vv. 7–9) and the gift of God's Spirit as evidence that the new age of redemption has arrived (vv. 1–6). At the same time, the verse again emphasizes that faith is the means by which these blessings are received and, anticipating a key idea to come, that all this takes place "in Christ."

The prepositional phrases "through faith" and "in Christ Jesus" find a similar emphasis to come in v. 26, "In Christ Jesus you are all sons of God through faith." So already the Galatian Christians have been born again in Christ, were sons of Abraham by faith, blessed with justification and redeemed from the curse and possessed of the enabling Spirit, all through the cross. Why then the need for circumcision and submission to the Mosaic law as the Judaizers proposed? As Longenecker[115] affirms, "Paul's theology is a theology of the cross, of the Spirit, of faith, and of being 'in Christ' … he begins at v. 1 with the cross and in v. 13 lays stress on it again." These convictions will go back to Paul's whole transformation at his conversion on the Damascus Road, with the new understanding of the reason for the crucifixion of Jesus, the true Messiah. When Paul writes of the blessing of Abraham being "in Christ," as McDonald[116] explains, "This is more than saying 'by His agency,' although it is that; but it is for those linked in indissoluble union with Christ. Thus the blessing of Abraham is not got by being *in* Israel but by being *in* Christ."

Dunn[117] writes here of "the reformulation" of the blessing of Abraham with regard to the promise of the Holy Spirit. Receiving "the promised Spirit" points to the prophecies of OT hopes as Isa 32:15; 44:3; 59:21; Ezek 11:19; 36:26–27; 37:1–14; Joel 2:28–29. These prophecies point to the coming of the age of fulfilment (see 3:8; 23–25; 4:1–7). Paul affirms that this Spirit is received "through faith" – literally "through the faith," the faith referred to in vv. 2, 5, 7, 9, 11 or as Moo,[118] "The Galatians have experienced the Spirit by means of 'hearing accompanied by faith' (3:2, 5); so they have received 'the promise of the Spirit' by faith." We should note in passing that this faith is NOT about the faithfulness of Christ.

Because of the Promise vv. 15–18

To Abraham God gave a promise in terms "I will," "I will," "I will"; to Moses God gave a law, "You shall," "You shall not." Stott[119] presents the contrast, "The promise sets forth a religion of God – God's plan, God's grace, God's initiative. But the law sets forth a religion of man – man's duty, man's works, man's responsibility." Paul is advocating that the Christian religion is a religion of Abraham and not Moses, of promise and not law. In fact, Paul calls for the first time this promise a covenant (vv. 15, 17). This covenant was unconditional – Abraham simply believed God would do

---

[115] Longenecker, *Galatians*, 124.

[116] McDonald, *Freedom in Faith*, 77.

[117] Dunn, *The Epistle to the Galatians*, 180.

[118] Moo, *Galatians*, 216.

[119] Stott, *The One Way: The Message of Galatians*, 87.

what he had said – rather than the covenant at Sinai with its "burdensome requirements, a code of behaviour that makes demands and issues threats."[120]

Fung[121] explains that here Paul is still basing his arguments on the biblical story and that the promise to Abraham "temporally preceded" the covenant given at Sinai. So even "this historical fact supports" what he is affirming, namely, that justification is by faith and not through the works of the law. The emphasis here is that the law which came in 430 years later does not annul, nor can it even modify the promise of God. Paul uses again the word "brothers." He is continually expressing his deep affection for them and appeals for their particular attention. For George[122] it is a particularly appropriate term to use here at the commencement of a passage where he is seeking to demonstrate that they may be those who are part of the family of God, true children of Abraham and heirs of the promise. For Witherington,[123] they are still Christian, albeit "confused Christians" and so, precious.

Paul writing "as a man" gives an everyday illustration, taken from the realm of human promises (Longenecker[124] suggests the translation, "Let me take an example from everyday life.") Paul refers to a will – διαθήκη *diathēkē* here used in the secular sense, but so suitable since it was used in LXX (and in the NT) of a Biblical covenant. There is really a play on words here. In ancient law a will once "having been ratified" – the perfect tense – could not be annulled or added to by someone else (which is the argument here), neither before, or particularly after, the testator had died.[125] So Paul uses an *a fortiori* argument – if a man's will cannot be set aside, how much more *the promises of God* by a law which was introduced later.

Paul in v. 16 writes of the promises made to Abraham and to his offspring. God's purpose was to give the land of Canaan to the Jews (Gen 15:18–21; 17:2–14), but also to give a spiritual inheritance to believers in Christ who share Abraham's faith (see v. 7). One part of the promise of God was that he would make him "the father of a multitude of nations" (Gen 17:4). Earlier in Gen 12:3 God promised that in Abraham and through his "offspring" all the families of the earth would be blessed. It should be recognised that while generally this is understood as a plurality of descendants, sometimes the reference concerns an individual (Gen 4:25; 21:12–13; also 1 Sam. 1:11). This fact is affirmed again here in the use of the word "offspring" or literally σπέρμα *sperma* "seed" by God, rather than "seeds." Paul sees the reference pointing to Christ the seed or "offspring" of Abraham and, of course, those who are

---

[120] George, *Galatians*, 245.
[121] Fung, *The Epistle to the Galatians*, 153. He commences this section with the heading "The Priority of the Promise."
[122] George, *Galatians*, 244,
[123] Witherington 111, *Grace in Galatia*, 242.
[124] Longenecker, *Galatians*, 227.
[125] The commentaries have quite a lot of discussion of the inheritance laws in the Greco-Roman world and in Judaism. See Longenecker, *Galatians*, 128–130; Bruce, *The Epistle to the Galatians*, 169–174. The basic argument, whatever laws Paul may be alluding to, is that the covenant God made with Abraham was irrevocable and could not be either annulled, added to or altered later.

in Christ by faith. Wilcox[126] quotes some late texts as Jub. 16:17–18 and Ps.-Philo *LAB* 8:3 which point to one pre-eminent descendant of Abraham (likely Isaac in the first, identified as "the eternal seed" and then Jacob, although possibly a later Messianic figure) in which the promise made concerning an individual "seed" could be fulfilled. One should not forget that σπέρμα *sperma* "seed" is a collective noun[127] and will allow us to see in Christ, the seed of Abraham, the new family or community for whom he died, who are heirs of the promise (4:29).

These points are discussed by Moo.[128] He notes that the phrase "and to his seed" occurs in Gen 13:15; 17:8 and 24:7 (LXX), while the phrase "to your seed" is in Gen 12:7; 15:18; 22:18 and 24:7. He suggests that since in Galatians here the focus is on testament/covenant Paul may have been drawn to Gen 15:18 or 17:8, where these concepts are also found. For Moo, Paul is not engaged in some kind of "forced interpretation" – the word σπέρμα *sperma* while singular in form is plural in meaning – for in this very context he makes clear how he understands the collective sense of σπέρμα *sperma* i.e., v. 29, as we noted above. In addition, "Paul's application of the 'seed' language to Christ may also reflect the later traditions about a 'seed' of David; for example, see 2 Sam. 7:12 where σπέρμα refers to David's immediate descendant Solomon, but ultimately to the Messiah, who would come from David's line."

Paul insists therefore in v. 17, in a concluding statement, that a law which came 430 years later "does not annul a covenant previously ratified by God, so as to make the promise void."[129] The verb "annul" which is often used by Paul in this context, for Moo,[130] will mean unable to "render inoperative" or "make powerless" or lose its validity and power e.g., Rom 3:3; 6:6; Gal 5:4, 11; Eph 2:15. The 430 years, the time mentioned in Exod 12:40, is generally understood to cover the time from the establishing of the covenant with Abraham and Moses' actual reception of the law on Sinai, while the figure in Gen 15:13 of 400 years refers generally to the period Israel spent in Egypt.[131]

If the Judaizers were right, our Christian "inheritance" (v. 18), implied in vv. 15–17, is given to those who keep the law. However, if it is by law i.e., the law of Moses, then it is no more by promise and Paul insists that it was given earlier by a promise affirmed – note ὑπο του θεου *hupo tou theou* "by God," contrasting v. 19 with the

---

[126] M. Wilcox, "The Promise of the 'seed' in the NT and the Targumim," *JSNT*, Issue 5 (October 1979), 15. For other examples of Rabbinic interpretation of "seed" as singular, see D. Daube, "The Interpretation of a Generic Singular," in *The New Testament and Rabbinic Judaism* (London: Ayer, 1956), 438–44.

[127] Witherington 111, *Grace in Galatia*, 244.

[128] Moo, *Galatians*, 230.

[129] Fung, *The Epistle to the Galatians*, 157 quotes W. Foerster, *TDNT* III: 784, n. 36. "Paul's point is that what God has said is already in force by the mere fact that He has said it."

[130] Moo, *Galatians*, 231.

[131] H. Strack and Billerbeck, *Kommentar zum Neuen Testament* (Munich: Beck, 1926–28), Vol. 2 670. Hendriksen, *Galatians*, 139, suggests that the time is reckoned from the final confirmation of the promise to Jacob (Gen 28:14). In Scripture Abraham, Isaac and Jacob are mentioned "in one breath." Again, he maintains, "In nearly every case when it occurs *it is in connection with the divine promise that the three patriarchs are grouped together as if they were one.*"

law "through angels." "God gave it (the Greek word emphasises that it was a free gift and the tense – perfect tense – that it was given for good), to Abraham by a promise." God has not gone back on a promise; it is as binding as a Greek will.[132] If by "law" it would belong to the people of the law, the Jewish nation; but being based on a promise made many, many years before the law was given,[133] it belongs to both Jews and Gentiles, the people of faith, true children of Abraham (v. 7) to whom God continues to give it. The inheritance which is being highlighted by God at this point comes more into prominence here in the letter – see also "heir" 3:29; 4:1, 7 and "inherit" in 4:30; 5:21; 6:16. There are different facets to our inheritance; new birth of the Spirit, justification (3:2, 11 already affirmed), the promise of blessing in Abraham, the Jerusalem which is above, sonship, a kingdom and being a member of the Israel of God. The true Christian life is not about supplementing one's faith in Christ with Torah obedience. We have all through the cross, in Christ and by the power of the Holy Spirit, 5:16–26. Paul is continuing the theme of the foolishness of the Galatians from v. 1 as he progresses into the next section.

Because of the Transgression vv. 19–22

Paul now explains the true function of the law in relation to God's promise. He asks and answers two questions (vv. 19, 21) said to be rhetorical in nature, and his argument, extending through to v. 25, shows the limited time and specific purpose of the law. The problem is that if, as Paul has affirmed, one receives the promise (involving justification) and the inheritance by faith in Christ and not by works of the law, what purpose could the law really have? Here now is his Christian understanding of the limited role of the law in the history of salvation.[134] Paul uses ἄχρις *achris* "until." Witherington[135] explains that this is a remarkable statement for a first-century Jew (especially a former Pharisee like Paul). He notes that early Jews believed that the law had a permanent and eternal purpose (2 Bar. 4, 1; 2 En. 99.2; Wis. 18.4; Jub. 1.27; 3.31; Josephus *A* 2.227). But from Paul's perspective, he will show that it had "a temporary, not a permanent role"[136] or "an important parenthesis between the Abrahamic covenant and the fulfilment of the promises to Abraham in Christ"[137] i.e., "until the offspring should come" (v. 19). As Moo[138] summarizes, if the law had a definite beginning – "it was added", it also had a definite end; it was to be in force

---

[132] George comments, "The law demands, 'Do this!' The promise grants 'Accept this!' Here in v. 18 Paul drew the two into sharpest antithesis: If law ... not promise; if works ... not grace." George, *Galatians*, 250. Moo explains that a promise by its nature involves "a free and unconstrained decision to commit oneself, or specific objects to another," Moo, *Galatians*, 231.

[133] The temporal nature of the establishing of the promise long before the law is seen in the use of the verb προκυρόω *prokuroō* "to establish before or previously."

[134] As George points out, Paul is not dealing here with the role of the law in the life of the believer but would come to this in 5:14f. and 6:2. The law has many uses, which must be carefully defined. George, *Galatians*, 251.

[135] Witherington 111, *Grace in Galatia*, 254.

[136] Witherington, 111, *Grace in Galatia*, 254, quoting here from Gyu Hong, *The Law in Galatians* (Sheffield: JSOT Press, 1993), 149–56.

[137] Witherington 111, *Grace in Galatia*, 254, quotes L. Bellville, "'Under Law': Structural Analysis and the Pauline Concept of Law in Galatians 3:21–4:11," *JSNT* 26 (1986), 71.

[138] Moo, *Galatians*, 233.

only until "the offspring" came or as the NIV puts it, "until the Seed to whom the promise referred had come." See also the exegesis of 3:24–25; 4:2–4.

Some questions should be addressed regarding this subject of the Law. Firstly, "Why then the law?" (vv. 19–20). Some of the Judaizers would accuse Paul of so fusing Abraham and Christ as to squeeze Moses out altogether. There is no room for the law in Paul's gospel – or so it appeared (see Acts 21:28). But Paul was quite clear that the law had an essential part to play. However, the function of the law was not to bestow salvation, but to convince men of their need of it. Paul says, "It was added because of transgressions" (v. 19).

Longenecker[139] presents two possible meanings to this statement: to multiply transgression or to bring about a knowledge of transgression. Because of the immediate context and particularly what is to come in vv. 21 and 24–25, the law is understood generally as "given to bring about a consciousness of sin in a sin-hardened humanity," although he is open to a "causative" interpretation (to increase the sin) as also a possibility. It is clear that the law was intended to make plain the exceeding sinfulness of sin as a revolt against the will and authority of God.

Bruce[140] explains this statement in v. 19 in even clearer terms. The law rather than being "added" to the promise as a kind of supplement, it was introduced into the situation for a special purpose, totally different from the promise. The verb "added" here has the same sense as in Rom 5:20 i.e., the law literally "came in by a side road" and as 2:4 here, the false brethren who "slipped in to spy out." The introduction of the law was with the purpose of multiplying, even stimulating transgressions. See also Rom 4:15; 5:20–21; 7:7–25 and 1 Cor 15:56 "the power of sin is the law."[141] Hendriksen[142] explains that the law acts as a magnifying glass which does not actually increase the number of dirty spots that defile a garment but "makes them stand out more clearly and reveals many more of them than one is able to see with the naked eye."

So, the law was to remain in force "until the offspring should come to whom the promise had been made." The word σπέρμα *sperma* (lit. "seed") now is used as a title of Christ and reminds us of v. 16b. The perfect tense of the word "promise" found in v. 18 assures us that the promise which had been given is permanently now in effect. So, the law looked on to the promise, to Christ, Abraham's seed, as the person through whom the transgression would be forgiven. Bruce[143] explains that:

---

[139] Longenecker, *Galatians*, 138.

[140] Bruce, *The Epistle to the Galatians*, 175–76.

[141] See also C.E.B. Cranfield, "St. Paul and the Law," *SJT*, 17 (1964), 46 "in order that there might be transgressions, the conscious disobeying of definite commandments," also quoted by Bruce here who adds, commenting on χάριν *charin* "The law was brought into the situation in order to produce transgressions ... to increase the sum total of transgressions," 175. So also Moo, *Galatians*, 234, where, after a discussion of other possibilities, χάριν *charin* will mean "for the sake of" turning sins into transgressions.

[142] Hendriksen, *Galatians*, 141,

[143] Bruce, *The Epistle to the Galatians*, 178.

There was an early Jewish doctrine of three epochs in world-history – the age of chaos, the age of law, and the messianic age – each lasting for 2000 years, after which the eternal Sabbath rest would be enjoyed (b. Sanh. 97a; m. Tamid 7:4).... But the logic of Paul's earlier instruction is of minor importance: the logic which impelled him to the conviction that Christ had displaced the Torah was the logic of his Damascus-road conversion.

Fung[144] also shares this view. The validity of the Mosaic law has ceased with the coming of the seed. It had an interim role, temporally restricted and temporally valid. So also Moo[145] who writes concerning vv. 19b–25:

He (Paul) makes two basic points. First, the law and the promise serve distinct purposes: the law was given to exacerbate and reveal sin (vv. 19b, 22a) and was not intended to, or able to, give the life that only the promise and faith could achieve (v. 21). Second, all along the law was intended to last only until the promised Messiah came (vv. 19b, 23–25).... It is the movement of redemptive history that explains why the law is no longer necessary ... he also views the coming of Christ – "Christ crucified" (3:1; cf. also 2:19–20; 6:14) – as a climactic moment that introduces a significant shift in the history of salvation.

Verses 19b–20 have caused some discussion, Paul states that the law was "put in place through angels by an intermediary." Witherington[146] makes the point that there is nothing in the context that would suggest that Paul is viewing these angels in a negative light. He discusses preposition διά *dia* which "expresses intermediate agency.... The law was ordained by God, but came to Moses through angels." In the LXX Deut 33:2 "holy ones" are mentioned as coming to Sinai, but it probably was Ps 68:17–18 which Paul has in mind. Callan[147] explains, where the chariots of God were often interpreted as "a large number of angels accompanying God at Sinai." See also Stephen in Acts 7:53 and Heb 2:2 "the message declared by angels" and of course other works which suggest that the idea was commonly understood, Jub. 1:29ff.; Philo (*Som.* 1.141–143); Josephus (*Ant.* 15.136).

Some scholars have suggested Paul is likely adding further support for the primacy of Abraham over the law of Moses, i.e., the promise came to Abraham first-hand or directly from God; the law it appears, comes to the people third-hand – from God to angels to Moses[148] the mediator and only then to the people. There is a contrast. The

---

[144] Fung, *The Epistle to the Galatians*, 157

[145] Moo, *Galatians*, 225.

[146]Witherington 111, *Grace in Galatia*, 257.

[147] 1. Callan, "Pauline Midrash: The Exegetical Background of Gal 3:19b," *JBL* 99 (1980), 55.

[148] The writer of Hebrews in 2:1–2 brings together the message spoken by angels which if rejected resulted in judgment and compares it with the greater certainty of such judgment in neglecting the salvation spoken by the Lord himself. On the question of the identity of the intermediary or mediator, some Early Fathers and Reformers understood this to be Christ. The words ἐν χειρί *en cheiri* lit. "in the hand" or "by means of" a mediator is a Hebraism regularly used in the LXX of Moses as a spokesperson for God and this role

whole point being made, Longenecker[149] suggests, after a full treatment of the various options, is "the inferiority of the law because of its indirect introduction into the people's experience." George[150] can write of the law's "creaturely mediation." Also, McDonald[151] commenting upon v. 20 the "intermediary" and about "God is one," mentions the vast number of proposed interpretations. He gives some helpful insights:

> A "mediator" ... has the character of a "middle-man," an intermediary.... As already observed, the law came through the mediation of Moses; it came only indirectly from God. But the law did not end the estrangement between God and the people.... In the giving of God's covenant, no human mediation stood between.... Of the promise God is the one, and the only one, who originated and executes it. He, the giver, is everything; the recipient is nothing, for such stands before the One as a transgressor. God in the promise acts alone.

Hendriksen[152] also suggests that Moses served as a human link between God and the people, but "such an intermediary lacks independent authority. God however is *One*. When he made his promise to Abraham ... he did this on his own sovereign account, directly, personally."

I now turn attention to the second question regarding the Law: "Is the law then contrary to the promises of God?" Here we have a supplementary question following on from v. 19 where Paul sets out a possible logical conclusion i.e., the law is in opposition to the promises of God.[153] So the relationship of the God-sent law to Moses and the God-given promise to Abraham must be clarified. Even the suggestion of conflict between the law and the promises is met with the strong emotional response of the optative – used thirteen times in Paul – "Certainly not!" How could they be in opposition? The same God is the source of both – the law indirectly and the promise directly. Longenecker[154] explains that Paul, in a contrary to fact condition (which assumes the condition to be untrue), makes plain that "the association of 'law' and 'life' is a false one. 'Life' in Paul's thought is 'spiritual life' (cf. Rom 8:11; 1 Cor 15:22, 36; 2 Cor 3:6; see also John 6:63), which stands in antithesis to 'death' with which the law is associated." So, Paul affirms, "If a law had been given that could give life, then righteousness would indeed be by the law." But no such law could be

---

of mediator on behalf of Israel is commonly used of him in first century Judaism. Hendriksen, *Galatians*, 142, points to Deut 5:5 where Moses said, "I stood between the LORD and you at that time."

[149] Longenecker, *Galatians*, 142. So also Fung, *The Epistle to the Galatians*, 161, to show the law's inferiority as that which was not given directly from God.

[150] George, *Galatians*, 256. He further explains that Gnostic commentators interpreted the angels as evil cosmic powers. Marcion and Heracleon advocated that the giving of the law was the work of the demiurge. But in the text the subject of the aorist participle "put in place" should be understood as God, 257.

[151] McDonald, *Freedom in Faith*, 84.

[152] Hendriksen, *Galatians*, 143.

[153] Some MSS omit του θεου *tou theou* "of God" but evidence is still strong for their inclusion.

[154] Longenecker, *Galatians*, 144.

given. In spite of what is stated in Lev 18:5 and later in Rom 7:10[155] the law could not bring life because of sin in man. In fact, men break it every day and so it could never justify. McDonald[156] again maintains that, " Paul, by omitting the article before 'law', here fastens attention upon the inability of any of law's provisions to be life-giving. Among all the laws of Moses not one was ordained to accomplish that end. To give life belongs to the life-giving Spirit."

The only possible way to create a harmony between the law and the promise is to see that men inherit the promise because they cannot keep the law, and that their inability to keep the law makes the promise all the more desirable, indeed vital. As Hendriksen[157] explains:

> Only then when law and promise (works and grace) are both regarded as means whereby the sinner obtains salvation, can they be viewed as opponents. But as soon as it is understood that the two differ in their objectives – *the law* aiming to lead the sinner to Christ and his gracious promise; *the promise* "in Christ" aiming to save him – it becomes clear that they cannot be in conflict with each other.

Furthermore, Silva[158] suggests; "God did not give the Israelites a law that provided an alternative source of righteousness and thus thwarted the promise. No, the law *aided* the promise by shutting, imprisoning, locking up everyone under sin (3:22–23)." [Italics his]. This fact Paul goes on to affirm.

In v. 22 Paul makes plain that the Old Testament, "the Scripture," plainly declares the universality of sin so that the grace which was promised could come through faith to all who believe. He begins with a strong adversative particle, ἀλλά *alla*, "but" which sets out the contrast between the impossible hypothesis in v. 21 and the actual reality here. The reference to "Scripture" may look back to the quotation of Ps 143:2 in 2:16 or more likely to the immediate reference to Deut 27:26 in 3:10. The ὑπό ἁμαρτίαν *hupo hamartian* everything imprisoned "under sin" here can be equivalent to ὑπό κατάραν *hupo kataran* "under the curse." We are all in fact "confined" or "imprisoned" – the phrase τὰ πάντα *ta panta* (neuter), is being used to include people. Longenecker[159] explains that the Greek here:

> Has the effect of obliterating every distinction and referring to all humanity as an entity (so "all people" or perhaps better "everyone without distinction") ... Paul saw the law as functioning in a negative fashion ... and it brought condemnation in bringing all humanity under its curse. In effect, it was, as Lutheran theologians often call it "God's strange work" instituted to

---

[155] Lev 18:5 "If a person does them, he shall live by them" and Rom 7:10 the "commandment that promised life ... "
[156] McDonald, *Freedom in Faith*, 85.
[157] Hendriksen, *Galatians*, 143.
[158] Silva, *Explorations in Exegetical Method*, 188.
[159] Longenecker, *Galatians*, 144–45.

bring us to "God's proper work." It was not opposed to God's promises, for it operated in the economy of God on a different level or plane than did God's promises.

McDonald[160] maintains:

> The pregnant expression rendered "consigned all things to sin" is very emphatic. It means to shut up (cf. Rom 11:32), without any way of escape from the lordship of sin. ... The "all" is in the neuter – "all things." That makes the declaration all the more comprehensive; all without a single exception."

Witherington[161] also helpfully suggests we understand the neuter phrase "all things" apocalyptically. The reference can then be to the whole created order *including* humans. All feel the effects of the fall.

Therefore, Paul explains that we were all "under sin" and helpless to change that. We remember also his later affirmation in Rom 11:32 "God has consigned all to disobedience, that he may have mercy upon all." In fact, earlier in Rom 3:10–18 he quotes three books from Scripture, Psalms, Isaiah and Ecclesiastes to demonstrate that people everywhere are sinners. Because of this condition, blessing has to come not through the law (which we transgress) but through God's grace and because of the cross, i.e., through the one made a curse for us. Hendriksen[162] translates the statement here in v. 22 to show that Scripture has "locked up the whole world." He sees that Scripture and of course in this context, the law, "has shut in from every side without possibility of escape" the whole world (he takes the neuter τὰ πάντα *ta panta* to refer to "all mankind"). Sin is the "jail-keeper" which through the law holds all men under the sentence of condemnation. He adds to the OT references mentioned above Isa 1:5–6; Jer 17:9; Gen 6:11–12; 8:21; Job 40:4; Dan. 9:4ff.; Zech 3:3. He explains, "But with the help of the Holy Spirit, the prisoners' very consciousness of their galling bondage and of their total inability to burst their chains, causes them to yearn for a divine Deliverer and to shout for joy when they hear his approaching footsteps."

God has graciously provided such a deliverer. Paul affirms, "so that the promise by faith in Jesus Christ might be given to all who believe" (v. 22). The phrase, "by faith in Jesus Christ," is not a reference to the faithfulness of Christ, but to the fact that through the same "hearing with faith" as Abraham who "believed" (it appears that all of 3:6–29 is pointing back to 3:6) the blessings outlined in Galatians might come in all their fullness to us. The statement in the verse "to all who believe" is then being used to emphasise the words "through faith." The law brings us down, so that we

---

[160] McDonald, *Freedom in Faith*, 86.
[161] Witherington 111, *Grace in Galatia*, 260. See also Moo, *Galatians*, 239, who also sees the neuter form as indicating a broader reference to the whole cosmos i.e., Rom 8:18–22 where it is made subject to decay, the reversal set out here in Gal 6:15 with the "new creation."
[162] Hendriksen, *Galatians*, 144.

might be led to look away from ourselves and then by faith up to him whose work on the cross is all we need. Bruce[163] concludes, "The establishment of righteousness by faith as the way to life implies the inability and displacement of the law.... Far from being against the promises, then, the law drives men and women to flee from its condemnation and seek refuge in the promises." For Hendriksen,[164] "This wonderful Redeemer does something for sinners that the law was not able to do. He sets the prisoners free from the curse by taking it upon himself.... The term 'promise' used here, must be interpreted in its fullest, richest sense." Paul will set out an understanding of this "fullness" arising from our justification later in the chapter and in the following chapters. Certainly, this blessing of the promise is vitally important, but Paul will later discuss other blessings too.

Because of the Role of the Law vv. 23–24

Paul explains that God's purpose for our spiritual pilgrimage was that men should move from the law to the promise. The law is likened to a gaoler or prison in which we were held captive and then to a tutor whose discipline is harsh.

Firstly, Paul takes the reader back in time: "Now before faith came" (v. 23). Note that the article is here i.e., the verse can be read before "this" faith, or "the" faith came. There are different shades of meaning here concerning the interpretation of what Paul means by "before faith." These need some comment.

Excursus: Before Faith Came

Note first Dunn's[165] view; he mentions the use of the article, "the" faith, or "this" faith. He suggests however that it is not a reference to the body of belief, "the" faith, but "this" faith i.e., the faith just referred to in v. 22, that faith in Christ which is the proper focus for the fulfilment of the promise. Moo[166] also seems to understand this as human faith in its object, Christ; and Witherington[167] sees this reference "the faith" simply as a reference to Christ as he is also described as "the Seed" (3:16).

Bruce[168] however, maintains that we read it in the context of v. 22, "the promise by faith in Jesus Christ ... given to those who believe." This opens up two possibilities for him and both appear important. The phrase can be understood, "on the plane of

---

[163] Bruce, *The Epistle to the Galatians*, 180. See also Fung, *The Epistle to the Galatians*, 164–66.

[164] Hendriksen, *Galatians*, 145. Moo, *Galatians*, 240, sees the promise here as the justification which was originally promised to Abraham (v. 8) and sealed by the Spirit (v. 14), now extended to Gentiles, "to those who believe." We note with Hendriksen the idea of justification in "its fullest sense." This fullness is yet to be revealed in Galatians.

[165] Dunn, *The Epistle to the Galatians*, 197.

[166] Moo, *Galatians*, 241.

[167] Witherington 111, *Grace in Galatia*, 268.

[168] Bruce, *The Epistle to the Galatians*, 181. He first rejects Howard's suggestion that these statements about faith in Christ mean "through the faithful act of Christ," i.e., his death. The final phrase in v22 "to those exercising such faith" rules this out. See G. Howard, *Paul: Crisis in Galatia*, SNTSM 35 (Cambridge: Cambridge University Press, 1979), 58, 65.

salvation history," in which the coming of faith coincides with the appearance of Christ, "in which the parenthetic age of law was displaced with the age of faith (cf. 4:4)." But the phrase should also be understood, "in the personal experience of believers," coinciding with their abandonment of any attempt to achieve a righteous standing through law, rather than the righteousness that comes by faith in Christ. Actually, in summary, the fact that he relates the phrase to v. 22, the coming of faith in Jesus Christ means that Paul is thinking of "the gospel" in this age of faith as that in which believers place their trust – as Abraham in the past, he heard and believed.

Paul has already highlighted the fact that in the regions of Syria and Cilicia he had been preaching "the" faith he once tried to destroy (1:23). So here in 4:23 we should think in terms of "the" faith which has been revealed (not the experiential faith of the believers, either individually or collectively) i.e., the gospel is in view (note also 3:8, God preached "the gospel" beforehand to Abraham). Here it is a gospel which is focused on "the promise" (also mentioned in v. 22 as Bruce points out) and its fulfilment in Jesus Christ, through his bearing the curse for us on the cross. One needs to note not just the phrase in v. 23 itself, "until the coming faith would be revealed," but also v. 25, "now that faith has come." We are moving here from the age of law to the age of fulfilment (4:4f.); we are exercising "faith" in "the faith" i.e., the gospel as revealed in the coming of Christ.

In our understanding, the types and figures of the OT age have been seen in reality. What God decreed has come to pass; before our very eyes Christ has been portrayed as crucified; the work of the cross is accomplished. All that needs to be done for our salvation has been done by Christ at Calvary. The gospel is the fulfilment of the promise. We, like Abraham, need to believe God's word to us, the good news, and place our faith in Christ! As Hendriksen[169] explains, believers of the old dispensation "looked *forward*" while Paul and his converts "look *back*" and we "look *up*" to the exalted one.

To continue, George[170] actually translates v. 25 in this way, "Now that faith has come, we are *no longer under the supervision of the law*." Here Paul is maintaining that before the coming faith i.e., before the time of the fulfilment of the promise, we[171] "were held captive under the law." The verb will generally mean to confine or imprison using military guards. It was used of Paul when he was in Damascus (2 Cor 11:32; Acts 9:24; see another use also in Phil 4:7 of peace "guarding" our hearts and minds). Paul also writes of us being "imprisoned." In v. 22 we were all (Jews and Gentiles) "imprisoned under sin"; now we are confined (again Jews and Gentiles, see 3:13–14) under law which is also affirming the guilt of men, as the law only shows

---

[169] Hendriksen, *Galatians*, 145.

[170] George, *Galatians*, 250.

[171] Fung, *The Epistle to the Galatians*, 167, n. 1 makes clear that the text is referring to both Jews and Gentiles, although the latter did not have the law in the same form. "The statement 'we are no longer under a custodian' … is explained by the sentence 'you are all the sons of God in union with Christ Jesus' (v. 26); this suggests that the 'we' includes the 'you.'" See also v. 28.

up our sinfulness (Rom 3:20). Moo[172] points out that there are some scholars who wish the verb should also here have a positive meaning – a protective and benevolent role as in Phil 4:7 above. However, he notes: "yet the parallel between 'under the law' in this verse and 'under sin' in verse 22 as well as the obvious point that Paul views being *not* 'under the law' as a good thing, suggests that the idea tends toward the negative." So, many consider that the phrase "under the law" means that all are under condemnation, since they cannot keep the law i.e., they are under "the curse of the law" (3:13). Again, George[173] explained that in Jewish thought the law was considered a fence, a protective wall for the chosen people from the corruption of the ungodly nations. Paul used the same idea but "radicalized it" into a prison wall which would enclose, condemn and punish. He not only radicalized it but universalised it.[174] So we were imprisoned "until the coming faith would be revealed." Paul is drawing again, as we also noted above, on the apocalyptic concept of the two ages (1:4) in the use of "revealed" following "the interim epoch of the law."[175]

Hendriksen[176] comments on how the *moral* law brought to Jews a sense of guilt – while obliged to fulfil it, they were unable to do so. Rather than grasping the hope in the promised seed, they looked to obtain salvation *for* and *by* themselves. The law, the ceremonial, the embellishments by the rabbis, became an oppressive burden. "Because of their own stubbornness the law, in its most comprehensive sense, thus *held* the Jews *in strictest custody*."

Jews and Gentiles were kept "imprisoned" so that we cannot escape, by the law. However, Paul also speaks of the relationship with the law as being under a "guardian," using the term παιδαγωγὸς *paidagōgos*. Longenecker[177] explains that, "in antiquity a *paidogōgos* was distinguished from a *didaskalos* ("teacher") and had custodial and disciplinary functions rather than educative or instructional ones." Where there were well-to-do parents the new-born would first be placed in the care of a nurse or a "nanny" who would be in charge until they were around six years of age. They were then put under the supervision of the *paidogōgos*, who must oversee his continuing development. We are thinking about possibly an older slave not able to carry out more strenuous tasks, but having the wisdom and experience that comes with age, charged with the duty of conducting the boy to and from school, carrying his tablets, scrolls etc., not so much his teacher as his disciplinarian. He would be regarded as an important figure in the ancient household and was often harsh, administering the directives of the father, usually depicted in ancient drawings with a rod or cane in his hand. He would test his charge on his return from school to see for

---

[172] Moo, *Galatians*, 242.

[173] George, *Galatians*, 263.

[174] Hendriksen, *Galatians*, 145, having translated v. 22, "locked up the whole world under (the power of) sin," now adds "before this faith came, we were kept in custody under law, being locked up with a view to the faith that was to be revealed." He comments, "If *sin* is the jail-keeper, then so is *the law*, for sin derives its power from the law (1 Cor 15:56). It is through the commandment that sin becomes exceedingly sinful (Rom 7:13; see also 7:9 and 4:15)."

[175] Dunn, *The Epistle to the Galatians*, 198.

[176] Hendriksen, *Galatians*, 146.

[177] Longenecker, *Galatians*, 146.

himself what he had learned that particular day. He would therefore play an important role imposing discipline and necessary restraint during the boy's "minority," before his coming of age in his teenage years. Witherington[178] sees him as having a "confining and restrictive" role, in the light of v. 23. For Longenecker,[179] the picture of the law presented here by Paul is also a negative one:

> The point of the analogy is not that the Mosaic law was a positive preparation for Christ.... Rather, the focus here is on the supervisory function of the law, the inferior status of one under such supervision, and the temporary nature of such a situation in the course of salvation history.

The translation of the word *paidogōgos* as "schoolmaster" (KJV) has led many interpreters to think in terms of educating one's charge or seeking their moral advancement. It is true that when we get to Gal 5–6 we will find that advancement etc., is expected of the believer – as the fruit of the Spirit – and in fulfilling the "law of Christ" (6:1), but as George[180] affirms, "that function is clearly not within the scope of Paul's meaning here." The law expressed the will of God for his people, but men disobeyed and fell under its just condemnation. It rebukes, condemns and punishes us for our transgressions. But God did not intend that the oppression to be permanent; he gave the law in order to make the promise more desirable. "Before faith came" (v. 23) this was the case. So, the oppressive work of the law was temporary, intended ultimately to lead on to blessing. As Stott[181] explains the aim was, "to shut us up in prison until Christ could set us free, or to put us under tutors until Christ should make us sons." As v. 24 states, "until Christ came, in order that we might be justified by faith." Again, Moo[182] states:

> Probably, then, we should read verses 23–25 as a description of salvation history and especially of the movement of the old era when the law had a central role in governing the relationship between God and his people to the new era, in which the law no longer continues to function in this way.

The Greek reads, εἰς Χριστόν *eis Christon* "to Christ" but is best not understood as NIV "to lead us to Christ." The word εἰς *eis* is used in the same sense as in v. 23 meaning "until," not "to."[183] We were confined under the law in our sin "until" God took the initiative in love for lost humanity and sent his Son. For Longenecker and Bruce[184] the temporal sense is in view, as apparently also with Moo. Again "in order

---

[178] Witherington 111, *Grace in Galatia*, 266. Fung, *The Epistle to the Galatians*, 169, agrees that custody under the law is here a negative, not neutral state, hemming them in with its directions and judgments.
[179] Longenecker, *Galatians*, 148.
[180] George, *Galatians*, 266.
[181] Stott, *The One Way* 98. For Hendriksen, *Galatians*, 148, the law had "a preparatory and disciplinary nature."
[182] Moo, *Galatians*, 241.
[183] Moo, *Galatians*, 242–43 suggests a different translation for εἰς *eis* i.e., what he calls the "outdated" English "unto" as KJV. Paul is seeing salvation history as a series of events that lead up to or "with a view to" an eschatological climax. This is a helpful insight.
[184] Longenecker, *Galatians*, 149; Bruce, *The Epistle to the Galatians*, 183.

that we might be justified by faith" expresses the ultimate purpose of the law; not only does it bring about a knowledge of sin, increase sin and condemn men before God, but ultimately, still emphasising the temporal sense, points us to Christ and his coming, to the effecting of the promise through Christ's death for us to bring us by faith into justification.

Finally, in v. 25, as Paul affirms, "now that faith has come, we are *no longer* under a guardian" [italics mine]. This concept of guardian describes the role of the law before the gospel age. Since the coming of the Christ, the fulfilment of the promise, through the work of the cross and the gift of the Holy Spirit, as Bruce[185] explains "believers have come of age." We will see this in 4:1–4. So Longenecker[186] insists:

> The law no longer has validity as a *paidagōgos*, regulating the life of faith … no longer could it be argued that circumcision, Jewish dietary laws, following distinctly Jewish ethical principles, or any other matter having to do with a Jewish lifestyle were requisite for the life of faith. Certainly not for Gentile Christians in any sense, though Paul and the Jerusalem apostles for cultural, national, and /or pragmatic reasons allowed Jewish believers in Jesus to live a Jewish lifestyle, but not as required spiritually.

George[187] commenting upon an earlier verse – v. 19, the law was added until "the offspring should come" maintains:

> Paul here spoke of the temporal parameters and limited duration of the law. Just as it had a point of origin on Mount Sinai, so also it had a point of termination – Mount Calvary … Paul interpreted the law eschatologically in terms of its fulfilment and cancellation (cf. Col 2:14) in the messianic mission of Jesus.

Note that Paul again uses the article with πίστεως *pisteōs* "*the* faith has come," the full gospel now revealed "in Christ," which believers have embraced. As McDonald[188] succinctly puts it, "the custodian has withdrawn; the schoolmaster has stepped aside." We are a new creation, born again, justified in Christ and enabled of the Holy Spirit who now can guide and direct us – all through accepting the word of the gospel, as Abraham first believed. Again, we will see, as Witherington[189] affirms, that this is really what Gal 5:18 is saying "if you are led by the Spirit, you are not under the law." It is no accident that the verb "led" there is the verbal form of ἀγωγός *agōgos* which is part of the word pedagogue.

* * *

---

[185] Bruce, *The Epistle to the Galatians*, 183.
[186] Longenecker, *Galatians*, 149.
[187] George, *Galatians*, 254.
[188] McDonald, *Freedom in Faith*, 88.
[189] Witherington 111, *Grace in Galatia*, 266.

Finally, to recall our main stream of thought, the Galatians were foolish to seek salvation by "works of the law" for another reason.

Because of the Blessing of Faith vv. 25–29

Paul writes of what we are in Christ in the concluding verses of this section. Actually, for Moo,[190] these verses are the critical focus of Galatians and the heart of Paul's argument in chapters 3–4, "perhaps of the letter as a whole" – although regarding 6:14 he can still affirm the centrality and exclusivity of the cross. With regard to these verses, he suggests that the beginning of the paragraph (v. 7) makes the same point, introducing for the first time the language of "sons of God" and "by implication," sons *by faith*, not through the law (see vv. 15–25). No doubt becoming "sons of God," including heirship (3:29; 4:4–7) is the greatest gospel blessing.

Paul uses the explanatory particle γαρ *yar* "because" or "for." The law of Moses is no longer imprisoning or serving in the role of a pedagogue or custodian, *because* in Christ we are all sons of God[191] through faith. It is important to stress again that those addressed "we" in vv. 23–26 taken as Jews and Gentiles in v. 26 can now be among the "you" of v. 26 – through faith. Stott[192] makes the point regarding "all sons of God" that God is certainly the universal Creator who brought all things into existence; and universal King ruling over all, but he is the Father only of the Lord Jesus Christ and those adopted into his family through Christ. So also for George,[193] Paul was not advocating here:

> The Fatherhood of God and the brotherhood of man. He did not say that all persons were by nature children of God. He pointed to a decisive difference within the human family, the distinction between those who know God as Father through faith in Jesus Christ and others who remain under the curse of the law.

Note again that the emphatic "all" stresses the fact that Jews and Gentiles both share in this standing.[194] God is now our Father who in Christ has accepted and forgiven us. We shall see shortly (4:1–6) that we are neither prisoners awaiting final execution or minors but sons of God and heirs to his glorious kingdom. Earlier in this letter Paul has used "Son of God" as a title for the Lord Jesus (1:15–16; 2:20). He sees him as

---

[190] Moo, *Galatians*, 248.

[191] Fung, *The Epistle to the Galatians*, 166, reminds us that in 3:7–14 Paul has been largely focusing upon sonship to Abraham and has demonstrated that the men of faith are the true sons. The verses on law and promise had a different focus (3:15–22); but now sonship comes to the fore again (3:23–4:7); we are the true offspring of Abraham and sons of God.

[192] Stott, *The One Way: The Message of Galatians*, 99.

[193] George, *Galatians*, 292.

[194] "sons of God" was seen by Jews as true of them exclusively, because of God's election (Exod 4:22–23; Deut 14:1–2; Hos 11:1; see also e.g., in other Jewish books, Sir. 36.17; 3 Macc. 6.28; 4 Ezra 6.55–59; Ps. Sol. 17.26–27; Jub. 1.22–25 where it was applied to the Israel of the end-time, i.e., the eschatological gathering of God's people). Sonship in the Greco-Roman world also symbolised a certain status and rights of inheritance. Through faith believing Gentiles can be so described and now have this status with God.

uniquely and exclusively the Son of God, having equality with the Father. Yet he now uses this term of believers, Jews and Gentiles! Note as was stressed, Paul points out that this sonship of God is "in Christ," a description which is found 172 times in Paul affirming our participation in and union with him. Hendriksen[195] points out that this description is "not only a repeatedly recurring Pauline theme but also the central thought in the immediate context (verse 27)."

Paul now points out that this blessing is to "as many of you as were baptised into Christ." Dunn[196] expresses the view that this reference is "a metaphor drawn from the rite of baptism to describe the entry of the believer into Christian experience." It is however, faith that secures the union (v. 26 "through faith"), so that by this means one is "baptised into Christ." We should note that the symbolic act of water baptism, signifying cleansing and being raised again to new life (Acts 22:16; Rom 6:3–4) is a witness by all believers to their spiritual experience. As Stott[197] makes clear:

> This cannot possibly mean that the act of baptism itself unites a person to Christ, that the mere administration of water makes him a child of God. We must give Paul credit for a consistent theology. This whole epistle is devoted to the theme that we are justified through faith, not circumcision. It is inconceivable that Paul would now substitute baptism for circumcision and teach that we are in Christ by baptism! ... Faith secures the union; baptism signifies it outwardly and visibly.

For Moo[198] also water baptism is almost certainly in view here and was "the normal culminating event in a person's coming to Christ." However, it must be noted that baptism was not, in and of itself, a means of salvation:

Faith, which Paul repeatedly highlights in this passage and in his other letters, is the only means of coming into relationship with Jesus Christ. However, baptism is more than simply a symbol of that new relationship; it is the capstone of the process by which one is converted and initiated into the church. As such, Paul can appeal to baptism as 'shorthand' for the entire conversion experience.

What does v. 27 mean when it states that believers have "put on Christ?" One is reminded of the use of a similar idea in the LXX, "I put on righteousness," Job 29:14; Ps 132:9; being clothed with salvation, 2 Chron 6:41; of the "excellent wife," "strength and dignity are her clothing," Prov 31:25; also Zech 3:4, the High Priest Joshua who is "clothed in pure garments." Paul can use the metaphor elsewhere of putting on the Christian armour, Rom 13:12, Eph 6:11–17 and see also Col 3:10–12, Eph 4:24, putting on "the new self"; and as here, Rom 13:14 "putting on Christ."

---

[195] Hendriksen, *Galatians*, n. 109, 148–49. Moo also sees "in Christ" as "a fundamental concept of the letter (as it is in Paul's theology generally)," Moo, *Galatians*, 33.

[196] Dunn, Baptism in the Holy Spirit, 109.

[197] Stott, *The One Way: The Message of Galatians*, 99. See also Hendriksen, Galatians, 149.

[198] Moo, *Galatians*, 251.

When they were converted they knew, as Paul has just stated, what it was to be "baptised into Christ." The phrase, "putting on Christ" certainly has ethical implications. They must now seek to live like Christ, seeking to follow the example of Christ. Paul affirms in 4:19 that Christ is being "formed" spiritually in them, transforming their mind, attitudes, will. They are now called to live out a true Christian lifestyle, imitating Christ in their behaviour; this they can do because of the gift of the Holy Spirit (5:22–23). Witherington[199] maintains: "This pattern, and not the Mosaic law, is what Paul means when he speaks later of the 'law of Christ' which is fulfilled when one acts in Christ-like fashion, bearing one another's burdens."

In v. 28 Paul first speaks negatively of distinctions of race, social standing and biological gender; then positively that we are "all one in Christ Jesus." In addition, in Christ we belong not only to God (as sons) but to each other (as brothers and sisters). This presentation of triple equality will stand in marked contrast to the patterns of privileged status in the Jewish and Hellenistic culture of the ancient world. But while we need to recognise that these distinctions remained in first century society – Paul did not cease to be a Jew when he became a Christian – the whole Christian community had found an equality of acceptance in Christ.

So negatively, Paul writes, there is no distinction of *race:* "There is neither Jew nor Greek." Stott[200] explains:

> God called Abraham and his descendants (the Jewish race) in order to entrust to them His unique self-revelation. But when Christ came, God's promise was fulfilled that in Abraham's seed all the families of the earth would be blessed. This includes the nations of every race, colour and language. We are equal, equal in our need of salvation, equal in our inability to earn or deserve it, and equal in the fact that God offers it to us freely in Christ. Once we have received it, our equality is transformed into a fellowship, the brotherhood which only Christ can create.

Again, there is no distinction of *rank:* "Neither slave nor free." We are all now on the same level. Although we have this statement it is important to stress again that these verses are not affirming that these distinctions in society no longer will be recognised; but in the context the message is that there is an equality of acceptance in Christ regardless of one's status. George[201] explains that Paul did not anywhere argue outright for the abolition of slavery yet he gave guidance as to how Christian masters and slaves should relate to each other:

> Nowhere did Paul treat slavery as a divinely ordained institution, and, at least on one occasion, he declared that a slave could properly become "free" (1 Cor 7:21) ... Paul waged no campaign to eradicate slavery from the Roman Empire. Rather he simply gave instructions on how to carry out

---

[199] Witherington 111, *Grace in Galatia*, 278.
[200] Stott, *The One Way* 100.
[201] George, *Galatians*, 289. See also Moore, *The Letters to Timothy and Titus*, 151–52.

assigned work duties with appropriate Christian attitudes in *the then-existing institution of slavery.* [Italics mine].

Neither is there distinction of *sex:* "There is no male and female." If the Galatian churches were ever to revert to acceptance of a nomistic lifestyle, circumcision, ceremonial commitments and practices involving cleanness and uncleanness, things would become very different, as there were different requirements for men and women. All this had been done away with in Christ!

The change in construction – male *and* female no doubt will reflect the statement in Gen 1:27, "male and female he created them." Longenecker[202] notes the change in construction but suggests that it "implies no real change in meaning." We should note that these are not the Greek words just for man and woman but bring out the gender distinctions of male and female which is grounded in the ordinance of creation, prior to the fall.

Fung's[203] comments on these statements are helpful. He maintains that the three antitheses which reflect the distinctions of ancient society have been deliberately chosen because of the three-fold privilege a pious male Jew would daily thank God for – he was not created a Gentile, a slave, or a woman. These were categories who were excluded from certain religious privileges. As far as the third grouping, the more technical terms "no male and female," does not mean that in Christ mankind is restored to some "pristine androgynous state, nor even that male-female distinctions have been obliterated in Christ, any more than that there is no racial difference between the Christian Jew and the Christian Gentile."

Excursus: on Christian Equality

Today Gal 3:28 is often removed from its context and imported into arguments in either liberation or radical feministic theology. As far as egalitarian and complementarian arguments concerning a women's role in ministry, this verse cannot legitimately be used in the debate – rather those passages that directly concern the issue. As George[204] has pointed out:

> It is regrettable that recent discussions of this theme have obscured the amazing good news Paul set forth in this verse. There is a unity in the body of Christ and an equality of access to salvation through faith in Jesus.... Thus in respect to our standing before God, Jewish blood, free birth, and male sex count for nothing. The call of the gospel is radically egalitarian and completely universal.

---

[202] Longenecker, *Galatians*, 157.
[203] Fung, *The Epistle to the Galatians*, 175.
[204] George, *Galatians*, 292.

So as far as these distinctions are concerned, Paul is *not* saying that they do not exist but that they do not create barriers of fellowship. As McDonald[205] states, "sin levels all men to the same low position; grace lifts all men to the same high privilege." There is "a triad of Christian equality."[206] This equality means that we all have equal standing, equal acceptance, whether male and female. However, to again make the point, we know from other scriptures that while "male and female" have equality of acceptance they also may still have different roles in ministry.[207]

One final point mentioned by Moo is relevant.[208] He notes that the other places where these terms are used are allusions to the creation account (Matt 19:4; Mark 10:6; cf. Rom 1:26–27). One reason he suggests for Paul to include these terms here is, "his concern in Galatians to recast the fundamental nature of the world in light of Christ: his coming means a 'new creation,' 'in which neither circumcision nor uncircumcision mean anything' (Gal 6:15)." So, Paul is highlighting what it means to be part of the "new creation"; also emphasising that there was no marginalizing of women.

Note that v. 29 should not be treated as just an afterthought; it is the concluding statement. It is a condition of fact ("if … then") which assumes the truth that is being affirmed. Paul can say in v. 29 "And if you are Christ's," literally "if you are of Christ," which will be identical in meaning to the phrase, "in Christ Jesus," then again, you are Abraham's offspring[209], v. 29, whether male or female, in slavery or free, Jew or Greek. We remember again, that in v. 16 the promises were spoken "to Abraham and his seed." As Moo[210] explains:

> In that verse, Paul interprets "seed" σπέρμα *sperma* in its singular sense, referring to Christ. But Christ is a corporate person. By faith one can enter into union with Christ and be counted, with him, as the "seed" to whom the promises were made. At the same time being the "seed" of Abraham is equivalent to being his "sons" or "children" (3:7). And so the argument comes full circle.

Believers are heirs, not of the inheritance of any land provisions of the covenant with Abraham (these are not mentioned in Galatians), but of the blessing of new birth, justification; also, as we will see, of full sonship and heirship and the enabling power

---

[205] McDonald, *Freedom in Faith*, 90.

[206] George, *Galatians*, 285. He also makes reference to commonly accepted patterns of the time. Hellenistic men would thank the gods that they were born as humans and not as beasts, slaves or women. He finds a similar attitude among Jews in the "benedictions" found in Jewish morning prayers i.e., that God did not make the worshipper a foreigner, a slave or a woman. See *The Authorized Daily Prayer Book of the United Hebrew Congregations of the British Commonwealth of Nations*, tr. S. Singer (London: Eyre & Spottiswoode, 1962), 6–7.

[207] See Moore, *The Letters to Timothy and Titus*, 98–105.

[208] Moo, *Galatians*, 254.

[209] As McDonald states, "You are of Abraham's family, even if you are not of Abraham's nation," McDonald, *Freedom in Faith*, 90.

[210] Moo, *Galatians*, 255.

of the Holy Spirit all through the cross! Without circumcision we take our place in the succession of faith down the centuries, spiritual heirs to the promise which God made to Abraham. Of "heirs according to promise," McDonald[211] says, "This is the peak of the promise." There is therefore more than simply justification here, contra Hendriksen. Fung[212] takes the three blessings just mentioned as, "intimately linked together as different expressions for the fulfilment of the promise. From this we may infer that these three are not separate and distinct experiences but closely interwoven parts or aspects of the single experience of faith-union with Christ." Oh the foolishness of the Galatians to go back to the works of the law! If we are "under the law," we are still imprisoned, like children under a pedagogue. But if "in Christ" then we need to understand that we are the inheritors of the promise, involving the above three-fold experience, regenerated by the Holy Spirit who moves in our hearts and brings us to "the hearing of faith,' we are justified, heirs of the promise and constituted sons of God; the cross has perfectly met our need. And we will yet see that our relationship to the law is different. These final verses of this chapter, as we mentioned, conclude the argument begun in 3:6 and now look forward to Paul's affirmations about our full status as sons and heirs.

* * *

---

[211] McDonald, *Freedom in Faith*, 90.
[212] Fung, *The Epistle to the Galatians*, 177.

GALATIANS FOUR

Gal 4:1–31. What we are in Christ

The opening verses of chapter 4 show no real break as far as the thought is concerned. Paul has set out what it meant for people to be living "under the law" (3:23–25) and then living "in Christ" (3:26–29); while he employs λέγω δέ *legō de* ("but I say") to introduce the clarification and progression of his argument regarding the heir (3:29). He now illustrates this in 3:23–29 through the analogy of a "child" or a "minor" νήπιος *nēpios*[1] growing up in a household, although he is κύριος *kurios* lit. "Lord" or "owner of everything" (4:1–7). There is also a contrast between being "no different from a slave" and a son. In the first state, "the guardians control his person and the trustees his property."[2] As Hendriksen[3] explains, "he is heir *de jure* (by right) but not as yet *de facto* (in fact)." But there is "a date set by his Father" (v. 2). For Longenecker,[4] the basic message is clear:

> The guardianship of the Mosaic law was ... when God's people were in their spiritual minority; but now with the coming of Christ, the time set by the Father has been fulfilled and Christians are now to live freely as mature sons "in Christ," not under the law's supervision.

We will see that v. 2 "the date set by his Father," parallels the eschatological time set by God and highlighted in v. 4.

Sons and Not Infants vv. 1–7

Where we were

Paul writes of man's condition under the law (vv. 1–3), where the man was regarded as an heir during his childhood. In Roman law,[5] only when a young man reached the age of fourteen would he become a free agent. Paul explains until that time like a minor – literally νήπιός *nēpios* "infant" in a great estate although lord of all by title, he is no better off than a slave – the ἀλλά *alla* "but" in v. 2 brings out the contrast. He

---

[1] Paul elsewhere uses the word for spiritual immaturity (1 Cor 3:1; 13:11; Eph 4:14; 1 Thess. 2:7; also see Heb 5:13). Here the meaning is an infant who has not yet reached maturity or adulthood. Moo suggests that it is understood here as a technical legal term meaning "one who is not yet of legal age, *minor, not yet of age,"* Moo, *Galatians*, 258.

[2] McDonald, *Freedom in Faith*, 91.

[3] Hendriksen, *Galatians*, 156.

[4] Longenecker, *Galatians*, 161.

[5] Commentators are not certain which inheritance laws Paul has in mind here, whether Roman, Greek or the Phrygian cities of South Galatia. Longenecker suggests that since the latter allowed the appointment of both "guardians" and "managers" and were flexible about the age when a boy reached maturity, Paul may well have these laws in mind. Longenecker, *Galatians*, 163. Let us not forget that Paul is simply using an illustration, whatever the source or combined sources.

is under "guardians" or restraint and "managers"[6] and will remain like this until the date set by his Father. Paul makes a comparison; so in the same way "we also" were enslaved – the phrase is emphatic. It can be suggested, in the discussion of who Paul has in mind writing of "we," that it is not Jews but the Christians or believers that are in view i.e., he is writing inclusively. McDonald[7] explains, "It is descriptive of their pre-Christian days." We were enslaved although heirs of the promise God gave to Abraham. But we had not inherited it yet. We were like children in a form of bondage – bondage to what Paul refers to as the "elementary principles of the world" or, noting other suggested translations, "elemental spirits" or "elemental forces."[8] George[9] comments that "a more sinister shadow falls across the page" with this particular verse.

The Greek word στοιχεῖα *stoicheia* ("elements" in v. 3), can have a range of basic meanings. Firstly the term was used of stakes set out in rows, a boundary or a place to hang nets[10], but developed to refer to "elementary or primary things" e.g., as letters of the alphabet, the ABC's which we learn at school. Secondly, since the ABCs are regarded as the "elements" out of which words and sentences are built up, the word was then used of "elements" which make up the material world, things associated in the ancient world, either the physical elements (earth, fire, air and water) or the heavenly bodies (sun, moon and the stars). It is in connection with this latter sense that the word can refer to the spiritual powers or cosmic forces which lie behind the heavenly bodies. Furthermore, it can mean the basic and rudimentary teachings of any religion, as for example, in Heb 5:12, "For though by this time you ought to be teachers, you need someone to teach you again the basic principles of the oracles of God." But in Col 2:8, 20 the phrase is translated "the elemental spirits of the world."[11]

How then do we see the term being used by Paul in the letter to the Galatians? Firstly, we must consider its use in v. 3; later we will return to how Paul uses it in vv. 8–11. In the context, the reference must be to everyone who was living "under law" (v. 5).

---

[6] Witherington suggests that the former term has the specific meaning of the guardian of an *orphaned* child, taking on the task of the development of character and education voluntarily, while the latter, an estate manager, refers normally to a trusted slave in the master's household (Luke12:42) who would oversee the minor's property. Witherington, 111, *Grace in Galatia*, 284. This distinction is not all important; the main emphasis is that the minor is under supervision and not free. Moo also makes the point that Paul is using sufficient analogies to the experiences of his readers to make the illustration meaningful, perhaps taking a few liberties to make a particular impact in their situation. Moo, *Galatians*, 259.

[7] McDonald, *Freedom in Faith*, 92. For Fung also, *The Epistle to the Galatians*, 181, the "we" of vv. 3–5 includes the "you" of v6, "the Galatian converts of Gentile origin."

[8] The first translation is by Stott, *The One Way*, 103; the second by Bruce, *The Epistle to the Galatians*, 191.

[9] George, *Galatians*, 295.

[10] McDonald, *Freedom in Faith*, 92.

[11] Bruce, *The Epistle to the Galatians*, 193, with regard to seeing the στοιχεῖα *stoicheia* as elements in the material world, refers to Philo (*Aet. Mund*, 109, *Vit. Cont.,* 3 and *Decal* 53) and Callisthenes in Ps.-Callisthenes (*Alexander Romance*, 1.1). He notes in these writings how these elements have often been deified and given the names of divinities. Some scholars accept that the word was being used for spiritual beings on Paul's time; others e.g., Moo, that the word appeared only in the post-NT period – see Test. of Solomon 8.2; 18.2 (first-third century AD. Moo, *Galatians,*, 261.

Bruce[12] points out that this time was not merely a time of elementary education but was also a time of bondage. He also asks, "Why are they called the στοιχεῖα *of the world*? … In what sense could it be said that the Galatian Christians in their pagan days were under the same στοιχεῖα as had controlled Paul and his fellow-Jews?" He will explain this in vv. 9–10. Yet at this point in his exposition of Galatians he can affirm it is clear that law ranks or is included as one of the στοιχεῖα *stoicheia* and is an instrument of spiritual bondage!

Longenecker[13] also comments on the phrase "the elementary principles of this world" and points out that while the phrase would have been understood by Greeks "cosmologically" (elements of the natural world), Paul may be thinking of "worldly" principles, in the same way as Hebrews 9:1, when focusing upon the tabernacle, refers to a "worldly sanctuary" (KJV, or ESV "an earthly" place of holiness). So "to return to life 'under the law' is to return to living 'under the basic principles of the world'… it was the Mosaic law in its condemnatory and supervisory functions that comprised the Jews' 'basic principles' of religion."

George[14] explains that there have been three basic interpretations when it comes to the *stoicheia*. These have been highlighted already: (1) Basic principles, which for the Gentile Christians to go back to the Mosaic law would be like a university graduate going back to kindergarten; (2) The material elements of the universe, earth, water, air and fire, which became personified deities; (3) The elements as spiritual powers, which is the interpretation he favours. The spiritual powers are real, existing still under the permissive will of God; they are under the orders of a personal devil; while Christ has dethroned them, men and women are still in a lifelong struggle against the evil designs of these elemental spirits. We will see in v. 9 that for the Gentile Christians to add to their faith in Christ, circumcision and the ceremonies of the law, would be no different to succumbing again to their former subservient status under the elemental powers![15]

Excursus: The Galatians and the Law

Further consideration must be given to the relationship of the Galatian Christians to the law. It has already been noted in chapter 2 that when the law was first given it was not with the purpose of obtaining God's favour, since Israel already had a relationship with God by means of election and by redemption from Egypt. Therefore, the law did not make them God's people, but set out in ten statements with the rest of the covenantal stipulations how they should live *because* they had this

---

[12] Bruce, *The Epistle to the Galatians*, 194.

[13] Longenecker, *Galatians*, 166.

[14] George, *Galatians*, 298–99.

[15]George, *Galatians*, 315. Hendriksen, *Galatians*, 157, explains that although there was nothing wrong in principle with the law, the Jews and proselytes to the Jewish religion began to look upon law observance as the way to achieve salvation. Also, the same was happening with regard to the prescriptions and ordinances by which the worshippers of pagan deities were seeking redemption. "By all such means, whether Jewish or pagan, men were putting themselves in bondage."

relationship with God. Here we have learned that, as Longenecker[16] explains, the law served: (1) a condemnatory function, revealing God's standard and the means of repentance were the sacrifices; and (2) a custodial function as a religious system instituted by God until Christ should come. So, the teaching of Paul here is that those who are now "in Christ" are to live as mature sons of God, no longer under slavery to legal prescriptions. Since the coming of Christ Paul tells us we are no longer under a supervisory guardian (3:25).

It must be remembered, as noted earlier, that the Ten Commandments were only a part of a broader covenantal agreement required of the people of Israel – there were over 600 stipulations which they were expected to observe![17] Paul's teaching in Rom 7:6 stresses that we do not walk in the oldness of the letter. We must not understand our responsibility to be like the old situation of the Israelites. Regarding covenantal stipulations, four of the OT books contain these stipulations, Exodus, Leviticus, Numbers and Deuteronomy. But none are binding upon us *unless* they are renewed in the new covenant.

It is clear that some stipulations of the old covenant have clearly not been renewed in the new covenant. *Civil law,* with its various penalties when one was tried in Israel; *Ritual law*, which gave details of the priest's duties, details of the sacrifices, animals to be used, their ceremonial killing, cooking and eating, all part of the OT worship of God. Jesus, by his once for all sacrifice has brought these sacrifices to an end. But there are certain aspects of the *Ethical law* actually restated in the new covenant – see Matt 5:21–48, Eph 6:1–3. Can these not be considered part of the New Testament "law of Christ" (Gal 6:2)? Fee and Stuart summarise as follows:

> Included in such a category would be the ten commandments, since they are cited in various ways in the New Testament as still bearing upon Christians (see Matt 5:21–37; John 7:23), and the two great commandments from Deuteronomy 6:5 and Leviticus 19:18. No other specific Old Testament laws can be proved to be strictly binding on Christians, valuable as it is for Christians to know all of the laws.[18]

It should be noted that the commandments that are part of the new covenant do not include the 4th commandment. Believers met from the beginning on the 1st day of the week (John 20:19; Acts 20:7), although the principle of rest one day a week is something that should be considered. Actually, the rest of God into which we enter by faith in Hebrews 4:9–11 is the fulfilment of the Sabbath. So, Sabbath observance (Saturday) is NOT required of Christians – it was not one of the stipulations agreed at the Council of Jerusalem which Gentile Christians were asked to observe to maintain harmony or social contact with their Jewish brethren. In fact, there was no requirement to general submission to the Jewish law and in particular no need either for circumcision; only the bare minimum of requirements was laid upon the church,

---

[16] Longenecker, *Galatians*, 177.

[17] See, Moore, *The Letters to Timothy and Titus*, 62.

[18] G. Fee and D. Stuart, *How to Read the Bible for All it is Worth* (Bletchley: Scripture Union, 1993), 54.

abstinence from idol meat, from blood, from things strangled and from immorality (Acts 15:28–29), but no Sabbath observance.

The commandments of the law, as noted in Gal 2 are really filled out in the teaching of Jesus e.g., the Sermon on the Mount and in the rest of the NT. In this sense, but only in this sense, we have part, as we will see later, of what Paul calls in Gal 6:2 "the law of Christ." We will discover that in Paul generally, and in Galatians in particular, the Christian life is basically life in the Spirit which is living a life of obedience to the Lord and producing the spiritual fruits of the Holy Spirit through his enabling. This will be clearly reflected as we proceed in our exposition of Galatians. One needs to stress that Christians will first trust Christ and his work on the cross alone for their salvation; a life of obedience in the power of the Holy Spirit is *not* to accomplish their own salvation; it is obeying Christ in love. Shortly we will return to the theme of the στοιχεῖα *stoicheia* when we reach v. 10. We will see that when one seeks to obtain acceptance through works i.e., obedience to the law, one will become trapped in Satan's deception. The law which remaining "holy and righteousness and good" (Rom 7:12) can still become not just an instrument of death (Rom 7:9–11), but an instrument of Satan. See the earlier reference concerning Col 2:8, 20 to "elemental spirits" – the rarity of the phrase will make it more likely that it has the same meaning in both books.

* * *

What He Did

Here in vv. 4–7 we learn of God's action through Christ.

WHEN? Verse 4 marks a new beginning or epoch "the fullness of time," the time before set in the providence of God. For McDonald,[19] it was a time not only divinely fixed but "historically fitting." It was an age when there were good Roman roads, the *pax Romana*, a single language in the empire, the presence of Jewish synagogues in many places, enabling Christian missionaries to reach Jews, proselytes and Godfearers to hear and also at that time, a certain cohesion to society. One could conclude that the old gods of Greece and Rome were losing their hold on the people and man's inability under the law was clear (Mal 4:4–6). All was getting ready, and it was the coming of Christ (3:24) which brought the arrival of the divinely ordained epoch.[20] At this time the people of God would enter into their mature status.

---

[19] McDonald, *Freedom in Faith*, 93.

[20] Longenecker has explained that the idea of the arrival of this moment in the plan of God is evident in Jesus' consciousness (Mark 1:15; Luke 1:21; the early church, Acts 2:16–36; 3:18; see also Matt 1:22; 2:15, 17, 23; 3:15; 4:14; 5:17; 8:17; 13:35; 21:4; 27v9; John's quotations, 2:17; 12:15, 38, 40; 19:24, 36, 37; Paul, Acts 13:27; Rom 3:26; 5:6; Eph 1:10 and the quotations in Galatians itself, 3:6, 8, 10, 11, 12, 13, 16; 4:27, 30; 5:14, *Galatians*, 170. Moo also can add that the phrase can refer to "the moment in salvation history when God deemed it appropriate to initiate the work of redemption." Moo, *Galatians*, 265.

WHO? "God." He did two things: he took the initiative when we could do nothing to save ourselves and sent his Son. This concept of the "sending" of the Son in found clearly in four passages of the NT (Gal 4:4–5; Rom 8:3–4; John 3:16–17; 1 John 4:9–10).[21] The sending of the Son will imply also his pre-existence – he was there to be sent.[22] As Bruce[23] claims, "If the Spirit was the Spirit before God sent him, the Son was presumably the Son before God sent *him*." Hendriksen[24] points out that, "Other children do not exist in any real sense before they are conceived in the womb. It is by means of conception and birth that they come into existence. But God's Son existed already from eternity with the Father." He is "Son" of course in an ontological sense. For George,[25] in this statement "God sent forth his Son" we have:

> Divine intentionality and eternal deity…. Not only was the incarnation the fulfilment of myriads of Old Testament prophecies, but it was the culmination of a plan devised within the eternal counsel of the triune God before the creation of the world.

HOW? "Born of woman, born under the law." Here is the way he was sent. God's Son was born of a human mother.[26] He took upon himself humanity. McDonald[27] states, "He came both born of woman and born under law. The word for 'born' is the same in each place." Moo[28] can point out that, "the participial clauses describe the nature of the sending, a sending that involved *taking on* the state of being human and Jewish." So, he submitted to all the requirements of the law, taking its yoke upon himself. His perfect obedience to the law meant that he could become the redeemer of those who failed to keep it. Longenecker[29] looks at the two participial clauses; the first, "'born of a woman,' speaks of Jesus' true humanity and representative quality, – i.e., that he was truly one with us … to stand in our place." The second, coming not just as "the Man" but "the Jew," meant he "was under obligation to God's Torah, so fulfilling the requirements of the law in his life (Matt 5:17–18) and bearing the law's curse in his death (cf. Gal 3:13; Phil 2:8)." This, of course was "for us" (3:13). Hendriksen[30] also points out the significance of these statements about Jesus Christ. He was one person, divine and human – *divine* to give his sacrifice "infinite value"

---

[21] Some scholars point to the influence of Wisdom 9:10–17 upon Paul here. There is of course the Christian tradition of Jesus' own self-consciousness expressed in the parable of the Wicked Tenants e.g., Mark 12:6. Here also one finds links between sonship and inheritance.

[22] George, *Galatians*, 301, notes Paul's other references to the pre-existence of the Son, 1 Cor 8v6; 10:4; Col 1:15–17; Rom 8:3; Phil 2:5–9.

[23] Bruce, *The Epistle to the Galatians*, 195. Elsewhere Paul can refer to his pre-existence as the wisdom of God in relation to creation (1 Cor 1:24, 30; 8:6b; Col 1:15–17) and whose presence was continually with Israel in the wilderness (1 Cor 10:4).

[24] Hendriksen, *Galatians*, 159.

[25] George, *Galatians*, 301.

[26] Luther points out that "Christ was made true and very man of womankind. As if he said, he was born not of man and woman, but only of womankind. Therefore when he nameth but only the womankind, it is the same when he saith: 'made of a woman,' as if he said: 'made of a virgin.'" Luther, *A Commentary on St. Paul's Epistle to the Galatians*, 353.

[27] McDonald, *Freedom in Faith*, 94.

[28] Moo, *Galatians*, 266.

[29] Longenecker, *Galatians*, 171.

[30] Hendriksen, *Galatians*, 159.

and *human* since it was man who sinned "it is also man who must bear the penalty and render his life to God in perfect obedience." Concerning "born under law" and therefore under *personal* obligation to keep the law, he adds, "but also of being duty-bound (with a duty to which he had voluntarily bound himself) *vicariously* to bear the law's penalty and to satisfy its demand for perfect obedience."

WHY? Two reasons are here, expressed in two ἵνα *hina* "in order that" clauses; Fung[31] explains, "the second will show the purpose or intended result of the first."

The first clause states that the Son came "to redeem those who are under the law." Paul uses an appropriate term here. Firstly, the word "redeem" reminds us of how we were slaves and in bondage of the law even as Gentiles (Rom 2:14–15). This term "redeem" also points us back to 3:13; there the way of our redemption is clearly expressed as Jesus "becoming a curse for us." The sinless one took the place of the guilty; on the cross, he took the curse for us. Then the second reason he came, the result of our redemption, "that we might receive the adoption of sons." Note McDonald has stressed that the adoption is not something which everyone naturally becomes through the cross; it has to be "received" and "received" by faith as 3:26 has expressed. Longenecker[32] finds here in these two statements first, God's purpose "to redeem" and the need for humanity's response "that we might receive."

As Stott[33] has explained, the divinity, the humanity and the righteousness of Christ uniquely qualified him to be man's perfect redeemer:

> If He had not been man, He could not have redeemed men. If He had not been a righteous man, He could not have redeemed unrighteous men. And if He had not been God's Son, He could not have redeemed men for God or made them the sons of God.

Bruce[34] explains therefore that 4:4 "constitutes the divinely ordained epoch for the people of God to enter into their inheritance as his mature and responsible sons." This takes in both Jews and Gentiles.

What we Received

We are placed as sons and heirs. This has been in Paul's mind in 3:18, 29; now he sets it out again. Is this not the highest gospel blessing? Note as Moo[35] explains, there is a chiastic structure in vv. 4–5. The text says: God sent his *Son* (A) ... born *under the law* (B) in order that he might redeem *those under the law* (B'), in order that we might receive the adoption as sons (A').

---

[31] Fung, *The Epistle to the Galatians*, 182.
[32] Longenecker, *Galatians*, 172.
[33] Stott, *The One Way*, 106.
[34] Bruce, *The Epistle to the Galatians*, 194.
[35] Moo, *Galatians*, 266.

Paul (and only Paul in the NT) uses this word υἱοθεσία *huiothesia* of believers in various contexts (Rom 8:15, 23; Eph 1:5). His use of it of Jews in what appears to be almost a traditional description of special status suggests that it would be recognised within Judaism (Rom 9:4–5). It is clear that adoption terminology was also used in contemporary practice among Roman emperors in the 1st century, with men not related directly by blood being adopted to succeed them, giving them heirship and the power to govern. Adoption is the "twin truth" of regeneration. Regeneration is about nature (2 Pet 1:4); adoption is about our status as sons. With regard to the Jews, in addition to the above, the truth of adoption is seen in the OT in Yahweh's relation to Israel his "first-born son" (Exod 4:22; Hos 11:1). The Hosea reference is then applied to Christ in Matt 2:15 – he was the Son who was all that Israel was meant to be but failed to be. By his death he brings "many sons to glory" (4:7; Heb 2:10). Hendriksen[36] comments that God sent his Son "that we might not only be delivered from the greatest evil but might also be crowned with the choicest blessing." Moo,[37] in his discussion of the concept, while he acknowledges that it "undoubtedly alludes" to the Greek and/or Roman practice of adoption, stressing legal rights and privileges, and "the legal practice of adoption has no real precedent in the OT or Judaism, the concept of being God's son, or sons is "deeply rooted" in the OT. See Exod 4:22; Jer 31:20; Rom 9:4, for the status of Israel; 2 Cor 6:18; 2 Sam. 7:14 "in terms of all Christians." He states:

> In claiming that Christians enjoy υἱοθεσία, then, Paul is claiming not only that we believers become his adopted children, with all the rights and privileges pertaining to their status, but also that we have become his own people, inheriting the status and blessings promised to his people Israel.

Who we Have

Being now sons, we have the Holy Spirit; as the Son was "sent forth," so the Spirit is also "sent forth" (same word) into our hearts. The "heart" here is the seat of the will or one's intellectual, moral and emotional life. God has sent "The Spirit of his Son."[38] Hendriksen[39] notes in light of the phrase "his Son," that, "all three persons" of the Holy Trinity are indicated in this passage, and their harmonious co-operation as the one true God is beautifully set forth.... He is the Spirit of the Son because he proceeds from the Son (John 15:26), as well as from the Father." For Bruce,[40] this phrase is emphasising that believers are indwelt by the same Spirit that indwelt him. Witherington[41] is of the opinion that it is rather that the Holy Spirit is the one who

---

[36] Hendriksen, *Galatians*, 160.

[37] Moo, *Galatians*, 268.

[38] The phrase "the Spirit of his Son," is unique in Paul and in Galatians, and so omitted in P46, Marcion, Augustine. Paul however can use other similar expressions "Spirit of Christ" (Rom 8.9), "Spirit of sonship" (Rom 8:15), "Spirit of the Lord" (2 Cor 3:17), "the Spirit of Christ Jesus" (Phil 1:19). See also Acts 16:7; 1 Pet 1:11.

[39] Hendriksen, *Galatians*, 161. He adds "the salvation that was *bought* for God's people by the Son will not avail unless it is also *wrought* in their hearts by that Son's Spirit."

[40] Bruce, *The Epistle to the Galatians*, 199.

[41] Witherington, 111, *Grace in Galatia*, 290–91.

forms Christ in the believer, who remodels us (see 3:27; 2 Cor 3:17) enabling us to live a life following the pattern of the Son. Once again Paul is highlighting the importance of us initially having the Holy Spirit (as in 3:2, 5, 14). Regarding this eschatological ministry of the Spirit, Moo[42] points out that the concept of sending the Spirit "into our hearts" continues:

> The allusion to the prophetic expectation of the ministry of God's Spirit: 'I will give you a new heart and put a new spirit within you; I will remove from you your heart of stone and give you a heart of flesh. And I will put my Spirit in you … and move you to follow my decrees and be careful to keep my laws' (Ezek 36:26–27; see also Jer 31:31–34). The ministry of the Spirit, as Paul will argue explicitly in 5:13–6:10, is what enables God's people in the new covenant to 'follow his laws'; no longer, however, to fulfil the will of God as found in torah, but as found in the eschatological torah, the 'law of Christ' (6:2).

What is the significance of the cry "Abba, Father?" Jesus himself used this term in addressing his Father in Mark 14:36. "Abba" αββα from אַבָּא is here an Aramaic diminutive, a term used expressing the affectionate intimacy of a family relationship. George[43] makes the point that the word "is not so much associated with infancy as it is with intimacy. It is a cry of the heart, not a word spoken calmly with personal detachment and reserve, but a word we 'call' or 'cry out' (*krazō*)." As here, Rom 8:15 also affirms this of believers. In Romans the believer cries out to God the Father; here the neuter participle agreeing with the neuter gender "spirit," presents the Spirit as crying out from within us. The point is that the Holy Spirit makes us conscious of, or gives us assurance of, our new relationship as we draw near to God. Hendriksen[44] explains:

> In reality the outcry of joyful recognition, sweet response, appropriating love, overwhelming gratitude, and last but not least, filial trust, is ascribed to the Spirit. Nevertheless, this must be understood mediately…. Similarly, in connection with the church's yearning for Christ's return we read, "And the Spirit and the bride say Come" (Rev 22:17). Here, too, the bride is moved by the Spirit. Spirit and bride always work together (Rom 8:16).

Moo[45] also explains regarding the Spirit who "cries" that the apostle, "undoubtedly thinks of the Spirit crying out through our own voices: see the parallel in Rom 8:15 … Paul perhaps uses a word picture to convey the deep and emotional reaction within the believer's heart to the joyful conviction brought by God's Spirit, that we are, indeed God's sons."

---

[42] Moo, *Galatians*, 269–70.
[43] George, *Galatians*, 307.
[44] Hendriksen, *Galatians*, 162.
[45] Moo, *Galatians*, 270.

Here we have non-Aramaic speaking Christians also – the Greek equivalent ὁ πατήρ *ho patēr* is placed alongside "Abba;" they are also "prompted by the Spirit"[46] to express their acceptance and nearness to God. Stott[47] explains:

> He (God) sent his Son that we might have the *status* of sonship, and He sent His Spirit that we might have an *experience* of it. This comes through the affectionate, confidential intimacy of our access to God in prayer, in which we find ourselves assuming the attitude and using the language not of slaves, but of sons.

Clearly, we have a changed status, not through our own merit, or our own efforts. Rather than imprisoned under law (enslaved by the *stoicheia* of this world), in the control of a slave attendant, the contrast is that "through God," i.e. his initiative of grace in his Son, who redeemed us, sent his Spirit to regenerate and live in us, now we are delivered from the curse of the law, and are adult sons and heirs. But we must not forget that it took the *giving* of a Son for the *making* of a son! Our blessing is through his work and not ours. This is why we glory in the cross.

Here v. 7 can affirm concerning us, "so, you are no longer a slave, but a son." The word ὥστε *hōste* is the conclusion of all that Paul has been teaching, not just the illustration in 4:1–6 but throughout what some have identified as his *probato* from 3:1. He refers to what we have left behind and then what we have received. The employing of the second person singular here (εἰ *ei* "you"), is making this personal for every Galatian believer (and ourselves) – see a similar use in 6:1. In 3:25 Paul has stressed that when we are "in Christ" then "no longer" are we under the law as a guardian; here he also emphasises that we are "no longer" a slave. As Hendriksen[48] has affirmed, "For him the way to the Father's heart is no longer blocked. Every valley has been raised, every mountain and hill made low, the crooked turns have been straightened, and all rough places have been made smooth. There are no longer any obstructions. Grace has removed them all."

As we will now see (v. 7b), literally, "and so," through Christ's death we are free as sons and heirs with the power to live a different lifestyle through the indwelling Holy Spirit.[49] Fung[50] reminds us, "For the Galatian Christians to put themselves under the law (or the *stoicheia* of the world) would, therefore, be to revert to spiritual infancy, whereas they were already God's full-grown sons and heirs." Note not just "a son" but the repetition of "an heir," as was stressed in v. 1 and also 3:29. All this has come about "through God."[51] Hendriksen[52] reminds us that "the sovereign, divine, nature of

---

[46] Witherington, 111, *Grace in Galatia*, 291.
[47] Stott, *The One Way*, 107.
[48] Hendriksen, *Galatians*, 162–63.
[49] Note the εἰ δέ *ei de* ("and so") here in v7. The "and" is expressing a continuance of, or further blessings we have received and the "so" is a condition of fact affirming the truth of the statement.
[50] Fung, *The Epistle to the Galatians*, 186.
[51] Moo points out that regarding "the clipped διὰ Θεοῦ" (*dia theou*), "it is just the difficulty of the brief phrase that testifies to its origionality…. The preposition διά *dia* (through) usually denotes instrument …

the work which made a man a son and an heir is stressed throughout Scripture (Deut 7:7, 8; Isa 48:11; Dan 9:19; Hos. 14:4; John 15:16; Rom 5:8 Eph 1:4; 1 John 4:10, 19)." Paul now again stresses that to return to subjection to the law was not just a return to infancy but to slavery and not just any slavery but the slavery of the *stoicheia* of the world. But he had more to reveal to them about what they were in Christ.

Free and Having Fellowship, No Longer Slaves vv. 8–20

Here we have the first exhortation in the letter, as Paul makes a direct appeal to the Galatians. His arguments in what many see as the *probato* are concluded and now we have this direct word to them, expressing his deep concern (vv. 8–20). For Longenecker[53] 3:1–5 and 4:8–11, with their direct address, "form an *incluso* for all that is argued in the *probato*." For Witherington,[54] 4:8–20 gives us Paul's appeal to the experiences of the Galatians; 4:21–5:1 is also an appeal but through the sacred text. Moo[55] suggests that Paul's appeal in these coming verses falls into three distinct sections; the first two are focused upon the past, their own (4:8–11), and that of Paul's relationship with them (4:12–20). The third section will take us forward to 4:21–31, where Paul uses the Sarah/Hagar allegory to remind the Galatians of their present status and to challenge them in the light of this to resist the Judaizers.

He begins by reminding them where they once were with God, "formerly" (v. 8). Witherington[56] points out the strong "but" here and that vv. 8 9 should be read together as the contrast – "on the one hand … on the other" i.e., what was true before their conversion and what is the reality now. They formally did not know God;[57] but into this glorious position of sons and heirs they have now come through the gospel, i.e., through the cross, the redemption of v. 5. Longenecker makes the point that knowing God is not being used by Paul in some mundane sense of perceive or acquire knowledge about. This is not to deny that because of how man is created there is a certain kind of knowledge of God through general revelation of his attributes (Rom 1:19–20) and the law written in man's heart (Rom 2:14–15). However, as Longenecker[58] explains, it is "in the biblical sense of 'to experience' … Galatian Christians have come to experience God in the intimacy of a family relationship."

Paul urges them not to turn back (vv. 8–11). This would be to renounce the knowledge of the true God they had come to know. In their former pagan days they

---

can also at times denote ultimate cause, or author … and that meaning is undoubtedly intended here." Moo, *Galatians*, 271.

[52] Hendriksen, *Galatians*, 163.

[53] Longenecker, *Galatians*, 178.

[54] Witherington, 111, *Grace in Galatia*, 292.

[55] Moo, *Galatians*, 273.

[56] Witherington, 111, *Grace in Galatia*, 296.

[57] Moo points out that "not knowing God" is Paul's way of describing non-Christians and especially Gentile non-Christians (2Thess. 1:8; Titus 1:16; note 1 Thess. 4:5. Moo, *Galatians*, 275.

[58] Longenecker, *Galatians*, 300.

had served beings whom they considered to be gods, but were not really so (cf. 1 Cor 10:20). They did not know God and were in bondage to evil spirits; now they know God.[59] We should note that when Paul considers the standing of sinners in God's sight he has three basic ways of describing their serious situation. Here in Galatians it is *universal enslavement* to the elemental spirits; in Rom 3:22 it is *universal sinfulness* and in 1 Cor 15:22; Rom 5:18 *universal death* in Adam. Why should they go back into the slavery from which they have been delivered?

In v. 9 Paul includes a correction to his statement that they had known God. McDonald[60] points out that, "The 'rather' of self-correction is a feature of his writings" – as in Rom 8:34. "Rather" they have come "to be known by God," which stresses the divine initiative in salvation. As Hendriksen[61] explains, in grace God had sent Paul and Barnabas to bring the good news to the Galatians and by the moving of the Holy Spirit they were brought to repentance. God had set his love upon them. "There is, accordingly, a renewed emphasis on God's sovereignty in the effectuation of man's salvation." Moo[62] also explains that the language used here has the sense of intimate relationship or even election:

> Humans do indeed come to know God, but they do so only because God first determines to 'know' us in Christ. In this context Paul may want to stress the divine initiative to highlight God's grace as the foundation for the Galatian's relationship to Christ and the foolishness of turning away from the rich experience of that grace.

Paul's deep concern is expressed now in a rhetorical question – how now they could contemplate turning back to what he terms "the weak and worthless elementary principles of the world?" Remember that v. 3 included the life "under law" as part of the *stoicheia*. The serious situation then is that, for Bruce,[63] the Galatians who were in the past enslaved to counterfeit deities:

---

[59] We should note the suggestion that the Roman colony cities led the way at this time in promoting Emperor worship. In Paul's day the most prominent building in Antioch would be the temple of Augustus in the very centre of the city. So, in places like Iconium and Derbe also, the life of the city would often have special days of celebration connected with the Emperor cult. Witherington, 111, *Grace in Galatia*, 298, makes reference among others to S. Mitchell, who affirmed that the ruler cult pressed the citizens "into observing days, months, seasons and years which it laid down for special recognition and celebration," S. Mitchell, *Anatolia: Land, Men and Gods in Asia Minor*, Volume 2, *The Rise of the Church* (Oxford: Clarendon Press, 1993), 10.

[60] McDonald, *Freedom in Faith*, 98.

[61] Hendriksen, *Galatians*, 165.

[62] Moo, *Galatians*, 276.

[63] Bruce, *The Epistle to the Galatians*, 202, George, *Galatians*, 310–312, points to the Galatians' former religious commitments; some perhaps devotees of various mystery religions, others the Roman Imperial cult or pagan deities of ancient Greece, worshippers of star gods. He notes the experience of Paul and Barnabas at Lystra (Acts 14:11–15) and mentions the goddess Dindimene at Iconium. Their conversion would mean breaking free from such worship of the non-gods. Later Christians, as Justin Martyr confessed, were accused of being atheists because they did not believe in such gods. But as George maintains, "This does not mean, however, that either Paul or Christians of Justin's generation believed that

Would be enslaved to the στοιχεια all over again if they "reverted" not to their former paganism but to Jewish religious practices ... For all the basic differences between Judaism and paganism both involved subjection to the same elemental forces.

This was a remarkable affirmation for one who was a former Pharisee (1:13–14). To take on circumcision and what was being urged upon them was to revert to the service of the *stoicheia*! Fung[64] explains that, "Paul calls the *stoicheia* 'weak and beggarly' (RSV): 'weak' because they have no power to save or justify their devotees and 'beggarly' (literally 'poor,' as in 2:10) because they have no spiritual riches to bestow upon the Galatians."

Atkinson[65] quotes Col 2:8, the verse we noted above was concerned with being taken captive by philosophy and empty deceit, which states, "according to the elemental spirits of the world, and not according to Christ." He affirms:

> The reference from Colossians is most helpful in understanding what Paul is talking about in Galatians 4:3. The law is being put in to the general category of rudimentary religion that includes even the former paganism and philosophies of the Galatian Gentiles. Paul says that in comparison to the perfect gospel, the law along with pagan religions, is simple, primitive, ineffective and enslaving. The law was as useless as pagan religion in regard to its ability to save from sin.

Barrett[66] also finds here "as extraordinary a statement as is to be found anywhere in (Paul's) letters.... Here in Galatians he virtually equates Judaism with heathenism. To go forward into Judaism is to go backward into heathenism."

Paul's deep concern is expressed in his appeal in v. 9, "How can you turn back again?" The verb is in the present tense, suggesting that, as with 1:6, the process had begun. They may have been accepting Jewish practices (v. 10), although they were not yet at the point of submitting to circumcision. Their religion was in danger of degenerating into an external formalism and the old bondage, under the influence of the false teachers, so that they would not be experiencing the fellowship with God into which Christ came to bring them. Paul was not all head and no heart. He calls them again "brothers" (v. 12) and "my little children" (v. 19) in this context he is like a mother who is in labour until Christ is formed in them.

It must be noted that Longenecker[67] highlights the attempts of the Judaizers of Galatia to persuade the Christian communities to add law observance to grace or justification

---

these false gods were merely projections of the human mind. Clearly, they understood them to be existent beings, fallen angels, the *ta stiocheia tou kosmou* described earlier."

[64] Fung, *The Epistle to the Galatians*, 192. Moo suggests that the first in translation be accepted as "weak" but the second as meaning "lacking in spiritual worth," Moo, *Galatians*, 277.

[65] B. Atkinson, *No More Law: A Bold Study in Galatians* (Milton Keynes: Paternoster, 2012), 171.

[66] Barrett, *Freedom and Obligation*, 61.

by faith. They were urging a life of Jewish nomism upon Paul's converts, reflected first in an act of submission to circumcision and a commitment to observe the law. "As they saw it a lifestyle of Jewish nomism was necessary for full acceptance before God."[68] But now we must ask this question. Is it not likely that Paul saw in this attempt to turn his converts away from grace alone, Christ and his cross alone, the activity of Satan or the "elemental spirits" who certainly were at work in the teaching which was being brought by the Judaizers to the Galatians? They were being duped by false doctrine (see 3:1, "Who has bewitched you?") Here is the answer. In this there is also a warning concerning the origin of any attempt today to add anything to grace alone or the cross alone for salvation. Are "elemental spirits" still at work?[69] John Piper[70] affirms:

> Satan and his demons specialize in taking the commandments of the law and alluring people in the church to make those commandments a basis of self-righteousness. And therefore Paul saw behind the legalistic teaching of the Judaizers an age-old demonic scheme to destroy genuine faith and with it the church.

Stott's comments are helpful here. He asks how we can really understand Paul conceiving that bondage to the law could be called bondage to evil spirits or the law be an evil design of Satan? Paul has written here that the law was given by God (through good angels) to Moses (3:19). He explains that the devil has taken this "good" thing and employed it for his own evil purpose. Stott refers to John Wesley when he was a post-graduate student at Oxford. He was a clergyman himself, the son of a clergyman, in the Holy Club, practising good works as he ministered in prisons and work-houses. He observed both Saturday and Sunday as the Sabbath, fasted, prayed and went to the province of Georgia for two years as a missionary. However, he was trusting in himself and his religion for salvation, trapped by Satan. Only later was he set free on 24th May 1738 as he sat in a Moravian meeting in Aldersgate Street. In his Journal[71] he recounts:

> In the evening I went very unwillingly to a society in Aldersgate Street, where one was reading Luther's Preface to the Epistle to the Romans. About a quarter before nine, while he was describing the change which God works in the heart through faith in Christ, I felt my heart strangely warmed. I felt I did trust in Christ, Christ alone for salvation, and an assurance was given me

---

[67] Longenecker, *Galatians*, 176–77.

[68] Longenecker, *Galatians*, 177. Hendriksen, *Galatians*, 165, shows us that many of them having formally been enslaved to the teachings of pagan priests seeking, "the discovery of the will of the gods by means of omens ,,, afflicting the body   submission to fate," now they were "to become enslaved all over again," this time by Judaistic regulations."

[69] One needs to remember and reflect upon passages like 1 Tim 4:1 "deceitful spirits and teachings of demons" and 1 John 4:1–3 warning us to "test the spirits, because many false prophets have gone out into the world." Is Paul not giving a similar warning here in Galatians?

[70] John Piper's message on Gal 4:1–11, delivered on May 8th 1983 "Spiritual Warfare."

[71] See http://www.ccel.org/ccel/wesley/journal.vi.ii.xv. html. Accessed December 2017.

that he had taken away my sins, even mine, and saved me from the law of sin and death.

We forget that there is a spiritual battle raging today for the souls of men. 2 Cor 11:13–15 reminds us of this. "Satan disguises himself as an angel of light. So it is no surprise if his servants, also, disguise themselves as servants of righteousness." Any message apart from the message of grace alone, by the cross alone is not the gospel and is not of God but is through the spirit of antichrist (see also 1 John 4:1–3; 2 John 7). Satan can dupe men to think that by their own efforts or self-righteousness they are acceptable to God. This is an example of what Paul is warning of in Galatians.

In vv. 10–11 Paul says, "You observe days and months and seasons and years. I am afraid I may have laboured over you in vain." George[72] suggests that Paul is referring to four measurements of time – "days," like the weekly Sabbath observance or other one day feasts; "months," new moon rituals as in Num 10:10; "seasons," the great annual festivals such as Passover, Pentecost and Tabernacles (2 Chron 8:13; Zech 8:19); and "years," the Year of Jubilee, the sabbatical Year and the New Year celebrations. There is no particle connecting this statement of the use of the cultic calendar with enslavement under the elemental spirits, but for many in the ancient world there were said to be forces that control the planets by which the calendar was regulated. McDonald[73] points out that the word "observe" in its compound form means doing all that is required down to the final minutia and in fullest measure.

It is true that after conversion many Jewish Christians still kept the sacred occasions – even Paul himself (1 Cor 16:8; Acts 20:16). But as Bruce[74] has pointed out, for Gentile Christians to adopt them, "as matters of legal obligation was quite another matter." The sinister fact was that for Gentiles in accepting the Jewish calendar was as Fung[75] maintains, "a form of subservience to the *stoicheia* which could neither save not justify its adherents but only cast them into bondage." Again, while there may be the promises of blessing by the Emperor through observing the cult or from others, but as Lightfoot[76] affirms, "they have no power to rescue from condemnation."

Paul in v. 11 is making an appeal to the emotions of the Galatians. Witherington[77] points out that this will become stronger as the verses continue. Also, the verb "have

---

[72] George, *Galatians*, 317.

[73] McDonald, *Freedom in Faith*, 99. So also Witherington, 111, *Galatians*, 301, who writes of "scrupulous observance."

[74] Bruce, *The Epistle to the Galatians*, 205.

[75] Fung, *The Epistle to the Galatians*, 193.

[76] Lightfoot, *Saint Paul's Epistle to the Galatians*, 171.

[77] Witherington, 111, *Galatians*, 302. He again points out that the appeal to advantage or benefit and the exhortation to imitation (see v. 12) are particularly characteristic of deliberative, rather than forensic rhetoric, which of course he sees as the hermeneutical key for reading Galatians. See also 295–96, 303–04. Moo also notes the tone of these verses as characteristic of the ancient rhetoric – the use of "pathos," moving an audience by appealing to their emotions and shared personal experience. Paul has brought a complex theological argument (3:1– 4:7), appealing to the mind; now he makes a direct appeal to their hearts (vv. 12–20). Moo, *Galatians*, 280.

laboured" is in the perfect tense, referring to Paul's past ministry and what should be its ongoing effect. But would there be any lasting spiritual benefit for the Galatians? Had his labour been "in vain?"[78] See also the use of the word in 2:21 – if righteousness is by the law Christ's death was "for no purpose" or "in vain." The legalistic approach of the Judaizers and the message of salvation by grace through the cross were irreconcilably opposed to each other. Would all his labour have been of no benefit to them? Hendriksen[79] notes Paul's use of μή πως *mē pōs* "perhaps" or "somehow" often missed in a number of translations, which means that "one of Paul's gloomiest utterances in the entire epistle" still holds out the hope of the perseverance of those truly regenerate.

Paul therefore urges them (v. 12) in a very personal way, "Be as I." He at one time had been zealous to have a legal righteousness, but that was before God met him in grace on the Damascus Road. He had discovered that he had nothing to commend himself to God, but stood in need of mercy (1 Tim 1:15–16). This is surely the meaning of the affirmation (an imperative) and the attitude they must adopt. Paul had "died to the law" (2:19) and was no longer "under the law" (3:23–25) and they must follow suit. He affirms, "For I also have become as you are." Paul was on the same level with them; he had forsaken any attempt to obtain righteousness through the law. His own righteousness meant nothing and had brought him no acceptance before God. He himself must look to the cross alone for his means of acceptance by God. The Galatians should not allow themselves to be in bondage to ordinances but continue in faith as free sons of God and heirs, as Paul himself was. With an "imploring intensity,"[80] he writes, "Brothers, I beseech you" (note also 1:11; 3:15; 4:28, 31; 5:11, 13; 6:1, 18). The agitators (see again vv. 17–18) were involved in attempts at "persuasion" which was finding some success; Paul was on the other hand in his letter (particularly in chapters 3–6) bringing heartfelt arguments of "dissuasion" for them not to be impacted by any such influence.

He confesses that they have never treated him badly, "You did me no wrong," reveals his own heart and commences a single Greek sentence which continues through vv. 12–14. Paul reminds them of the time he preached the gospel to them "at the first," τὸ πρότερον *to proteron*, means "on the former occasion."[81] It can refer to the eastern mission trip (Acts 13:14–14:20), followed by the western journey along the same route (Acts 14:21), as explained in the Introduction. Although Luke in Acts does not mention it, here we learn that when he first came he was suffering some "bodily ailment." Fung[82] explains that Paul will have come to Pisidian Antioch from Perga in Pamphylia, which would take him across the Taurus Mountains to high country some 3,600 feet above sea level. Paul's ailment may have been some ophthalmic problem; in v. 15 Paul will acknowledge that they would almost have plucked out their own

---

[78] See also Gal 2:2; 1 Thess. 3:5; 1 Cor 15:14; Phil 2:16 for similar concerns of ministry without lasting results.
[79] Hendriksen, *Galatians*, 166.
[80] McDonald, *Freedom in Faith*, 101.
[81] See 16, 18.
[82] Fung, *The Epistle to the Galatians*, 196.

eyes for him (see 2 Cor 12:7). Witherington[83] explains that the eyes would be understood as the organ of greatest value, "being the windows on the world (cf. Deut 32:10; Ps 17:8; Zech 2: 8)." With regard to Gal 6:11, he asks what kind of person needs *large letters* – surely someone with a visual impairment. He suggests that this may be why Paul used scribes especially for his larger letters, always travelled with someone to act as his amanuensis from place to place and his bodily presence was considered to be weak (2 Cor 10:10). Again, did his "blinding" on the Damascus Road leave him with recurring eye problems? Is it significant that with regard to the "vision" of 2 Cor 12:1, 7, when he was caught up into heaven he can record that he "heard" things not to be repeated – why does he not write "saw?" So, for Witherington, taking into account all of these clues, no other view suits the evidence as much.

Some other scholars suggest the possibility that Paul may be referring to the time he came to Lystra and was stoned. But God raised him up. They suggest that this is actually what Paul is referring to in 2 Cor 12:1–10, when he writes of the "thorn in the flesh?"[84] Dunn,[85] having discussed the possibilities can propose, "given the train of thought (4:13–15) the most obvious implication is that Paul's ailment affected his eyes most of all, presumably leaving him with greatly restricted vision and in a painful condition which excited the pity of the Galatians." It appears that whatever ailment Paul had it was of such a nature that the Galatians could have been repelled by it and so "despised" him[86]; but (using ἀλλὰ *alla* as a strong contrast) and even using an exaggeration in v. 14, "received me as an angel of God, as Christ Jesus"[87] they rather in love valued him highly. Because of his grace and power he seemed "to be worthy of such honours as becomes an unearthly visitant."[88] They had treated him with such respect, but now things seemed to have changed.

Paul questions them in v. 15, "What has become of the satisfaction you felt?" He reminds them of the blessing they had received when he was with them; of what they had grasped through his preaching of grace and the cross of Christ. They had felt that God was truly at work among them. They would have done anything for him. Such was their regard for him that "if possible, they would have "gouged out" their eyes and given them to him (v. 15). Paul must have been aware that things had changed in

---

[83] Witherington 111, *Grace in Galatia*, 309. Note also with reference to Paul's poor insight, Acts 23:1–5.

[84] Hendriksen, *Galatians*, 171, is doubtful about it being an eye affliction and asks his readers to note the references in Acts 13:50; 14:5, 6, 19 to persecution "experiences … never erased" from Paul's memory – even to the time of his final letter, 2 Tim 3:10–11. Other suggestions have been made, fleshly desire, spiritual trials, malaria, or epilepsy. See McDonald, *Freedom in Faith*, 102 and Longenecker, *Galatians*, 191.

[85] Dunn, *Galatians*, 236. Moo, after a full discussion of the usual possibilities, also suggests the possibility of "some kind of eye problem." Moo, *Galatians*, 282–85.

[86] Hendriksen, *Galatians*, 172, discusses the literal sense "spit out" and links it with the reaction when someone has an epileptic fit. There is no evidence anywhere in the NT that Paul suffered from this affliction and so he affirms that we ought to understand this phrase as it was taken from earliest times "in a metaphorical sense – to loathe."

[87] This statement will add extra support to the South Galatian Theory as we learn from Acts 14:11–13 of the intention to sacrifice to Paul and Barnabas as heavenly beings come down among men.

[88] McDonald, *Freedom in Faith*, 103.

their attitude towards him and so he challenges, rather than questions,[89] them in v. 16 whether they now saw him as their enemy[90] as he sought to reveal to them the serious and stark reality of their present course of action, telling them "the truth" in his letter.[91] Stott[92] makes the point applying it to today; "We cannot, when we like what an apostle (the preacher today) teaches, defer to him as an angel, and when we do not like what he teaches, hate him and reject him as an enemy."

It is clear that others are now operating among them and have their ear. Their aims were very different from that of the apostle. He writes of the false teachers, v. 17f. "They," (Paul will not even name them) "make much of you" or flatter you to win you over to their gospel. They claim to have this fuller understanding of what God requires. Yet Paul makes clear that their influence was "for no good purpose." In reality, they "shut you out" – they were excluding the Galatians, not just from fellowship with the apostle, but from God (cf. 1:6) and from Christ (5:4) and the freedom in him. So, the aim of the Judaizers was that they (the Galatians) would have nowhere else to look other than to them – therefore they gain in their importance and would desire to be their exclusive teachers. As McDonald[93] has stated, "By being shut out from Christ the Galatians are shut up to them – a false enclosure." Not as John the Baptist desired, "He must increase, but I must decrease" (John 3:30). They turned this upon its head.

In v. 18 Paul acknowledges that he does not have a problem with others wishing to help the Galatians. In fact, it is always good for them to be receiving attention from others; yet it must be only if it was sincere and had their best interests at heart, i.e., in contrast to v. 17, now "for a good purpose" i.e., if they were being helped and not deceived. Fung[94] explains that "Paul has already explicitly stated that the agitators intentions were dishonourable; he now implies that his own intentions were honourable – for he sought nothing but that his converts be built up (edified, cf. 2 Cor 10:8; 13:10; Rom 15:2) in the truth of the gospel."

Here we see the intensely personal nature of Paul's travail for them (v. 19). Witherington[95] notes that the vexation and anger of vv. 17–18 have been replaced by a tenderer and compassionate tone. There is real love and affection as he calls them

---

[89] McDonald explains that "Therefore" does not introduce a question elsewhere in the New Testament, *Freedom in Faith*, 104.

[90] Witherington 111, *Grace in Galatia*, 313, n. 55, points out that this was a description given to Paul later by the Ebionites because of their particular form of Jewish Christianity. See Pseud. Clem. *Hom. E Pet*. 2.3; Pseud. Clem. *Recog*. 1.70.

[91] Moo points out that the reference to "telling you the truth" (v. 16) is more than "simply truth telling" but "truth proclaiming, namely, the 'truth of the gospel' that is at stake in Galatia (Gal 2:5, 14;5:7)." A gospel "offered freely by grace … accepted and lived out by means of faith alone," Moo, *Galatians*, 286.

[92] Stott, *The One Way*, 115.

[93] McDonald, *Freedom in Faith*, 105. Again, Hendriksen, *Galatians*, 174, makes the point that the aim of the false teachers was to "*exclude*" the Galatians from all influences except their own and "*isolate*" them from Paul.

[94] Fung, *The Epistle to the Galatians*, 201.

[95] Witherington 111, *Grace in Galatia*, 314.

"My little children"[96] – however they now think of him. For McDonald,[97] this phrase is more than "an expression of endearment" since the Galatians were really Paul's spiritual children (see also 1 Cor 4:15; Phlm 10; 1 Tim 1:18; 2 Tim 2:1; Titus 1:5). He is again "in travail" for them, having renewed pangs as when he first saw them coming to Christ. Fung[98] explains that he had suffered in bringing the gospel to them at the beginning and notes the references to the persecutions Paul and his fellow labourers had endured (Acts 13:45, 50; 14:2, 5f., 19). Now he was experiencing apprehension (v. 11) and perplexity (v. 20), the pangs of labour "over again" in his efforts to recover them to the truth of the gospel. It is not enough that Christ dwells in them but he must be formed in them. The preposition means that Christ is not being held up as some kind of model to which they should conform; he lives "in" them and by the power of the Holy Spirit they can be changed more and more into his likeness (Gal 3:14; 5:22–23).

George[99] comments upon the use of the image of a mother here by Paul, a mother who goes through the pains of childbirth for her children. Elsewhere in his letters he can employ the image of a nurse caring for her little children (1 Thess 2:7); also one finds the more common image of Paul as a father begetting sons and daughters in Christ through the preaching of the gospel. Only in Galatians does he use the image of a mother, "in the anguish of childbirth." "This image bears witness to the deep personal anguish Paul was experiencing for his spiritual offspring in Galatia.... The anguish of his labor over them was to continue, he said, 'until Christ is formed in you.'" Hendriksen[100] also writes of the "warm, pastoral" and "parental" affection in Paul's writing. He can say that he is "again in the anguish of childbirth" for them. "Once before he had endured these labor pains for them" as he had formally done in Acts 13–14. He had been God's instrument bringing them to not just love and trust him, but to love and trust Christ and turn from all reliance on self or on law-works. They need to provide evidence that they were continuing to look to the cross alone.

Paul in v. 20 wishes he could visit them again. He would certainly change his tone. Would this be a change from severity to gentleness or vice versa? Some will suggest that he has been passionate, blunt and stern (e.g., 1:6, 9; 2:6, 11, 14, 21; 3:1, 3–4, 9; 5:3–4, 12; 5:21; 6:7). He was deeply perplexed about them; he has a strong affection for them; he may have given them the impression that he was their enemy but that was not the case. If he was there he would display his love and gentleness.

---

[96] Longenecker, *Galatians*, 195, discussed two possible vocatives here, "my children" which Paul can use in 1 Cor 4:14, 17; 2 Cor 6:13; 12:14; 1Thess. 2:7, 11; Phlm. 10, but opts for the diminutive "my *little* children" which is a harder reading, nowhere else in Paul, in keeping with the unusual imagery of giving birth here. So also Moo, *Galatians*, 290.

[97] McDonald, *Freedom in Faith*, 106.

[98] Fung, *The Epistle to the Galatians*, 202.

[99] George, *Galatians*, 329–30. Stott, *The One Way*, 116 also makes the point that the mother-metaphor is used here by Paul, "not to illustrate their dependence upon him, but his travail for them ... to see them transformed into the image of Christ."

[100] Hendriksen, *Galatians*, 175.

However, his affection for the Galatians was clear (1:11; 3:15; 4:12, 19, 28, 31; 5:11, 13; 6:1, 18). It was because of serious concern for them that he wrote.[101] If he had been able to go again, he would have used sterner reasoning and more passionate argumentation. The difference is clear between him and the false teachers. They wanted themselves to be prominent and dominate the Galatians; Paul wanted to sacrifice himself for them that Christ would mean everything to them and be formed in them.

We should note by way of summary Witherington's[102] discussion of how various commentators have approached 4:8–20. He suggests that if one misses the rhetorical force of the argumentative appeal (especially in vv. 11–20) Paul will be presented as losing control of himself and the logic of the whole argument. On the contrary, if one can recognise Paul's use of rhetoric here, as Moo also has pointed out, we can see that it would be particularly effective. Paul has appealed to the Galatians' own feelings, of the kindness and fairness in their past relationship, feelings of pity for his physical condition, his "parental" love and painful labour for them, his concerns and fears for them, his strong warnings of the motives of those who would zealously lead them astray.

This is not an erratic argument, or miscellany of ideas, it is a touching of all the major emotional bases in a masterful way, by using all the rhetorically appropriate sort of key terms listed under *pathos* and the tactics listed in the literature on appeals to *pathos* or the deeper emotions.

Moo[103] also notes Paul's use of "perplexed" concerning the Galatian believers – a word also found in Mark 6:20; Luke 24:4; John 13:22; Acts 25:20. He ends this paragraph expressing the same deep concern as in the previous one (v. 11). "The Galatians have experienced the blessing of Abraham (3:14) and the powerful ministry of the Spirit (3:2–5): how can they turn their backs on these?"

Hagar-Sarah Allegory, Ishmael and Isaac vv. 21–31

Paul now moves on to issue another direct appeal, as he has done in 4:8–11 and 4:12–20, this time in the Hagar-Sarah allegory. Here he seeks to reaffirm his whole argument from 3:7–29, that those who belong to Christ are the sons/seed of Abraham and inheritors of the promise. As Moo[104] explains, "What is implicit in the earlier argument becomes explicit here: it is not biological descent from Abraham that marks the true children of Abraham but decent through the line of promise."

---

[101] Although he is deeply concerned for his converts in Galatia it appears that he is not in a position to visit them. We have suggested that the timing of the writing of the letter will be just before Paul leaves Antioch for the Council of Jerusalem in Acts 15. There *is* a crisis already where he and Barnabas are. So, while he would prefer a visit, only a letter can be sent.
[102] Witherington 111, *Grace in Galatia*, 305–06.
[103] Moo, *Galatians*, 290.
[104] Moo, *Galatians*, 292.

Excursus: The Hagar-Sarah Allegory

The apostle, unlike Philo,[105] who finds in the Abrahamic narrative the philosophic concepts of higher wisdom and sophistry, here using the same narratives sets forth the affirmations of the great blessings of salvation over against the captivity which the law brings. Paul is drawing a parallel between the Genesis narrative of chapter 16–21 and the situation in his own day. Some scholars as Longenecker, Barrett, Moo and George suggest that Paul may very well be responding to another interpretation of the whole Hagar-Sarah story from that presented by the Judiazers themselves – the need to be connected physically (through circumcision) with Isaac, whose descendants received the enlightenment of the law, rather than, as they counselled, remaining with those of Ishmael, who were in darkness.[106]

Using the Genesis narrative of 16–21 Paul, as Moo[107] points out, mixing argument with appeal, distinguishes two lines of descent from Abraham, one from Hagar and the other from Sarah – although, as we will see, only one of them is really named. He is focussing upon the birth of the two sons of Abraham, Ishmael and Isaac, vv. 21–23. The use of the article, "*the* slave woman" and '*the* free woman" while pointing to the two familiar women in the narrative, and the fact that Paul does not name them (the second only in vv. 24–25), says something about his interpretative approach in this context.

Stories about Ishmael, Isaac, Hagar and Sarah were often found in various Jewish writings.[108] Paul's argument here is identified as allegorical, the kind that would have been common in the rabbinical schools; but its message is up to date. Paul uses the term ἀλληγορούμενα *allēgoroumena*, a compound of ἄλλος *allos* "another" and ἀγορεύειν *agoreuein*, "to say;" so that an allegory is, when one thing is said, a further meaning, something generally more excellent, is intended. Luther[109] comments about the use of allegory here by Paul:

> Allegories do not strongly persuade in divinity, but as certain pictures they beautify and set out the matter. But because he had fortified his cause before in invincible arguments, taken of experience, of the example of Abraham, of the testimonies of the scripture, and similitudes: now in the end of his disputations he addeth an allegory, to give a beauty to all the rest. For it is a seemly thing to add an allegory when the foundation is well laid and the

---

[105] e.g., *Abr.* 68; *Fug.* 128, 209f.; *Mut.* 255.

[106] George, *Galatians*, 334; Longenecker, *Galatians*, 200–06; C. K. Barrett, "The Allegory of Abraham, Sarah and Hagar in the Argument of Galatians," *Essays on Paul* (Philadelphia: Westminster, 1982), 541–70. Moo also considers that Paul's argument is likely "defensive, a response to the agitators' use of the same texts," and that it belongs with 4:8–11 and 12–20, as part of the "appeal" section of the letter, Moo, *Galatians*, 292.

[107] Moo, *Galatians*, 292. Paul uses both the indicative and the imperative mood here.

[108] See the Excursus in Longenecker, *Galatians*, 206, where he explains that there were "tendencies within the various streams of Judaism generally to contemporize the persons and places of the biblical narrative for their own purposes, whether … understood as allegorical or typological treatments."

[109] Luther, *A Commentary on St. Paul's Epistle to the Galatians*, 417.

matter thoroughly proved. For as painting is an ornament to set forth and garnish a house already builded, so is an allegory the light of a matter which is already otherwise proved and confirmed.

Bruce[110] explains, "he (Paul) has in mind that form of allegory which is commonly called typology ... an aspect of the new covenant is presented in terms of an OT narrative. Typology presupposes that salvation-history displays a recurring pattern of divine action." He supplies examples of such typology, among which he refers to the Red Sea passage, the manna, the water from the rock and the wilderness wanderings (1 Cor 10:1–11), and in particular, to 2 Cor 3:7–4:6, with reference to Exod 34:29–35, the fading glory on Moses' face, with the administration of the law compared to the new covenant and the administration of the Spirit. "The contrast between law and Spirit is identical with the contrast between legal bondage and spiritual freedom which Paul illustrates by his present 'allegory.'"[111]

Moo[112] also considers that in Paul's day the term "allegory" did not carry the technical sense understood in later centuries, but simply referred to an interpretation that would be called "figurative." We should note also that the participle of the verb ἀλληγορέω *allēgoreō* is being used not with reference to the narrative but the women themselves with the meaning, "this is allegorically speaking." Moo wishes to emphasise that Paul has drawn upon a historical narrative in making reference to Sarah and Hagar. He affirms, "It would be a mistake to think that Paul is claiming to do what Philo is doing. Paul gives no indication that he is calling into question the historical referentiality of this narrative. What he is doing is showing how the narrative can be seen to foreshadow the realities of the new covenant that he is defending." So here Paul is using a form of typology and "His reading is based on the direction that salvation history has taken." He will link this in v. 27 with Isa 54:1 to arrive at the following conclusion:

> He (Paul) knows that Christ is the climax of salvation history and that access to Christ is given by faith (alone!) and through the eschatological gift of the Spirit (see esp. 3:1; 5:5). It is therefore by faith in Christ that the "many children" Isaiah has promised to eschatological Zion/Jerusalem have been born.

Paul is actually returning to his argument in 3:7–29 about what it means to be children of Abraham. Here he is taking a second step in distinguishing two lines of descent from Abraham, one from "the slave woman" (Hagar) and the other from "the free" (Sarah). Basing all his argument on the Scripture (first from the Genesis story of chapters 16–21 and then from Isaiah's prophesy in 54:1), Moo declares, "The

---

[110] Bruce, *The Epistle to the Galatians*, 217. One should remember of course that here it is not Hagar who is an actual "type" of Mount Sinai or of Jerusalem, but it is in the experience of bondage that they have a similarity. The miraculous birth of Isaac, as we have highlighted throughout, also reminds us of the regenerating power of God's Spirit.

[111] Bruce, *The Epistle to the Galatians*, 218.

[112] Moo, *Galatians*, 292, 294, 299 – 300.

Galatians, Paul argues, belong to this second line of descent, children of Spirit, born through the promise." This is not a biological line of descent, but, as we noted, spiritual.

Finally, Witherington[113] also discusses Paul as an exegete and allegorizer. Helpfully he explains:

> If the eschatological age has come, if follows now that one can and should go back and look for pre-figurements and types and prophesies and promises of what was to come in the Scriptural record of all previous ages of the history of Israel. This also implies that all which has come before was preliminary, not final ... the law and indeed all of the Hebrew Scriptures are to be read not just ecclesiologically but also and perhaps primarily Christologically.

Paul in v. 21 calls for their attention using the imperative, "tell me." He addresses those who desire to be under the law i.e., to live under the Mosaic legislation, written law and oral tradition. The present participle used here reveals that the Galatians were on the verge of submitting to circumcision and the law but could yet pull back from that commitment. In a play on words he urges those who wish to be "under the law" to listen to the law, for that very law, if they place themselves under it, will be their judge, issuing in condemnation.[114] Yet his real aim in these closing verses is to affirm the glorious blessings of those who have been born of the Spirit, redeemed and free, placed as sons and heirs.

There are others of course, not Jews or Judaizers, about whom Stott expresses genuine concern i.e., religious people today:

> People whose religion is legalistic, who imagine that the way to God is by the observance of certain rules. There are even professing Christians who turn the gospel into law. They suppose that their relationship to God depends on a strict adherence to regulations, traditions and ceremonies. They are in bondage to them.

It is clear that they need to listen not to the law but to the message of Galatians as a whole. The law only condemns but the cross meets our need. There is salvation by grace through the finished work of Christ. It is not the cross plus law, or Christ plus law, but Christ alone.

---

[113] Witherington 111, *Grace in Galatia*, 220.

[114] Moo explains that the phrase "under the law" is found earlier in Gal 3:23; 4:4, 5; also, phrases expressing a similar idea, "under a guardian" 3:24, 25 and "under the elements of the world," 4:3. To be "under the law" is to be under "the ruling authority of the Mosaic law" which leads to condemnation ("the curse of the law"; cf. 3:13). Moo, *Galatians*, 297. Also George, *Galatians*, 335, points out the use of two senses for the word "law"; First the law of Moses that they would put themselves under; next in hearing the law, he was referring to the Old Testament Pentateuch, which contained this particular story of Abraham, Sarah, Hagar and their two sons.

Stott[115] is helpful in his overall treatment of the Hagar-Sarah, Ishmael-Isaac narrative. He finds three stages in Paul's argument: The Historical Background (vv. 22–23); The Allegorical Argument (vv. 24–27); The Personal Application (vv. 28–31). Our references to his work will be noted as we continue looking at this passage. The Galatians are:

Children of Miraculous Birth, Not Just According to Nature

While "it is written" (v. 22) is normally used to introduce an OT quotation, here Paul is using it not to point to a particular passage but to refer, as we have stated, to the Abrahamic historical narrative covering a number of chapters, particularly Gen 16-21. This teaching which is presented by the apostle is a complete reversal of what would have been expected of Paul the Pharisee.

"Abraham had two sons." Stott[116] explains that the Jews were proud that they could claim to be descended from Abraham and were sons of Abraham (see Matt 3:9; John 8:31–44). However, Paul now unfolds what John the Baptist and Jesus had maintained i.e., that true descent from Abraham is not physical but spiritual. Galatians affirms that it is not those who only have an impeccable Jewish genealogy are Abraham's true children, but those who believe as he believed and obey as he obeyed (see 3:14, 29). So Stott insists that they cannot claim to belong to Abraham unless first they belong to Christ. Paul is presenting an argument which picks up on what he has already written in chapter 3.[117]

This double decent from Abraham Paul sees illustrated in the two sons of Abraham, Ishmael and Isaac. They may have had Abraham for their father, but two things were different. Firstly, they had different mothers – one a slave, Hagar, the other a free woman. So, Ishmael was born into slavery – he shares his mother's status – and Isaac was free. Secondly, their births were different. As Stott[118] explains, Ishmael was born according to nature, "according to the flesh"; but Isaac was rather "not born according to nature, but against nature, supernaturally," when you consider the age of Abraham and especially Sarah. Clearly, he was born miraculously, through the promise of God (Gen 15:4–6; 17:15–21; 18:10–15; note also 21:1 – "The Lord did for Sarah what he had promised"). George[119] explains that Abraham and Sarah were childless into their old age. There was no word of God concerning the birth of Ishmael, just Sarah's prompting or plan to which Abraham listened and a child born who was a source of contention and suffering in their future lives. But fourteen years later God's promise was fulfilled in the birth of Isaac "not a son by proxy, according to the flesh; Isaac was his son by promise, a living witness to divine grace."

---

[115] Stott, *The One Way*, 122–128.

[116] Stott, *The One Way*, 122–123.

[117] Hendriksen, *Galatians*, 180, also makes the point that Abraham had *two* sons, Ishmael by Hagar and Isaac by Sarah. "If physical decent from Abraham is so all-important, then they who are Jews by birth are not any better off than are the Ishmaelites."

[118] Stott, *The One Way*, 124.

[119] George, *Galatians*, 338.

Moo[120] has included in his discussion two particular translations of "born according to the flesh" which would point us in the direction of the agitators and their aims regarding submission to the law: TNIV "as a result of human effort" and the more expansive NLT "in a human attempt to bring about the fulfilment of God's promise." But no "human effort" can bring about salvation. It involves God's initiative in sending his Son for helpless sinners and also his initiative through the work of the Holy Spirit is the human heart bringing us to faith.

Hendriksen[121] stresses that Isaac was born through Abraham's faith in the promise, "spirit-born (verse 29), for it was the Holy Spirit who caused the promise to be realised. The conclusion, therefore that Isaac is a symbol of all Spirit-born (now in the sense of *regenerated*) men is not far-fetched." This is an important point for whole of Galatians – as we have stressed, the initiative of God, rather than human effort. God by his Spirit works in regeneration and this blessing leads on to the empowering and enabling of the Spirit which is set out in chapters 5–6. Therefore Paul, in using an allegorical argument, is actually teaching that it is the people of the law, or those being encouraged to be circumcised and submit to that law who are like the offspring of the slave woman! Hendriksen[122] makes it clear, as was noted earlier, that the law was not given as a means of achieving salvation as the Judaizers erroneously interpreted it. One can note that God could still dwell in the midst of a failing people through the sacrifices offered in the tabernacle. Individuals could be forgiven. But "when it (the law) is, nevertheless, viewed as a force by means of which a person achieves deliverance and salvation, as the Jews and Judaizers actually viewed it, then it enslaves. It then not only leaves men in their bondage but more and more adds to their heavy burden."

The children of the free are those who have received the promised justification by faith. In reality, his readers are all an Ishmael or an Isaac, either still what they were by nature, a slave, or through the blessing of Abraham, by the new birth and the grace of God, set free. This is basically what Paul's purpose is as Witherington[123] points out. Sarah is not mentioned by name for:

> What is important here for Paul is not who Sarah is as a person but the fact that she was a free woman and bore free children. In other words, what is going on here is a contrast between freedom and slavery, two conditions the Galatians must choose between.

We note the point that Sarah (v. 22), Isaac (v. 23), the Jerusalem above (v. 26) are all said to be "free" (cf. 5:1 of the Galatian Christians; also earlier, 2:4). The fact that

---

[120] Moo, *Galatians*, 299.

[121] Hendriksen, *Galatians*, 181.

[122] Hendriksen, *Galatians*, 182.

[123] Witherington 111, *Grace in Galatia*, 326, n. 15. Hendriksen, *Galatians*, 181, gives the text a "double" interpretation, wishing to include the idea that Ishmael was born by nature i.e., "his parents' natural power of procreation," what Abraham and Hagar could accomplish themselves (cf. John 1:13; Rom 9:7–9). Ishmael represents "all those who base their hopes for eternity on what they themselves are able to effectuate, that is, on their good works."

Ishmael is also not mentioned by name supports this view that it is what the individuals *represent* that is in Paul's mind as we mentioned earlier in the excursus.

Children of the New Covenant, Not the Old

Paul suggests in v. 24–25 that the two women stand for two covenants (also two Jerusalems, as we will see). The old covenant was based upon law; he mentions "Mount Sinai" which of course is where the law was given. Paul writes "she is Hagar;" both Sinai and Hagar[124] are linked. As Hendriksen[125] affirms, "both can produce nothing but slaves." However, the new Christian covenant which was first of all foreshadowed through Abraham was based upon promises. As Stott[126] explains, in the law the responsibility was based upon men – "thou shalt not." But in the promise, God himself accepts the responsibility, "I will." As we noted, Sarah is not mentioned by name, but naturally she is meant, although the promise is the focus and the fact that she was "the free woman."

People of the Jerusalem Above, Not the Jerusalem Beneath

The women in vv. 25–27 also stand for the earthly and the heavenly Jerusalem. The meaning is of course two peoples, as Moscow, Tokyo and London can stand for the respective peoples. So, Hagar stands for the covenant of law and also corresponds to the present Jerusalem who is in slavery with her children.[127] Bruce[128] explains it is not actually the literal city which is in view but "the whole legal system of Judaism, which had its world-centre in Jerusalem." Note that Paul uses here the more Hebraic (and LXX) form of the word "Jerusalem" (compare 1:17–18; 2:1) since he is emphasising the religious significance of the city. This is true for both the earthly and heavenly Jerusalem. Longenecker[129] also observes that:

> For Jews generally, the salvation-historical line of Scripture began with Abraham, Sarah, and Isaac, extended on through Moses and the Torah given

---

[124] Moo points out how the early scribes supplied a range of readings for this verse. Following a full discussion of the various possibilites, he suggests we understand the use of "quasi-adjectives" i.e., "the Hagar Sinai mountain" and so paraphrases: "Now the mountain that is Sinai and that is represented by Hagar is, to be sure, in Arabia; nevertheless ... she [or it] represents the present Jerusalem." Moo, *Galatians*, 302–304, 313. Bruce, *The Epistle to the Galatians*, 219, tells us more about "the slave woman." He points out that Hagar (Heb *Hāgār*) is similar to the Semitic word "rock" which also reminds us of Mount Sinai.

[125] Hendriksen, *Galatians*, 183.

[126] Stott, *The One Way*, 124.

[127] George, *Galatians*, 341 also comments upon the textual possibilities here in this verse. He explains that some early MSS omit the word "Hagar" from the text. The twenty-sixth edition of the Nestle-Aland Greek NT prefers the longer reading which enables us to keep the link "with her children" in the concluding clause.

[128] Bruce, *The Epistle to the Galatians*, 219.

[129] Longenecker, *Galatians*, 213. McDonald, *Freedom in Faith*, 112, also stresses the contrast, "The Jerusalem which now is, is the home of the religion of bondage, which shuts up God in a temple made with hands and substitutes for His spiritual worship a scrupulous observance of legal enactments."

at Mt. Sinai, and came to focus in the present city of Jerusalem as the epitome of Israel's hopes regarding the law, the land, and the temple.

Paul now affirms that the natural descendants of Abraham are in bondage through their dependence upon law-works![130] George[131] points out that the word "corresponds" (v. 25) is only here in the NT. "It means 'stand in the same line' or 'place in the same column'." He sets out how things "correspond."

HAGAR	SARAH
Ishmael, son of slavery	Isaac, son of freedom
Birth "according to the flesh"	Birth "through the promise"
Old Covenant New Covenant	Mount Sinai (Mount Zion)
Present Jerusalem	Heavenly Jerusalem

He affirms that the efforts of the Judaizers "to make circumcision and observance of the law an entrance rite into the Christian faith was nothing less than a futile attempt to reverse the divinely ordained course of redemptive history."

Hendriksen[132] also makes the point that Hagar and Mount Sinai is the Jerusalem of Paul's own day – certainly all of carnal Israel who had rejected Christ and his glorious gospel:

> These have enslaved themselves to Sinai's law, for they imagine that by strict obedience to this legal code – with emphasis on its ceremonial regulations, expanded by man-made additions – they can work their way into the kingdom of heaven. But they are wrong. Mount Sinai is in Arabia, and Arabia is a desert. It is not the land of promise; it is not "Zion" (Heb 12:22; Rev 14:1).

Longenecker[133] also admits we have here from Paul, the former Pharisee, "undoubtedly a shocking realignment of personages and places in a Jewish understanding of salvation history." Sarah, Isaac's mother, whose son was born supernaturally according to promise and free, stands for the heavenly Jerusalem, the new people of God, Gentiles and some Jews, the Christian Church!

---

[130] One must recognise that the nature of Palestinian Judaism being identifed here is akin to that described in the excursus in chapter 2:16. The traditional viewpoint of the Judaism of Paul's day, as explained there, is seen as largely legalistic with a perverted understanding of the role of the law. This is the "Jerusalem" also being described here.

[131] George, *Galatians*, 342.

[132] Hendriksen, *Galatians*, 183.

[133] Longenecker, *Galatians*, 213.

Hendriksen[134] again writes of the phrase "the Jerusalem above." The concept is not just a reference to the "Church Triumphant," but includes "the church here below" who receive heavenly blessings "producing conditions on earth which in measure reflect those in heaven." He considers how the true children of God, whether Gentiles or Jews, who have been born from above, receive "heaven's peace" (Isa 11:6–9; cf. Jer 23:6; 31:31–34); heaven is "their homeland" (Phil 3:20) and they seek to live by its standards. "Are not their names inscribed in heaven's register? ... Is it not to heaven that their thoughts and prayers ascend? ... Their Savior dwells there, living evermore to make intercession for them." Moo[135] also takes the same position:

> It is fundamental to Paul's argument here, and to NT teaching in general, to claim that the eschatological realities to which the image of "new Jerusalem" refers have, in fact, entered into history in the work of Christ: the "fullness of the time" has arrived (4:4).... Paul is convinced, of course, that the "New Jerusalem," representing the age to come, has come into being and that it is through his Spirit-empowered preaching of the gospel that this new Jerusalem is being populated. And this gospel, Paul is convinced, is only truly the gospel if it is a matter of a freely offered gift, apart from any human contribution.

Therefore, Paul is affirming that this gift of salvation is possible solely through the cross and by faith alone in the Christ who died and rose again.

Concerning the "Jerusalem above" Paul adds, "she is our mother"[136] – the "our" is emphatic – and we are citizens who are in the new covenant and free! Note that the possessive pronoun ἡμῶν *hēmōn* "our" refers to all true believers in Christ, the children of promise (3:29), not just the Galatian Christians. So, Stott[137] stresses that Paul is arguing it is not enough to claim Abraham as our Father. "The crucial question concerns who our mother is." As McDonald[138] affirms, "From this heavenly Jerusalem come the children of the free woman; here is the home of free worship of God in the Spirit – of sons serving in love, not slaves working in fear."

Paul, using faithfully the LXX and Hebrew text, quotes Isaiah 54:1[139] employing the normal method in a quotation, "For it is written." The reference is where the prophet

---

[134] Hendriksen, *Galatians*, 184.

[135] Moo, *Galatians*, 305, 307. While scholars will revel in all these affirmations about the Christian church by Longenecker, Hendriksen and Moo, some may still look outside Galatians to find other statements which they will interpret as also affirming a future for Israel as a nation, e.g., Rom 11:25. Also, is there another future earthly Jerusalem to come with another ultimate fulfilment not the focus here in Galatians?

[136] Longenecker, *Galatians*, 215, briefly lists the rich Jewish heritage associated with Jerusalem as "our mother" referring to Ps 87; Isa 66:7–11; also in 4 Ezra 10:7, 25–57. "Here in his Hagar-Sarah allegory, therefore Paul conflates two Jewish traditions: the first that of Sarah, the barren free-born wife of Abraham, who was destined to be the mother of nations: the second, that of the holy city of Jerusalem, the eschatological Zion, who symbolically is the mother of God's own."

[137] Stott, *The One Way*, 126.

[138] McDonald, *Freedom in Faith*, 113.

[139] Some have noted that Isaiah 54:1 is "altogether allegorical," finding a link to Hannah's song in 1 Sam. 2:4ff. on barrenness and fruitfulness. Luther, *A Commentary on St. Paul's Epistle to the Galatians*, 422.

is addressing prophetically the exiles in the Babylonian captivity. Stott[140] explains that Paul sees their state in exile, under divine judgment to that of a barren woman finally deserted by her husband, and their future state after the restoration to that of a fruitful mother with more children than ever. God promises that his people will be more numerous after their return than they were before. So, the two women here both refer to Jerusalem or Zion at different stages of its existence. "This promise received a literal but partial fulfilment in the restoration of the Jews to the promised land. But its true, spiritual fulfilment, Paul says, is in the growth of the Christian church, since Christian people are the seed of Abraham." Moo[141] affirms that:

> The contrast in 54:1, then, is between the "present" Jerusalem, apparently "barren" and "desolate" and the same city renewed and repopulated by God's own intervention on behalf of his people.... Paul's quotation of Isa 54:1 in this verse provides the lens through which he interprets and applies the narrative about Hagar and Sarah.

It seems clear that the introductory formula (above) may use the quotation of Isaiah 54 as the hermeneutical justification of all the verses, vv. 22–26, where Paul has been affirming his argument.

The Jerusalem that is above has many, many more children than ever the old Jerusalem had. As Hendriksen[142] explains, this blessing and acceptance has come about not by human exertion, but through "the work of the Lord, the result of his enduring loving-kindness (cf. Isa 54:7–8)" actually, through the realization of "the very promise that gave Isaac to Abraham and Sarah." At this time (the writing of Galatians) Paul's mission ministry had just begun with the first missionary journey (Acts 13:1–14:28); but he was appointed by God as apostle to the Gentiles (Acts 9:15–16; Gal 2:7–9). God was going to use him and his missionary team in a remarkable way (Rom 15:16–24); and now we know that there was much more expansion to come – through the cross and by faith. All this is part of the Christological fulfilment as both Moo and Witherington consider.

In v. 28 Paul now sets out the conclusions of his Hagar-Sarah allegory in vv. 22–27. He applies the story's personal application to the current situation. He affirms, "Now you (the "you" is emphatic), brothers (the Galatians) like Isaac, are children of promise." How affectionately he addresses them. They had fellowship links in the family of faith; they were not just sons of Abraham by nature; they were children of promise, brothers by grace.[143] Responding to the preaching of Christ crucified (3:1) in Jesus Christ they have received "the blessing of Abraham" and "the promised Spirit through faith" (3:14). "Like Isaac." Here Isaac is mentioned by name. The

---

[140] Stott, *The One Way*, 126; see also Fung, *The Epistle to the Galatians*, 211, for the fulfilment of the Isaianic prophecy in the gathering of all believers in Christ into the church.

[141] Moo, *Galatians*, 306.

[142] Hendriksen, *Galatians*, 185.

[143] Fung, *The Epistle to the Galatians*, 212, points out that the word "promise" is emphatic and placed before "children"; therefore, "its qualitative aspect is stressed through the absence of the article."

Judaizers were advocating that they could only become part of the family of Abraham through circumcision; Paul insists that they were by faith *already like Isaac.* Moo[144] points out that κατα *kata* means "like" or "just as" or "in the pattern of." The Galatian believers, just like Isaac, were children born as a result of the promise of God. For Moo:

> The likeness includes both the means ("as God graciously does what he has promised") but also perhaps the outcome ("as God gives life to Sarah's 'dead' body, so in conjunction with the resurrection of Christ, he gives life to people 'dead in trespasses and sins'"; Eph.2:1; see Rom 4:17–21).

Paul continues to make clear the situation and consequences through their link with Isaac – as Moo[145] puts it, "Paul raids the Genesis narrative one more time to suggest a parallel between the Galatians and the agitators/Jews, on the one hand, and Isaac and Ishmael, on the other; on the basis of this comparison, he calls on his readers to take action (v. 30)." The Galatian churches should expect persecution. The ἀλλά *alla* "but" of v. 29 is best translated as having its usual adversative meaning – they had received great blessings through their link with Abraham and Isaac, *but* they should not assume that they would also not experience suffering.

Isaac, it appears, was the object of Ishmael's scorn and resentment, as Sarah had been in the past from Hagar (Gen 16:4–5). Genesis 21:9 states that Ishmael was "laughing" ESV; the KJV has "mocking."[146] McDonald[147] comments, "Hagar's feelings toward her mistress were continued in her son; and the same attitude of spiteful opposition and of hateful antipathy was taken up by him who was born according to the flesh to him who was born according to promise. And so it ever is." The theme of laughter therefore is clearly there in the whole conception of Isaac (Gen 18:12; 21:6). Here Sarah is convinced that when Abraham would be gone the child Isaac would not be safe from his older half-brother – probably around seventeen, with Isaac, a boy of three years of age at that time.[148] George[149] can state, "He (Paul) clearly saw a corresponding historical parallel between the mistreatment of Isaac by Ishmael and the persecution being inflicted on Christians in his day."

---

[144] Moo, *Galatians*, 309.

[145] Moo, *Galatians*, 308.

[146] Hendriksen, *Galatians*, 185–86, explains that the Hebrew text lacks the words after "mocking" i.e., "her son Isaac." but "this object, added by the Septuagint and thus also by the Vulgate, etc., undoubtedly expresses what the writer had in mind, as the context clearly indicates." He rejects the RSV rendering of Ishmael "playing with" Isaac. Nowhere in the OT does the verb refer to "innocent fun" (cf. Gen 19.14; 39:14; Exod 32:6; Jud. 16:25).

[147] McDonald, *Freedom in Faith*, 115.

[148] Hendriksen, *Galatians*, 185, points out that the weaning of a child took place usually at around three years of age. Here Abraham celebrated this moment by organising a great feast. Ishmael, as was noted, would be around seventeen years of age.

[149] George, *Galatians*, 346.

Note how Paul refers to Ishmael and Isaac, "He who was born according (κατὰ *kata*) to the flesh persecuted him who was born according ((κατὰ *kata*) to the Spirit" (v. 29). Moo[150] points out that:

> The preposition (κατὰ *kata*) probably here indicates "the nature, kind, peculiarity or characteristics" of the births of Ishmael and Isaac.... Ishmael's birth "according to the flesh" suggests that he was born in the natural way and by the power of human decision. In contrast, then, Isaac's birth "according to the Spirit" would be a birth characterized by the work of the Spirit, which may mean "took place by the power of the Spirit"...

How fitting a description of the birth of Isaac this is, in light of the parallel to Galatian believers "born" or regenerated by the Spirit of God!

Regarding the persecution of the "Spirit-born," it is clear from Acts 13:50; 14:2–5, 19 that the Galatian Christian community experienced real hostility from the Jews of Antioch, Iconium and Lystra. Sarah urges Abraham to "cast out this slave woman with her son" (Gen 21:10). While God would make of Ishmael a nation, it was Isaac who was heir and must receive the inheritance. Abraham had first wanted Ishmael to be the heir, but God had chosen to establish his covenant with Isaac (Gen 17:18–21). Now God told Abraham to do as Sarah desired and "cast out" Hagar and her son (Gen 21:12). Isaac was the heir of the promises.

McDonald[151] affirms that Paul is not thinking here of the rejection of Israel as a nation as he understands in Rom 11, but the stark contrast between two irreconcilable systems, law and promise, salvation by works and salvation by grace. Others will suggest that the contrast is not between Christianity and Judaism, but between the Christian mission of Paul and the Christian mission of the agitators i.e., this is Paul's way of referring to the "persecution" of the Gentile believers in the pressure that was being brought to bear upon them to be circumcised and commit themselves to submit to the law, otherwise they would not be reckoned among God's people. But the context seems greater than just a reference to the agitators – is the teaching not given following the references to "the present Jerusalem" which is in slavery with her children? Again, this pressure from the agitators does not adequately describe the concept of persecution here. As Moo[152] affirms:

> The contrast between the "present Jerusalem" and the "Jerusalem above" better fits the fundamental salvation-historical contrast between Judaism as a whole, which is continuing to find its basic identity in a view of election that is tied up with law observance – and the emerging Christian movement,

---

[150] Moo, *Galatians*, 309–10.
[151] McDonald, *Freedom in Faith*, 116. Stott, *The One Way*, 127, adds a further insight. The Jews would interpret this verse as God's rejection of the Gentiles. Here Paul boldly reverses this and applies it "to the exclusion of unbelieving Jews from the inheritance." So, for the true Isaac's, while there is the pain of persecution, there is also the privilege of inheritance. (4:7; 2 Cor 6:8–10).
[152] Moo, *Galatians*, 310.

which insists on the presence of eschatological realities and orients its view of election to the person of Christ.

It is imperative to point out that there is absolute mutual incompatibility between the two systems of salvation. Bruce[153] maintains, "Legal bondage and gospel freedom cannot coexist." The way of salvation is not submitting to legal necessities but by grace, through the Spirit's initiative in regeneration, grasping by faith the blessings of justification, sonship and heirship and experiencing the daily power of the Holy Spirit – all because of the cross. No doubt that the reason why some commentators shy away from seeing the clear rejection of Judaism here is because of the fear of anti-Semitism, as George[154] explains:

> We must however for the sake of the souls of men recognise the reality of the situation. Stott[155] quotes Lightfoot as commenting, "the Apostle thus confidently sounds the death-knell of Judaism." The teaching with clear convictions and the stark choices Paul has expressed throughout Galatians reflects the phenomenal change which happened in his life on the Damascus road when he met the risen Christ. He was finished with Judaism as a way of salvation once and for all. The whole epistle gives evidence of his deep concern for the churches he had founded in Galatia, who were now in danger of accepting circumcision and turning back to law-keeping – they must realise the serious implications of this (1:6, 8–9; 2:21; 5:2–4).

The statements in v. 30 are also significant. Paul affirms what is expected of the Galatians. They are to "cast out the slave woman and her son." Paul retains the singular form of the OT text – is this only because he wishes to quote accurately, or to reflect the individual responsibility of every believer to reject this teaching of another gospel (1:6)? We can also ask whether Paul is not encouraging his Galatian converts to cast out every one of the Judaizers and their influence from the Christian congregations of Galatia. Paul again refers to the inheritance (see earlier 3:29; 4:1–2, 7). Moo explains that while both Ishmael and Isaac are "sons" (v. 22), and from both will come nations, only one is affirmed "heir" to all the spiritual blessings. So it is with the Galatians. As Hendriksen[156] states, "The inheritance (see on 3:9, 18, 29), is not for mockers or persecutors. It is for believers, for them alone."

Clearly v. 31, with the use of διό *dio* "therefore" and the direct address to the "brothers" is a fitting conclusion, confirming the whole point of the allegory, that the

---

[153] F. F. Bruce, "'Abraham Had Two Sons': A Study in Pauline Hermeneutics." In *New Testament Studies: Essays in Honor of Ray Summers* (Waco: Baylor University Press, 1975), 79.

[154] George, *Galatians*, 347, warns us of the danger, which has happened at different times through history of taking statements out of context and using them as an excuse for adopting anti-Semitic attitudes and activity against Jews. Such thinking forgets Paul's deep concern for his own nation (Rom 10:1). "No Gentile Christian who has truly grasped what Paul meant by grace will have any reason to boast or feel superior to the Jews," 347, n. 269.

[155] Lightfoot, *Saint Paul's Epistle to the Galatians*, 184 in Stott, *The One Way*, 128.

[156] Hendriksen, *Galatians*, 187.

true children of God are not those in bondage to law observance for acceptance[157] i.e., generally Abraham's natural descendants, but the children of promise, children by spiritual descent, free,[158] both Jews and Gentiles who share Abraham's faith. In fact, this verse itself seems to sum up the whole teaching of the letter. Stott[159] can apply the doctrine to the modern situation:

> The Ishmaels of this world trust in themselves that they are righteous, the Isaac's trust only in God, through Jesus Christ. The Ishmael's are in bondage, because this is what self-reliance always leads to; the Isaac's enjoy freedom, because it is through faith in Christ that men are set free. So we must seek to be like Isaac.

Note how Moo compares the conclusion of the argument in 3:29 with the conclusion of this paragraph:

> In Gal 3:7–29, Paul argued that Christians are, in Christ, the true "seed" of Abraham, heirs to the promises he was given. In this paragraph he has shown that Christians are the "children of the free woman," Sarah, and thus like Isaac are heirs of all the promises that God gave to Isaac and his descendants. Believers can trace their privileged status to both their paternity and their maternity.

Of course, the reason for Paul's use of the Sarah argument is surely to contrast the children of Abraham and Sarah with those of Abraham and Hagar. The inheritance is only because of Abraham.

In the next chapter he will expand on the concepts of "slavery" and the "freedom" which believers have. But what about the chapters to come? Longenecker[160] can explain that here in chapter 4:22f. there is an emphasis on two types of people represented by the two sons, those who live out their lives in terms of legal ordinances and those who live their lives by the Spirit's direction. He also notes as we have how Isaac is referred to as "born according to the Spirit." Paul has already introduced the Holy Spirit (3:2, 3, 5, 14), but followed that with "promise" or "promises" (3:16, 17, 18, 21, 22, 29;4:28), "inheritance" (3:18; 4:1–7, 21–31). From this point the references "become focused here and throughout the rest of the letter in

---

[157] Hendriksen, *Galatians*, 188–89, points out that the Greek text of v. 31 has "children of slave woman" omitting the article before "slave", "to emphasise her *slavish* quality" and to picture slavish dependence upon the law which cannot bring salvation; the text then has "of *the* free woman," to affirm our freedom. We are free in Christ, delivered from the curse of the law and having the freedom of access to the throne of grace.

[158] We should note that in v. 31 the statement in the LXX and MT of Gen 21:10 "my son Isaac" is replaced by Paul with "the son of the free woman." Is is not just because Paul has made the required change with Sarah speaking, but, in addition, "the free woman" actually adds emphasis to the whole "freedom" argument?

[159] Stott, *The One Way*, 129.

[160] Longenecker, *Galatians*, 216–17.

terms of the Spirit's presence and guidance in the believer's life." As George[161] explains:

> Paul is now ready to move on to the third major section of his letter in which he would set forth the goal of the gospel as God intended for it to be realized in the Spirit-controlled lives of the Galatian believers.

---

[161] George, *Galatians*, 348.

GALATIANS FIVE

Gal 5:1–26. Free at Last!

This chapter begins without any kind of transitional particle or phrase leading to difference of opinion about whether it still belongs to chapter 4. Some take v. 1 as the conclusion of 4:21–31– we can note how Paul makes reference again to himself in v. 2; others as the heading of the new chapter – it follows on with further teaching on the theme of freedom which is the focus in v. 13f. Can v. 1 be regarded as a transitional verse? Some identify it as a "Janus" from the Roman god with two heads, facing both ways. It will point back to "the free woman" (4:22, 23, 30, 31), in fact back to 1:4; 2:4, but still opens up the whole discussion in chapter 5 of the freedom believers now have in Christ and through the power of the Holy Spirit. This is the position taken in this commentary as the following pages will demonstrate.

Longenecker sees 5:1–12 as an *incluso* with 1:6–10 forming Paul's whole argument concerning the threat of the Judaizers. He points to the severity of both passages in 1:6–10 and 5:2–12; the reference to "the one who calls you" 1:6, 5:8; the use of "grace" 1:6, 5:4; "again" 1:9, 5:3; and the judgment references 1:8–9, 5:10b. This is quite a persuasive listing. Betz[1] also affirms, as Witherington and Moo,[2] that "freedom" is basic in the whole letter and "is the central theological concept which sums up the Christian's situation before God as well as in this world. It is the basic concept underlying Paul's argument throughout the letter." One can comment that "freedom" does play a significant role – but how do we receive it and upon what ground is it given? Of course, it comes to us through the cross.… We will see that it is Christ who delivers us from sin (1:4; 2:4; 3:14) by his redeeming death – this is the basis of everything – and the regenerating and empowering Spirit who makes this freedom real in our lives (3:14; 4:30; 5:5–25). Moo[3] also points out that Paul is returning here to many of the themes in 3:1–6: "so 3:1–6 and 5:1–12 bracket the argument in this part of the letter." We see that as one opens with the cross (3:1), so the other also ends with reference to the cross (5:11).

Circumcision has so far only been briefly mentioned (2:3); now we see that it is beginning to emerge as a real point of contention. Witherington[4] claims that this approach is often used as "a rhetorical strategy" which is known as *insinuatio*. It means that circumcision has special prominence in the letter and Paul will revisit it in a more prominent way when it comes to what he calls the *peroratio* (6:12–17). So, for Moo,[5] while the agitators pressed on the Galatian churches the necessity of circumcision not just as a "marker" of Jewishness in the pluralistic Greco-Roman

---

[1] Betz, *Galatians*, 255.
[2] See comments on 2:4 "false brothers who slipped in to spy out our freedom."
[3] Moo, *Galatians*, 316.
[4] Witherington 111, *Grace in Galatia*, 364.
[5] Moo, *Galatians*, 318.

world of the first-century, but a vital step if they were to be covenant people and found "righteous" he maintains:

> Circumcision is bound up with a commitment to obey the entire law (5:3). If they become circumcised the Galatians would tie themselves to a law that is outmoded (3:15–18; 4:1–3), demanding works that sinful humans cannot adequately produce (cf. 3:10, 12) and therefore subjecting its "doers" to a curse (3:10, 13; 4:4–5).

The first verse then gives us an assertion, "For freedom Christ has set us free," and a command, "stand fast therefore." Longenecker[6] takes the opening assertion as a dative of goal or purpose. Paul is urging us in the imperative which follows the dative to maintain our freedom. Witherington[7] reminds us of an inscription found at Delphi:

> For Freedom Apollo the Pythian bought from Sooibus of Amphissa a female slave whose name is Nicaea.... The purchase, however, Nicaea has committed unto Apollo for freedom.

The focus is the sacral redemption of slaves who pay money into the temple treasury. While the slave could not initiate his own freedom, the god could then purchase the slave out of his bondage. He then belongs to the god whose service is perfect freedom. So, the suitability of all this imagery is clear in that God in Christ initiated our redemption and set us free.

Stott[8] also comments upon the importance of these opening verses for the whole of the epistle. He explains that Galatians is essentially a polemical epistle as Paul responds to the introduction of erroneous teaching into the local churches. The contrast is basically between "two religions, one false and the other true." In this chapter first, in vv. 1–6, the focus is upon those who practise these two religions; second, vv. 7–12, between those who preach them. He is keen to stress that the theme of Christian freedom is basically, "freedom of conscience, freedom from the tyranny of the law, the dreadful struggle to keep the law, with a view to winning favour with God. It is a freedom of acceptance with God and of access to God through Christ."

Hendriksen[9] suggests that there are many different aspects to our freedom in Christ. First there is deliverance, a deliverance from the guilt and power of sin (Rom 6:18); from an accusing conscience (Heb 10:22); from the wrath of God (Rom 5:1; cf. Heb 10:27); the tyranny of Satan (2 Tim 2:26; cf. Heb 2:14 and Gal 5:1, 13); but he considers that Paul is likely thinking in the Galatian context of freedom from "the curse which the law pronounces upon the sinner who has been striving – unsuccessfully, of course – to achieve his own righteousness (Gal 3:13, 22–26; 4:1–

---

[6] Longenecker, *Galatians*, 224.
[7] Witherington 111, *Grace in Galatia*, 340 quoting M. Eugene Boring, Klaus Berger, and Carsten Colpe, eds., *The Hellenistic Commentary of the New Testament* (Nashville: Abington, 1995), 463.
[8] Stott, *The One Way*, 131–32.
[9] Hendriksen, *Galatians*, 192.

7)" and is now free from fear and has access to God. In addition, positively, the individual is free to walk and live in the Spirit (Gal 5:25 with all that this entails). Finally, he has freedom *plus.* Not only has the accused been declared not guilty, the slave has been emancipated but the judge or emancipator has gone beyond in grace to "adopt the acquitted individual as his son." He is free indeed!

We mentioned above that the chapter opens with the dative. How should we understand it? Some have taken it as an instrumental dative i.e., by the freedom (already spoken of in 4:21–31) Christ has made us free. Others, as Longenecker above, see it as a dative of purpose i.e., for the sake of, or with the goal of freedom, Christ has set us free. The second may be a better approach as Paul proceeds to outline for us the kind of freedom we have in this chapter. Here first he will remind them that they must "stand fast"[10] in it. This positive command is then followed by a negative which highlights the central problem which Paul is warning them of in this letter.

Free Not to Return to Bondage, the Bondage of the Law

Their former state is seen as one of slavery (v. 1). For many of them in Galatia their former slavery was to pagan gods – the *stoicheia* (4:9). They had been brought into freedom through regeneration, justification and basically, through the preaching of the cross. They were now being encouraged to return to bondage, this time the bondage of Judaism! "Do not submit again to a yoke of slavery" (v. 1). The verb here "Do not submit" means "do not be subject to" or "be burdened by." Longenecker[11] also explains that the noun "yoke" could be used in an honourable sense of Torah study or various kinds of social or family responsibility but "was also used figuratively in antiquity for any disagreeable burden that was unwillingly tolerated like slavery." One recalls 1 Tim 6:1 and Peter's statement in Acts 15:10, "why are you putting God to the test by placing a yoke on the neck of the disciples that neither our Fathers nor we have been able to bear?" Paul has reminded them earlier in this letter in 3:13, "Christ has redeemed us from the curse of the law by becoming a curse for us." How can we think of putting on the yoke again? As Moo[12] explains, the imagery of the yoke could sometimes be used by Jews to describe the law (e.g., *m. 'Abot* 3.5; cf. Matt 11:29–30; as above, Acts 15:10). "Of course, Jewish teachers would never have called the law a "yoke of slavery": this is Paul's summary of the effect that submission to the law would have for Galatian Gentile believers."

It is true that as Christians we were once under condemnation because we came short of the law's demands. When we could do nothing to change this, God himself took the initiative for us in sending his Son to the cross to bear the condemnation in our

---

[10] Moo points out that Paul elsewhere uses the same word for Christians to stand fast in the blessings they have received in Christ, in the new realm of salvation, Phil 1:27; 4:1; 1 Thess. 3:8; 2 Thess. 2:15. "It has a military flavor: the rendering 'stand firm' found in many English versions, is quite justified." Moo, *Galatians*, 320.

[11] Longenecker, *Galatians*, 225.

[12] Moo, *Galatians*, 320.

place. So, as was noted above, through our faith in him we now have freedom of conscience from the guilt of sin, freedom from the tyranny of the law. We must "stand fast" in this freedom and not be persuaded that we have to win our acceptance with God through our own obedience.

Free Not to Require Circumcision

In v. 2 Paul focuses directly upon the issue of circumcision and his Galatian converts for the first time. As we noted, it has been in the background until this point (2:3, 7–9, 12). Now Paul writes pointedly and personally to them. Longenecker[13] translates "Mark my words! I Paul...." The word "Look!" stresses this, as does the emphatic ἐγὼ *egō* "I" linked to his own personal name "I Paul" (see also 2 Cor 10:1; Eph 3:1; Col 1:23; 1 Thess 2:18). What he will write to them is from his own authority as an apostle, not the views of the "brothers who are with me" (1:2) and as their spiritual father (4:11–19). The whole tone becomes more severe and is sustained up until v. 12. The way the issue of circumcision is presented suggests that it had not happened yet (the conditional clause bears that out, "if you accept circumcision." It appears that the false teachers were still urging the converts to be circumcised, but they had not yet taken that step. Hendriksen[14] accepts that the Galatians were at this point "already yielding" to the Judaizers in observing the special days etc. (4:10) and "the danger was great" that they would yield also in the matter of circumcision.

Stott[15] makes the situation clear that while to some it may have seemed just a trivial matter – only a minor surgical operation on the body – Paul sees it as serious because of its doctrinal implications. "As the false teachers were pressing it, circumcision was neither a physical operation, nor a ceremonial rite, but a theological symbol. It stood for a particular type of religion." He reminds us of the insistence of the brothers from Judea in Acts 15:1, "Unless you are circumcised according to the custom of Moses, you cannot be saved." He continues, "Thus they were declaring that faith in Christ was insufficient for salvation. Circumcision and law-obedience must be added to it. This was tantamount to saying that Moses must be allowed to finish what Christ had begun." George[16] also explains the seriousness of this. It was in effect, a rejection of "God's all-sufficient provision for salvation through faith in Jesus Christ and his finished work on the cross." We should note that in 6:10 Paul will make clear that even those calling for circumcision, do not keep the law themselves.

Paul stresses the point "I testify again" (v. 3). The verb "testify" without the accusative means that it is not being used in the sense of bearing witness to

---

[13] Longenecker, *Galatians*, 225.

[14] Hendriksen, *Galatians*, 195.

[15] Stott, *The One Way*, 133. Moo explains that Paul's prohibition of circumcision is "contextually determined." Paul is strongly opposed to Gentiles being circumcised to qualify them for full membership of the people of God. As we have already noted earlier, he has no problem with the circumcision of Jews "when it is not a matter of a requirement for salvation" as in Timothy's case (Acts 16:1–3). Moo, *Galatians*, 322.

[16] George, *Galatians*, 357.

something, but means to make a declaration. With the use of "again" he is not referring to when he was formally with them, rather, he is either reminding them of what he had just said in v. 2 or, just emphasising or reinforcing the seriousness of the present situation – that those who receive circumcision are "bound to keep the whole law" (v. 3), are seeking "to be justified by the law" (v. 4). Bruce[17] points out the implications of the verb in the middle voice "get yourselves circumcised." Every Jewish male infant would be circumcised as a child – involuntarily. However, for these Gentile converts to accept circumcision now was to commit themselves to a whole way of life of which circumcision was the introductory rite.[18] In effect, they were placing themselves under the obligation of keeping the whole law to be accepted with God, a salvation through law keeping which was impossible! Paul has already made the situation clear in 3:10–11 that those who seek acceptance or justification by submission to the law cannot attain it but rather come under its curse.

A further warning is apparent in v. 4, "You are severed from Christ you who would be justified by the law; you are fallen away from grace." Paul is writing about whoever is thinking or trying – he is speaking about the present – to be justified "by the law," the instrumental use of the dative, they are "severed from Christ" or "have fallen away from (the) grace." The articular use "the" grace will mean the grace which according to Longenecker[19] "was distinctive to his (Paul's) proclamation of the gospel (1:6)." Stott[20] makes the point:

> You cannot have it both ways It is impossible to receive Christ thereby acknowledging that you cannot save yourself, and then receive circumcision, thereby claiming that you can. You have got to choose between a religion of law and a religion of grace, between Christ and circumcision. You cannot add circumcision (or anything else for that matter) to Christ as necessary for salvation, because Christ is sufficient for salvation in himself. If you add anything to Christ, you lose Christ. Salvation is in Christ alone, by grace alone, through faith alone.

Witherington[21] often highlights the spiritual immaturity of the Galatians. They were so easily led astray (3:1) and had received into their number those who were spreading the false teaching (5:9; 6:7–8). Here, he comments on the seriousness of the direction in which they were moving.

Christ by his death endured the curse of the law covenant so no-one else would have to endure it, and by doing so rendered the covenant's sanctions fulfilled, finished, over and done with, and thereafter null and void.... In Paul's view God has only one covenant one agreement about relationship between himself and his people at a time.

---

[17] Bruce, *The Epistle to the Galatians*, 229.
[18] Moo points out that circumcision is bound up with doing the law. Also, the δέ *de* here is explanatory, "now," not "but." Moo, *Galatians*, 322.
[19] Longenecker, *Galatians*, 228.
[20] Stott, *The One Way*, 133–34.
[21] Witherington, 111, *Galatians*, 367.

To submit to the law covenant is to imply clearly that the covenant inaugurated by Christ is null and void ... that Christ's death did not accomplish what Paul says it did.... Thus the Galatians are confronted with a choice between two covenants, the question is which covenant and covenantal stipulations will they live by?

The stark reality was that if they choose to submit to circumcision, they commit themselves to observe the whole law covenant. Christ's death has not brought it to an end. They lose Christ and his death has accomplished nothing. So as Bruce[22] also maintains. "Christ will provide unlimited help to those who place their unlimited trust in him, but no help at all to those who bypass his saving work and think to become acceptable to God by circumcision or other legal observances." Again[23] referring to 1:6 "called ... in the grace of Christ" he maintains as was already noted above, that "to forsake his call for the way of law involved self-expulsion from his grace, because they no longer relied on it."

Moo[24] also comments upon the use here of the phrase "severed from Christ" (using ἀπό *apo* "from" with the verb), which is found in Paul in just one other context i.e., Rom 7:1–6. Believers, once bound by the law, have been "released from" the law to be joined to Christ and serve in the new way of the Spirit (vv. 5–6). "Tragically, the Galatians are flirting with the possibility of reversing this situation; binding themselves to the law and becoming alienated from Christ." Of course, as George[25] has maintained, "Paul did not here contemplate the forfeiture of salvation by a truly regenerated believer." We must note the "confidence" (5:10) the apostle still had in them – if they really had come to know the Lord when he was first with them.

Free to Live in the Power of the Spirit

In vv. 5–6 the pronoun changes and Paul includes himself – the "we" in the Greek text at the beginning of the sentence is emphatic and inclusive of all who are trusting in Christ, not law. Longenecker[26] agrees with other scholars like Betz and Burton that these verses almost sum up all that Paul has been unfolding in his past argumentation, see 2:15–21; 3:1–4:11. He quotes Burton, in whose opinion "there is no more important sentence in the whole epistle, if indeed in any of Paul's epistles. Each term and construction of the sentence is significant."

First Paul has highlighted "through the Spirit." The Holy Spirit was first introduced in 3:2–5. In 4:6 Paul again joins the sending of the Spirit into our hearts with the sending of God's Son. Also, in 4:29 as true believers, Jew and Gentile are linked with Isaac, who is described as the son "born according to the Spirit." We should also note

---

[22] Bruce, *The Epistle to the Galatians*, 229.
[23] Bruce, *The Epistle to the Galatians*, 231.
[24] Moo, *Galatians*, 326.
[25] George, *Galatians*, 360.
[26] Longenecker, *Galatians*, 229. Also Betz, *Galatians*, 262; Burton, *Galatians*, 279.

as George[27] pointed out, "The mention of the Spirit in this present verse anticipates the increasingly prominent role Paul would assign to the Spirit in his depiction of the Christian life in the closing two chapters of this letter." So, while he was there at the initiation of our spiritual life, the reference here points more to his enduement and enabling power for daily living (5:16–6:10).

The mention of "by faith" recalls the other major emphasis of the letter. We remember 2:16, the example of Abraham's faith in 3:6 and the fact that we are "all sons of God through faith" (3:26). Then we have the "hope," "we ourselves eagerly wait for the hope of righteousness." We must remember as we discussed in 1:4 Paul's apocalyptic perspective. Although we still live in this present evil age, through his work on the cross Christ has already brought to his people the blessings of the new age – justification, the gift of the Holy Spirit, the blessing of being part of the "Jerusalem above" – in fact, in 6:16, they are already part of "the new creation." So as Stott[28] explains the statement here refers to:

> The expectation for the future which our justification brings, namely spending eternity with Christ in heaven.... We do not *work* for it; we *wait* for it. We do not strive anxiously to secure it, or imagine that we have earned it by good works. Final glorification in heaven is as free a gift as our initial justification. So, by faith, trusting in Christ crucified, we wait for it.

Note also Bruce's helpful comments concerning the "hope of righteousness." He links it with the final verdict on the last day. "For those who believe in Christ such a verdict is assured in advance by the present experience of justification by faith ... In their case the eschatological verdict of "not guilty" is already realised." So, the whole emphasis of Paul's message of justification in Galatians and beyond is that divine righteousness is imputed here and now in the present through the cross and by faith in Christ (Gal 2:16; 3:22; 1 Cor 6:11; Rom 3:24; 5:1, 9). Rather than understand this as some suggest, the expectation is of entering into the fullness of our justification *in the future*, one can interpret the statement as Fung,[29] i.e., it is the hope to which the justification of believers, *which they already possess*, points them forward. The verb "wait for" is used elsewhere by Paul of eschatological expectation (Rom 8:19, 23, 25; 1 Cor 1:7; Phil 3:20; but here also, 4:5–7; 26–29). This is the ultimate accomplishment or glory of the cross, not the law. Hendriksen[30] maintains that what Paul has in mind is the fact that "our righteousness will be declared *publicly* (Cf. Matt 25:31–40; Luke 18:1–8; 1 Thess 3:13; 11 Thess 1:10)."

---

[27] George, *Galatians,* 360. This seems a clearer understanding of the teaching on the Spirit than in Moo at this point who suggests with 3:1–6 that "these two texts provide the rhetorical bookends to Paul's theological argument and appeal to the Galatians," Moo, *Galatians,* 34.

[28] Stott, *The One Way,* 134.

[29] Fung, *The Epistle to the Galatians,* 26.

[30] Hendriksen, *Galatians,* 197.

The main point Paul has made is signalled by the fact that he puts "through the Spirit" and "by faith" early in the Greek sentence, modifying the verb. As Moo[31] explains, "Paul's real concern in 5:5 is not to tell us something new about justification or righteousness but to insist that our right standing with God is finally confirmed for us though the Spirit and by means of faith." The word faith will echo the earlier occurrences (2:16; 3:8, 11, 24; indirect in 3:7, 9; see also 3:12, 22) and Paul has already emphasised the believers have graciously received the *experience* of the Spirit, 3:2, 5, 14 (his presence marking them out as recipients of God's covenant blessings) and the *work* of the Spirit is to come ((5:13–6:10). How we live "through the Spirit" is presented in v. 6.

Free to Live in Faith and Loving Service

Paul affirms in v. 6 that it is faith that is the key matter, not circumcision and the law. In fact, what matters is being "in Christ Jesus" (cf. 3:26–29) by faith. When a person is in Christ, nothing else or more is necessary. Neither circumcision nor uncircumcision can improve our standing before God (cf. 6:15). This state of circumcision or uncircumcision was all-important in the old order but not now in the new. As Moo[32] points out:

> His (Paul's) reference to both fundamental religious states (see the similar "neither Jew nor Greek" in 3:28; and 1 Cor 7:19) suggests that Paul is implicitly appealing to a fundamental theological conviction that undergirds the argument of Galatians: the fact that a new world has come into existence, a "new creation" so radically new that all human claims and status cease to have significance.

Salvation is not Christ plus anything, but Christ alone. We are in Christ by faith and so the Christian life is "faith working through love," as we saw, in the power of the Spirit (v. 5). Stott[33] makes clear that "it is not that works of love are added to faith as a subsidiary and secondary ground of our acceptance with God." It is important to stress that Paul never has implied that we are justified by love, either our love for God or others. We are justified by grace through faith in Christ crucified – his death for us. Bornkamm[34] insists that we never lose sight of the fact that our salvation is through God's grace – not through some expression of our love leading to justification. If anything else, other than faith he writes, "This represents a serious distortion of the relationship between faith, love, and justification. In speaking of justification Paul never talks of faith *and* love, but *only* of faith as receiving. Love is not therefore an additional prerequisite for receiving salvation." But we *can* add that the faith which saves is a faith which will manifest itself in works, or a faith which

---

[31] Moo, *Galatians*, 329. Moo throughout his commentary appears to stress the future dimension of justification. But if that is the case, he still affirms that faith is the means of entering, maintaining and also finally confirming that relationship on the final day.

[32] Moo, *Galatians*, 330.

[33] Stott, *The One Way*, 134.

[34] G. Bornkamm, *Paul* (New York, Harper & Row, 1971), 153.

issues in love, in acts of service. As Fung[35] asserts, "He (Paul) is saying simply that the faith which justifies is of such a nature that it will express itself through love." Moo[36] explains that these words "act as something of an anticipatory bridge between the central and concluding sections of the letter. 'Faith' plays a key role in 2:16 – 4:31, while 'love' is a prominent theme in 5:13 – 6:10." Thus, there is a strong link between "the theological section of the letter and the so-called ethical section."

As Witherington[37] explains, this is the first mention of love in the letter and here it is "an action word for Paul, referring not primarily to feelings but rather loving activities." The word is ἀγάπη *agape* which, while it is not used often in the LXX or extra-Biblical Greek literature, is found 75 times in Paul and 116 times throughout the NT. It expresses "the wholly generous, sacrificial and actively outreaching concern on their behalf shown by God in Christ (2.20)."[38] This is the love Christians are to show to others. As Witherington[39] stresses, their faith must be manifested, not by "doing works of the Mosaic law, but by doing works of piety and charity." This focus anticipates the future emphasis later in 5:13–6:10. McDonald[40] points us forward here to v. 14 explaining the real implication of what Paul is saying, "By this statement, Paul implies that the law had been set aside by being fulfilled in the one word "love" (cf. 5:14)."

Free to Rest in Our Acceptance With God

The apostle is going back to the concerns he expressed in 3:1–6 – in fact back to the opening paragraph, 1:6–9. The text in v. 7 resumes abruptly, – there is no particle or connecting conjunction. It continues with what Dunn[41] calls, "a series of abrupt expostulations, like snorts of indignation" as Paul challenges them: "You were running well. Who hindered you from obeying the truth?" He again reminds them of their past witness, their previously faithful spiritual condition, introducing an athletic metaphor which he used already of his own service (2:2) and would often use in his forthcoming letters of spiritual advancement (cf. 1 Cor 9:26; Phil 3:14; 2 Tim 4:7). The verb is imperfect, which was to remind them that they were running well in the past, but someone had "hindered" them. The verb was used initially to mean to "break up" a road and so to hinder, but came to mean to cut in across a runner or the placing of an obstacle which was thrown in the way to deviate them from the path. The churches in Galatia had had such a glorious "first lap" as Acts 13–14 documents, but someone from the crowd had cut in among them or other runners were causing them to stumble. From what he writes it seems that Paul does not have all the facts or a complete picture of the false teachers, but he does know that they had contradicted "the truth" (shorthand for "the truth of the gospel," 2:5, 14) his Galatian converts had

[35] Fung, *The Epistle to the Galatians*, 230.
[36] Moo, *Galatians*, 331.
[37] Witherington, 111, *Galatians*, 370.
[38] Dunn, *Galatians*, 271 in Witherington, 111, *Galatians*, 370.
[39] Witherington, 111, *Galatians*, 370.
[40] McDonald, *Freedom in Faith*, 126.
[41] Dunn, *Galatians*, 273.

first believed. The τις *tis* 'who" referring to the one who hindered might hint at a reference to Satan (1 Thess 2:18), but likely the indefinite pronoun will leave it with the Galatians themselves to identify the trouble-makers. The churches must remain committed to the truth they had initially received.

Paul in v. 8 writes about the source of the false doctrine: "This persuasion is not from him who calls you." As Longenecker[42] states, as far as the Judaizers were concerned, Paul believes "their work and influence to be without divine backing and totally of their own making." As far as the Christian community was concerned, God had called them in grace; the false teachers were advocating a doctrine of merit. This means that their message was totally inconsistent with the Galatians' call. Moo[43] makes the point with reference to the "call." "The one who calls them is God. As often in Paul, 'call' has the sense of God's effectual call, his powerful reaching out to bring people into relationship with himself." We should ask the question that if the message was not from God, what or rather who was its real source? Remember 3:1.

Next he deals with its influence; it "hindered" v. 7, "troubled" v. 10 and "unsettled" them, v. 12. It of course, came from the agitators. In v. 9 Paul warns that the error was spreading in the community like leaven. Yeast, or leaven was used to make the bread ferment – it appears Paul is using a well-known proverbial saying which carries the idea of the extensive effects that something small can have. If the apostle did not take action the danger was that it would spread even further and the whole could become contaminated. Witherington[44] points out that while in Matt 13:33/Luke 13:21 most scholars would interpret the concept positively of the growth of the kingdom of God, more often "leaven" in the NT and elsewhere in Greek and later Christian literature is used to describe corruption or evil (cf. Mark 8:15; *Quaest. Rom.* 109; 1 Clem. 5:6; *Magn.* 10.2). Also in Matt 16:6, 11–12 Jesus uses it of "the teaching" of the Pharisees. Paul himself can later use the concept of leaven of the possible spread of sin in the Corinthian church (1 Cor 5:6). Just as leaven was removed from the house at Passover time, so the teaching of the Judaizers involving faith plus circumcision and law keeping must be given no place among them.

Now its Ultimate Failure. Paul is sure the error will not triumph. The Galatians will continue to adhere to the truth of the gospel – "I (Paul's personal emphatic ἐγώ *egō*) have confidence in the Lord" (see also Rom 14:14; Phil 2:24; 2 Thess 2:3). The thoughts of George[45] are relevant in relation to Paul's statements in 5:4, 7. He explains that:

> From God's omniscient perspective, of course, no person who has been genuinely regenerated will ever utterly and finally fall away from the faith (cf. John 10:28; Eph 1:4–6; Rom 8:29). From our limited point of view, however, persons who appear as bona fide Christians do abandon the truth

[42] Longenecker, *Galatians*, 230.
[43] Moo, *Galatians*, 334.
[44] Witherington, 111, *Galatians*, 372.
[45] George, *Galatians*, 364.

of the gospel (cf. 1 John 2:19; Rom 1:22–23). Paul had "confidence" that the Galatians could be won back and thus laboured strenuously to that end. So must every minister of the gospel who counsels with those who may be tempted to abandon the race they have begun.

Paul recalls with much confidence how they had initially responded to the preaching of the cross, the power of God which had been demonstrated among them, their baptism and the forming of local Christian communities in south Galatia. The confidence he expressed concerning their perseverance was not just a wishful hope but reliance on the Lord and the reality of his grace and the presence of the Holy Spirit at work at least in the majority of them. For Hendriksen[46] Paul's confidence in them is expressed in other texts in the letter (3:4b; 4:6, 7); and in the frequent use of the "endearing form of address: 'brothers' (1:11; 3:15; 4:12, 28, 31: 5:11, 13; 6:1, 18)."

Concerning "the one who is troubling you," while elsewhere Paul could refer to the Judaizers in the plural (1:7; 5:12), here he focuses on the leader "whoever he is" – or however exalted his rank. He will fall ultimately under the judgment of God. The word here is κρίμα *krima* and points to the final judgment (see also 1:8–9; see also e.g., Rom 2:2, 3; 3:8; 5:16; 13:2; 1 Tim 5:12).

It appears that these false teachers were even claiming that Paul was an advocate of their views. He denies it. He was not "still" preaching circumcision[47] and asks how he could then "still" be persecuted (see 4:29)? He would surely have been spared this at the hands of the Jews. It was they who were preaching circumcision; he was preaching the cross (6:14). The only possibility concerning Paul preaching circumcision would be in his former life within Judaism.

If he was preaching circumcision as they suggest "In that case the offence of the cross has been removed" (v. 11), or "is abolished." Paul focuses again on the cross and what Christ accomplished there. The offence of the cross or the stumbling block of the cross was of course the unacceptable idea for Jews of the possibility of a crucified Messiah. But while that still remained true there is something more meant here. When one preaches circumcision with the following commitment of keeping the law to be saved, one is nullifying the message of the cross. To trust in the cross alone was for Paul and the Galatians to confess that they are hopeless sinners who cannot save themselves by anything or everything that they could do. All notions of self-help and any possibility of saving themselves is ruled out. This was an "offence" to the pride of man. Just as for example, in the Book of Hebrews the once for all sacrifice of

---

[46] Hendriksen, *Galatians*, 203.

[47] It is possible, even practically certain, that *before* his conversion because of his great zeal for the Jewish tradition (1:14), he did preach circumcision to the Gentiles or God-fearers and proselytes in the Jerusalem and Judean synagogues (1:23). But that was before 1:16, the Damascus Road, over twenty years earlier. 1 Cor 7:18–19 reveals Paul's thinking since his conversion regarding circumcision, as was noted earlier. A Christian should remain in the condition in which God saved him. Gentiles need not seek to become Jews, not Jews Gentiles. The circumcision of Timothy, who had a Jewish mother, as he joined Paul's mission team in Acts 16:3, was to give him greater opportunity in the evangelisation of Jewish communities.

Christ (Heb 10:12) brought the sacrifices in the temple to an end or "abolished" them (Heb 10:18), so to reinstate circumcision and law-keeping was in effect saying that the cross meant nothing and had no power to save. It was effectively nullified! Fung[48] emphasises also the difference, "justification through legal works would enable one to speak of a 'righteousness of my own', whereas the preaching of the cross offers only 'the righteousness which comes from faith in Christ.'" Barrett[49] makes the point very clearly:

> You cannot preach both the cross and circumcision for the cross is the enemy of all rights and institutions to which men cling for salvation, in which they suppose they can make their salvation secure. It is circumcision as security, not as an example of a national custom, that Paul opposes. And the cross is a denial of all security.... The man who hangs on the cross has surrendered every kind of human security, and those who follow him must surrender it too. There is nothing so wounding as this to man's pride.

So as Stott[50] again stresses, circumcision stands for a religion of *human* achievement, of what man can do, but Christ "stands for a religion of *divine* achievement, of what God has done through the finished work of Christ."

Paul was so concerned at the damage they were doing and his deep love for these people he wished that these false teachers would "emasculate themselves." This statement has generated much discussion and many different English translations.[51] Bruce[52] translates the text here, "I wish that those who are upsetting you would complete their cutting operation – on themselves!" George[53] refers to the worship of Cybele, a popular cult in Asia Minor, where, in devotion to the Mother goddess, the worshippers would emasculate themselves. The Judaizers were no better guides than these priests. Fung[54] highlights Deut 23:1, which refers to those who are to be excluded from entering the assembly of the Lord because of physical mutilation. It is better if the false teachers shut themselves out i.e., it refers to self-excommunication, or they were similarly excluded. Hendriksen[55] however considers that a "more reasonable interpretation" which reflects the use of the verb in contemporary sources

---

[48] Fung, *The Epistle to the Galatians*, 241. He actually entitles the section 5v7–12 "THE CROSS VERSES CIRCUMCISION." Stott, *The One Way*, 137, also agrees, "To preach circumcision is to tell sinners that they can save themselves by their own good works; to preach Christ crucified is to tell them that they cannot and that only Christ can save them through the cross."

[49] C.K. Barrett, *Freedom and Obligation: A Study of the Epistle to the Galatians* (Philadelphia: Westminster, 1985), 69.

[50] Stott, *The One Way*, 138.

[51] Various suggestions are e.g., RSV, "mutilate themselves"; NEB, "make eunuchs of themselves"; JB, "see the knife slip", Moffatt, "get themselves castrated"; or a more drastic translation, KJV, "I would they were cut off which trouble you." Some suggest this means to be "cut off" from the church, but that is not the most likely meaning when the KJV was translated in 1611!

[52] Bruce, *The Epistle to the Galatians*, 233.

[53] George, *Galatians*, 372. Also W. Durant, *Caesar and Christ* (New York: Simon and Schuster, 1944).

[54] Fung, *The Epistle to the Galatians*, 242.

[55] Hendriksen, *Galatians*, 205.

is to follow the NEB translation i.e., "make eunuchs of themselves." Moo[56] points out that it should be recognised that "ancient authors frequently used language that today would be considered overbold" and again, that self-castration was a "more widespread phenomenon in Paul's day."

It has been pointed out that the statement is a reminder of Paul's opening anathema against those who disturb the church through the promulgation of a false gospel (1:6–9). His converts must not let themselves be troubled or tortured but rest in the assurance of their salvation – through faith in Christ and him crucified, without circumcision or law-keeping. They are free, accepted and can rest – and in fact, rejoice in their acceptance with God.

Free, But Not to Indulge the Flesh or Live as We Choose

The ψάρ *yar* should be taken as just the beginning of the next stage of the argument. Paul again uses the affectionate term "brothers" since the appeal is applied to them all. For Longenecker[57] the term is constantly appearing at "the epistolary seams of Galatians (1:1; 3:15; 4:12, 28, 31; 5:11 and 6:18)" which are more significant than has been noted. Also, the concept of serving others begins here and concludes with the same theme in 6:10 – an *inclusio*?

Once more in vv. 13–15 we are reminded about the true nature of Christian freedom, that to which God had "called" them. Stott[58] again explains that Christian freedom, "is a freedom of conscience. According to the Christian gospel no man is truly free until Jesus Christ has rid him of the burden of his guilt." Again, "Our Christian life began not with our decision to follow Christ but with God's call for us to do so. He took the initiative in his grace while we were still in rebellion and sin. In that state we neither wanted to turn from sin to Christ, nor were we able to. But he came to us and called us to freedom." As we noted from Moo in the last section, all this is an effectual call, by grace – Paul had experienced this call by grace (1:15) and so had the Galatians (1:6). This is true of all born again Christians. We were living in sin, rebels, but God took the initiative not just in sending his Son, but in moving in our hearts by his Spirit, calling us to Christ and to himself. Stott then explains more about our Christian freedom. "In brief, it is freedom from the awful bondage of having to merit the favour of God; it is not freedom from all controls." Let us consider this fact.

Moo[59] also outlines what Paul means by the blessing of Christian freedom in Galatians; it involves freedom from the powers of the old age, sin, the elements of this world, false gods and from the bondage to the law. Now "Paul uses the theme of freedom effectively to create a transition into the ethical concerns that dominate 5:13–6:10." But now alternatively, he will stress that Christian freedom is not

[56] Moo, *Galatians*, 338.
[57] Longenecker, *Galatians*, 236.
[58] Stott, *The One Way*, 139.
[59] Moo, *Galatians*, 343.

libertinism or licence, freedom from all moral restraints. We will also learn that it is a freedom which is characterized by love, service and a life empowered by the Spirit of God. As Moo explains, "The freedom that Christ has won for us (v. 1) and to which we have been called by God (v. 13) is a freedom to be what God originally made us to be. And as Paul will explain, God has called his people to live in loving, sacrificial service with one another."

Paul uses an emphatic "you" which clearly distinguishes them from the Judaizers and also reminds them that they were not just delivered from condemnation and the guilt of sin, having an assurance of acceptance with God, justified, a new creation, having received the gift of the Holy Spirit, sons of God but they were also "called to freedom."[60] He has warned them in the opening verses of the chapter that they must not return to slavery – which would be the case if justification and life depend upon their circumcision and the performance of certain requirements of law. But now, as we noted, he writes of the opposite extreme. They must realise that freedom does not mean excess or what Moo[61] calls, "the abuse of freedom." The Christian can never say, "I am free to do as I like." Paul had been accused of teaching this. However he has made clear in this letter that by freedom he means freedom from the condemnation of the law; from the awful bondage of having to merit the favour of God, but *not* freedom from all controls. This is clear in his use of the adverb μόνον *monon*, "only" which limits the freedom – also with the inclusion of the article with the second use of the word i.e., "the freedom." Therefore, Paul is not writing about freedom to sin i.e., a self-seeking and sinful use of freedom – what he calls giving "opportunity for the flesh."

The word σάρξ *sarx* "flesh" has different uses in Galatians. In 1:16; 2:16, 20; 4:13–14, 23, 29; 6:10–18 it refers to what is human or physical; here it has an ethical sense. As Longenecker[62] explains, "It has often been noted that σάρξ used ethically has to do with humanity's fallen, corrupt, or sinful nature as distinguished from human nature as originally created by God." This is the sense in which we understand it in this passage. A fallen, sinful nature which is self-centred, self-seeking and self-asserting. While other English translations have suggested a more descriptive rendering,[63] ESV just uses the word "flesh." For Silva[64] the use of "flesh" in this ethical sense is a reminder of the life of the old aeon, i.e., "the present evil age (1:4)." McDonald[65]

---

[60] This call came through the gospel (1:6) and is grounded on the work of Christ on the cross (5:1).

[61] Moo, *Galatians*, 37. Moo explains that for four chapters Paul has argued for "freedom." He now warns of how it may be abused, following the dictates of the flesh. He doubts whether, as some commentators think, that having contested with the legalists, now he turns to another group among the churches with a libertine attitude. It can be maintained that Paul in his argumentation, is simply continuing to set out the glory of the cross, which as part of our salvation, supplies the Holy Spirit who enables the believer to live a holy life.

[62] Longenecker, *Galatians*, 239.

[63] NEB "lower nature," Knox "corrupt nature," NIV "sinful nature," JB "self-indulgence." Note the use of an adjective often to express man's present condition that is in opposition to "the Spirit."

[64] Silva, *Explorations in Exegetical Method*, 176. The "present age" is the old age of the flesh and the law, 183.

[65] McDonald, *Freedom in Faith*, 131.

explains that Paul, using the word "opportunity" as in Rom 7:8, 11; 2 Cor 5:12;11:1; 1 Tim 5:14, stresses that the flesh or our basic human nature must not be allowed to become a "base of operation", as the word is generally understood, for sin to extend its mastery over us. To emphasise this warning again, Christian freedom is freedom from sin, not to sin. It is a freedom which among other blessings involves the freedom of unrestricted access to God; not unrestricted licence to self-indulgence.[66] We will see that, rather, we are to have "crucified the flesh" (5:24), since we have been "crucified with Christ" (2:20).

Paul continues in v. 13 and in contrast to the preceding negative statement, introduces the positive alternative, using the strong adversative – "but through love serve one another." Witherington[67] points out that there is a deliberate paradox here or a significant contrast in enslavement from what is set out in v. 1. Rather than going back into slavery to the Mosaic law (v. 1), the hearers of the letter are urged to "slavery" to other Christians through self-sacrifice, loving actions and committed service. The expression "through love" has the definite article, "through *the* love" or "through *that* love." Longenecker[68] considers that it may "probably" refer to 2:20 – Christ's love for us, or 5:6 (the Christian love highlighted here) "or both." Or is it not simply "love" within the believer through the fact that he is reborn of the Spirit and then motivated by the power of that same Holy Spirit?

Bruce[69] sets out Paul's exhortation in the following way, "If you must live in slavery here is a form of slavery in which you may safely indulge – the slavery of practical love for one another."[70] The present tense of the imperative "through love *serve*" emphasises that this obligation continues for all of our lives. McDonald[71] makes the point:

> This is the apostles' answer to the legalism of the Judaizers and to the licence of the antinomians.... Paul has been asserting that the Galatians are not to be led into bondage; now he asserts that the only bondage is love. Free as to legalism we are bound as to love. To act in love as slaves for our fellows is to be really free.

Moo[72] reminds his readers of Luther's famous statement, "A Christian is a perfectly free lord of all, subject to none. A Christian is a perfectly dutiful servant of all,

---

[66] Bruce, *The Epistle to the Galatians*, points out that the particular sin to which the Galatian community was prone at the time was quarrelsomeness, 240.

[67] Witherington, 111, *Galatians*, 378.

[68] Longenecker, *Galatians*, 241.

[69] Bruce, *The Epistle to the Galatians*, 241.

[70] Fung, *The Epistle to the Galatians*, 245, suggests that Paul is possibly influenced by the example of Jesus' love demonstrated in his act of lowly service for the needs of his disciples in the upper room (John 13:2, 5, 12).

[71] McDonald, *Freedom in Faith*, 131.

[72] Moo, *Galatians*, 345, from J. Dillenberger, ed. *Martin Luther: Selections from His Writings* (Garden City, NY: Doubleday, 1961), 53.

subject to all." Love is not so much the means as the motivation and the manner in which we serve.

These actions which we will see are to be energised and guided by their life "in the Spirit," are again set in contrast to the disunity of v. 15. If we love one another, we will not "bite and devour one another" (v. 15) with malicious talk and spiteful action. In v. 22 Paul will show us some of the marks of love.

Free, But No to Exploit Our Neighbour

Paul continues with the theme of love in vv. 14–15. Christian freedom, as we have seen, is not freedom to do as I please regarding the flesh; neither is it freedom to do as I please irrespective of the good of my neighbour. Paul tells them that the "whole law is fulfilled in one word" and then quotes Lev 19:18.[73] This must be handled with care here. Paul is reminding them that his teaching about loving service to fellow believers "fulfils" what was stated concerning the Mosaic law. This surely does not mean that after writing over four chapters to the Galatians that they were *not* to submit to the Mosaic law now he is urging them fulfil that same law. We cannot accept that Paul is contradicting himself from letter to letter or even worse, in this one epistle.[74] The word "fulfils" is the key here. We have already seen from 4:4 that we are now in the age of fulfilment. Paul is not suggesting that the people of God were still under the Mosaic covenant and governed by the Mosaic law. In the phrase "the whole law" it is, as Bruce[75] points out, "the spirit and intention of the law"; or as Longenecker,[76] the love ethic fulfils "the real purport of the law." Witherington[77] explains further:

> Paul can speak of the basic substance of the law being fulfilled in the community of Christ, not because the law continued to be the rule for believers' behaviour and not by their submitting to that law. Rather this fulfilment is what happens quite naturally when Christians follow the example and teaching of Christ. If the Galatians will continue to walk in the Spirit, pay attention to the law of Christ, and run as they had already been running, they will discover *that a by-product of this effort is that the basic*

---

[73] It must be remembered that in Lev 19:18 the command to love your neighbour was understood as referring to the Jewish people. The Lord expanded its scope in Matt 22:39, 40; Mark 12:31; Luke 10:29f and of course so did Paul (here and Rom 13v8–10).

[74] Contra H. Räisänen, *Paul and the Law* (WUNT 29; Tübingen: Mohr, 1983) 10–11; Sanders, *Paul, the Law and the Jewish People*, 93–114. Already in this letter (see particularly chapter 2) Sanders' views on seeking to fulfil the law have been noted; "getting in" is a matter of grace; "staying in" is based upon obedience to the law, expressed in "covenantal nomism." George, *Galatians,* 380 explains this view as "getting in" by faith; "staying in" by faith plus works. "For Paul to have adopted this position, however, would have meant that he was rejecting his confidence in the triumph of grace from first to last and was adopting the posture of a semi-Judaizer himself." So here we must look carefully at what Paul is meaning when he writes of "fulfilling the law."

[75] Bruce, *The Epistle to the Galatians*, 241.

[76] Longenecker, *Galatians*, 243. See the full discussion in 241–44.

[77] Witherington, 111, *Galatians*, 381.

aim and substance of the law has already been fulfilled in their midst.
(italics mine)

Paul therefore makes the point that if the Galatians follow his teaching concerning not submitting to circumcision and going back into slavery and on the other hand of not falling into licence, but in love sacrificially serve one another they will be fulfilling what God was looking for from his people, without taking on again the "yoke" of the law.[78] Moo[79] makes this clear:

> Paul carries over this focus on the law from earlier in the letter because he needs to assure the Galatians that the Christian life as Paul understands it is fully able to provide that conformity to the will of God that the agitators were apparently claiming could be found only by submission to the law of God.

He also proposes that the verb here refers to an eschatological completion of the law – in a "salvation-historical sense," as in other texts where Paul speaks of "fulfilling" the law (Rom 8:4; 13:8, 10). "Paul is not enjoining obedience to the law: he is claiming that, in some sense, the love command results in the law's being fulfilled." For Hendriksen,[80] love is both a "*summary*" and the "*realization in practice* (italics his) of the entire God-given moral law, viewed as a unit."

The present tenses of the verbs biting and devouring expose what was actually happening in the Christian communities in Galatia.[81] They were engaged in an unholy, fierce struggle. Paul had written bluntly about the Judaizers (v. 12); now he warns the believers also plainly that if they continue with this loveless aggression to one another they will end up "consumed" by each other – as Longenecker,[82] "wild beasts fighting so ferociously with one another that they end up annihilating each other." The communities could be described as fractured fellowships, tearing one another apart. That these things were really happening is supported by the fact that Paul focusses upon such attitudes and actions among the list of "the works of the flesh" in vv. 19–21. But they had the power to be different.

---

[78] This understanding is in keeping with Paul's teaching elsewhere in his letters (cf. Rom 8:4; 13:8–10). His emphasis is *not* about the "doing" of the law, but the law being "fulfilled" (the perfect tense is here in 5:14 meaning "stands fulfilled") by those in this age through the gift and empowerment of the Holy Spirit. Is this not also one of the aspects of the fulfilment Christ has brought by his coming and death for us (Matt 5:17)?

[79] Moo, *Galatians*, 346–47.

[80] Hendriksen, *Galatians*, 211.

[81] Bruce, *The Epistle to the Galatians*, 242, points out that they were "like a pack of wild animals preying upon one another," Paul's concern for the Galatian believers, the spiritual, any who have stumbled, the burdened etc., continues through into 6:10.

[82] Longenecker, *Galatians*, 244.

Free to Live in the Power of the Holy Spirit vv. 16–25.

Galatians is the first example of what would become a pattern in Paul's letters – doctrinal or theological argumentation followed by ethical instruction or practical guidance (Rom 12–15; Phil 4; Col 3–4; Eph 4–6). Paul here explains that the Christian life and true Christian liberty is possible through the Holy Spirit i.e., through knowing the power of the Spirit. We should note the importance of this particular chapter and that of chapter 6 in the overall argument of Galatians. Fee[83] has affirmed that 5:13ff is a vital part of the teaching in Galatians, not just some paraenesis at the end of the theological arguments. The letter presents the contrast not between faith and the works of the law but between life in the Spirit – lived out by faith and life on the basis of Torah observance. "The ethical result of the life of the Spirit is part of the essential argument of the letter, since this is the burning question, 'How do believers *live*?'"

Paul has in chapter 5, as Bruce[84] has explained, set out the hopelessness of their plight – if they rely on law-keeping, over against the blessedness of the life in the Spirit, to which they are now called. So, while in 3:2, 5 Paul has reminded them that they were born of the Spirit when they were converted and his continued presence was attested by mighty works, Bruce[85] now points out that Paul wants to see that same presence attested by their manner of life. George[86] also writes of the resources which can bring victorious Christian living. It is not a winsome personality, advanced theological degrees, special seminars on the Christian life, social activism, or spiritual psychotherapy. "Paul's answer is the Holy Spirit." The one through whom we were regenerated can enable us to experience the power of sanctification as we walk in him. This is what is absolutely vital in witness – a Christian lifestyle. Moo[87] explains that:

> Paul now goes into detail about the Spirit's role in enabling believers to finish what they had begun (3:3).... And the Spirit whom Paul now celebrates as the power of the new life is nothing other than the Spirit that the prophets predicted would take possession of God's people in the eschatological age, providing for the wholehearted obedience to the Lord that the law could not secure ("the promise of the Spirit" in 3:14; see e.g., Jer 31:31–34; Ezek 36:24–28; Joel 2:28–32).

Paul in v. 16 makes a personal appeal and in fact a positive emphasis about what really is the true nature of the Christian life, "But I say." These words, as also in 3:17; 4:1 and 5:2 seem always to mark a new step forward in his argument. Again, his affirmations here end with the same appeal in vv. 25–26. First, in v. 16 we find here

---

[83] Fee, *God's Empowering Presence*, 385.
[84] Bruce, *The Epistle to the Galatians*, 229.
[85] Bruce, *The Epistle to the Galatians*, 243.
[86] George, *Galatians*, 386.
[87] Moo, *Galatians*, 351.

the promise that those who walk in the Spirit will overcome the flesh and this really is the theme of all that follows in these verses. Next, there is set out the conflict between the flesh and the Spirit and the contrast between the works of the flesh with the fruit of the Spirit (vv. 17–23). There follows a final assurance that the people who belong to Christ will enjoy a freedom from the power of the flesh as they crucify the flesh and walk in the Spirit (vv. 24–25).

Paul proceeds to compare a number of common Gentile vices characteristic of Galatian society with what he expects when it comes to Christian behaviour. Both lists are not meant to be complete – see v. 21 "things like these." The first sets out the sort of behaviour which took place at pagan feasts when people have drunk too much. But Paul first writes of:

(a) True Deliverance v. 16

Note as Longenecker[88] points out, here we have an exhortation followed by a promise, namely, "Walk by the Spirit and you will not gratify." Note that "by the Spirit" is given emphasis as it is placed before the verb. Again, the double negative adds emphasis – "definitely will not," affirming the Spirit's power. The Greek word (only here in Galatians) "walk," literally, "go about," "walk around," as Longenecker[89] explains, is frequently found in Paul and occasionally in the Johannine letters in the figurative sense of "live" (cf. e.g., Rom 6:4; 8:4; 13:13; 14:15; 1 Cor 3:3; 7:17; 2 Cor 4:2; 5:7; 10:2, 3 ; 12:18; Eph 2:2, 10; 4:17; 5:2, 15; Phil 3:17, 18; Col 2:6; 3:7; 4:5; 1 Thess 1:12; 4:1, 12; also 1 John 2:6; 2 John v. 4, 6; 3 John vv. 3–4). It should be noted that with this statement we have really an echo of an OT phrase "walk according to the statutes of the law" (Exod 16:4; 18:20; Lev 18:4; Jer 44:23; Ezek 5:6–7). There appears to be a deliberate contrast here. As Dunn[90] suggests, in a "walk by the Spirit Paul is deliberately posing an alternative understanding of how the people of God should conduct themselves." His direction is life by the Spirit's power, rather than life under the Mosaic law. Rom 8:3 would later state, "God has done what the law weakened through the flesh could not do."

Actually, the Holy Spirit is mentioned 7 times in these verses. They are, as Stott[91] maintains, "full of the Holy Spirit." He alone is the one who can, as we will see, oppose and subdue the flesh (vv. 16–17), and cause the fruit of righteousness to grow in our lives (vv. 22–23). Moo[92] also explains, that to counter the flesh (v. 13), "Paul now brings onto the stage, front and center, the Spirit." "Walk," emphasises the point that effort or positive determination is required if one is to know this. But it is equally true that it is, as we shall see, the Spirit who alone enables us to do the walking. The present tense of the imperative in v. 16 "walk," emphasises that this is to be a

---

[88] Longenecker, *Galatians*, 244.
[89] Longenecker, *Galatians*, 244.
[90] Dunn, *Galatians*, 295.
[91] Stott, *The One Way*, 145.
[92] Moo, *Galatians*, 352.

continuing experience day by day. "be always walking by the Spirit." Fung[93] makes the point that this experience of the Spirit in the life of the believer is a sign that Jeremiah's prophesy of the new covenant has been fulfilled (Jer 31:31–34; Heb 8:8–12). "God's will is now an inward principle, the result of the leading of the Spirit within the believer. To 'walk by the Spirit' means to be under the constant moment-by-moment direction, control, and guidance of the Spirit." In this way believers will not carry out or fall under the control of their fallen nature. As the NLT puts it, you will not do "what your sinful nature craves."

(b) Inner Conflict vv. 17–18

The view of some Christians is that there will be no inner conflict because of the eradication of the flesh and also that the old nature is dead. This is clearly not what this passage teaches. The flesh remains but the Holy Spirit can still give us the power not to act out those fleshly desires of the sinful nature i.e., they can be subdued. As Witherington[94] explains, "while sin remains in the Christian life, Paul is reassuring his converts that … sin need not reign." He again makes the point that "the Christian lives in a tension between the urgings of the eschatological Spirit and inherent fallen desires." As George[95] explains, "As long as we remain in this present life, we never outgrow or transcend the spiritual conflict Paul is describing in this passage." For Longenecker,[96] "the flesh" is a captive to sin:

It produces "desires and passions" that are at work against the Spirit … and so ethically speaking "the flesh" continues to be a potential threat. Thus the Christian may choose to use his or her freedom in Christ either as "an opportunity for the flesh" or in response to "the Spirit." Paul calls on his converts to renounce the former, thereby being open to the latter.

Taking the purpose clause to mean literally, "in order to keep you from doing," means Paul is making the point that to walk in the Spirit means that they will not succumb to their sinful desires. As Fung[97] explains, in this conflict it is impossible for the believer to remain neutral or to be some kind of helpless spectator or pawn. He must "actively choose to stand on the side of the Spirit over against the flesh." McDonald[98] makes the same point that the reference is to "the restraining action of the Spirit on the constraining attitudes of the flesh." Moo[99] also helps us here. He explains that it is a conflict in which human beings are caught up, but the conflict is not really between natures – although he is not ruling out the flesh. It is what the flesh produces:

---

[93] Fung, *The Epistle to the Galatians*, 249.
[94] Witherington, 111, *Galatians*, 394. So Bruce also, *The Epistle to the Galatians*, who writes of the "eschatological tension which, as long as believers remain in the body, is inseparable from their life in Christ," 244. Hendriksen, *Galatians*, 215 writes of "the intensity of the life-long tug of war."
[95] George, *Galatians*, 387.
[96] Longenecker, *Galatians*, 241.
[97] Fung, *The Epistle to the Galatians*, 251.
[98] McDonald, *Freedom in Faith*, 134.
[99] Moo, *Galatians*, 354.

The conflict is between God's Spirit and *the impulse to sin* [italics mine], an impulse that no longer rules in the believer but still exerts influence and must be resisted. Paul brings to our attention the fundamental spiritual battle that Christians must be aware of so that we will take with the utmost seriousness Paul's command that we "walk in the Spirit."

Paul also affirms in v. 18 that being led by the Spirit "you are not under the law." This of course, is a reference to the law of Moses and the phrase is reminding us of the earlier references (3:23; 4:4, 5, 21). Again, is this not a reminder of the teaching in 3:25 about in the past being "under a guardian?" Here we have the verbal form – we are not "led by a paidagogos." We are now regenerated, adopted as sons and heirs and the Holy Spirit is sufficient to enable us and to provide for us – from the further teaching of the NT, of course, or the "law of Christ" 6:1 – all the guidance we need. Note Hendriksen's[100] point that to be "led" by the Spirit is not only about being guided but "indicates *leadership*" in which the Holy Spirit "becomes *the controlling influence* in their lives." Here is the positive influence and enabling in the believer's life day by day.

(c) Evil Works vv. 19–21

Paul lists in vv. 19–21 the lusts/works of the flesh which are all the sinful desires/practises of our fallen nature. These are said to be "evident," obvious, easily identified. Such "vice lists" were common in the literature of the time. (see in Pauline writings, e.g., 1 Cor 5:9–11; 6:9–10; Rom 1:29–31; Col 3:5–8; Eph 4:17–19; also 1 Tim 1:9–10; 6:4–5; 2 Tim 3:2–4; Titus 1:7). "Virtue lists" in the NT include Eph 6:14–17; Phil 4:8; Col 3:12; 1 Tim 3:2–3; 6:11; Titus 1:7–8; James 3:17; 2 Pet 1:5–9). It was noted that the list is not exhaustive, but provides examples. It falls into four categories.[101]

In the area of SEX, Paul lists three sins; "sexual immorality," which is normally fornication, sexual intercourse between unmarried people, but may here be used in a more general sense of any kind of unlawful sexual behaviour, including adultery and incest (1 Cor 5:1); "impurity" has a wider range of meaning. Longenecker[102] explains that in a physical sense it means "dirt" or "dirtiness"; infection or impurities in a medical sense and is used in Leviticus in the LXX twenty times for uncleanness which shuts one out from the presence of God. Paul uses it generally for sexual impurity (Rom 1:24; 6:19; 2 Cor 12:21; Eph 4:19; 5:3; Col 3:5; 1 Thess 4:7 and in 1Thess 2:3 of "error"). It therefore refers to the defilement before God that results from the misuse of sex, unnatural vice and licentiousness, a defilement from which God can "cleanse" us (1 John 1:9). For Hendriksen[103] also the word has a

---

[100] Hendriksen, *Galatians*, 217.
[101] George, *Galatians*, 392, first highlights Lightfoot's division of these sins; sensual passions; unlawful dealings in things spiritual; violations of brotherly love; intemperate excesses, *Galatians*, 210. He himself writes of "sins of immorality, idolatry, animosity and intemperance."
[102] Longenecker, *Galatians*, 254.
[103] Hendriksen, *Galatians*, 219.

"comprehensive" sense and "includes not only uncleanness in deeds but also in words, thoughts, and desires of the heart." Then "sensuality" (elsewhere in Paul in Rom 13:13; 2 Cor 12:21; Eph 4:19), involving contempt for propriety, throwing off all restraint or as Witherington[104] explains, "extreme and public debauchery of a kind that would be shocking even to a pagan." We remember the total excess of Israel in Jeremiah's day, as he writes, "No, they were not at all ashamed; they did not know how to blush." (Jer 6:15). Fung[105] explains that this sin is likely meant to represent an advance on the first two, being a vice paraded without regard for the rights or feelings of others, or for public decency. We could say that here there is a violation of all the bounds of what is socially acceptable. The above three sins are brought together in 2 Cor 12:21 as Paul expresses his sadness over the "many" in Corinth who had committed such evil acts.

In RELIGION there are deviations from true religion, with offences against God as well as against men. First, "idolatry," or the brazen worship of other gods and the practices associated with such worship. We note that conversion in 1 Thess 1:9 involved a turning from idolatry to serve "the living and true God." Such idolatry consists in a society which "worshipped and served the creature rather than the Creator" (Rom 1:25). Bruce[106] suggests a reference not only of the worship of graven idols, but "of any substitute for the living and true God." Even covetousness (Col 3:5) "because the thing coveted becomes an object of worship." Also "sorcery," which Bruce points out was first of all a neutral word for "pharmacy" involving the dispensing of drugs but finally took on the sense of the use of drugs in witchcraft.[107] The reference will be to the secret tampering with the powers of evil and of the occult. Fung[108] reminds us of Acts 19:19, where the burning of the books of the practitioners of the magic arts came to a considerable sum, giving evidence of the popularity of such practices. Also George[109] explains that in the NT the word is invariably associated with the occult, both here in Galatians and Revelation (Rev 9:21; 18:23). While the various English translations do express the link with the idea of black magic and demonic control "they miss the more basic meaning of drug use."

In the area of COMMUNITY. Paul gives eight examples of the breakdown of personal relationships! Does this list of eight items as compared with two or three in the other categories suggest that these sins were more prevalent in the Galatian Christian communities? For Moo,[110] it is clear that this was a special concern of

---

[104] Witherington, 111, *Galatians*, 398.
[105] Fung, *The Epistle to the Galatians*, 255. He points out that there is clear evidence that the sexual habits of the Greco-Roman world were chaotic – even pagan writers were disgusted at the unspeakable nature of the immorality prevalent in the culture.
[106] Bruce, *The Epistle to the Galatians*, 247. Moo, *Galatians*, 359, writes of this word as "a general word for the worship of anything apart from the one true God."
[107] Bruce, *The Epistle to the Galatians*, 247; Hendriksen, *Galatians*, 219, also comments on the understanding of *pharmakeia* "in an unscientific age – "a mixer of drugs" – could be viewed as a "magician."
[108] Fung, *The Epistle to the Galatians*, 257.
[109] George, *Galatians*. 394.
[110] Moo, *Galatians*, 359.

Paul's at that time. These include, "enmity," the plural form giving evidence of repeated occurrences of this hateful attitude and the manifestation of such hostile acts; in the context here, more against other people than God; "strife" which is used nine times in the NT, all in Paul. Fung[111] explains that he uses it as a characteristic of pagan society (Rom 1:29; cf. 13:13) but also the sin gains entry into the Christian church and is a word which highlights the strife and discord which troubled so many of the communities (cf. Rom 1:29; 13:13; 1 Cor 1:11; 3:3; 2 Cor 12:20; Phil 1:15; 1 Tim 6:4; Titus 3:9).

Next is "jealousy," a word which is used elsewhere in a good sense for "zeal" for God (Rom 10:2), for individuals (2 Cor 7:7) and for the collection (2 Cor 9:2). Even in Galatians itself we find the use of the verb "be zealous" in a positive sense, seeking the good of the believers (4:17–18); and the adjective in a usage particularly common in Judaism of a passionate commitment, as Paul himself, to the "tradition of the fathers" (1:14). But there are other references where, as here, the word is associated with "strife" (Rom 13:13; 1 Cor 3:3; 2 Cor 12:20) meaning a kind of self-centred or envious spirit. As Bruce[112] suggests it means, "a sense of resentment that another has enjoyed success or distinction (thus far) denied to him." An envious desire to have for yourself what someone else possesses and enjoys. George[113] states, "At the root of all sentiments of jealousy is the basic posture of ingratitude to God, a failure to accept one's life as a gift from God. To envy what someone else has is to fling one's own gifts before God in unthankful rebellion and spite." Then, "fits of anger" or rage. The word can have different shades of meaning – in Rom 2:8; Rev 14:10; 19:15 it refers to God's wrath. But the plural here suggests repeated outbursts of rage, uncontrolled verbal violence (cf. 2 Cor 12:20; Eph 4:31; Col 3:8); "rivalries" or contentions; a term first used in the political world of Ancient Greece of "office seeking" or the manipulation that springs from a self-promoting lifestyle. Here in its plural form, the reference will be to repeated occurrences of this promotion of oneself through selfish ambition, self-seeking, as Longenecker,[114] "selfish devotion to one's own interests ... as is evident in its use in the NT where it appears more often than in all other ancient writings (cf. Rom 2:8; 2 Cor 12:20; Gal 5:20 [here]; Phil 1:17; 2:3; James 4:14, 16.)" Fung[115] explains that the references point to contexts that involve "competing parties" or "factions" within the church; "dissensions," found again only in Rom 16:17, may refer to the results of the introduction of the false teaching into the churches and the "disputes" which it caused. Also, "divisions" which are often the result of the former sin, because rather than overlooking differences, splits are formed, disunity is manifested. Hendriksen[116] refers to groups "working and scheming against each other (cf. 1 Cor 11:19)"; for Moo,[117] the second word "divisions" may suggest "a more formally organised party." He observes that these last two just

---

[111] Fung, *The Epistle to the Galatians*, 257. For Hendriksen, *Galatians*, 220, it occurs when people begin to choose sides and worship their hero.
[112] Bruce, *The Epistle to the Galatians*, 248.
[113] George, *Galatians*, 395.
[114] Longenecker, *Galatians*, 256.
[115] Fung, *The Epistle to the Galatians*, 258.
[116] Hendriksen, *Galatians*, 220.
[117] Moo, *Galatians*, 361.

mentioned are not found in any other NT "vice list" and so they must have "particular relevance to the situation in Galatia." Then finally, "envy," a word similar to the sin of "jealousy" mentioned earlier, but here in the plural, literally "envyings." For Bruce[118] it signifies "a grudging spirit which cannot bear to contemplate someone else's prosperity." The plural will refer to the manifestations of a malicious attitude rooted in ill-will (cf. Matt 27:18; Mark 15:10; Rom 1:29; Phil 1:15; 1 Tim 6:4; 1 Pet 2:10). Longenecker[119] points out that the omission of "murders" here from some translations reflects that it is missing from some important Greek MSS and its inclusion in others probably is "an attempt to harmonize Paul's list with the catalogue of vices found in Mark 7:21–22 (cf. Matt 15:19); perhaps also influenced linguistically by Rom 1:29."

Then we have the fourth group of sins Paul includes in the "works of the flesh." The effects of ALCOHOL. George[120] explains that alcohol abuse was common in urban life in the Roman Empire and there was also the cultic abuse (religious intoxication) practised e.g., in the mystery religion of Dionysus, the wine god. Paul employs the use of the plural term μέθαι *methai* which is more than drinking or drunkenness but regular bouts of drinking, binging and the like (also used in Luke 21:34; 1 Cor 5:11; 6:10; Eph 5:18; 1Thess 5:7). Fung[121] points out that:

> Drunkenness is a nocturnal activity, ill-becoming those who belong to the daylight (1 Thess 5:6f.). Getting drunk before partaking in the Lord's supper was an especially culpable act; it made a farce of what ought to be a sacred and solemn occasion (1 Cor 11:20f.).

In fact, such drinking was totally incompatible with life in the kingdom of God (see below), life in the Spirit. The last term follows the same theme "orgies," which occurs three times in the NT (here; Rom 13:13; 1 Pet 4:3) and is, as Fung[122] explains, "a characteristic feature of the pagan way of life." The word is for Bruce[123] always found in close association with drunkenness in which people lose moral control. The NLT actually translates it as "wild parties." It is a term which Witherington[124] points out, was similar to the name Komos, the Revel, who was made a Greek god and whose rites, both novel and varied in their revelling, were known to be carried on in pagan temples.

Paul then would be telling his converts that through the Holy Spirit, they could resist the lure to return again to the social milieu they left behind when they converted and especially the social location where one regularly found these sorts of things happening.

---

[118] Bruce, *The Epistle to the Galatians*, 249.
[119] Longenecker, *Galatians*, 248.
[120] George, *Galatians*, 397. The AV translated the word as "witchcraft"; ESV as "sorcery."
[121] Fung, *The Epistle to the Galatians*, 259.
[122] Fung, *The Epistle to the Galatians*, 260.
[123] Bruce, *The Epistle to the Galatians*, 250.
[124] Witherington, 111, *Galatians*, 399.

In v. 21 Paul affirms that those who indulge in these works – we noted that the list of vices is representative but not total or exclusive, as Paul uses "such things" – or manifest such evil attitudes or actions[125] are excluded from God's kingdom, for such works give evidence that they are not really in Christ. He has not mentioned the kingdom in this letter, but the theme had no doubt figured in his preaching when first he was with them (see Acts 14:22). His warnings here are also very similar to what he wrote in 1 Cor 6:9–10. Fung[126] explains that:

> Insofar as the kingdom of God and the kingdom of Christ may be distinguished in Paul's usage, the kingdom of Christ seems to denote the present phase of the divine kingdom (as in Col 1:13), which is mediatorially administered by Christ, while the kingdom of God refers to its future consummation in glory when Christ "delivers up the kingdom to God the Father" (1 Cor 15:24).

As George[127] maintains, those who behave in such ways will be excluded from the eternal blessedness of God's final kingdom. "This is not an idle threat but a solemn warning from the pen of a divinely inspired apostle of Jesus Christ." Yet we are not without hope. We can "inherit" this blessed kingdom. The whole letter has the theme of the cross and a God who himself – in our helplessness ever to get right with him or make up for such sins of our past lives – took the initiative in sending his Son "to redeem," to become a curse for us (3:13). The gift of faith, repentance and trust can by grace bring justification (3:8–9), acceptance as sons and the gift of the indwelling Holy Spirit (4:4–7), which can result in a transformed Christian lifestyle, as we live in the present form of the kingdom of God. This new lifestyle is now the theme of the verses which follow.

(d) Christian Graces vv. 22–23

Following the listing of fifteen sinful "works of the flesh," Paul now gives us a list of nine Christian contrasting graces (using δέ *de*, "but") which ought to characterize the Christian communities in Galatia. Many of them, as we noted earlier, can be found elsewhere in Paul (e.g., 2 Cor 6:6; 1 Tim 4:12; 6:11; 2 Tim 2:22). George[128] observes that the catalogue of evil was:

---

[125] Fung, *The Epistle to the Galatians*, 251, makes the point that the present participle will stress that here we have not "occasional lapses but habitual behaviour."

[126] Fung, *The Epistle to the Galatians*, 261. For Fung, Bruce, *The Epistle to the Galatians*, 251, also suggests this possible distinction – although the kingdom is still "the kingdom of Christ and God" (Eph 5:5).

[127] George, *Galatians*, 398.

[128] George, *Galatians*, 399. George, *Galatians*, 212, mentions Lightfoot who again lists the graces as habits of the Christian mind; social intercourse and neighbourly concern; principles of conduct. Also, Stott, *Only One Way*, 148 writes of the Christian's attitude to God, to other people and to himself. George accepts that these divisions may be helpful, but should not be pressed too far as the nine qualities "flow into one another, mutually enriching and reinforcing the process of sanctification in the life of the believer."

disorderly, chaotic, and incomplete, corresponding to the random and compulsive character of sin itself. In stark contrast now, the character traits contained in the catalog of grace appear in beautiful harmony, balanced and symmetrical, corresponding to the purposeful design and equilibrium of a life filled with the Spirit and lived out in the beauty of holiness.

Dunn[129] makes the point that here we ought to find a kind of "character-sketch" of Christ – see also 4:19 where Christ was being "formed" in them and they are in 6:2 to seek to "fulfil the law of Christ." We should not forget that these Christian virtues are said to be the "fruit of the Spirit." We remember the challenge to Israel in the OT regarding "fruitfulness (Isa 5:2–4; Hos 14:6). Also, we have the lifestyle of the godly man in Ps 1:3. Here this fruitfulness is the result of the transforming power of God in the lives of those who are indwelt and energised by the Holy Spirit – for Longenecker,[130] "the spontaneous quality of a life directed by the Spirit as opposed to human efforts to live according to the directives of the law or the flesh." Note also that "the flesh" *encourages* sin but "the Spirit" *produces* likeness to Christ. One should note that Paul uses the singular "fruit" to emphasise that *all* of these Christ-like features should be seen in the Christian, not love in one, joy in another etc.

Paul begins with what has been identified as the primary virtue "love" (see 1 Cor 13).[131] The noun "love" ἀγάπη *agape* is used seventy-five times in Paul, the verb ἀγαπάω *agapaō*, thirty-four times. This love was to characterize relationships between God and themselves and also between them as brothers and sisters in Christ. It is true that Paul could have stopped there without any more listing, for love is the source or fountainhead from which all the rest flow.[132] Paul has already illustrated elsewhere in this letter some features of this Christian quality (5:6, 13, 14). One recalls that only on two occasions does Paul write about the Christian's love for God (Phil 3:1; 4:4). Here in Galatians and elsewhere the emphasis is upon the believer's love for one another – note the present context, 5:13–15, 26. George[133] makes the important point that "while the horizon of the love of neighbor is by no means restricted to fellow-believers, it is supremely important that Christians learn to live together in love." Bruce[134] writes of it as "God's own love, as manifested in Christ (cf. Rom 8:25, 38f.) which floods their lives and springs up in a responsive love to God and Christ and to one another, and overflows to all mankind (cf. 6:10)."

Fung[135] helpfully lists how vital this love is. To summarize, it is:

---

[129] Dunn, *Galatians*, 301.

[130] Longenecker, *Galatians*, 259.

[131] Hendriksen, *Galatians*, 223, suggests that Paul "gives priority to this grace" as does John (1 John 3.14, 4:8, 19) and Peter (1 Peter 4:8); in this they follow the example of Christ himself (John 13:1, 34; 17:26).

[132] Luther, *A Commentary on St. Paul's Epistle to the Galatians*, 523, makes this point, "It had been enough to have said 'love,' and no more; for love extendeth itself unto all the fruits of the Spirit."

[133] George, *Galatians*, 401.

[134] Bruce, *The Epistle to the Galatians*, 252.

[135] Fung, *The Epistle to the Galatians*, 264.

The atmosphere in which believers are to conduct their lives (Eph 5:2); the garment they are to put on (Col 3:14); the consistent motive of all their actions (1 Cor 16:14) … the proper restraint on the exercise of Christian liberty (Gal 5:13; Rom 14:15; 1 Cor 8:1, 13) … love is accompanied by practical action; it leads, for example, to magnanimous giving (2 Cor 8: 7f., 24) and genuine forgiveness (2 Cor 2:7f.) … it is capable of true discrimination (Phil 1:9f.) and does not refrain from censure and warning, when such is demanded by the situation (2 Cor 2:4; cf. 1 Cor 16:24).

McDonald[136] suggests that the term "love" which heads the list of the Spirit's fruit, "should not be regarded merely as one of a cluster; it is rather the stem upon which all the rest hangs. Love stands at the head of the list, but is the heart of the whole." He takes "joy" and "peace" as "love's attitude" towards God. Patience, kindness, goodness, faithfulness will be "basic" attitudes towards others. "While gentleness and self-control are love's acceptance of restraint upon ourselves." This will now become clear. What Moo[137] calls this "headline placement" of love in the listing of the Spirit's fruit, "is due both to the centrality of love within new-covenant ethics" and "because it is the most important bulwark against the factional infighting that seems to be racking the Galatian churches."

Next, "joy," for Dunn,[138] was "a feature of the earliest Christian movement" (Acts 8:8; 2 Cor 7:4, 13; Phil 1:4; 2:29; Phlm 7; 1 Pet 1:8). This "joy" Witherington[139] suggests, involves contentment, the ability to not be overcome by difficult circumstances, even of health, an eschatological joy because of the Christian hope (Rom 5:2, 11; 15:11). In Rom 14:17 Paul picks up the theme of the "kingdom of God" which is "not a matter of eating and drinking but of righteousness and peace and joy in the Holy Spirit." Hendriksen[140] affirms:

> Since all things work together for good to those who love God (Rom 8:28), it is evident that believers can rejoice even amid the most distressing circumstances, as Paul himself proved again and again (Acts 27:35; 2 Cor 6:10: "as sorrowful, yet always rejoicing"; 12:9; Phil 1:12, 13; 4:11; 2 Tim 4:6–8).

The quality "joy" is found only here in the NT "virtue lists." Moo[141] explains, as others, that in the Greco-Roman world "joy" is an emotion closely related to pleasure. "In Paul, however, 'joy' is a settled state of mind that arises from a sense of God's love for us, produced by the Spirit (1 Thess 1:6) and that exists even in the face of difficulties and trials (2 Cor 7:4; 1 Thess 1:6)."

---

[136] McDonald, *Freedom in Faith*, 137.

[137] Moo, *Galatians*, 364.

[138] Dunn, *Galatians*, 310.

[139] Witherington, 111, *Galatians*, 409.

[140] Hendriksen, *Galatians*, 224.

[141] Moo, *Galatians*, 364.

Then "peace," which is related to the Jewish concept of *shalom* and expresses the experience of positive relationships with others which are first rooted in a right relationship with God. For Dunn[142] it is in direct contrast to "divisive factionalism" which was prevalent among them. Paul in Rom 14:17–19 urges the Roman believers to recognise that this harmony is characteristic of the kingdom of God and so they must "pursue what makes for peace and for mutual upbuilding." There is need for a commitment to seek to maintain loving relationships with others in the community.

These are followed by 3 social virtues which exhibit, first "patience" which means longsuffering or endurance of difficulties, wrongdoing, without responding in anger or seeking to take revenge. To put up with people even when at times it is difficult to do. Bruce[143] reminds us that God shows patience over his elect (Luke 18:7); towards the impenitent (Rom 2:4; 9:22). Paul urges his Christian friends to show a similar patience with one another and towards all (Eph 4:2; Col 1:11; 3:12; 1 Thess 5:14). George[144] insists "Paul's point is clear: if God has been so long-suffering with us, should we not display this same grace in our relationships with one another?" There are times when we ought to refrain from responding in anger to wrong done to us. Again, Paul can in 2 Tim 4:2 exhort Timothy in his preaching to "exhort, with complete patience and teaching."

This is followed by "kindness," a word found only in the NT in Paul (the adjective is in Luke 6:35; 1 Pet 2:3). It is used as an attribute of God (Rom 2:4; 11:22; Titus 3:4), and therefore ought to be reproduced by his Spirit in his people, rather than the evil works being manifested (5:15, 26).[145] Paul elsewhere appeals to Christians to be "kind to one another" and to clothe themselves with this spiritual quality (Eph 4:32; Col 3:12). Fung[146] can make the point that "Kindness is also among the qualities displayed by Paul as a servant of God (2 Cor 6:6). It is an essential ingredient of love (1 Cor 13:4) and, like love expresses itself in action; those who are kind treat others in the same way as God has treated them (Eph 4:32; cf. Luke 6:35)."

Next, "goodness." Perhaps when seen as a spiritual dynamic of a Christian, it is first, a focusing on speech or word and then on deed or action (Rom 15:14; Eph 5:9; 2 Thess 1:11). Then there is "faithfulness" πίστις *pistis*. It is used in three ways in Galatians. In 1:23 it is used of the basic content of the Christian message – Paul was preaching *the* faith he once tried to destroy. Again, in his argumentation throughout Galatians Paul can insist that the way of justification is "by faith" (*pistis*) (cf. 3:8–9). But the word has a further meaning; George[147] explains it means "faithfulness, fidelity, that is, the quality of being true, trustworthy, and reliable in all one's

---

[142] Dunn, *Galatians*, 310.

[143] Bruce, *The Epistle to the Galatians*, 253.

[144] George, *Galatians*, 403.

[145] Hendriksen, *Galatians*, 224, points out that we are admonished to be like God in this respect (Matt 5:43–48; Luke 6:27–38). He reminds us of the kindness of Christ to sinners e.g., Mark 10:13–16; Luke 7:11–17; 36–50; 8:40–56; 13:10–17; 18:15–17; 23:34; John 8:1–11; 19:25–27.

[146] Fung, *The Epistle to the Galatians*, 268.

[147] George, *Galatians*, 403.

dealings with others." So as Bruce[148] maintains, πίστις *pistis* is generally more often used in the NT for the act or attitude of believing, but it also stands for faithfulness, or trustworthiness and given the fact that the list is about ethical qualities, this is its sense here. It will refer to someone in whom one can place great confidence. "Faithfulness" is again another attribute first found in God (Rom 3:3; 1 Cor 10:13) and "Because God is faithful, because he can be relied upon, his people are to be faithful too, and the Spirit enables them to be so." Paul was one who could be trusted (1 Cor 7:25; 1 Tim 1:12); others have been found faithful e.g., Timothy (1 Cor 4:17); Tychicus (Eph 6:21; Col 4:7); Epaphras (Col 1:7); Onesimus (Col 4:9).

This quality is followed by (inward) "gentleness," being considerate toward others, rather than aggressive. The term does not suggest some kind of weakness; rather strength under control – respectful action. Fung[149] explains that gentleness is the spirit in which we receive God's word (James 1:21); restore the erring brother (Gal 6:1); correct with sound doctrine (2 Tim 2:25); should be reflected in our Christian lifestyle (James 3:13; 1 Pet 3:4); it was the outstanding feature of Christ himself (Matt 11:29; 21:5; 2 Cor 10:1). The quality did not however rule out indignation in certain circumstances (Jesus – Matt 11:29; Mark 3:5; Paul – 2 Cor 10:1; Gal 1:8; 5:12). In Titus 3:2 Paul writes to the believers on Crete, "to be gentle, and to show perfect courtesy towards all people."

The final term is "self-control," which involves self-mastery, control of the passions.[150] One finds "self-control" in the list of virtues to be sought in 1 Pet 1:5–7, urged upon the "spiritual" athlete, 1 Cor 9:25–27 and is the quality necessary for eldership, Titus 1:8 (using the adjective). Fung[151] suggests that self-control may be taken as being in contrast to all the sexual offences involving the uncontrolled sensual passions included as "works of the flesh", 5:19–21. Hendriksen[152] explains that the word used here means the power to keep oneself in check; the enabling must come from the Holy Spirit, as Paul lists the quality as part of the "fruit" of the Spirit.

The closing statement in v. 23 "against such things there is no law" needs careful attention. The meaning will be that such people, manifesting such Christian qualities through the gift (3:2) and enabling power (5:22) of the Holy Spirit do not need to return to or require something like the Mosaic law to regulate or control them (see also 5:18). We also remember 1 Tim 1:9, where we read "the law is not laid down for the just but for the lawless and disobedient." Dunn[153] explains further, "the overall thrust of the argument would seem to point to a sense like this: no law is required in order to produce such virtue. That is, in order for the fruit of the Spirit to flourish in the lives of the Galatians it was *not* necessary to refer to or put oneself 'under the

---

[148] Bruce, *The Epistle to the Galatians*, 254.

[149] Fung, *The Epistle to the Galatians*, 270.

[150] Stott, *The One Way*, 148, sums up these nine Christian graces in three groups: Godward, "love, joy, peace"; manward, "patience, kindness, goodness"; selfward, "faithfulness, gentleness and self control"; all the fruit of the Spirit.

[151] Fung, *The Epistle to the Galatians*, 271.

[152] Hendriksen, *Galatians*, 225.

[153] Dunn, *Galatians*, 313.

law.'" So, they already had the Holy Spirit (3:2) to produce this fruit. They needed no circumcision and submission to the Mosaic law to manifest the spiritual qualities which God was looking for in their lives. Moo[154] likewise, examines the possibilities for interpretation and finally suggests that the "finale" on the fruit of the Spirit passage should match the one that ends the works of the flesh list in v. 21. This fruit "enables a person to avoid the curse of the law and enter the kingdom.... The Spirit produces fruit in the lives of believers and thereby provides all that the law requires."

But how can these Christian graces be manifest rather than the works of the flesh? Paul teaches here that the way is to "crucify" the flesh and "walk" in the Spirit.

(e) Enabling of the Spirit vv. 24–25

Remember that all the above graces (which are not an exhaustive list), as has been mentioned, are the "fruit of the Spirit" which appears in the lives of Spirit-led and Spirit-filled Christians. Paul explains this here and finally issues an appeal in vv. 25–26.

He first writes of "those who belong to Christ Jesus" which should be seen to recall deliberately the teaching of 3:26–29, the community of those who are in Christ Jesus and share his life. McDonald[155] can identify them as, "a redeemed family (cf. 4:5) ... collectively Abraham's offspring and inheritors of the promise (cf. 3.29)."

They have "crucified the flesh with its passions and desires." Dunn[156] makes the point that to use crucifixion as a metaphor in any positive sense was probably unheard of at that time and the Christian usage "is thus entirely dependent on the Christian evaluation of Jesus' death on the cross." Witherington[157] explains that the aorist tense used here will convey that this action began at the time of their conversion in the past and, as we will see, ought still to be happening at the present time. To clarify, there was first of all something done FOR US at the cross. We were "crucified with Christ" Gal 2:20; the verb is passive, referring to a past act, something, as we have noted, done for us by another: God judged us in Christ and we died in him. But now Paul is writing of something using an active construction which was (at the moment of conversion) and still is to be done BY US – we have "crucified the flesh"; and so we must continue to "crucify" or turn our back on the old life of sin or as here "its passions and desires." For Bruce,[158] the desires are the source by which the passions are directed this way or that and if unchecked will express themselves in the "works of the flesh." But this is only half of what Paul is saying here.

---

[154] Moo, *Galatians*, 367.
[155] McDonald, *Freedom in Faith*, 137.
[156] Dunn, *Galatians*, 314.
[157] Witherington, 111, *Galatians*, 412.
[158] Bruce, *The Epistle to the Galatians*, 256; see also Fung, *The Epistle to the Galatians*, 274–275, who notes the active force of the verb, which when contrasted with the passive in 2:20, seems to put the emphasis on the believer's actions.

As v. 25 explains, "if" meaning "since" they now "live by the Spirit" from the time of their conversion (3:2–3), having "crucified the flesh," they must also "walk by the Spirit," or they ought to actively and progressively "walk" in the enabling of the Holy Spirit; the tense here is present continuous. The meaning of the phrase is "to be in line with" NIV "keep in step with."[159] Note the tenses of the verb Paul uses here. Bruce[160] reminds us: "Here too we have the characteristic interplay between indicative and imperative: we live in the Spirit (granted); therefore let us keep in step with the Spirit." The same Spirit, the source of the believers' spiritual birth, can also enable and effect in us a truly Christian lifestyle. This is how the desires of the flesh can be overcome. Here we have an accomplished fact – we live by the Spirit; then an appeal to be obedient – to keep in step with that same Spirit every day of our lives. Hendriksen[161] points out that there is a chiastic structure here which should be preserved. He follows the A.R.V. and translates "If we live by the Spirit, by the Spirit let us walk." Therefore, the phrases "by the Spirit" are "at the center and receive the strongest emphasis." Also with this order the words "we live" stands at the beginning of the sentence and "we walk" at the end, "so the contrast between *living* and *walking*, as the terms are here employed, is brought out with full force." The message is that as we have life in the Spirit, we have the obligation to walk by his power.

As Stott[162] explains:

> We must "walk in the Spirit", setting ourselves to follow what we know to be right. We reject one path and follow another. We turn from what is evil in order to occupy ourselves with what is good.... This will be seen in our whole way of life – in the leisure occupations we pursue, the books we read and the friendships we make ... in a disciplined practice of prayer and Scripture meditation, in fellowship with believers ... and in attending public worship and the Lord's Supper.... It is not enough to yield passively to the Spirit's control; we must also walk actively in the Spirit's way.

This of course is not just an individual matter. McDonald[163] points out that the word "walk" in this verse is different from that of v. 16. He explains, as Moo also noted, that the literal meaning of the verb here is "to walk in rank." So, McDonald adds: "The reference is not, then, so much to individual conduct as to the life of a community under the Spirit's direction and dynamic." What a goal for the local church community!

---

[159] Moo translates this phrase "with the Spirit let us also stay in step." The verb was also used in military contexts meaning "stay in line with" and also metaphorically to "fall in line with" as in Polybius (*Hist.* 28.5.6): "After these speeches, Gaius and his colleague, seeing that the populace disliked the idea of having garrisons, and wishing to follow the line [στοιχειν *stoichein*] of policy marked out by the Senate, expressed their adherance to the view of Diogenes." See also for the same idea, Acts. 21:24; Rom 4:12; Gal 6:16; Phil 3:16. Moo, *Galatians*, 372.

[160] Bruce, *The Epistle to the Galatians*, 257.

[161] Hendriksen, *Galatians*, 226.

[162] Stott, *The One Way*, 154.

[163] McDonald, *Freedom in Faith*, 138.

Witherington[164] also notes that the verb στοιχῶμεν *stoichōmen* "walk in step" to which we have just referred will not have been chosen by accident in view of the previous use of *stoicheia* (4:3, 9). He explains that:

> Paul is reminding the Galatians that they do not need to place themselves under any elementary principles of the universe, either pagan or Jewish ones precisely because they already live in and by the Spirit of God and should follow the Spirit's lead, staying in line or step with the Spirit, not the law.

The law could never provide the power or even the life to be all that God wants us to be – only the Holy Spirit enabling us to follow the law of Christ, as we shall see. The principles therefore we follow lead us to walk in the way which the Spirit leads. We live by the Spirit – walk in the Spirit. In this way, the desires of the flesh are overcome. As Fung[165] affirms, "believers can overcome the flesh if they submit to the leading of the Spirit, with whom victory belongs."

By way of summary we note how Moo[166] can also stress the importance of the Holy Spirit in the Christian life:

> Essential to Christian existence, Paul has argued, is the Holy Spirit. The Spirit fulfils God's promise that he will transform the hearts of his people in this eschatological age (3:14), producing among them those character traits that please God and build up his people (5:22–23a). The Spirit is the power that inaugurates Christian existence (3:3) and brings it to completion (5:5).... When Paul now says "If we live by the Spirit," he is summing up in one succinct clause this Spirit-dominated existence that fundamentally characterizes believers who live in the age of fulfilment.

This is part of the reason why we glory in the cross – not just that it brings to us the blessing of justification, and of course sonship and in the future, heirship; but *in the present age* it gives us regeneration and the power to live in the enabling of the Holy Spirit. So, as we have maintained, the cross is the central theme of all of Galatians, and as Longenecker[167] can explain, identifying with Christ in his crucifixion means a deliverance which is two-fold; from any legalistic dependence on the Mosaic law or the challenge to be caught in any libertine lifestyle. He stresses, "one cannot espouse a lifestyle that expresses either a legalistic or a libertine orientation."

(f) Loving Harmony

Finally, in v. 26 Paul includes an important practical application which ties the whole discussion of the works of the flesh and the fruit of the Spirit to the actual situation in

---

[164] Witherington, 111, *Galatians*, 413.
[165] Fung, *The Epistle to the Galatians*, 276.
[166] Moo, *Galatians*, 371.
[167] Longenecker, *Galatians*, 264.

the Galatian Christian communities. In fact, he sets out an ugly contrast for them. It is still possible for true believers to live in a way that is not God-glorifying. We are reminded again of v. 15, as Paul warns them of the fact that, in light of the ministry of the Holy Spirit in their lives, they should not continue to become conceited. The participles which follow set out what Paul does not wish to see in them – "provoking one another and envying one another." There should rather be harmonious personal relationships and care as to how they should treat one another as the result of Paul's teaching here. It is in these personal contacts that Dunn[168] claims "the acid test" will come. Paul's examples will demonstrate what a community is *not* to look like, if it manifests the reality of the power of the Spirit.

Hendriksen[169] explains the meaning of "conceited" in his own words, "Let us neither brag about what we have (or think we have)." Moo[170] explains further, that the word is composed of κενός *kenos*, "empty" and δόξα *doxa* "praise," "renown." "It connotes the attitude of persons who think they have a right to praise and renown when, in fact, they have no such right: hence 'conceited' (most English versions)." We should not "provoke" – almost challenge another. This comes from the fact that being conceited will often result in such aggressive challenges of others, their actions and views. Or, as already highlighted among the "works of the flesh" (v. 21), they must not be envious of another's gifts and attainments.

True Christian relationships are not about "crossing swords" with others but serving others. George[171] quotes Stott here who noted, "This is a very instructive verse because it shows that our conduct to others is determined by our opinion of ourselves."

Paul has set out the fact that the Christian community have the clear teaching about recognising that they were crucified with Christ and so they can say "no!" to the desires of the flesh, through positively seeking to live in the power of the Holy Spirit enabling each one to adopt a godly lifestyle; in practical terms, the standard is not looking back to the law of Moses but on to the "law of Christ" as chapter 6 will affirm. All this the cross has won for us.

---

[168] Dunn, *Galatians*, 318.
[169] Hendriksen, *Galatians*, 227.
[170] Moo, *Galatians*, 373.
[171] Stott, *Only One Way*, 156 in George, *Galatians*, 406.

GALATIANS SIX

Gal 6: 1–10 Individual and Community Responsibilities

The change to the second person "you" and the direct address "brothers" points to the new section. So what do we have in this final chapter – is it just a collection of various sayings loosely put together? This of course, is the approach of some scholars.[1] However, it is possible to find here rather a carefully presented concluding section, with significant final insights about what life in the Spirit involves (cf. v. 8, sowing to the Spirit, rather than the flesh with 5:16–23), a most important final affirmation (6:14, glory in the cross) in the light of all the former argumentation[2] and a final appeal not to forsake the true gospel. So, this is a very important part of the letter. Firstly, in vv. 1–10 he writes about what the Spirit enabled life involves. Longenecker[3] identifies both personal and corporate responsibilities. As McDonald[4] reminds us, "spiritual freedom issues in specific obligations."

A Life of Sympathy

First of all, he calls them all "brothers." Paul reminds them again, as he often has done throughout the letter that they are family and this should affect all their attitudes and actions towards one another. Fung[5] points out that the vocative coming first in the Greek will be a "reminder to the readers that their membership in the same spiritual family involves mutual obligations." Again, George[6] explains that in this reiteration of his affection for his readers, Paul thus reinforced his earlier expression of confidence that they would "take no other view" (5:10), i.e., because they were after all true believers or children of God, "they would not utterly and finally fall away from the truth of the gospel."

So, he exhorts them to attempt compassionate restoration of any who have fallen into sin. Here we have an individual appeal – Paul writes, "you (sing.) who are spiritual" which will refer to all those who have responded to his teaching in 5:16–25. It is not likely that he is speaking ironically or with sarcasm.[7] The "spiritual" are those who

---

[1] J.C. O'Neill, *The Recovery of Paul's Letter to the Galatians* (London: SPCK, 1972) finds in 5:13–6:10 material from other authors being used; M. Debelius, *A Fresh Approach to the New Testament and Early Christian Literature*, Ferdinand Hahn, ed. (Westport, CT: Greenwood, 1979), also treats this section as he does other passages in various epistles as comprising paraenetic material which are insertions.

[2] Witherington, 111, *Galatians*, 444, points out that in the use of rhetoric the *peroratio* which he finds in 6:11–16, is generally used to sum up matters, not to introduce new arguments. This is exactly what it appears is happening here, as we will see when we reach that section.

[3] Longenecker, *Galatians*, 268.

[4] McDonald, *Freedom in Faith*, 140.

[5] Fung, *The Epistle to the Galatians*, 284.

[6] George, *Galatians*, 409.

[7] See R. A. Cole, *The Epistle of Paul to the Galatians*, TNTC (Grand Rapids: Eerdmans, 1965), 172.

already have the Spirit (3:2–5, 14; 4:6, 29; 5:5). Now they must live in his power; they must manifest the fruit of the Spirit, keep "in step" with the Spirit.[8]

Paul writes of the possibility of someone who is "caught" in any transgression. The generic "man" ἄνθρωπος *anthrōpos* is well attested but still will refer to someone within the church as "of you" makes clear. The verb "caught" in the passive means to be "overtaken" or "trapped" and suggests the idea of being taken unawares. The NEB rendering of the Greek is "do something wrong … on a sudden impulse." This is how things often happen – sin creeps up on us or we are put in unexpected circumstances and suddenly we have fallen! Hendriksen[9] explains that this verb προλαμβάνω *prolambanō* is used elsewhere in 1 Cor 11:21 for eating "before" the less-privileged arrive; Mark 14:8 for anointing Christ's body "before" his burial. So here "Before he even realizes to the full extent the ethically reprehensible or injurious nature of the act he has already committed it." The particular sin is not specified. But the word "transgression" as Longenecker[10] explains, is "a late word in Greek literature that literally means 'fall beside' or 'false step'… (cf. elsewhere in Paul's letters at Rom 4:25; 5:15–18, 20; 11:11–12; 2 Cor 5:19; Eph 1:7; 2:5; Col 2:13)." Witherington[11] points out, Paul has been calling the believers to "keep in step with," to stay in line with the Spirit, while here he warns by the use of "transgression" of a *false* step. That this can happen to anyone is suggested as Paul uses, as we have noted, the term "a man" – we cannot stand alone.

It is very possible that Paul is referring to a real situation which had occurred among the churches, a transgression such as had been listed among the "works of the flesh." It may very well have been disrupting the Galatians' fellowship with one another and with God. Paul urges that we must seek to "restore" such a person. Longenecker[12] explains that the verb "restore" is quite common in Greek literature and can be translated "put in order," "repair," "restore," or "make complete":

In the NT it appears (1) in material contexts to signify the "repair" of nets to their former usable condition (cf. Matt 4:2; Mark 1:19) (2) in religious contexts to signify the "completion" or "perfection" of one's faith (cf. 2 Cor 13:11; 1 Thess 3:10; Heb 13:21), and (3) in ethical contexts to signify moral "restoration" to a former good state (cf. 1 Cor 1:10). Here in Gal 6:1 it is evidently used in an ethical sense to mean "restore" to a former good state.

Paul is not asking here for punishment or discipline at this moment[13] but that they act in "a spirit of gentleness." George[14] makes the point that while no particular

---

[8] Moo translates the Greek as "You who are Spirit people." But he suggests that Paul is not trying to single out a "particular segment" within the Galatian churches. Rather he is seking to remind them that they all ought to be determined to "stay in step with the Spirit" (5:25). Moo, *Galatians*, 374.

[9] Hendriksen, *Galatians*, 231.

[10] Longenecker, *Galatians*, 272.

[11] Witherington, 111, *Galatians*, 421.

[12] Longenecker, *Galatians*, 273.

[13] The situation here of seeking to restore someone overtaken, or caught in a transgression is different from the godly discipline to be exercised by the Corinthian church in 1 Cor 5 where we have evidence of an

procedure is mentioned, Paul "likely knew and presupposed the one given by Jesus in Matt 18:15–17." Here there is a one–to–one encounter first; if this fails, a small group discussion; then "tell it to the church," and if necessary formal excommunication i.e., withdrawal from the fellowship of the Lord's table and expulsion from participation in the leadership or even membership of the church body. But we should note that "from Paul's perspective the purpose is always remedial and never punitive, even in the drastic case of the immoral brother at Corinth who was to be handed over to Satan, 'for the destruction of the flesh, that his spirit may be saved in the day of the Lord Jesus' (1 Cor 5:5)."

This direction in v. 1 will provide them all with an opportunity to manifest the fruit of the Spirit highlighted in 5:23 – the same word "gentleness" is used on both occasions. Such an approach is so important, where there are guilty, grieving souls. As George[15] explains, by using the word "gentleness," Paul is not calling for leniency that overlooks the transgression… "he is saying that the work of restoration should be done with sensitivity and consideration with no hint of self-righteous superiority." McDonald[16] explains that "nothing will be accomplished by denunciation."

The verse closes with the concessive clause, "keep watch on yourself, lest you too be tempted." Now again the singular "you" is being used, which makes the challenge more pointed and very personal. The word "tempted" here is the common word used in the NT, whose meaning will be determined by the context. Sometimes it will mean "try" or "test," but on many occasions, it will carry the sense of "tempt" (e.g., James 1:13) and this will be the meaning here. No-one can stand by their own strength; all must "watch" for all need the help of God and the enabling of the Spirit.

Bruce[17] comments, "The realization of one's personal vulnerability to temptation should prevent self-righteousness in the treatment of those who have yielded to it. Cf. 1 Cor 10:12…. This cautionary word is directed to each individual." Each must remember that they also could fall. The appeal therefore is for all to maintain a critical self-scrutiny in any such ministry. As Dunn[18] reminds us, "those who become involved with a person guilty of some (presumably) moral failure (cf. 1 Cor vii:5; x:9; James i:13–14) become vulnerable to the same failure precisely because of their genuine sympathy with that person." This warning here is so important.

---

ongoing persistent sin. Here the "transgression" is not a continuing course of action but an isolated incident. For Hendriksen, *Galatians*, 231, the trespass probably also was of a less serious nature, compared to what we have in the Corinthian context.

[14] He makes reference to C. H. Dodd, *"Ennomos Christou,"* in *More New Testament Studies* (Grand Rapids: Eerdmans, 1968), 148, who he suggests has "argued convincingly that Paul had access to the tradition of the words of Jesus in the gospels." One can add the important article in this area by K. E. Bailey, "Informal Controlled Oral Tradition and the Synoptic Gospels," *Asia Journal of Theology*, 5.1 (1991) 34–54 and *Themelios* 20.2 (January 1995), 4–11.

[15] George, *Galatians*, 411.

[16] McDonald, *Freedom in Faith*, 141.

[17] Bruce, *The Epistle to the Galatians*, 260.

[18] Dunn, *Galatians*, 321.

In v. 2 Paul also urges them to manifest their concern by bearing one another's burdens (the word order in the Greek puts the emphasis here). The word burden means literally "weight" but its figurative use is found in the NT where it carries various meanings (Matt 20:12; Acts 15:28; Rev 2:24). For some scholars Paul was concerned about the serious burden of poverty experienced by many in the Christian community (2:10), but Longenecker and Witherington[19] are doubtful about this verse being applied or limited to the idea of financial support. This is the focus of 6:6. Neither should the burden be limited to the burden of the one overtaken by sin – the immediate context, as Luther[20] suggests.

We all have burdens and God does not design that we should carry them alone. In Ps 55:22; 1 Peter 5:7 we are to cast our burdens upon him. But we should note that one of the ways he carries our burdens for us is through human friendships. See 2 Cor 7:5–6 concerning Paul himself, where he later wrote, "For even when we came into Macedonia, our bodies had no rest, but we were afflicted at every turn—fighting without and fear within. But God, who comforts the downcast, comforted us by the coming of Titus." Paul was afflicted, indecisive, fearful but help came through a friend. As Stott[21] has reminded us "God's comfort was not given to Paul only through private prayer and waiting upon the Lord, but through the companionship of a friend and through the good news which he brought. Human friendship, in which we bear one another's burdens, is part of the purpose of God for his people." We live in an uncaring world where it seems everyone is too busy to really take time to get involved with other needy souls. However, so many individuals need thoughtfulness, concern, sympathy and love, expressed especially to other members of the family of God.

Witherington[22] explains that the word ἀλλήλων *allēlōn* "one another" is in an emphatic position in the text stressing the importance of placing others first. To be a burden bearer is a great ministry. Considering the need for the church to be a continuing "supportive family community" – the present tense of "bear" suggests that burden bearing should be a constant practice. Dunn[23] can observe. "It was such mutual concern and support which caused not a few in the ancient Mediterranean world to exclaim, "see how these Christians love one another!'"

This sympathy or concern, this burden bearing is said to "fulfil the law of Christ." As has been mentioned already earlier in the letter, this fulfilment has nothing to do with the imposition of the Mosaic law. It was explained that Christ carried over into his own teaching some of the principles already stated in the law of Moses and even elaborated them; Paul did the same; this means that the original law is filled out in the whole of the NT. But the law of Christ is not the old law – as we should take a moment to reaffirm.

---

[19] Longenecker, *Galatians*, 275; Witherington, 111, *Galatians*, 423.
[20] Luther, *A Commentary on St. Paul's Epistle to the Galatians*, 540.
[21] Stott, *The One Way*, 158.
[22] Witherington, 111, *Galatians*, 422.
[23] Dunn, *Galatians*, 322.

Excursus: The Law of Christ

It is important to focus again[24] on the whole subject of "law" particularly in light of this phrase "the law of Christ" and consider how certain scholars have understood it.

There are a number of attempts at definition. First Thielmann,[25] who has maintained:

> Aspects of Moses' law such as the famous summary in Leviticus 19:18 are absorbed into this new law, but the covenant made with Moses at Mount Sinai is considered obsolete, and in its place Paul has substituted "the law of Christ."

Bruce[26] also considers that: "the 'law of Christ' is for Paul the whole tradition of Jesus' ethical teaching, confirmed by his character and conduct (cf. Rom 13:14; 2 Cor 10:1) and reproduced within his people by the power of the Spirit (cf. Rom 8:2)." Dunn[27] concurs with all of this. In both Galatians and Romans the call about loving your neighbour, "in echo of Jesus' teaching, is followed by a series of practical exhortations illustrating that love. In Romans the climax comes with clear allusion back to xiii.8–10 and with explicit evocation of the example of Christ (xv. 2–3)." Should we then not interpret this phrase as a reference to the teaching of Christ, his example of love and compassion and, in fact, even the principles built upon these which have been elaborated in the rest of the NT? As far as the Galatian Christians are concerned (and ourselves) they can "fulfil" that law by heeding Christ's teaching, emulating the pattern of his life of loving concern through our own dedicated self-giving and self-sacrificial action.

Fung[28] also helps us here in our interpretation of 6:2. He maintains that the "law of Christ" is the commandment of love – see first of all Lev 19:18 – considered by Jesus as the greatest of the commandments (Matt 22:36–40). He gave this commandment to the disciples as "a new commandment" (John 13:34; 15:12; 1 John 3:23) and he also demonstrated it in his own life. Fung writes:

> Paul regards love as both the summary and fulfilment of the law (Rom 13:8–10). The merit of this interpretation of "the law of Christ" is that it reasonably links the "law" with the "commandment" of Jesus and agrees with the emphasis on love in the preceding section of the letter (5:13f., 22;

---

[24] See chapter 2, the discussion on the law.

[25] F. Thielmann, *Paul and the Law* (Downers Grove: InterVarsity Press, 1994), 142.

[26] Bruce, *The Epistle to the Galatians*, 261. See also Longenecker. Here we have, "principles stemming from the heart of the gospel (usually embodied in the example and teachings of Jesus), which are meant to be applied to specific situations by the direction and enablement of the Holy Spirit, being always motivated and conditioned by love," *New Testament Social Ethics for Today* (Grand Rapids, Michigan: William B. Eerdmans Publishing Co.), 15. See also George, *Galatians*, 416.

[27] Dunn, *Galatians*, 322–323.

[28] Fung, *The Epistle to the Galatians*, 289.

6:1) ... Jesus reinterpreted the law in terms of love both in his teaching and by his example.

Again, Moo[29] gives us some important reflections. First, the genitive qualifier Χπιστοῦ *Christou* "of Christ" can be a deliberate counterpart to the "law of Moses." Second, 1 Cor 9:20–21 provides a close parallel to this text. Paul is no longer "under" the law that was valid for Jews while he is still obligated to the law of Christ, which he distinguishes from the law of Moses. He acknowledges that the love command must be part of what Paul intends and also there must be more. "Precisely because the phrase serves as the new covenant counterpart to the "law of Moses," we should expect the reference to include all those teachings and commandments set forth by Christ and by his inspired apostles – including Paul."

In summary, as to meaning then, fulfilling the law of Christ can be defined as follows. It is first of all following the example of Jesus' loving character and conduct. There is little here that points us directly back to the OT and the Mosaic law. As Bruce[30] suggests, "It is as though he (Paul) said 'If you must live under law, live under the law of love – that is, the law of Christ.'" This "law" is exemplified in the life of Christ and set out in his teaching but also fully and finally elaborated in the ethical teachings of Paul and the rest of the NT. Therefore, we can say that in 6:2 the whole example and teachings of Christ is being set in stark contrast to the errant behaviour of the self-seeking Galatians in 5:15, 26. Only the power of the Holy Spirit in their lives would make this Christ-like love, example and ethical teaching a reality. Yet this love and example is what can be seen expressed in "burden bearing."

* * *

A Life of Humility

In v. 3 Paul uses a verb he used earlier in 2:2, 6 meaning "to be important" "to be esteemed,"– by others. Here rather it is to think *oneself* to be important; the danger of an inflated self-esteem. This is surely related to Paul's exhortation in the previous verse – following the pattern of Christ. In Phil 2:6–8 the one who was in the very "form of God," who could not have a higher status, "made himself nothing, taking the form of a servant." But we are nothing to begin with; we must not be deceived or lifted up in pride as that would not help us in our commitment to reach out to others. The problem for Moo[31] are those believers who "take credit for their own accomplishments without recognising their absolute dependence on God's grace and Spirit for anything useful that is done for the Lord." If we only are thinking of ourselves we will not be ready to be involved practically with others in dire need. The

---

[29] Moo, *Galatians*, 378.
[30] Bruce, *The Epistle to the Galatians*, 241. For Hendriksen, *Galatians*, 233, the "law of Christ" is simply "the principle of love for one another laid down by Christ (John 13:34; see also on Gal 5:14; cf. James 2:8)." It was a principle which he himself exemplified.
[31] Moo, *Galatians*, 379. He queries if here we find a further discrete development of the warning about "conceit."

more we recognise our own feebleness the more we will be willing to have a concern and an openness to reach out to others in their need.

A Life of Responsibility

For Moo, "In contrast, then, to a superficial and deceptive view of themselves as more than they really are (the δέ [*de*] is adversative: "but"), every believer should 'test their own work'." In fact, vv. 4–5 are verses which can be considered together; they highlight two aspects which should be closely connected – self-examination and our future reckoning before the judgment seat where "each will have to bear his own load."

Paul begins by reminding the Galatians of their personal responsibility – "each one." Longenecker[32] points out that the verb "test" has in Paul "three different, though complimentary, senses." (1) "test" or "examine" (1 Cor 3:13; 11:28; 2 Cor 3:5; 1 Thess 5:21; 1 Tim 3:10); (2) "accept as proven" or "approve" (Rom 2:18; 14:22; 1 Thess 2:4; 2 Cor 8:22); and (3) "think best" or "choose" (1 Cor 6:3). Rom 12:2 is not easy to place. Here 6:4 falls into the first category. Therefore v. 4 emphasises that the basis for "the boasting" (the article makes it restrictive, as does the use of "himself alone") is that we must test our own actions before God, rather than comparing ourselves with others around us.[33] The phrase "his own work" is emphasised as it is placed first in the sentence. Note in passing also, that the word "work" can be understood as a collective term, referring to all that Christians do. Dunn[34] suggests that the idea is "the act of critical self-comparison of oneself as though a spectator of one's own conduct." Therefore, rather than assessing others you must ask yourself about your own work or the task you have been set by God. You are responsible to God for your work and must give account of it to God in that day. This is affirmed as we have noted in v. 5 in the statement about "each one … will bear his own load." Everyone will give account of HIMSELF to God – each is responsible for his own particular task.

Lightfoot[35] highlights Paul's use of two words here for "burden." While acknowledging the difficulty in establishing precise distinctions, βάρος *baros* in v. 2 suggests the idea of an oppressive burden which could be relieved, while φορτίον *phortion* is more a "load" of responsibility[36]. The use of "his own" and not someone else's, emphasises the idea of personal responsibility – only for himself. Can this not refer to one's own labour for the Lord, i.e., service for the lost or in the church? It must be surely the "work" referred to in v. 4. Also, let us not forget about the burden of prayer. When you do not bear *your* load the whole fellowship suffers. The question of course is how our service will be seen in the "day of Christ." At the judgment seat

---

[32] Longenecker, *Galatians*, 277.

[33] As McDonald, *Freedom in Faith*, 142, has stated, "the best check on pride is for each one to check his own work."

[34] Dunn, *Galatians*, 325.

[35] Lightfoot, *Saint Paul's Epistle to the Galatians*.

[36] Note that the ESV here translates "For each will have to bear his own load."

each one shall bear (the future tense is here) his own burden or render his own account to God (Rom 14:12; 2 Cor 5:10).

A Life of Liberality

In v. 6 we learn there is one "burden" we should not forget. The one taught is to impart a share of his good things to the one who teaches the word. As Bruce[37] states:

> The teacher relieves the ignorance of the pupil; the pupil should relieve the teacher of concern for his subsistence. This is another way of stating the principle that "the Labourer deserves his wages" (Luke 10:7; 1 Tim 5:18; cf. Matt 10:10).

Elsewhere when Paul writes about financial support it is the *right* of the teacher he stresses (1 Cor 9:3–14; 1 Tim 5:18)[38]; here it is the *duty* of those who are taught. George[39] explains that Paul and Barnabas had appointed elders in every church and some may then have been singled out to be the first pastors and teachers of the growing congregations. Had the Galatians withdrawn material support from these church leaders in their infatuation with the new theology advanced by Paul's opponents? The churches were built upon "the word" – an important emphasis here; the word includes all the apostolic traditions or doctrines of the faith (1 Cor 11:2; 2 Thess 2:15; 3:6). Teachers themselves have the responsibility to prove to be "faithful" in their instruction of it. But the question is about local teachers in the Galatian Christian community who are not being supported as they should.

Have we personally noted the church's responsibility in this? What about our personal giving in the local church to support the ministry? Do we only tip God? Is there a work, a pastor we should be helping to support? It is not said to be the duty of the state to provide such support but the duty of "the one who is taught." The verb κοινωνέω *koinōneō* here "must *share* all good things" is a present imperative which affirms an ongoing responsibility. This language of "sharing" as Dunn[40] names it, had been a feature of the Christian movement from earliest days (Acts 2:42, 44–45; 4:34–35). Note that "all good things," as Longenecker[41] has maintained, is a general expression, "it certainly cannot be understood apart from material sustenance – probably more directly financial support." Moo[42] also emphasises this. It is clear that "all good things" must be material in nature – he suggests that Phil 4:15 can furnish a parallel. This is not a spiritual sharing but rather material, "since it better explains

---

[37] Bruce, *The Epistle to the Galatians*, 263.
[38] Fung, *The Epistle to the Galatians*, 293, explains that Paul did not always exercise that right. In fact, he consistently refused such support in order to be an example to his converts not to be "parasites" living off others (2 Thess. 3v6–13; Acts 20:33–35) or that he was driven by mercenary motives (2 Cor 11v7–12; 1 Thess. 2:5–9). Such support "was a right to be claimed – or not claimed", depending on each situation.
[39] George, *Galatians,* 420.
[40] Dunn, *Galatians,* 326.
[41] Longenecker, *Galatians,* 279.
[42] Moo, *Galatians,* 382. See also Dunn, *Galatians,* 327.

why Paul puts the responsibility on the one being taught rather than on the one who is teaching."

A Life of Purity

Paul again in vv. 7–9 refers to the Spirit's powerful ministry in the lives of his converts as he returns to the desires of the flesh-Spirit antithesis, which was central to his understanding of the Christian life. Also, as Moo[43] explains, "Paul seeks to motivate his readers to action by warning that their conduct will have consequences for the eschatological judgment."

Scholars have here, as with earlier verses in chapter 6, identified certain principles which can be compared with OT and philosophical wisdom. He begins in v. 7 with a warning in the present imperative which is often found in the NT, "Do not be deceived." (Luke 21:8; 1 Cor 6:9; 15:33; James 1:16). While Bruce[44] is not persuaded by Schmithals's understanding of Galatians having an anti-gnostic emphasis, he identifies with his comments regarding how some of the community were "mocking" God:

> Consciously stressing the possession of the divine Pneuma, for this reason held themselves to be perfect Christians and openly boasted of their piety (Gal 5:26; 6:3), but at the same time were sowing to the σάρξ (flesh) and were doing that equally consciously and emphatically.

Witherington[45] reminds us that "People assume that they can get away with certain things without God paying attention or without God finally holding them accountable." This is true of Christians as well, but Paul is clear, "God is not mocked." He cannot be taken in. The verb "mocked" is only here in the NT; it is common in the LXX (16x) and OT references about "turning up your nose" or treating others contemptuously are mainly about mocking God's prophets – see e.g., 2 Chron 36:16. Once there is a reference to blasphemously mocking God himself, Ezek 8:7. Bruce[46] affirms, that anyone who "thought that the law of sowing and reaping could be safely ignored, would indeed be treating God with contempt." Here Paul warns that God *cannot* be mocked; we inevitably reap what we sow.

Moo[47] also makes the point that this particular word picture of sowing and reaping is used because Paul was dealing with "societies dominated by agriculture" and the use

---

[43] Moo, *Galatians*, 384.
[44] W. Schmithals, *Paul and the* Gnostics, ETr. (Nashville: Abingdon Press, 1972) 54 in Bruce, *The Epistle to the Galatians*, 264.
[45] Witherington, 111, *Galatians*, 431.
[46] Bruce, *The Epistle to the Galatians*, 265.
[47] Moo, *Galatians*, 384.

of such imagery is "a natural way to speak of cause and consequence." George[48] now explains that in v. 8 Paul moves on from his general statements about the impossibility of mocking God and the principle of sowing and reaping, "to apply these truths to the Galatian situation in terms of his earlier antithesis between flesh and Spirit." He also makes the point that Paul's use of the agricultural metaphor was common in the Greco-Roman world, also in the OT, Job 4:8; Prov 22:8; Jer 12:13; Hos. 8:7 and in the NT as well, 1 Cor 9:11; 2 Cor 9:6; Luke 19:21–22; John 4:35–36). He assures us that the harvest depends upon where and what we sow.

The opening ὅτι *hoti* of v. 8 is not causal ("because") but is used by way of explanation "that is." The duty in chapter 5 was to walk in the Spirit; now it is presented as "sow to the Spirit" and not to the flesh. It is clear that when he refers to "the one who sows" he is focusing upon the community of faith in Galatia. The flesh is our unregenerated lower nature and to sow to it is to let it dominate.[49] Believers sometimes can focus upon things which feed the flesh and its desires, i.e., let our lower nature control. Paul is exhorting us not to sow to the flesh. Sowing to the Spirit is, as well as dependence upon him, to set our minds upon the things of the Spirit, to be open to his anointing or infilling, to foster disciplined habits of devotion in daily prayer and bible study and worship on the Lord's day. Therefore v. 8 is giving us directions about the way to Christian holiness of life. Such a life is really what the reformers would affirm as evidence of the presence or reality of saving faith, which, by grace and through the cross, leads us to eternal life. As Silva[50] explains, "When the apostle affirms that the future judgment grows out of one's mode of existence during the overlap of the ages…, he is in fact making explicit what may be deduced from the rest of the letter."

There are two life-styles set before us. The alternative to this Spirit filled life, fulfilling the sins of the flesh, is leading to a different harvest, "destruction," which, for Longenecker,[51] "picks up on and expresses in a graphic manner the warning of 5:21b." The word is φθόρα *phthora* meaning "corruption" "destruction" "decay." George[52] comments, "However, we should not be misled by this graphic depiction of utter decay and desolation into thinking that the final destiny of those who sow to the flesh is annihilation or nonexistence. Hell is both final and eternal." He points out the similar language found in Rev 21:8 with Paul's category of evil in Gal 5 and notes the state of eternal separation from God expressed as "the 'corruption' of the second death," "He that is unjust, let him be unjust *still*, and he that is filthy, let him be filthy *still*" (Rev 22:11 KJV). We are confronted with the reality of eternal misery in hell,

---

[48] George, *Galatians,* 423. One should note that Dunn, *Galatians,* 330 takes "flesh" in the sense it is used in 4:23, 29; 6:12–13 involving also the Judaizers' attempt to persuade the Galatians concerning circumcision. But the Spirit/flesh antithesis of 5:13–26 is difficult to set aside.

[49] The sowing metaphor is expressed in the translation of the NEB, "in the field of his lower nature … in the field of the Spirit."

[50] Silva, *Explorations in Exegetical Method,* 183–84.

[51] Longenecker, *Galatians,* 281. Harvesting elsewhere in the Scriptures often refers to judgment, Jer 12:13; Matt 13:24–30, 36–43; Rev 14:15–16.

[52] George, *Galatians,* 423.

as the rest of Scripture will affirm. For Moo[53] φθόρα *phthora* "destruction" is an adequate translation, "always remembering that, when applied to the eternal state in the NT, this kind of language refers not to annihilation but to eternal punishment."

Excursus: Eternal Punishment

It is important that this subject is highlighted in the teachings which we consider as fundamental for the Church today. Considering the future condition of the lost, Church leaders (and members) are often asked to unreservedly affirm "The conscious eternal punishment of those who die impenitent."[54] In this statement annihilationism or conditional immortality (only those who "believe" have life in the age to come) are ruled out by the words "conscious eternal"; universalism is challenged by the reality of "eternal punishment" and a second chance by the statement "those who die impenitent." Note the following Scripture passages:

(a) contra annihilationism – Matt 8:11–12; but some will ask about the word "perish" ἀπολλυμι *apollumi*. It does not actually imply non-existence (1 Cor 15:18; 2 Cor 2:15; 4:3; 2 Thess 2:10; 2 Pet 3:9; John 17:12; 1 Cor 15:18; Luke 19:19). ὄλεθερος *oletheros* "destruction," 2 Thess 1:9 is amplified by the words that follow about being shut out "from the presence of the Lord." Packer[55] affirms:

> In 2 Thessalonians 1:9 Paul … extends, the meaning of "punished with everlasting [eternal, *aionios*] destruction" by adding "and shut out from the presence of the Lord" — which phrase, by affirming exclusion, rules out the idea that "destruction" meant extinction. Only those who exist can be excluded. It has often been pointed out that in Greek the natural meaning of the destruction vocabulary (noun, *olethros*; verb, *apollumi*) is wrecking, so that what is destroyed is henceforth nonfunctional rather than annihilating it, so that it no longer exists in any form at all.

(b) contra universalism – Jesus speaks to two opposite but equally eternal destinies (Matt 25:46; cf. Col 1:20; Phil 2:10–11), where in the second passage, highlighting reconciliation, those "under the earth" are omitted. In Matt 25:46 the same word everlasting describes the end of the righteous and of the unrighteous. Universalists see two sets of texts in the NT (a) final division and also (b) restoration of all things. They will see (a) as "threats" or taken over by the apostle from the contemporary Jewish environment – unauthentic texts. This is to undermine the authority of the Scriptures and Jesus himself. In addition, Daniel 12:2 refers to the condition of the wicked AFTER the resurrection of the body and judgment.

---

[53] Moo, *Galatians*, 386.
[54] See Moore, *The Letters to Timothy and Titus*, 132–133.
[55] J.I. Packer, "Evangelical Annihilationism in Review," Reformation & Revival, Vol. 6, No. 2, Spring, 1997. 45. An assessment of the critique of Annihilationism in contrast to the biblical doctrine of everlasting punishment. See also www.the-highway.com/annihilationism-Packer.html accessed April 2015.

Some will say that surely hell fire destroys. But Rev 14:11; 20:10 are about eternal punishment. See 2 Peter 2:9 which also speaks of punishment, not being "cut off" as the teaching of the Jehovah Witnesses, or Seventh-Day Adventists affirm.

(c) contra second chance – see John 5:29; Acts 24:15; Rev 22:11; John 3:18. The Scriptures speak of a door shut (Matt 25:10–12); a chasm fixed (Luke 16:26).

Some find it difficult to reconcile God's love/punishment. But it is important to consider these facts.

(a)   Remember the seriousness of sin.

(b)   God has done everything apart from the outrage of his justice/righteousness to keep people from hell (John 3:16; 2 Cor 5:19; Rom 3:24–26; 2 Pet 3:9). All that needs to be done has been done – men only need to believe.

(c)   Before hell is an experience which is imposed by God, we must remember that we have opted for it ourselves – Judas went to "his own place," i.e., of his own choosing (Acts 1:25).

In light of all this, we must make our calling and election sure (2 Pet 1:10; 2 Cor 13:5); we need to be deeply concerned for the lost (Rom 9:1–3); we must realise that when we could not get right with God by our own actions – even circumcision and submission to the Mosaic law – God himself took the initiative in love (4:4) and all has been accomplished at the cross – we can be accepted by grace through believing as Abraham did. Our obligation is in proclaiming the good news of this message of the cross (6:14).

The Scriptures speak of conscious suffering of the entire re-constituted personality (Matt 10:28); conscious separation (Luke 16:19–31); conscious deprivation – of fellowship (Luke 14:24); of a place of usefulness (Matt 21:41); all worked for (Luke 12:20). However, in contrast and hope, they also speak of deliverance through the cross.

Packer[56] made this point respectfully but firmly:

> Jude 6 and Matthew 8:12; 22:13; 25:30 show that darkness signifies a state of deprivation and distress, but not of destruction in the sense of ceasing to exist. Only those who exist can weep and gnash their teeth, as those banished into the darkness are said to do. Nowhere in Scripture does death signify extinction; physical death is departure into another mode of being ... existence that is God-less and graceless; nothing in biblical usage warrants the idea ... that the "second death" of Revelation 2:11; 20:14; 21:8 means or involves cessation of being.

---

[56] J. I. Packer, "Evangelical Annihilationism in Review," 44.

Those who struggle with this doctrine and seek to hold to an alternative viewpoint which they consider should be acceptable among evangelicals surely must not avoid the clear teaching of the Bible here.

To mention again, the alternative to sowing to the flesh is sowing to the Spirit and the harvest is "eternal life." This is a concept that is found often in both the Johannine and Pauline writings (John 3:16; 11:22–23; 17:3; 1 John 1:2; 5:11; Rom 2:7; 5:21; 6:22–23; 1 Tim 1:16; Titus 1:3; 3:7). As George[57] clarifies, "Eternal life, of course, is not merely life that lasts eternally. It is rather God's very own life, the life of the Father, the Son, and the Holy Spirit, graciously bestowed upon the children of God through faith." It is a present possession (John 3:36; 11:25–26) but Paul can also use it of the final consummation of salvation, with the return of Christ – as Jesus in Luke 18:29–30.

So Hendriksen[58] can sum up:

> The two terms "corruption" and "life everlasting" must be understood in a double sense: quantitative and qualitative. With respect to the former, the two are alike: both last on and on and on … Qualitatively, and with this reference to both body and soul, the two – "corruption" and "life everlasting" – form a striking contrast. Those who have sown to the flesh will awaken unto shame and everlasting contempt (Dan 12:2). Their worm will not die, neither will their fire be quenched (Mark 9:48). Their dwelling place will be outside the banquet-hall (Matt 8:11, 12; 22:13; 25:10–13). On the other hand those who have sown to the Spirit will then shine as the brightness of the firmament and as the stars for ever and ever (Dan 12:3). They will bear the image of the heavenly (1 Cor 15:49), and physically will be conformed to the body of Christ's glory (Phil 3:21).

What a glorious future! All accomplished for us through the cross!

* * *

A Life of Ministry

Having dealt with holiness, Paul now turns attention to Christian well doing, v. 9. In fact, it appears that the teaching of v. 8 is brought to an encouraging practical conclusion – the δε *de* here translated "And," shows the connection with v. 7 i.e., you must "sow to the Spirit, therefore do good." There is a connection also in the harvest imagery with v8 – "reaping" if we do not give up.

Paul once again includes himself in the "let us" not grow weary[59] or be tempted to ever give up. Longenecker[60] wishes us not to lose sight of the context first of all:

---

[57] George, *Galatians*, 424.
[58] Hendriksen, *Galatians*, 237.

In particular, it has reference to those matters commanded in 6:1–6: restoring someone entrapped by sin (v. 1), bearing the oppressive burdens of others (v. 2), and sharing materially with those who teach the gospel message (v. 6).

Were they reverting to a selfish, self-seeking attitude with little concern for others, whether those who had sadly fallen into some transgression, those who were oppressed and burdened, or the serious needs of their teachers? Betz[61] wishes to extend the exhortation to include everything from 5:16. He maintains that the phrase doing good "includes everything the Christian is responsible for doing. Thus it is identical with the concepts of the 'fruit of the Spirit' (5:22–23) and of 'following the Spirit' (5:25; cf. 5:16)."

Paul continues to use the agricultural imagery of sowing and reaping. Understanding the exhortation in a general sense, sometimes we want to sow and reap in the same day. Only in the untiring work of well doing can one receive the commendation for doing well. For well doing there can one day be a "well done." The translation "in due season" reminds us of the need of sowing now in our lifetime and reaping in the future. George[62] reminds us that the word here for "season" or "time" is καιρός *kairos*, the same word Paul uses for the opportune moment when God sent his Son into the world (4:4). He also uses it of the *parousia*, the second coming in 1 Tim, 6:15. So while he will not dismiss the possibility of a harvest in time and earthly ministry, he still reminds us of the ultimate time of reaping. "Its larger fulfilment points to the eschatological consummation at the return of Christ." Therefore, we must not give up.

Should we understand this exhortation as commitment to ministry? Or rather as the need for perseverance? Longenecker [63] suggests, "For Paul, the fruit of a spiritual harvest comes through the concurring actions of both God and the believer, with the believer's perseverance being generally in response to the Spirit's work in his or her life." Dunn[64] also reminds us of how God has sown in them the seed of the Spirit which is followed by a lengthy period of growth "in adverse conditions, in which the human participants have a responsibility not to slacken in their own (co-operative) efforts." We must persevere.

Hendriksen[65] however takes the word "well-doing" in a general sense – as "comprehensive," as walking/being led by the Spirit, and also should include providing for the needy – in every sense, physical and spiritual. Commenting on not "growing weary" he considers Paul is referring to a well-known weakness in human

---

[59] The Textus Receptus translates "lose heart"; ESV, following the use of the MSS on which it is based where a different verb is used, translates "become weary."

[60] Longenecker, *Galatians*, 281.

[61] Betz, *Galatians*, 309.

[62] George, *Galatians,* 426. For Moo, "It probably means the appointed time of eschatological evaluation." Moo, *Galatians*, 388.

[63] Longenecker, *Galatians*, 282.

[64] Dunn, *Galatians*, 332.

[65] Hendriksen, *Galatians*, 237–38.

nature which "lacks staying power ... is easily discouraged." He sees this as especially true when the work is hard and people are unresponsive and the apparent delay for the Galatians in the fulfilment of the promise of Christ's return.

A Life of Opportunity

Paul is using in v. 10, as he often does elsewhere, "therefore then" to conclude his exhortations to them (cf. Rom 5:8; 7:3, 25; 8:12; Eph 2:19; 1 Thess 5:6). This statement serves as a conclusion and it is clear that the previous verses should be seen as all connected, involving the call to "sow in the Spirit" in v. 8 which is related to the life in the Spirit Paul has been setting forth from chapter 3 and especially in 5:14–26; 6:1–9. Do we have an *incluso* here with 5:13?

He urges, "as we have opportunity (life is full of such opportunity) let us (he includes himself) do good to everyone." Works do have their place, but not to save (2:16). We should show the love of Christ to all men. If others do not do it, it gives us the opportunity. One should however, as George[66] reminds us, take note of the word repeated from v. 9b καιρός *kairos*. As the "time" of reaping or the harvest will come, so now we must make use of this "time" to sow to the Spirit and not to the flesh; also we ought to be open for the present opportunities or "time" which we understand to be strategically significant, or God-given and set before us as part of God's purpose of ministry for us.[67] Looking back to the affirmation of 5:1, he stresses, "The freedom of the Christian is a freedom of service in the moment of opportunity ... let us faithfully fulfil the ministry God has given us to do." Christ is coming again; now is the opportunity!

The "everyone" means that his converts in Galatia (and ourselves) should reach out to all, regardless of national, cultural, social, religious distinctions. They should seize the mission opportunity to the wider community. Moo[68] states, "Amid the vital theological issue with which they are wrestling and the internal divisions this issue has created, the Galatian Christians are to manifest the love of Christ and the grace of God to all the people they come into contact with." Yet we should note how Paul stresses, "especially to those who are of the household of faith." Paul focuses upon a second obligation without reducing the responsibility for the first. Dunn[69] explains that there may well be a deliberate contrast here to the phrase "house of Israel" (e.g., Num. 20:29; 2 Sam. 1:12; Ezek 3:4), or "the house of truth in Israel" (1QS 5.6), "the house of holiness for Israel" (1 QS 8.5) or "the house of the law" (CD 20.10, 13). His comments here are significant for the whole letter. "In which case it will be significant once again that the bonding characteristic of this household is faith, and

---

[66] George, *Galatians,* 427.

[67] Dunn, *Galatians,* 332, makes the point that the concept of the time "has eschatological overtones in Paul (cf. Rom xiii.11; 1 Cor vii.29; 2 Cor iv. 5; Eph v. 16)."

[68] Moo, *Galatians,* 389.

[69] Dunn, *Galatians,* 333. Moo also reminds us that the use of "household" here brings to mind one of the key NT images of the church as an extended spiritual family, Eph 2:19; 1 Tim 3:15; 1 Pet 2:5; 4:17; Heb 3:6. Moo, *Galatians,* 389.

not membership of ethnic Israel, and not the Torah." Therefore, in having a genuine concern for all, they must have a special concern ("especially" ESV) for fellow believers in real need or for the Christian community which is a family of faith[70]. George[71] gives to us a challenging quotation from Brown:

> Every poor and distressed man has a claim on me for pity.... But a poor Christian has a far stronger claim on my feelings, my labors, and my property. He is my brother, equally interested as myself in the blood and love of the redeemer. I expect to spend an eternity with him in heaven. He is the representative of my unseen Savior, and he considers everything done to his poor afflicted as done to himself. For a Christian to be unkind to a Christian is not only wrong it is monstrous.

So generally, there needs to be a Christian lifestyle which is loving, caring and genuinely outgoing to meet the needs of others, especially God's people. Note that for Paul here the division of mankind is not into Jew and Gentile (this racial distinction is gone, Gal 3:28; 5:6) but between the believer and the unbeliever. Yet the primary claim on us towards the Christian community, does not exclude the wider responsibility to all.

In this opening section of chapter 6 the self-sacrificial lifestyle expected of the Galatian Christian community is made clear. In seeking to recover those who have fallen, in bearing another's burden, in dedicated living, in serving others they manifest the fruit of the Spirit (5:22–23) and "fulfil" the law of Christ, manifesting his love, following his example (6:2) and the principles of the NT. In this way Christ is truly being "formed" in them (4:19). They take on their own burden of responsibility, faithfully support their teachers and do not give up in their ministry. As Paul has stated, through sowing to the Spirit they will be more and more prepared for the final harvest (6:8).

The Subscription – Glorying Only in the Cross vv. 11–18

Usually in Paul the thanksgiving section at the beginning of an epistle points ahead to the major concerns to follow; on the other hand, the subscriptions will highlight and summarize the themes that have been the focus throughout. While Galatians may lack a thanksgiving section at the beginning, those verses do make clear the occasion and the issues at stake for the writing of the letter. But what of the final verses, 6:11–18? Do they function in providing a summary, an interpretative key to the themes of the body of the letter? It is important to discuss the claims made as to how significant they may be for the teaching in the whole letter.

---

[70] Fung, *The Epistle to the Galatians*, 298, makes the point that the phrase concerns "members of the family of those whose characteristic is faith – the last word being taken in the active and subjective sense of trust, not in the objective sense as equivalent to the gospel or Christianity (as in NEB 'the faith')."
[71] J. Brown *An Exposition of the Epistle to the Galatians* (Marshallton, Del.: Sovereign Grace, 1970) 348 in George, *Galatians*, 428.

Excursus: The Final Subscription

First, in interpreting this letter, as was discussed in the Introduction, we have acknowledged that many noted scholars affirm Paul's indebtedness to rhetorical style. This is also said to be influential in the final subscription. For example, when it comes to 6:12–17 we noted how Witherington[72] considers that the tone here to be extremely serious, not light-hearted or friendly, and that in these closing verses "we find a carefully crafted *peroratio*, the proper conclusion to a rhetorical composition," full of sound, fury and pathos. It should be clear by this stage that in our exegesis of Galatians we have accepted the use of rhetoric to some degree, but not adopted it as the letter's all-pervasive hermeneutical key.

It appears that some modern scholars have not given sufficient attention to an epistolary analysis of Galatians. As we noted in the text, at various stages Paul has employed Jewish forms of argumentation, Jewish exegetical practices, using Scripture, rather than Greco-Roman rhetorical conventions. What we have here certainly seems to be more than Witherington[73] suggests, when he proposes that Paul is giving "at least a nod in the direction of the rules of first-century letter writing." Paul has adopted popular methods of persuasion in the culture of the time, but has combined these with epistolary features in certain ways.

However we classify the style or genre of the subscription identified here as 6:11–18 – *peroratio* or not, it can be maintained that in these verses we have a final climatic summing up of the real issues and argumentation of the whole of the letter. We noted at the beginning that Christ's death on a cross was affirmed by Longenecker[74] as *the central soteriological theme of Galatians* (cf. 1:4; 3:1, 13; 6:12, 14) just as of course it was the focus of early Christian preaching. We need now to examine what role the theme of the cross has in this closing section. We will find among other elements a clear contrast between the cross and circumcision. For Fung,[75] they are set forth "as representing respectively the true and the false ground of boasting and thus carrying a stage further his (Paul's) polemic against the Judaizers and their way of legal observance."

Longenecker[76] points out that often subscriptions in Paul's letters have not received the attention they deserved – although Galatians has had more attention because it is longer and somewhat unique. He quotes from two earlier scholars who commented on the close links between the subscription and the main body of the letter – Lightfoot[77] who sees it as "summing up the main lessons of the epistle," and

---

[72] Witherington, 111, *Galatians*, 443.
[73] Witherington, 111, *Galatians*, 439.
[74] Longenecker, *Galatians*, 264. n. 6.
[75] Fung, *The Epistle to the Galatians*, 300.
[76] Longenecker, *Galatians*, see "Form/Setting/Structure," 286–89.
[77] Lightfoot, *Saint Paul's Epistle to the Galatians*, 220.

Deissmann[78] who, writing of the concluding words of Paul's letters generally, affirms that they ought to be seen as of "the highest importance" and the conclusion of Galatians as "a very remarkable one." Longenecker also focuses on Betz, who while he is emphasising the letter is not from an epistolary but a rhetorical perspective, can still, as we noted in the Introduction, write of 6:11–18 not only as a summation but also *the* hermeneutical key to the intentions of the Apostle. For Longenecker this is quite significant, as he finds, rather than forensic rhetoric, Jewish ways of argumentation as well as deliberative rhetoric in Galatians.

Galatians does have certain epistolary conventions which are to be found in the conclusion of a normal Hellenistic letter. One can acknowledge that it does lack certain features of other Pauline letters i.e., greetings, a call to rejoice, request for prayer, a doxology, but these can be explained because of the strained relationship which existed. Others do appear, the autograph (larger than normal), the peace and grace benedictions. It can be maintained that the subscription will provide a summary of central matters, plus a focus upon major issues discussed within the body of the letter, while it carries a note not of rejoicing or thanksgiving but of warning. So, when it comes to the final chapter, Longenecker[79] can conclude, "6:11–18 must be seen as something of a prism that reflects the major thrusts of what has been said earlier in the letter, or a paradigm set at the end of the letter that gives guidance in understanding what has been said before."

One also needs to note Witherington's[80] conviction as to how Paul has crafted what he considers as the whole *peroratio*. He sees two particular elements here, a summing up of the most essential points of the previous act of persuasion – helpful for any attempt to argue for the importance of this section – and an attempt to arouse the emotions – anger against the Judaizers and pity for the apostle (vv. 11, 12–13, 17).

Having examined the subscription in some detail and the views of a range of scholarship, what can we add by way of final comment? All that Longenecker writes about the summary, issues and theme of Galatians here is very significant and important for this present work. However, while highlighting the presence of a summary and a reminder of the issues in this final section, has he failed to mention again the all-important theme clearly expressed in v. 14? He did affirm a few pages earlier that the cross was the theme.[81] Again, as far as Witherington's work is concerned, it was accepted in the Introduction that Paul has no doubt used rhetoric in the letter but in the situation of great concern with the urgent need to respond quickly to the Galatian crisis, Paul has employed different elements of composition. We noted the short epistolary introduction 1:1–5 and now a very different subscription and a brief but particular benediction. So, there is some flexibility. Yet the elements of rhetoric do appear here in the conclusion, as in other parts of the argumentation of

---

[78] A. Deissmann, *Bible Studies*, Tr. A. Grieve (Edinburgh: T&T Clark, 1901), 347–48.
[79] Longenecker, *Galatians*, 288–89.
[80] Witherington, 111, *Galatians*, 443–45.
[81] See Longenecker, *Galatians*, 264.

the letter. However, one should also note Witherington's[82] expression of support for the study by Weima which again affirms in effect the very theme we are advocating, as he maintains that the agitators had no place for the offence, importance and sufficiency of the cross in their message. We will see that this section (6:12–17) has a series of antitheses between Paul's view and that of the Judaizers – namely, boasting in the cross, rather than boasting in circumcision, as Fung earlier stated. George can highlight, writing of these antitheses, "Just as Paul had placarded Christ crucified to the Galatians during his first preaching mission among them (cf. Gal 3:1–3), so it is (the cross) still the centrepiece in the final conclusion of the letter." Hence the title of this commentary, *Glory in the Cross*.

Finally, one takes note of Moo[83] who refers to how in Galatians Paul focuses especially on the cosmic significance of Christ's death. The reference in 1:4, Christ by his cross rescuing us from "the present evil age" and 6:14, the world being crucified to us and we to the world, are "the Christological bookends of the letter." Moo[84] further states concerning the antitheses between the agitators and Paul which we will see outlined in this closing section:

> They are motivated by selfish considerations while Paul is motivated by Christ's cross; they focus on the physical mark of circumcision, Paul on the "marks" of Jesus; they are bound to this world, and Paul is bound to the next world.... And the creator of all these antitheses is the cross of Christ (vv. 12, 14).

Once again we maintain, faith in the Christ of the cross is the all-important theme of Galatians; we glory in the cross.

* * *

Beginning the closing section, it can be noted that the reference to Paul's "own hand" in v. 11 and his grace prayer in v. 18 provides us with a formal framework. Here we see:

Paul's Pain v. 11

Most scholars are of the opinion that until this point Paul has been dictating to an amanuensis,[85] but now, as his custom was, he takes up the pen himself to add a personal postscript. Paul would not use a professional scribe, but personal fellow workers or travelling companions who would be well able to perform such a special task. It is clear that these would be from those named in the salutations of his letters,

---

[82] Weima, "Gal 6:11–18: A Hermeneutical Key to the Galatian Letter," *CalvTheoJourn*, 90–107 in Witherington, 111, *Galatians*, 444–45. As was noted in the Introduction, Weima calls for a renewed focus on the theme of the cross.

[83] Moo, *Galatians*, 33.

[84] Moo, *Galatians*, 391.

[85] For Paul's use of this practice see, 2 Thess. 3:17; 1 Cor 16:21; Col 4:18; Rom 16:22.

as we have noted in the footnote below; Silas and Timothy (2 Thess 1:1; Phil 1:1; Phlm. 1), Sosthenes (1 Cor 1:1), Tertius (Rom 16:22) and his faithful companion to the end, Luke (2 Tim 4:11). George[86] reminds us that:

> We should not imagine that these helpers were given such freedom and leeway as actually to compose the materials found in the Pauline Epistles. It is much more likely that he dictated to a secretary word for word. His signature at the end was his "apostolic seal" verifying that the foregoing content was precisely what he had intended to convey.

For an example of this kind of signature as a guarantee against forgery cf. 2 Thess 3:17, or a final exhortation or the grace composed in his own hand. But what of Galatians? Some scholars have cited Chrysostom[87] who proposed on the basis of the aorist "I have written," Paul is revealing, in the urgent situation that existed in the Galatian communities, with no amanuensis available, that he took on the painful task himself. Most scholars will suggest however that we read the verb as an epistolary aorist (cf. 1 Cor 5:11; Phlm. 19, 21) which can be translated "I am now writing," and so are content to ascribe the actual personal writing to only 6:11–18. But Witherington,[88] following a full discussion of the alternatives, proposes that, "Paul's own Gospel and the Christian life of his converts were believed to be hanging in the balance. It is hardly likely that Paul would have left the composition of this letter to another."

So, v. 11 states, "with what large letters." Not the sprawling untidy writing of an amateur, or baby writing for the immature, or the clumsy writing of a workman's hand twisted by toil, or to underline and emphasise[89] what he was saying, but due to his bad eyesight and in pain. In these closing verses as we noted, Paul will emphasise the stark choice between glorying in the cross or boasting in circumcision, the real contrasts between his gospel and that of the Judaizers.

Paul's Scorn

We noted above Witherington's[90] comments regarding a *peroratio* i.e., that here it was a normal thing to use emotionally charged and polemical language as a last attempt to persuade the listener to follow the advice and directions which were being given. This type of emotion is found in these verses, vv. 12–16.

---

[86] George, *Galatians*, 431.

[87] J. Bligh, *Galatians* (London: St. Paul Publications, 1969), 489, who cites Chrysostom (*PG* 61.678A).

[88] Witherington, 111, *Galatians*, 442. See also Calvin, *Galatians*, 115; McDonald, *Freedom in Faith*, 151, who also suggests that the "large letters" were just for "special emphasis"; also Bruce, *The Epistle to the Galatians*, 268, who admits that it is "just conceivable that he refers to the whole letter if (contrary to his custom) he wrote it all in his own hand." See the discussion in Moo, *Galatians*, 391–92, who also sets out the options.

[89] So Hendriksen, *Galatians*, 242; also Dunn, *Galatians*, 335, even suggesting the writing of letters large enough to hold up to be read by the various congregations!

[90] Witherington, 111, *Galatians*, 446.

We should recognise that these verses also are picking up on the whole discussion and exhortations of 1:6–5:12. One indication of this fact is the use of "flesh," similar to the earlier use, again understood in a physical sense as in 2:20; 4:13, 14, 23, 29. The agitators were concentrating on something outward, the external mark of circumcision rather than the Spirit's inward work in Paul's converts. It is possible from the participle used in v. 13, to understand "those who belong to the circumcision," to refer to "the circumcision party" of 2:12. Following the earlier discussion in that chapter we will understand them to be Jewish Christians who want to make "a good showing in the flesh ... that they may boast in your flesh," particularly to impress the zealotic Jews back in Jerusalem.

Hendriksen[91] makes the point that whatever Paul had said earlier of the opponents is here brought to a climax. "In a few crisp phrases he makes clear that these Judaizers are not at all interested in the welfare of the Galatians. On the contrary, they are concerned only about themselves: their own honor, their own ease (freedom from persecution)." It appears that in fact the Judaizers had two unworthy motives. First, they were motivated by religious pride and wanted to impress others with their external piety (see the same aims in e.g., Matt 6:1–7) and what they had achieved in the proselytization of the Galatian Christian community. The verb here in v. 12 is rare, meaning literally, "to have a good face." It can be translated "to make a good showing in the flesh" (ESV) or better, as the NIV, "to make a good impression." Here "in the flesh" obviously has the sense of publically, or before men. As Cole[92] says, "so many circumcisions in a year was certainly something to boast about." George[93] reminds us of 1 Kings 18:27, where David, in order to receive the hand of Saul's daughter Michal, brought "two hundred foreskins" of the Philistines – twice as many as the "bride price" Saul demanded. He writes of the Judaizers' intentions: "Figuratively, Paul's opponents were doing the same thing that David and his soldiers had done of old; presenting Gentile 'foreskins' as a mark of their own success and ingenuity." They felt that these ecclesiastical statistics in winning converts to Judaism would also be pleasing to God.

Again, they had another motive (see Hendriksen above) which was perhaps even more important to them – note in v. 12 the neuter pronoun μόνον *monon* "only" i.e., so that they would not suffer persecution. Dunn[94] explains that this persecution was not likely persecution from Roman authorities, but persecution by other Jews as Paul had carried out before his conversion (1:13, 23), and even had later experienced himself (2 Cor 11:24). So, they were more concerned about their own personal safety than correct doctrine. By persuading Paul's Gentile converts to adhere more to the Mosaic law than to the message of Jesus, they hoped to avoid Zealot vengeance,[95]

---

[91] Hendriksen, *Galatians*, 242–43. He reminds us that a Jew who departs from Jewish traditions to become a Christian could only expect "bitter persecution": ostracism, threats, physical and mental torture.
[92] Cole, *The Epistle of Paul to the Galatians*, 181.
[93] George, *Galatians*, 434.
[94] Dunn, *Galatians*, 337.
[95] We noted in the Introduction the suggestion of Jewett, "The Agitators and the Galatian Congregation," highlighted by Bruce of the resurgence of zealot activity in this period (AD 46–52). Also cf. Acts 12:2–3, where we have the martyrdom of James and the arrest of Peter. The circumcision of the Gentile Christians

social and financial ostracism from other Jews and also help the other Jewish Christian communities. As Bruce[96] also explains:

> If the trouble-makers could persuade the Gentile Christians to accept circumcision, that might preserve the Jerusalem Church and its daughter-churches in Judaea from reprisals at the hand of zealot-minded militants from being linked with uncircumcised Gentiles.

Longenecker[97] explains that the construction of 12b in the Greek text makes clear that Paul is highlighting something of importance here. The emphasis is on avoiding persecution "for the cross of Christ" which he will elaborate on in v. 14 "as the central focus of the gospel proclamation (cf. 3:1, 13)." How could the Judaizers avoid this persecution? George[98] explains:

> By insisting upon the circumcision of Gentile believers, the Judaizers could cast themselves in a favorable light with the local synagogue authorities: they were simply recruiting more Jewish proselytes for the nation of Israel, thereby mitigating, to some extent at least, the scandal of the cross with its particularistic emphasis on salvation through Jesus Christ alone.

However, you cannot have a Christianity without the cross. Dunn[99] stresses that it was this preaching, the proclamation of the cross alone, as Paul understood it, "the sole basis for acceptance with God" that would spark resistance. Or to be more precise, "faith in the cross which was wholly sufficient to remove sins (i.4), to neutralize the curse of the law so that the promise of Abraham might be extended to Gentiles as well (iii.13–14). To add circumcision to the cross 'made the cross of no effect.'"

Therefore, they tried to "force" the Gentile believers to submit – meaning that they put a great deal of verbal, or moral, rather than physical pressure upon them. It appears, as we have suggested throughout our exegesis, that the Judaizers had not yet succeeded and there was still the opportunity to dissuade his Galatian converts from succumbing to this action. One recalls that Judaism was still a religion which the state recognised as legitimate – circumcision and the commitment to keep the Mosaic law would give them a measure of safety. They were zealously working to seek to win Gentile converts to the law so they could, as we noted, brag about their effective proselytizing. We will see shortly that while God did give circumcision as a sign of the covenant to Abraham, Paul now makes clear that in itself it was nothing (v. 15).

---

might help them also to avoid the threat of vengeance or reprisals. Note again Moo, who also refers to Jewett, and explains that the sometimes violent resistence of the Zealot movement was gaining ground at this time. He refers to the pressure being brought to bear on Peter and other Jewish Christians in Antioch (2:11–14). Moo, *Galatians*, 394. See also note 13.

[96] Bruce, *The Epistle to the Galatians*, 269. See again Jewett, "The Agitators and the Galatian Congregation," 206; Longenecker, *Galatians*, 291.

[97] Longenecker, *Galatians*, 292.

[98] George, *Galatians*, 434.

[99] Dunn, *Galatians*, 336–37.

Here in v. 13 Paul makes the point that the very ones who were advocating circumcision and submission to the Mosaic law were themselves failing to keep it entirely (see earlier 2:16; 3: 10–13; 5:3). McDonald[100] makes clear, "In this one sentence the whole 'circumcision party' comes under condemnation." This point is also developed at length in the later work by Paul, i.e., Romans (Rom 1:18–3:23; 7:7–25; 8:3). See especially the discussion in Rom 2, where Paul challenges the Jewish people who have failed to "do' the law they have so much pride in. Bruce[101] affirms:

> Paul says that in practice they failed to keep it (the law) themselves. In his eyes they were as guilty of ὑποκρισις (hypocrisy) as were the "play-actors" at Antioch: their concern, he implies, was not for the law as a matter of principle but for the sake of boasting about those who followed their teaching.

Circumcision was not only an outward ritual but it was also a human work performed by one human being upon another. It also required the person who submitted to it to keep the law fully, as we noted. This really would mean that salvation was by human achievement, but Paul is insistent that a fallen sinner could never reach this standard. So, while the religion of the Judaizers was a human religion, with human effort, salvation is rather a Divine work, "God sent forth his Son ... to redeem." If Christ had not borne the curse, we would have been still under condemnation. Men do not like the cross, for it makes clear that they have no hope. Most want a Christianity without a cross, which relies on salvation through their works and not through the work of Christ. But Paul affirms that there is no other way. He will insist that what matters was, as he affirms in different texts in Galatians, the death of Christ for us (1:3; 2:20; 3:1, 13; 4:4–5; 5:11) and for the individual sinner, the experience of "a new creation," a birth from the Holy Spirit, an inward miracle performed by God. By contrast, as Moo[102] has pointed out, "the agitators, in taking pride in physical flesh, are also and ironically allying themselves with *the power of the old age*" (italics mine).

Therefore in v. 12 and 13 Paul has explained that the Judaizers wished by the circumcision of Paul's Galatian converts to make "a fair showing in the flesh" and to "boast" (the basic motive) in their flesh. Paul claims that there is only one thing we can boast in: the cross.

Paul's Glory

v. 14 "But far be it from me to boast except." The δὲ *de* indicates that Paul is setting out the crucial difference between himself and the Judaizers – a difference which determines one's eternal destiny! Note again the μὴ γένοιτο *mē genoito* common in

---

[100] McDonald *Freedom in Faith*, 142.
[101] Bruce, *The Epistle to the Galatians*, 270.
[102] Moo, *Galatians*, 395.

Paul and used in 3:21 of an emphatic denial. It carries the same sense here. He will "certainly not" boast in anything other than the work which Christ had accomplished for him on the cross. Longenecker[103] sets out the contrast, "What Paul depreciates as wrongful, misguided boasting in v. 13 he now dramatically contrasts in v. 14 with what he views as rightful, healthy exultation." Note also how Paul is speaking personally with the emphatic positioning of ἐμοὶ *emoi* "me."

What he was trusting in was totally different from that of the Judaizers. People must choose what they will boast in – themselves or the cross. If they will submit to circumcision they will in effect be saying that their law keeping is enough. But if they realise that they cannot save themselves they have to fly to the cross for salvation and spend all their lives glorying in the cross. As we will see, we are then crucified to the world, which has huge meaning; crucified to the world first, in its fleshly living (5:19–21), but also in its *way of thinking*, the world of an outward and human approach to salvation. Niebuhr[104] has observed concerning the liberal social gospel, that in such a message, "A God without wrath brought men without sin into a kingdom without judgment through the ministrations of a Christ without a cross." There will be more to come of the significance of his crucifixion. Now we must recognise that the whole epistle is about glorying in the cross and all that has been accomplished for us. The subject can be set out in these final verses as:

How Personally He Writes

Paul in fact twice emphatically uses ἐμοὶ *Emoi* – first of the one in whom his trust is placed and then of his resulting world-view.[105] They must, as 4:12 implored of them, "become" as he was. He insists that this is the only way of salvation.

How Seriously He Writes

"Far be it from me" or as in the AV, "God forbid!" Paul is deadly serious. Note again v. 11 where he expressed his deep concern in his confession, "with what large letters." We are talking about what these men are depending upon for acceptance with God. Where they will spend eternity is at stake, heaven or hell. Paul fully recognises the seriousness of the situation.

How Plainly He Writes

"But far be it from me to boast." What does it mean to glory or boast in the cross? Luther[106] appears to interpret this as glorying in suffering, our suffering with Christ:

---

[103] Longenecker, *Galatians*, 293.
[104] R. Niebuhr, *The Kingdom of God in America* (New York: Harper & Row, 1959), 193.
[105] Moo, *Galatians*, 395–96.
[106] Luther, *A Commentary on St. Paul's Epistle to the Galatians*, 558–59.

Moreover, the Cross of Christ doth not signify that piece of wood which Christ did bear upon his shoulders, and to that which he was afterwards nailed, but generally it signifieth all the afflictions of the faithful, whose sufferings are Christ's sufferings.... But let us think with ourselves, after the example of Paul, that we must glory in the cross which we bear, not for our sins, but for Christ's sake.

But is this not to miss the whole point here of the contrast between reliance on circumcision and reliance on Christ? Luther will apparently find this in another statement in this verse (see v. 14b). Paul is surely writing about what you put your confidence in, what you depend upon or trust in. People put confidence in many things. We began this book considering the Pharisee and the Tax Collector, Luke 18:9, 11–12. As he prayed, the Pharisee prayed only with himself. Remember Paul's former life in Judaism, Phil 3:3–11. But he would not boast in it; rather he knew what it was to "glory in Christ Jesus and put no confidence in the flesh" (v. 3). What are you depending upon? Where is your trust?

How Humbly He Writes

Paul boasts in "the cross of our Lord Jesus Christ." Paul falls down as it were at the cross. Moo[107] observes that the concept of "the cross" with its violence, shame even horror would be something strange to consider – even to mention in polite society in the ancient world and today. "Of course, it is not crucifixion per se in which Paul boasts, but the crucifixion of 'our Lord Jesus Christ'.... The singular event of Christ's crucifixion, where God was 'reconciling the world to himself' (2 Cor 5:19), is what transforms the cross for Paul."

"The cross" therefore, stands for the saviour's work. Regarding our salvation this humbles us. It is not our work but his. Not their circumcision but his crucifixion. In Gal 3:10 (cf. Deut 21:23) we noted that when a victim was hung upon a tree it was a sign that the man had been condemned, cursed by God. Christ took our condemnation. If you boast in the cross you are saying first that you cannot save yourself. Only Christ through what he did on Calvary can save. Hendriksen[108] makes this point when he discusses the cross. "The cross exposes man's desperate state, his utter bankruptcy that made such suffering necessary.... No one is ever able to see on that cross 'the wonder of God's glorious love' unless he also sees 'his own unworthiness' and 'pours contempt on all his pride.'"

Paul has written of many blessings in Galatians; a Christ who "died for our sins to deliver us from the present evil age" (1:4); who also has commissioned us to preach the one message to the circumcision and uncircumcision (2:7–9), which proclaims that we are "justified by faith in Christ and not by works of the law" (2:16). We "having begun in the Spirit" come to "the hearing of faith" (3:2–3), having learned of

---

[107] Moo, *Galatians*, 395.
[108] Hendriksen, *Galatians*, 243–44.

a Christ who "redeemed us from the curse of the law by becoming a curse for us" (3:13); who brings to us the "blessing of Abraham"... as we "receive the promised Spirit through faith" (3:14). More than this, we "receive adoption as sons" (4:5), cry "Abba Father!" (4:6), are also truly "an heir through God" (4:7), children of "the Jerusalem above" (4:26), by grace "called to freedom," in which we can "walk in the Spirit" (5:13–26) and "fulfil the law of Christ" (6:2). What a salvation! But all this can be entered into and experienced because of the cross, and only because of the cross. I emphasise again, it is not our work but his. His death is all-sufficient for us. It is faith in Christ, not circumcision and the works of the law. In Paul's gospel – the death of Christ is so central to the message that Paul can call it "the word of the cross," 1 Cor 1:18.

How Exclusively He Writes

Paul affirms that he does not boast in anything "except" or "only" in the cross. Only what Christ alone has done can save him. Longenecker[109] again observes, "Thus, as noted in 3:1, the gospel of Christ crucified so completely rules out any other supposed means of being righteous before God that Paul found it utterly incomprehensible for anyone who had once embraced such a gospel to ever think of supplementing it in any way." Dunn[110] comments that "it is precisely this shift in the ground and cause of boasting which marked Paul's transition from persecutor to apostle.... Characteristic of Paul's theology is the fact that it is the death of Christ which has become the primary ground of boasting before God (Rom v. 11; xv. 27; 1 Cor 1.31; xv. 31; Phil ii.16; iii.3)."

But this way was not only for him. As McDonald[111] states, "the 'our' before 'Lord Jesus Christ' serves to make the Galatians remember their oneness of fellowship with the apostle in the gospel, and the fact that they, no less then he, had reason for glorying in that same cross."

How Perceptively He Writes

"By which the world has been crucified to me and I to the world." We are back to the point of endeavouring to explore the full meaning of this statement introduced above.

Luther[112] mentioned that this statement has been wrongly and foolishly applied to monks entering into monasteries – cutting *themselves* off from the world! He affirms here how the trust of the faithful is in the real saving elements of the gospel – what has been understood in this work as "glorying" in the cross:

---

[109] Longenecker, *Galatians*, 294.
[110] Dunn, *Galatians*, 340.
[111] McDonald *Freedom in Faith*, 154.
[112] Luther, *A Commentary on St. Paul's Epistle to the Galatians*, 560.

Most foolishly and wickedly therefore was this sentence of the Apostle wrested to the entering into monasteries. He (Paul) speaketh here of a high matter, and of great importance, that is to say, that every faithful man that judgeth that to be the wisdom, righteousness and power of God, which the world condemneth as the greatest folly, wickedness and weakness. And contrariwise, that which the world judgeth to be the highest religion and service to God, the faithful do know to be nothing else but execrable and horrible blasphemy against God.

George[113] helps us understand that here the text really sets before us "a triple crucifixion" for there is "the crucified Christ, the crucified world and the crucified Christian." We have emphasised already throughout the whole letter the importance of the "crucified Christ" – through him and him alone there is salvation and blessing. George further explains that Paul's testimony (the world crucified to me) is not about the physical world of space and time but about the world-system with its orientation and philosophies from which Paul withdraws.

To be crucified to the world means to reject "the world" as it was described in 5:19–21(its lifestyle). Paul had died to that world in Christ and now was living "in the Spirit" keeping in step, seeking to produce the fruit of the Spirit (5:22–25).

However, there was more, as we have also noted, and it concerned Paul's new understanding of what God values and accepts. Being "crucified to the world" meant that he was turning his back on the way the world thinks and that upon which it depends i.e., the world's philosophy of acceptance, its systems of belief, or as Dunn[114] describes its "world of meaning." We are considering again what we discussed earlier – the teaching of the agitators which advocated the necessity of circumcision and the commitment to keep the whole law identified by Paul as the στοιχεια *stoicheia* or "elements of this world." Paul claimed that it all belonged to the evil world system! So, Paul affirmed that these world philosophies holding out what were considered possible ways of acceptance were dealt a decisive blow by the death of Christ on the cross. He, and he alone, through his work on the cross is "the hope of righteousness" (5:5)! Therefore, Paul did not follow the world's philosophy for acceptance but trusted in the cross, trusted in Christ alone. Witherington[115] notes that the genitive relative pronoun οὗ *ou* could possibly be translated "through whom" i.e., Christ, rather than ESV "by which" i.e., the cross. Either we have here the neuter pronoun or the masculine, referring to the saviour himself. But the Lord Jesus Christ and his cross can basically be identified; the Christ in whom we place our trust is Christ crucified. We should note as Dunn[116] explains the "decisiveness of that past event…. Here, as in ii.20, the tenses are perfect – denoting a continued state resulting

---

[113] George, *Galatians*, 437.

[114] Dunn, *Galatians*, 341.

[115] Witherington, 111, *Galatians*, 450, n. 28.

[116] Dunn, *Galatians*, 342. He adds what some would consider as unnecessary comment regarding a dying, not yet complete while his "belongingness to the world (his old nature) is not yet ended."

from that initial act.... Paul's whole Christian life was spent in a state of the world having been crucified to him and him to the world."

There is another emphasis here; in fact, it should take priority, the eschatological emphasis. As Fung[117] explains, Paul speaks first of the world being crucified to him and then of himself being crucified to the world:

> In that order; the thought thus clearly goes beyond that of his own subjective experience to that of two objectively existent worlds, from one of which he has been transplanted into the other.... The underlying thought then is that the cross – standing for the Christ-event as a whole – marks the end of the old world and ushers in the new (cf. on 4:4).

As we will see in the next verse, Christ by his coming and death on the cross has inaugurated and brought about a new creation. Fung[118] maintains the cross, marks the line of demarcation between the old world and the new creation. It "also marks the line of demarcation between circumcision and the law on the one hand and justification by faith on the other, in that it rendered the former inoperative as a means of justification and brought the principle of faith into effect."

Therefore, as we noted in our treatment of 1:4, Christ delivers us from "the present evil age," Paul's understanding is similar to that of other writers in the NT, namely that at his first advent, Christ invaded this age and through the cross brought to his people already the blessings of the new age. Moo[119] also writes of how Paul again stresses, using the first-person pronoun, "*to me* the world has been crucified, and I to the world." He sees here the fact that Paul's crucifixion means a decisive separation between the world and himself: he has a wholly new relationship with it. Paul can often use the term "world" for the world of human beings or the cosmos, but also of an "apocalyptically colored worldview" denoting the realm of sin, death and evil, similar to the "present evil age" (1:4). "Through their co-crucifixion with Christ, Paul and other believers are definitively freed from the baneful influences of this world, and they no longer owe that world their allegiance ... Christ's crucifixion is 'the transformative event that ended the old order of things.'"

So, Paul affirms that this present world has been "crucified unto me." In Gal 6:16 believers are part of the "new creation" – its fullness is in the future, but for those in Christ its blessings are already realized through the regenerating Holy Spirit.

How Decisively He Writes

Paul again in v. 15 refers to the problem which really led to the writing of this letter. The need to affirm, in fact to reaffirm, as he had already highlighted it in 5:6,

---

[117] Fung, *The Epistle to the Galatians*, 307.
[118] Fung, *The Epistle to the Galatians*, 309.
[119] Moo, *Galatians*, 396.

"Neither circumcision counts for anything, nor uncircumcision." What a statement for Paul the former Pharisee to make! As Witherington[120] states concerning circumcision or uncircumcision, "The former will add nothing to their status or condition and the latter will take nothing away." As Moo[121] also affirms, circumcision and uncircumcision stand for "those 'worldly' valuations that no longer matter in the new age."

It is not circumcision (followed by the keeping of the Mosaic law) or uncircumcision that counts for salvation. The blessing of salvation is first of all as he has emphasised, not a work done *on us* i.e., circumcision; or a work done *by us*, law keeping but a work done *for us* – by Christ on the cross – and a work done *in* us by the regenerating power of the Holy Spirit! So what people need is not something outward, but something inward, they need to become "a new creation."[122] The term κτίσις *ktisis* is used in Rom 8:19–22 of "creation" itself; but it can also be used of an individual being, a "new creature," 2 Cor 5:17. Here "new creation" refers to how we receive a new nature, with new desires, affections wrought in us by the regenerating power of the Holy Spirit. In Judaism proselytes were seen as "newborn" and this was the goal of the Judaizers for the Galatians – if they would be circumcised and commit to submit to the law. How wonderful it was for Paul to assure them that through the cross and by the work of the Spirit they were already new creatures and children of promise, children of God and their faith could be expressed (as 5:6 maintains) in the "household of faith," and beyond, "in love." The agitators could offer them nothing.

While what we have said above is true, we need also to consider that the term "new creation" may lend itself to a fuller interpretation. As Moo[123] explains, the expression can be seen as an established technical term in Jewish apocalypticism referring to a transformed creation expected to follow the destruction of the present world. Considering the context, he maintains that the concept new creation "most naturally functions, in contrast to the 'world' (v. 14) and 'the present evil age' (1:4), as a designation of the new state of affairs that the cross signifies and inaugurates." Fundamental to NT eschatology is that everything flows from the cross and what Christ accomplished there. As Bruce[124] affirms:

> The "new creation" in its fullness belongs to the future, but to those in Christ it is already realized through the Spirit. Christ is head of the new creation; in him they have been transferred from their former existence "in Adam," the head of the old creation, and await the final manifestation of the new creation on the day of resurrection when "in Christ all shall be made alive" (1 Cor 15:22).

---

[120] Witherington, 111, *Galatians*, 451.
[121] Moo, *Galatians*, 397.
[122] Hendriksen, *Galatians*, 245, notes the use of the conjunction "for" at the beginning of v. 15. It brings out the contrast between circumcision or even uncircumcision which cannot contribute anything regarding salvation and the cross which is absolutely vital.
[123] Moo, *Galatians*, 398.
[124] Bruce, *The Epistle to the Galatians*, 273.

Again, we must emphasise this link between the cross and the "new creation."[125] Weima[126] has made clear the importance of the closing verses here in establishing the centrality of the cross in the whole letter. He understands how significant the affirmations of 6:14 are in taking us back to the first chapter and to v. 4 – the cross delivering us from "the present evil age." He sees the cross as, "the decisive event in salvation history that marks an end of the old 'world' and ushers in the 'new creation.'" So, by our "glory" in the cross, we were crucified to the world and are already part of that new creation. The Judaizers were seeking to remain in the old world through circumcision; those who trust in the cross have entered into a new pattern of future existence – but now, in the present! Being Spirit born, they submit to Spirit-led conduct; as we will see below (v. 16), they are the new eschatological people of God.[127]

In v. 16 Paul encourages his audience to follow ("follow in line with" as 5:25) his teaching here and live in accordance with it. The word κανών *kanōn* here naturally is not employed of some list of books, which it would come to mean, but in its root sense of the measurement of something or a "rule."

These final words of Paul are a benediction which as George[128] points out, is "clearly targeted to a specific group," those who "walk" by this rule, i.e., the doctrine or apostolic teaching as expressed here. It is those who understand the all-sufficiency of the cross, trust in Christ alone for salvation, not circumcision followed by keeping the Mosaic law, live according to the law of Christ in the power of the Holy Spirit, as part of the new creation, who will be truly blessed, experiencing, as Paul explains, God's peace and mercy.

Here the verb στοιχέω *stoicheō* reminds us of the earlier teaching of the elements or "principles" of this world in 4:3. By way of contrast, Paul has set out a different "rule" or principles to live by (see also 5:25). In the opening section of his letter Paul has pronounced an apostolic curse on all those who adhered to and preached "another gospel" (1:9); now he pronounces an apostolic blessing upon those who rather trust in this "rule," the work of the cross (6:14–16). As Fung[129] points out, "The thesis of v. 15 is of such supreme importance to Paul that he makes it the rule of blessedness: the benediction of peace … and mercy is pronounced upon all 'who take this principle for their guide.'"

---

[125] Moo, entitled the closing section of his treatment of this book, "The Cross and the New Creation," 6:6–11, *Galatians*, 65–66.
[126] Weima, "Gal 6:11–18: A Hermeneutical Key to the Galatian Letter," *CalvTheoJourn*, 103. See also Silva, *Explorations in Exegetical Method*, 184. Dunn, *Galatians*, 343, also sees ultimately the "new creation" of which Paul writes as including the "larger meaning" predicted in Isa 65:17 and 66:22, the ultimate eschatological hope.
[127] Moo makes the point concerning the concept "new creation." "Foundational to this new state of affairs, of course, is the conversion of individuals; and central to it is the new community of Jew and Gentile." It has "cosmic scope" and all is "the outcome of Christ's death and resurrection." Moo, *Galatians*, 398.
[128] George, *Galatians*, 438.
[129] Fung, *The Epistle to the Galatians*, 309.

Moo[130] takes new creation as "a big idea," incorporating within it all those elements of the new era that Christ has inaugurated. Specifically, "new creation" as Paul has stressed throughout the letter, will prominently feature the work of the Spirit, faith, and the love to which faith gives birth (5:6). He explains:

> The reality of the new creation carries with it its own rule or standard of living. The old age – "the present evil age" (1:4), the "world" (6:14), the spatiotemporal state of affairs condemned at the cross – has its own set of values: flesh, circumcision, the law; the new creation carries its own values: the Spirit, faith, and love. Believers will experience God's peace and mercy only as they align themselves with these values.

In using "whoever" or "all who," in v. 16a Paul is challenging everyone, even the Judaizers to consider again how they stand before God and holding out to all who follow his teaching the possibility of this "peace" and "mercy." We should note again that the blessings are made conditional; it is only to those who follow this rule. So, just as he could not open the letter with his usual thanksgiving for the Galatians, so he cannot promise unconditional peace to his readers.[131] The situation is too serious for that.

This is a typically Jewish benediction and these blessings are now for all the "Israel of God." The reference is surely to those who are Abraham's spiritual offspring, for Paul has already expressed often in this letter his understanding as to who are the true people of God. Therefore, when Paul writes "upon them, and upon the Israel of God" he is not referring to two groups. Witherington[132] reminds us of the Nineteenth Benediction used in Jewish worship in the synagogue, "bestow peace, happiness, and blessing, grace and loving-kindness and mercy upon us and upon all Israel, your people." Here we have a reference not just to peace and mercy, but the distinction between "us" and "all Israel." Is there something similar going on here? Paul has been focusing on the local situation and what was true and possible for them was also true for all of God's people. So, when Paul in Galatians refers to "Israel" he means all who believe in Jesus e.g., 3:25–29; 4:21–31. He is surely not introducing another grouping – the whole context of the letter concerns both Christian Jews and Gentiles; all who depend upon the cross or the crucified messiah and his finished work are now "the Israel of God." As Hendriksen[133] affirms, one must interpret the phrase in its own particular context and *"in the light of the entire argument of this particular epistle."* Therefore *kai* must be interpreted as "even" and it is "All of God's true Israel, Jew or Gentile, all who truly glory in the cross," upon whom the blessing is pronounced. The

---

[130] Moo, *Galatians*, 399.

[131] Betz can write of the entire letter standing between the conditional curse of 1:8–9 and the conditional blessing of 6:16. Betz, *Galatians*, 321.

[132] Witherington, 111, *Galatians*, 452. He acknowledges that while the date of the benediction is uncertain, similar wording is found in Ps. 125:5.

[133] Hendriksen, *Galatians*, 247.

phrase "Israel of God" surely must be coextensive with "all who follow this rule," which includes not just believing Jews but believing Gentiles. As Moo[134] maintains:

> Throughout Galatians, Paul has argued strenuously that the old barriers distinguishing Jews and Gentiles, circumcision and the law, have been removed. In Christ, there is no longer a distinction between "Jew" and "Gentile/Greek" (3:18): both have equal access to God through faith. Moreover, Paul redefines the "seed of Abraham," insisting that his heirs consist of all who believe (3:7–29) and that the Gentile Galatians are "like Isaac, children of promise" (4:28). *Granted this central and critical argument, it is inconceivable, so it is argued, that Paul would here at the end of his letter suddenly re-erect ethnic considerations by pronouncing a blessing on an "Israel" distinct from Christians in general.* (italics mine).

Longenecker[135] suggests the possibility of the Judaizers themselves affirming to those Gentile Christians who would be circumcised and observe Jewish laws that they would more fully be "the Israel of God." So here Paul presents:

> In quite telling fashion that what the Judiazers were claiming to offer his converts they already have "in Christ" by faith: that they are truly children of Abraham together with all Jews who believe and so properly can be called "the Israel of God."

We should note the point again made by Silva,[136] considered by him as a fundamental criticism, that Paul's opponents failed to recognise the eschatological significance of the crucifixion, but wished the Galatians to remain in the old world of circumcision. His comments provide a useful summary of the teaching of these final verses:

> On the other hand, those who belong to the new creation (καινὴ κτίσις 6:15) share in Christ's crucifixion and are therefore no longer alive to the old age.... They live according to a different pattern of existence ... (6:16, alluding to Spirit-led conduct, 5:25) and constitute the true, eschatological people of God.

How Authoritatively He Writes

In v. 17 Paul, speaking of himself, requests that no man question his authority. The phrase Του λοιπου *Tou loipou* while ESV translates, "From now on," expressing a temporal sense, may simply be used in a logical sense to mean "finally" (cf. Eph

---

[134] Moo, *Galatians*, 403. Moo notes that by referring to all Christians as an "Israel *of God*" Paul "tacitly" recognises the existence of an ethnic/national Israel, but says nothing about any possible future for them.
[135] Longenecker, *Galatians*, 299. But see also Dunn, *Galatians*, 344–345, who favours more the view that Paul has in mind still ethnic Israel here. His desire is that God's covenant mercy and peace "be fully sustained and achieve its end for *all* the seed" but still "the seed of Abraham understood in terms of the argument of chs iii–iv." So, we have an Israel understood *not* as excluding Jews as a whole but as *including* Gentile believers. See Rom 11:17–26.
[136] Silva, *Explorations in Exegetical Method*, 184.

6:10; Phil 3:1; 4:8; 2 Thess 3:1). Here Paul has reached his concluding remarks. If he is thinking of the agitators who had troubled him the sense may still be temporal.

The noun κόπος *kopos* often can mean "work" or "labour," but also is used as here for "trouble" or "difficulty" (e.g., Matt 26:10; Mark 14:6; Luke 11:7; 18:5). He bluntly challenges them that they refrain from "continuing to cause" (the verb in a present imperative) him trouble (4:15–20). As McDonald[137] states, "it was a burden which should never have been added to his already anxious concern for all the churches (cf. 2 Cor 11.28)." Hendriksen[138] explains the pain and physical and mental exhaustion that "troublesome churches, and also troublesome individuals" can cause to those who are trying to set them straight. The apostle appeals to the Galatian churches to therefore take his message here in this letter to heart. As a Jew he had the mark the Judaizers were anxious to promote, but that counted for nothing. He bore the stigmata, not the manifestation of the wounds of Christ on his body,[139] and probably not the sign of ownership of a slave or one set aside for temple service, or that of soldiers (the name of their best general tattooed on their arms), but the wounds which he had received while being persecuted for Jesus Christ (2 Cor 8:9–10; 11:23–25). The scars which these beatings left behind, these were the "marks of Jesus." Paul was claiming that persecution, not circumcision as the Judaizers claimed, was the "authentic" Christian "tattoo." Witherington[140] again points to rhetorical style here to create "pathos"; Paul can say, "see my wounds!" Bruce[141] also makes the point that:

> In contrast to the now irrelevant mark of circumcision, Paul asserts that he has marks on his body στίγματα (*stigmata*) or scars which he had acquired as a direct consequence of his service for Jesus. ... Among them the most permanent were probably the marks left by the stoning at Lystra (Acts 14:19; cf. 2 Cor 11:25), and if the church of Lystra was one of those to which this letter was addressed, some at least of his readers would have a vivid recollection of that occasion.

Dunn[142] makes the point that here Paul is saying something similar to his claim elsewhere of sharing Christ's sufferings (Rom 8:17; 2 Cor 1:5; 4:8–10; Phil 3:10; Col 1:24).

So, true liberty of the Spirit brings: FRUITBEARING (5:22–23); BURDEN-BEARING (6:2); SEED-BEARING (6:7–9) and BRAND-BEARING (6:17).

---

[137] McDonald *Freedom in Faith*, 156.

[138] Hendriksen, *Galatians*, 248.

[139] Hendriksen, *Galatians*, 248, fn. 189, maintains that "these *stigmata* must not be identified in nature with the wounds in the hands, feet, and side of Francis of Assisi and many others after him.... As some see it, such marks are connected with nervious or cataleptic hysteria." For him this phenomenon has "nothing to do" with 6:17.

[140] Witherington, 111, *Galatians*, 454.

[141] Bruce, *The Epistle to the Galatians*, 276.

[142] Dunn, *Galatians*, 347.

How Singly He Writes

Note how Paul finishes; the "grace" at the beginning of the letter in the opening introduction (1:3, 6) is repeated again in the closing benediction, "the grace of our Lord Jesus Christ." This use of the word "grace" is of course normal in Pauline opening salutations and closing benedictions (Rom 16:20b; 1 Cor 16:23; 2 Cor 13:14; Eph 6:24; Phil 4:23; Col 4:18c; 1 Thess 5:28; 2 Thess 3:18; 1 Tim 6:21b; 2 Tim 4:22b; Titus 3:15; Phlm. 25). The wish that the grace be "with your spirit" is repeated again only in 2 Tim 4:22.

It is clear that here it is a simple but well-chosen benediction. For Longenecker[143] its appearance in Galatians is "particularly meaningful." In fact, the whole letter has been emphasising the theme of the grace of God in our salvation (1:3–4, 6, 15; 2:9, 21; 5:4). He points out that set between 1:3 and 6:18 Paul refers explicitly to how the Galatians were called by "the grace of Christ" (1:6); he himself being called "by his (God's) grace" (1:15); to how the Jerusalem apostles recognised the "grace" that had been given to him by God (2:9); also how God "graciously gave" the inheritance to Abraham through a promise and not on the basis of the law (3:18).

In fact, throughout Galatians grace and law are set out as opposite poles, certainly with regard to being accounted righteous before God (2:15–16, 21; 3:1–18), but also with regard to living a proper Christian lifestyle (2:17–21; 3:19 – 4:11).

Clearly Paul's whole goal throughout the letter is to appeal to them to continue to rely on grace. McDonald[144] asks us to note that "it is the grace of our Lord Jesus Christ – His grace, for there is no grace found elsewhere…. He is 'ours' says Paul, so giving the Galatians a parting reminder of their common unity and their united community in Christ." The grace to be "with your spirit" is not about the emphasis in the letter on life in the Spirit, but because the human spirit is that "God-conscious" aspect of the inner life.

But while this righteousness or salvation is certainly by grace, it is also through the cross of our Lord Jesus Christ. It is his work, not our own works or circumcision and submission to the Mosaic law. We have known his unmerited favour to sinners. George[145] can affirm:

> Likewise the "peace benediction" of v. 16 and the more typical "grace benediction" of v. 18 should not be read as mere stylistic devices at the close of the letter. They express the heart and soul of the apostle Paul summarizing in two majestic words the essence of the gospel he laboured so valiantly to set forth in this brief but powerful letter.

---

[143] Longenecker, *Galatians*, 300. Earlier we noted the same emphasis in Moo, *Galatians*, 30, in Chapter One, n. 17.

[144] McDonald *Freedom in Faith*, 157.

[145] George, *Galatians*, 429.

Paul ends on the same note. Hendriksen[146] also stresses that "This is the grace (love to the undeserving) that has atoned for their sin, had brought about the operation of the Holy Spirit in their hearts, and their adoption as children and heirs." He notes also that Paul gives Jesus his full title. He is the *Lord* who "owns us, governs and protects us, and we belong to him and should do his bidding." As *Jesus* "he, and he *alone*, is our savour (Matt 1:21; Acts 4:12)." Finally, as *Christ* the Mediator he is "our chief Prophet, only High Priest, and eternal King."

Note again Paul's use of "brothers" once more, as often in the letter (1:11; 3:15; 4:12, 28, 31; 5:11, 13; 6:1). Dunn[147] comments that this is an "unusual feature" in Pauline farewells – he emphasises his fellowship with them, as all are part of the household of faith, the family of God. Fung[148] suggests that by setting the word at the end of the sentence, Paul is emphasising that in spite of the Galatians' changed attitude to him (4:15f.) his love for them remained unchanged. His attitude from the beginning was as McDonald[149] has stated: "Even his most passionate passages reveal him, not as the offended master but as the agonizing mother (cf. 4:19)."

We can also note how Hendriksen[150] draws attention to the very similar final benediction in Philippians. They are identical – apart from the fact that in Galatians Paul includes this endearing term "brothers."

The Philippians did not need to be reassured of this. They knew it (Phil 1:12; 3:1, 13, 17; 4:1, 8). The Galatians must hear it once more; for the heart of Paul, that warm, throbbing heart, feels the need of once again embracing these erring "children" of his with his love!

The final ἀμήν *amen* as Bruce[151] observes, "would form the congregation's response to the reading of the letter; it would be pleasant to think that a well-meant and hearty 'Amen' was forthcoming from all the congregations to which the letter was sent." In response, there is some evidence that it did not go unheeded. We see this in the later references to the Galatians in Acts 16:6 and 1 Cor 16:1. We also have a responsibility to heed its message.

Summary

We must grasp the basic message that we are not saved by two means, commitment to Christ and then the obligation to law keeping. The cross is all sufficient. It is the underlying theme of all of Galatians. We need to glory in the cross. Our salvation is grace from beginning to end. We must continue to rely on the grace of God for the undeserving. But we must understand that we are not only justified, having been born

---

[146] Hendriksen, *Galatians*, 249.

[147] Dunn, *Galatians*, 347.

[148] Fung, *The Epistle to the Galatians*, 315.

[149] McDonald, *Freedom in Faith*, 141.

[150] Hendriksen, *Galatians*, 250.

[151] Bruce, *The Epistle to the Galatians*, 277.

again through the gracious operation of the Holy Spirit, but we have become sons of God through adoption and are now heirs. In addition, the Christian life is life in the Spirit, and this also is a blessing which is ours by virtue of the cross. By the enabling and enduement of the Spirit we can be delivered from the desires of the flesh, walk in the Spirit and cultivate his fruits. Finally, Paul is calling us not only to a life of holiness but also to a life of loving service in the enabling of that same Holy Spirit.

We must believe that the cross is a complete work and perfectly deals with sin and we must trust in the Christ who took the place of sinners and was crucified for them. All the blessings outlined in this letter become ours through faith alone in Christ alone. In addition, the cross is also the heart of the gospel and we must preach its glorious message. We close with a quotation from T. Crosby:[152]

> How many have been brought to Christ by reading Martin Luther upon the Galatians? What sledge-hammer words Martin uses! Only the other day I met a man who came to me like one of the old Puritans and said that he had traversed the line of the two covenants. He began to converse with me in that majestic style which comes of Puritanic theology. I thought, "Bless the man! He has risen from the dead. He is one of Oliver Cromwell's grey Ironsides.... So I said to him, "Covenant and law, where did you pick that up?" "Not at any church or chapel," said he. "There are none round about where I live who know anything at all about it. They are all in the dark together, dumb dogs that cannot bark." "How did you stumble on the true light?" I asked. The man replied, "In the good providence of God, I met with Master Martin Luther on the Galatians. I bought it for sixpence out of a box in front of a bookseller's shop." It was a good find for that man! Sixpenny worth of salvation according to the judgment of men, but infinite riches according to the judgment of God. He had found a jewel when he learned the truth of salvation by grace through faith. I recommend people, whether they will read Martin Luther or any other author, to be especially careful to read the Epistle to the Galatians itself. Paul hammers there against all hope of salvation by the law, and puts salvation on the basis of grace and grace alone, "through faith which is in Christ Jesus."

---

[152] T.P Crosby, *365 Days with Spurgeon,* 18th February Undated Sermon. (Leominster: Day One Publications, 2011).

BIBLIOGRAPHY

Askwith, E. H., *The Epistle to the Galatians* (London: MacMillan, 1902).

Atkinson, B., *No More Law: A Bold Study in Galatians* (Milton Keynes: Paternoster, 2012).

Aune, D. E., *Rereading Paul Together: Protestant and Catholic Perspectives on Justification* (Grand Rapids: Baker Academic, 2006).

Aus, R.D., "Three Pillars and Three Patriarchs: a Proposal concerning Gal 2:9," *Zeitschrift für die neutestamentliche Wissenschaft und die Kunde der älteren Kirche* 70 (1979), 252–61.

Bailey, K. E., "Informal Controlled Oral Tradition and the Synoptic Gospels," *Asia Journal of Theology,* 5.1 (1991) 34–54. Published also in *Themelios* 20.2 (January, 1995), 4–11.

Barrett, C. K., "Paul and the 'Pillar' Apostles," *Studia Paulina*, FS Johannis de Zwaan, ed. J.N. Sevenster and W.C. Unnik (Haarlem: Bohn, 1953), 1–19.

_____. "The Allegory of Abraham, Sarah and Hagar in the Argument of Galatians," *Essays on Paul* (Philadelphia: Westminster, 1982), 154–70.

_____. *Freedom and Obligation: A Study of the Epistle to the Galatians* (Philadelphia: Westminster, 1985).

Bellville, L., "'Under Law': Structural Analysis and the Pauline Concept of Law in Galatians 3:21–4:11," *JSNT* 26 (1986), 53–78.

Betz, H. D., "The Literary Composition and Function of Paul's Letter to the Galatians," *NTS*, 21 (1975), 353–79.

Galatians: A Commentary on Paul's Letter to the Churches in Galatia, Hermeneia (Philadelphia: Fortress, 1979).

Bligh, J., *Galatians* (London: St. Paul Publications, 1969).

Boice, J. M., "Galatians," *Expositors Bible Commentary,* F. Gaebelein Ed; Zondervan on CD ROM.

Boring, M. Eugene, Klaus Berger and Carsten Colpe, eds., *The Hellenistic Commentary of the New Testament* (Nashville: Abington, 1995).

Bornkamm, G., *Paul* (New York: Harper & Row, 1971).

Brinsmead's B. H., *Galatians as Dialogical Response to Opponents*, SBLDS 65 (Chico, CA: Scholars, 1982).

Brown, J., *An Exposition of the Epistle to the Galatians* (Marshallton, Del: Sovereign Grace, 1970).

Bruce, F. F., *The Epistle to the Galatians: A Commentary on the Greek Text*, NIGTC (Exeter: Paternoster Press, Grand Rapids: Eerdmans, 1982).

_____. "'Abraham Had Two Sons': A Study in Pauline Hermeneutics." In *New Testament Studies: Essays in Honor of Ray Summers* (Waco: Baylor University Press, 1975).

Burton, E. de W., *A Critical and Exegetical Commentary on the Epistle to the Galatians*, ICC (Edinburgh: T & T Clark, 1921).

Callan, T., "Pauline Midrash: The Exegetical Background of Gal 3:19b," *JBL* 99 (1980), 549–67.

Calvin, J., "Galatians," *Calvin's New Testament Commentaries*, Torrance, David W. and Thomas F. Torrance, eds. 12 Vols. (Grand Rapids: Eerdmans, 1959–70).

Carson D. A., Douglas J. Moo and Leon Morris, "Galatians," in *An Introduction to the New Testament* (Grand Rapids: Zondervan, 1992).

Carson, D. A., O'Brien, T., and Seifrid, M., eds. *Justification and Variegated Nomism: The Complexities of Second Temple Judaism*, vol.1 (Grand Rapids, Michigan: Baker Academic 2001).

_____. *Justification and Variegated Nomism: The Paradoxes of Paul*, vol. 2 (Grand Rapids, Michigan: Baker Academic 2004).

Cohn-Sherbok, D., "Paul and Rabbinic Exegesis", *SJT* 35 (1982) 117–132.

Cole, R. A., *The Epistle of Paul to the Galatians*, TNTC (Grand Rapids: Eerdmans, 1965).

Coppings, W., *The Interpretation of Freedom in the Letters of Paul*, Wissenschaftliche Untersuchungen zum Neuen Testament 261 (Tübingen: Mohr Siebeck, 2009).

Cranfield, C. E. B., "St. Paul and the Law," *SJT,* 17 (1964), 43–68.

_____. *On Romans and Other New Testament Essays* (Edinburgh: T&T Clark, 1998).

Crosby, T., *365 Days with Spurgeon,* 18th February Undated Sermon. (Leominster: Day One Publications, 2011).

Bibliography

Debelius, M., *A Fresh Approach to the New Testament and Early Christian Literature*, ed. Ferdinand Hahn (Munich: 1975).

Deissmann, A., *Bible Studies*, Tr. A. Grieve (Edinburgh: T&T Clark, 1901).

_____. *Light from the Ancient East: The New Testament Illustrated by Recently Discovered Texts of the Graeco-Roman World*, Tr. A. R. M. Strachan (London: Hodder & Stoughton, 1909).

Denny, J., "The Epistle to the Romans," *The Expositor's Greek Testament*, ed. W. R. Nicoll (5 vols.; 1897–1910; reprint, Grand Rapids, 1961).

Dever, M., Duncan 111, J.L., Mohler Jr., R. A., Mahaney, C. J., *Preaching the Cross* (Illinois: Crossway, 2007).

Dillenberger, J., ed. *Martin Luther: Selections from His Writings* (Garden City, NY: Doubleday, 1961).

Dodd, C. H., "*Ennomos Christou*," in *More New Testament Studies* (Grand Rapids: Eerdmans, 1968).

Drane, J., *Paul, Libertine or Legalist?* (London: SPCK, 1975).

Daube, D., "The Interpretation of a Generic Singular," *The New Testament and Rabbinic Judaism* (London: Ayer, 1956), 438–44.

Duncan, G.S., *The Epistle to the Galatians* (New York: Harper, 1934).

Dunn, J. D. G., *Baptism in the Holy Spirit* (London: SCM, 1970).

_____. "Works of the Law and the Curse of the Law (Gal 3:10–14)," *NTS* (1985) 523–42.

Manson Memorial Lecture (4.11.1982) "The New Perspective on Paul," *BJRL*, 65 (1983) 95–122.

_____. "The New Perspective on Paul," in *Romans*, Vol. 38A (Dallas: Word, 1988), lxiii-lxxii.

_____. *The Epistle to the Galatians*, Black's New Testament Commentaries (London: A&C Black, 1993).

_____. *The Theology of Paul's Letter to the Galatians* (Cambridge; Cambridge University Press, 1993).

_____. "Prolegomena to a Theology of Paul," *NTS* 40 (1994), 407–32.

_____. *Christianity in the Making*, Vol. 2, Beginning from Jerusalem (Grand Rapids: Eerdmans, 2009).

Durant, W., *Caesar and Christ* (New York: Simon and Schuster, 1944).

Eveson, H., "Justification: Is Wright Right?" in www.the-highway.com/justification.

_____. *The Great Exchange: Justification by Faith Alone in the Light of Recent Thought* (Facing the Issue) (Leominster, UK: Day One Publications, 1996).

Evans, A. C. & S.E. Porter (eds.) *Dictionary of New Testament Background* (Downers Grove, IL: InterVarsity Press, 2000).

Fee, G. D., *God's Empowering Presence: The Holy Spirit in the Letters of Paul* (Peabody MA: Hendrickson Publishers, 1994).

Fee, G. D., and D. Stuart, *How to Read the Bible for All it is Worth* (Bletchley: Scripture Union, 1993).

Kittel G., and G. Friedrich., *Theological Dictionary of the New Testament*, tr. G.W. Bromiley, index by R.E. Pitkin, 10 vols. (Grand Rapids: Eerdmans, 1964–1976).

Freese, J. H., Loeb Classical Library, *Aristotle*, vol. 22, no. 193 (Cambridge, MA: Harvard University Press, 1926).

Fung, R. Y. K., *The Epistle to the Galatians*, NIC (Grand Rapids: Eerdmans, 1988).

"Cursed, Accursed, Anathema," *Dictionary of Paul and His Letters*, G.F. Hawthorne and R. Martin (eds) (Downers Grove: Intervarsity Press, 1993), 199–200.

George, T, *Galatians,* The New American Commentary, Vol. 30 (Nashville, TN: Broadman & Holdman? Holman? Publishers, 1994).

Gorman, M. J., *Inhabiting the Cruciform God: Kenosis, Justification, and Theosis in Paul's Narrative Soteriology* (Grand Rapids, Michigan: William B. Eerdmans, 2009).

Guthrie, D., *Galatians (*London: Thomas Nelson, 1969).

_____. *New Testament Theology* (Leicester: Inter-varsity Press, 1981).

_____. *New Testament Introduction*, 4th ed. (Downers Grove, IL.: InterVarsity, 1990).

Hansen, G.W., *Galatians*, The IVP New Testament Commentary Series (Leicester: InterVarsity Press, 1994).

Harris, M. J., "Prepositions and Theology in the Greek New Testament," *NIDNTT* 111 ed. C Brown (Grand Rapids: Zondervan, 1975–78).

Harrisville, R.A., "Πίστος Χπιστοῦ: Witness of the Fathers" *Novum Testamentum* 36 (1994), 233–41.

Hays, R. B., "The Letter to the Galatians: Introduction, Commentary, and Reflection," vol. X1, 181–348 in *The New Interpreter's Bible* (ed.) L.E. Keck (Nashville: Abingdon, 2000).

_____. *Echoes of Scripture in the Letters of Paul* (New Haven state?: Yale University Press, 1989).

Hemer, C., *The Book of Acts in the Setting of Hellenistic History* (Winona Lake: Eisenbrauns, 1990).

Hendriksen, W., *Galatians* (Edinburgh: Banner of Truth Trust, 1974).

Hengel, M., *Judaism and Hellenism: Studies in Their Encounter in Palestine during the Early Hellenistic Period*, 2 vols. Tr. J. Bowden (Philadelphia, PA: Fortress, 1974).

A Pre-Christian Paul, in collaboration with Ronald Deines (London: SCM and Philadelphia: Trinity Press International, 1991).

Hong, I. G., *The Law in Galatians* (Sheffield: JSOT Press, 1993), 149–56.

Howard, G., *Paul: Crisis in Galatia*, SNTSM 35 (Cambridge: Cambridge University Press, 1979).

Jeremias, J., "Chiasmus in den Paulusbriefen," *ZNW*, 49 (1958) 145–56.

_____. "The Key to Pauline Theology," *Ex T*. Oct. 1964.

Jewett, R., "The Agitators and the Galatian Congregation," *NTS* 17 (1970–71), 198–212.

Jones, S. F., "Freiheit" in *den Briefen des Apostels Paulus: Eine historische, exegetische, und religionsgeschichtliche Studie*, Göttinger theologischer Arbeiten, 34 (Göttingen: Vandenhoeck & Ruprecht, 1987).

Kennedy, G. A., *New Testament Interpretation through Rhetorical Criticism* (Chapel Hill: University of North Carolina, 1984).

_____. *A New History of Classical Rhetoric* (Princetown, NJ: Princetown University Press, 1994).

Kümmel, W. G., *Introduction to the New Testament* (London: SCM Press, 1982).

Ladd, G.E., *Theology of the New Testament*, Rev ed. (Grand Rapids, Michigan: Eerdmans Publishing Company, 1993).Lightfoot, J. B., *Saint Paul's Epistle to the Galatians* (London: MacMillan and Co. Ltd., 1921).

Longenecker, R. N., *Galatians*, WBC 41 (Dallas: Word, 1990).

Lührmann, D., "Gal 2 9 und die katholischen Briefe. Bemerkungen zum Kanon und zur regula fidei," *ZNW* 72 (1981) 65–87.

Luther, M., ETr., *A Commentary on St. Paul's Epistle to the Galatians,* A revised and completed translation based on the "Middleton" edition of the English version of 1575 (ed.) Watson, S. (London: James Clarke & Co. Ltd., 1953).

Mc'Devitte, W. A. and W. S. Bohn, *De Bello Gallico* ET (New York: Harper & Brothers, 1869).

McDonald H. D., *Freedom in Faith: A Commentary on Paul's Epistle to the Galatians* (London: Pickering and Inglis, 1973).

McKnight, S., *Galatians*, The NIV Application Commentary (Grand Rapids, Michigan: Zondervan Publishing House, 1995).

Martyn, J. L., *Galatians: A New Translation with Introduction and Commentary*, Vol. 33A (New York: Doubleday, 1977).

Metzger, B. M., *A Textual Commentary on the Greek New Testament*, 2nd Ed. (New York: United Bible Societies, 1994).

Meyer, R., "Περιτέμνω" in *Theological Dictionary of the New Testament*, Volume 6. 72–84.

Mikolaski, S. J., "Galatians," *The New Bible Commentary*, Rev. Guthrie, D., J.A. Motyer, A. M. Stibbs and D. J. Wiseman (eds.) (Downers Grove, IL.: InterVarsity Press, 1970).

Mitchell, S., *Anatolia: Land, Men and Gods in Asia Minor, Volume 2, The Rise of the Church* (Oxford: Clarendon Press, 1993).

Moo, D. J., *Galatians*, Baker Exegetical Commentary on the New Testament (Grand Rapids, Michigan: Baker Academic, 2013).

Moore, H., *The Letters to Timothy and Titus: Missional Texts from a Great Missionary Statesman* (Belfast: Nicholson and Bass, 2016).

Bibliography

Morris, L., *Galatians: Paul's Charter of Christian Freedom* (Leicester: IVP, 1996).

Mussner, F., *Der Galaterbrief*, HTKNT, 9 (Freiburg, Basel and Vienna: Herder, 1974).

Nanos, M.D., "Paul and Judaism: Why Not Paul's Judaism?" 117–60 in *Paul Unbound: Other Perspectives on the Apostle*, M.D. Given (Ed) (Peabody, MA: Hendrickson,).

Neusner, J., and B. Chilton, "Uncleanness: a Moral or an Ontological Category" *Bulletin for Biblical Research*, 1 (1991), 63–80.

Neusner, J., "Introduction: 'The Four Approaches to the Description of Ancient Judaism(s): Nominalist, Harmonistic, Theological and Historical,'" in Alan Jeffery-Avery Peck and J Neusner, *Judaism in Late Antiquity: Death, Life-after-Death, Resurrection & The World to Come in the Judaisms of* Antiquity (Leiden; Boston; Köln: Brill, 2000), 1–34.

Niebuhr, R., *The Kingdom of God in America* (New York: Harper & Row, 1959).

O'Brien, T., "Was Paul a Covenantal Nomist?," D. A. Carson, Mark Seifrid, Peter T. O'Brien (eds), *Justification and Variegated Nomism*, Vol. 2 *The Paradoxes of Paul* (Grand Rapids: Baker Academic, 2004), 249–96.

_____. "Was Paul Converted?" in D. A. Carson, T O'Brien, and M. A. Seifrid (eds), *Justification and Variegated Nomism*, Vol. 2 *The Paradoxes of Paul (*Grand Rapids: Baker Academic, 2004), 361–91.

O'Neill, J. C., *The Recovery of Paul's Letter to the Galatians* (London: SPCK, 1972).

Orchard, B., "A New Solution to the Galatians Problem," *BJRL* 28 (1944), 154–74.

_____. "The Ellipis between Galatians 2, 3 and 2, 4," *Bib* 54 (1973) 469–81.

Packer J. I., "Evangelical Annihilationism in Review," in *Reformation & Revival*, Volume 6, Number 2 Spring, 1997, 37–51.

_____. *Celebrating the Saving Work of God (*Carlisle, UK: Paternoster Press, 1998).

Peterson, D. *The Acts of the Apostles* (Grand Rapids, Michigan: W. B. Eerdmans Publishing Co., Nottingham: Apollos, 2009).

Piper, J., *The Future of Justification: A Response to N. T. Wright* (Wheaton Ill.: Crossway Books, 2007).

Räisänen, H., *Paul and the Law* (WUNT 29; Tübingen: Mohr, 1983).

Ramsay, W., *Cities and Bishoprics of Phrygia*, 1–11 (Oxford: Clarendon, 1895–1897).

_____. *The Church in the Roman Empire before A.D. 170* (London: Hodder and Stoughton, 1897).

_____. *A Historical Commentary on St. Paul's Commentary to the Galatians* (Grand Rapids: Baker, reprint 1979).

Philipps, J. B., *The New Testament in Modern English* (New York: Macmillan, 1958).

Reymond, R. L., *Paul Missionary Theologian* (Fearn: Mentor, 2000).

_____. "The Sanders/Dunn 'Fork in the Road' in the Current Controversy over the Pauline Doctrine of Justification by Faith," www.semper-reformanda.org Accessed May 2015.

Ridderbos, H. N., *The Epistle of Paul to the Churches of Galatia* (London: Marshall, Morgan and Scott, 1961).

_____. *Paul: An Outline of His Theology* (Grand Rapids, Michigan: Eerdmans, 1977).

Sanders, E. P., *Paul and Palestinian Judaism: A Comparison of Patterns of Religion* (London: SCM 1977).

_____. *Paul, the Law and the Jewish People* (Philadelphia: Fortress, 1983).

Schmithals, W., *Paul and the* Gnostics, ETr (Nashville: Abingdon Press, 1972).

Scott, I. W., *Implicit Epistemology in the Letters of Paul: Story, Experience and the Spirit*, Wissenschaftliche Untersuchungen zum Neuen Testament 205 (Tübingen: Mohr Siebeck, date),

Scott, J. M., "Galatia, Galatians," in Evans, A. C., & Porter, S. E. (eds.), *Dictionary of New Testament Background* (Downers Grove, IL.: InterVarsity Press, 2000).

Silva, M., *Interpreting Galatians* (Grand Rapids, Michigan: Baker Book House, 2001).

_____. *Explorations in Exegetical Method: Galatians as a Test Case* (Grand Rapids, MI: Baker Books, 1996).

Stanley, C., "'Under a Curse': A Fresh Reading of Galatians 3:10–14" *NTS* 36 (1990), 481–511.

Bibliography

Stendahl, K., "The Apostle Paul and the Introspective Conscience of the West," *Harvard Theological Review*, 56, no 3 (July, 1963), 199–215.

_____. *Paul among Jews and Gentiles* (Philadelphia: Fortress, 1976).

Stott, J. R. W., *Only One Way: The Message of Galatians*, Bible Speaks Today (London: Inter-Varsity Press, 1974).

_____. *The Message of Romans,* The Bible Speaks Today (Leicester: Inter-Varsity Press, 1994).

Strauss, L., *Devotional Studies in Galatians and Ephesians* (Edinburgh: McCall Barbour, 1974).

Strack, H., and Billerbeck, *Kommentar zum Neuen Testament*, 4 Vols. (Munich: Beck, 1926–28).

Swanton, M.J., *The Anglo-Saxon Chronicle* (New York: Routledge, 1998).

Thielmann, F., *Paul and the Law; A Contextual Approach* (Downers Grove, IL.: InterVarsity Press, 1994).

_____. "Paul, the Law & Judaism: The Creation & Collapse of a Theological Consensus" in *Paul and the Law: A Contextual Approach* (Downers Grove IL.: InterVarsity Press, 1994).

Wakefield, A. H., "Summary and Analysis of Recent Scholarship: Paul and the Law," in *Where to Live: The Hermeneutical Significance of Paul's Citations from Scripture in Galatians 3:1–14* (Boston: Leiden Brill, Society of Biblical Literature, 2003).

Weima, J. A. D., "Gal 6:11–18: A Hermeneutical Key to the Galatian Letter," *CalvTheoJourn* 28 (1993), 90–107.

Wilcox, M., "The Promise of the 'seed' in the NT and the Targumim," *JSNT*, Issue 5 (October 1979), 2–20.

Witherington 111, B., *The Acts of the Apostles. A Socio-Rhetorical Commentary* (Grand Rapids: Eerdmans, Carlisle: Paternoster, 1998).

_____. *Grace in Galatia: A Commentary on Paul's Letter to the Galatians* (Edinburgh: T & T Clark, 1998).

Wright, N. T., *What St. Paul Really Said: Was Paul of Tarsus the Real Founder of Christianity?* (Grand Rapids: Eerdmans, 1997).

_____. *Justification: God's Plan and Paul's Vision* (Downers Grove, Ill.: IVP Academic, 2009).

_____. *Climax of the Covenant: Christ and the Law in Pauline Theology* (Minneapolis: Fortress, 1991).

Ziesler, J., *The Epistle to the Galatians* (London: Epworth, 1992).

Webpages

J.I. Packer, "Evangelical Annihilationism in Review," an assessment of the critique of Annihilationism in contrast to the biblical doctrine of everlasting punishment. www.the-highway.com/annihilationism-Packer.html accessed April 2015. This article appeared in *Reformation & Revival*, Volume 6, Number 2 – Spring 1997, 37–51.

Journal of Philosophy and Scripture, Vol. 2, Issue 2 Spring (2005) www.philosophyandscripture.org. Accessed May 2015. review of Pamela Eisenbaum, *Paul was not a Christian: the Original Message of a Misunderstood Apostle* (New York: HarperOne, 2009) in www.denverseminary.edu by J.D. Kim. Accessed May 2017.

Eveson, H., "Justification: Is Wright Right?" in www.the-highway.com/justification. Accessed Nov. 2016.

Journal of John Wesley http://www.ccel.org/ccel/wesley/journal.vi.ii.xv. html. Accessed December 2017.